35

After the Thunder

After the Thunder

Fourteen Men Who Shaped
Post–Civil War America

WILMER L. JONES, PH.D.

Taylor Publishing Company
Dallas, Texas

Copyright © 2000 Wilmer L. Jones

Published by Taylor Publishing Company
1550 West Mockingbird Lane
Dallas, TX 75235
www.taylorpub.com

Library of Congress Cataloging-in-Publication Data

Jones, Wilmer L.
After the thunder: fourteen men who shaped Post-Civil War America / Wilmer L. Jones.
     p. cm.
Includes bibliographical references (p.) and index.
ISBN 0-87833-176-X
1. United States—History—Civil War, 1861–1865——Biography. 2. United States—Histo-ry—1865–1898—Biography. 3. Generals—United States—Biography. 4. Presidents—United States—Biography. 5. United States. Army—Biography. 6. Confederate States of America. Army—Biography. I. Title.

E467 .J79 2000
973.7′092′2--dc21
[B]   99-055775

10 9 8 7 6 5 4 3 2 1

Printed in the United States of America

To my wife,
Carol J. Jones

Contents

Contents

With malice toward none; with charity for all; with firmness in the right, as God gives us to see the right, let us strive on to finish the work we are in; to bind up the nation's wounds; to care for him who shall have borne the battle, and for his widow, and his orphan—to do all which may achieve and cherish a just, and a lasting peace, among ourselves, and with all nations.

LINCOLN'S SECOND INAUGURAL SPEECH,

March 4, 1865

But I say to you that listen, Love your enemies, do good to those who hate you, bless those who curse you, pray for those that abuse you . . . Do to others as you would have them do to you.

LUKE 6:20–31

Introduction

I N 1880, Woodrow Wilson, a native of Virginia who lived four years of his childhood in wartime Georgia, expressed his feelings about the results of the Civil War: "Because I love the South, I rejoice in the failure of the Confederacy . . . [I cannot] conceive of this Union divided into two separate and independent sovereignties! . . . Slavery was enervating our Southern society . . . [Nevertheless] I recognize and pay loving tribute to the virtues of the secession . . . the righteousness of the cause which they thought they were promoting—and to the immortal courage of the soldiers of the Confederacy." Wilson's words contained themes that would help to reconcile Southerners to their defeat. *After the Thunder* carries these same themes in order to shed some light on the men behind the myths.

It was difficult for many Southerners to accept that they had lost the war. They blamed their loss on the superior size of the Union army and on the North's greater economic resources. The Lost Cause theme took on legendary proportions. Robert E. Lee became the leading hero, almost to the point of cult worship. To allow Lee to be completely virtuous and honorable, the Confederate defeat at Gettysburg had to be blamed on the officers under him. Recently another view about the outcome of the war has been presented. This perspective is critical of the Lost Cause, claiming the South failed because of its own shortcomings. Lee is no longer cast as the hero but is considered one of those contributing to the loss. *After the Thunder* does not glorify the Lost Cause position, nor does it focus on the South's failures. Rather, it takes the middle ground: It acknowledges some of Lee's faults, but still emphasizes his nobility and honor. Telling the stories of each of the war's heroes with honesty and fairness, *After the Thunder* strives for a balanced evaluation of each person's strengths and weaknesses.

Introduction

The Civil War was a long, deadly war. It lasted four years and resulted in over a million casualties. It was fought first to reunite the Union and then to free the slaves. And its repercussions are still felt today. *After the Thunder* illuminates the end of the Civil War and the Reconstruction period in the South by focusing on the lives of major participants in the war. It is taut and lean, limited to fourteen characters who played a critical role during the war and the Reconstruction period that followed. Conspicuous by their absence are Abraham Lincoln, Thomas J. "Stonewall" Jackson, J. E. B. Stuart, and John Reynolds. By necessity, the subjects included are only those who survived the war. Important events, battles, and people are included only to the extent that they are important to the subject in that chapter.

This book is the result of my forty years of interest in the Civil War. Having read a great deal about the Civil War, its battles, and its heroes, I was curious to know more about what happened to the participants after the war. *After the Thunder* is the result of my search for the answer. I hope you will enjoy reading it as much as I did writing it.

DR. WILMER L. JONES
Towson, Maryland
1999

After the Thunder

1   The Fall of Richmond

IN 1865, spring came gently to Richmond. Fruit trees bloomed in the city and in the scarred, desolate landscape beyond. After a cold winter and wet March, Sunday, April 2, dawned mild and pleasant. People strolled leisurely to church amid the cheerful ringing of bells and the faint distant booming of cannon. The siege of Richmond and nearby Petersburg was in its ninth month. General Robert E. Lee's Confederate army still held Petersburg, twenty-five miles to the south, and the defense lines five miles east of Richmond against General U. S. Grant's Union Army of the Potomac. Within a few days, the American Civil War would be four years old. It seemed unlikely that the Confederate capital would survive to celebrate the anniversary.

In May 1861, the Confederate Congress in session at Montgomery, Alabama, voted to move the capital of the Confederate states to Richmond. The move was dictated by political and military considerations. The prestige of Virginia, richest and most populous state in the South, was considered necessary for the success of the Confederacy. For political reasons, it was believed that the capital should be near the border states and the heavy fighting expected there.

Richmond was destined to become the political, military, and manufacturing center of the South, and the very symbol of secession to the North. For four years, it remained the primary military objective of the Union armies in the East. During all that time, Richmond remained a beleaguered city. As one Southern newspaper stated: "To lose Richmond is to lose Virginia, and to lose Virginia is to lose the key to the Southern Confederacy."

When the war began, Richmond underwent dramatic changes. Hundreds of regiments from farther south poured into the city, giving it the appearance of a vast military camp. At night the glow from thousands of campfires lit up the sky. People came by the thousands from all over the South to work in the various government departments. Refugees from the battle areas crowded into the city, along with others seeking wounded and sick loved ones and friends. These were followed by speculators, spies, deserters, furloughed soldiers, gamblers, bandits, prostitutes, and derelicts of every kind. This conglomeration of people, some 100,000 in number, was packed into private homes, rooming houses, and hotels—where they were housed two to a bed and six to a room. The population of Richmond would double again, to 200,000, by the end of the war.

The inevitable outcome was a critical shortage of food and supplies, resulting in rampant sickness and disease. Inflation ravaged the city and threatened the unfortunate with starvation. Flour sold for $1,500 per barrel, live hens for $50 each, butter for $20 per pound and beef for $15. One woman said, "You can carry your money in your market basket and bring home your provisions in your purse." Some suffered more than others. Young A. R. Tomlinson, a wounded soldier serving as a hospital guard, was so weak that he could hardly stand watch, but he could not bring himself to eat as his companions did: "The surgeons and matrons ate rats and said they were as good as squirrels, but having seen the rats running over the bodies of dead soldiers, I had no relish for them."

Richmond was once active with commercial and industrial activities. Now in the spring of 1865, a slow, steady rumble of the carts bearing the dead and ambulances on their way to the cemeteries and hospitals had become familiar sounds in the war-weary city. The past few days in the capital had been quiet despite growing pressure from Ulysses Grant's Federal besiegers so near at hand. Although it was clear that the city would soon fall, a stranger new in the city might have assumed all was well. By now Richmond's population had swelled to 200,000. The populace had grown accustomed to the perils about them and went about their affairs as if everything was normal. For the past few months, the Confederate government had been sparing with military news, and the public had been left to imagine what it pleased. Indeed, the atmosphere on the street was "rather pleasant and assuring." Richmonders had not the slightest inkling of the situation as the Confederate capital neared its hour of doom.

On Saturday evening, Postmaster General John Reagan had spent most of the night at the War Department in Richmond, following the bleak news from the Petersburg front. Early on Sunday morning, April 2, at 10:40 A.M. a telegram arrived from Lee addressed to Secretary of War John Breckinridge.

> *I see no prospect of doing more than holding my position here till night. I am not certain I can do that . . . I advise that all preparations be made for leaving Richmond to-night.—R. E. Lee*

Reagan was on the way to the presidential mansion when he met Jefferson Davis and his aide, Francis Lubbock, strolling toward church. When he reported Lee's dispatch to the president, Reagan was surprised by Davis's reaction. Davis seemed "oddly distracted," as if he didn't understand the reality of the dispatch. Despite the urgency of the message, Davis and Lubbock continued on to St. Paul's church, having taken little note of Reagan or the information he had brought them.

Davis and Lubbock arrived at the eleven o'clock service at St. Paul's Episcopal Church and entered the presidential pew. It was Communion Sunday. The Reverend Charles Minnigerode, a German immigrant who had become a beloved figure in Richmond, opened the service, raising his voice so he could be heard over the rumble of distant guns from the front.

The service was underway when a young man entered the church and insisted on seeing the president. As soon as the prayer was over, a message was delivered to Davis. Sallie Putman, an eyewitness, described what happened: "The service was progressing as usual, no agitation nor disturbance withdrew the thoughts from holy contemplation, when a messenger was observed to make his way up the aisle and to place in the hands of the President a sealed package. Mr. Davis arose, and was noticed to walk unsteadily out of church. An uneasy whisper ran through the congregation, and intuitively they seemed possessed of the dreadful secret in the sealed dispatch—the unhappy condition of General Lee's army and the necessity for evacuating Richmond. . . ."

The service was hastened to a close, and people emerging from St. Paul's joined others on street corners. There they learned that Lee's lines had been broken, and Richmond would be evacuated that day. It was difficult to accept, but slowly reality set in "upon the stricken people that the four year struggle was nearing its end."

The city had lost its peaceful appearance—a scene of frenzied activity replaced it. Government clerks frantically packed or burned records on the sidewalks; others rushed loaded boxes and crates to the Richmond & Danville Railroad depot. Piles of unsigned paper money burned brightly in front of the Capitol. Government bonds were tossed into the street and blew across the city like confetti. Rumors spread and grew: "Richmond has fallen—the Yankees are coming."

Fear swept the city. It was partially due to the war-long propaganda depict-

Richmond, with the Capitol in the background, 1862

ing the enemy as "Yankee mudsills and degraded foreigners," all beneath the contempt of true Southerners. Already, as if to confirm Southerners' belief, William Sherman's "bummers" were advancing from the south. Behind the bummers was a thousand-mile trail of fire and destruction, adding to the fear of Richmond's citizens. Tales of looting and pillage were commonplace. Sherman understood the phenomenon of total war. He realized that he and his troops would be reviled by Southerners for generations to come, but he believed he could shorten the war by his scorched-earth policy. Although it was Grant's army and not Sherman's that battered at Richmond's gates, Sherman's past actions were foremost on the citizens' minds. They didn't know what to expect from Grant, and this added to their fears.

At noon, Davis and his cabinet met in the president's office with Governor William Smith, former Governor John Letcher, and Richmond's mayor, Joseph Mayo. Davis read the latest message from Lee, and preparations were made for their departure from Richmond. They agreed to meet at the train depot at 7 P.M., ready for the 140-mile trip to Danville, a small town near the North Carolina border.

Davis left his executive office and walked to his home for the last time. Many people stopped him along the way to ask what was happening and what they should do. In the streets, he saw women clad in black, weeping and mourn-

4 |

Richmond in ruins, with the Capitol in the background, 1865

ing the loss of loved ones from the war. When asked if Richmond was to be evacuated, Davis admitted the painful truth but said he hoped they would be able to return under better conditions. One woman, speaking for the group, declared, "If the success of the cause requires you to give up Richmond, we are content." Davis was deeply touched. "The affection and confidence of these noble people in the hour of disaster," he later wrote, "was more distressing to me than complaint and unjust censure would have been." To everyone he met, Davis appeared as he had to Reagan that day, full of "calm and manly dignity, devoted to the public interest, and courageous."

When Davis reached the Confederate White House, he found that several of his slaves had fled—and the four who remained were drunk. Davis asked one of the remaining servants to wrap some of his most prized artifacts. John Grant, a friend of Davis, agreed to store the president's valuables in his farmhouse, but declined to take his wife Varina's carriage. "I don't believe I'd risk that sir," he said. Davis realized that Grant feared retaliation by federal troops should they discover the carriage in his possession. Davis's mind turned to the women and children who must remain behind in the city. He sent his most comfortable chair to Mrs. Robert E. Lee, an arthritic invalid who was to remain behind to face the enemy. The president left his mansion only when a messenger came with word that the cabinet was waiting for him at the depot.

In the afternoon, the banks opened so that owners of valuables could retrieve them before the Yankees arrived. No one bothered picking up their Confederate money or bonds; the streets near the banks were littered with them. Instead they took jewelry, federal currency, deeds, and stock certificates. They returned home with their valuables and buried them in boxes in their basement, hid them in furniture, or stuffed them into secret places in their clothing.

When the official evacuation order was posted, pandemonium broke loose. Trunks, boxes, and bundles of every description were piled on sidewalks and in the streets. Wagons, carts, buggies—anything with wheels that could move—were loaded and raced toward Mayo's Bridge in a mad dash to cross the James River and flee south with the army.

Those who didn't head for the bridge crowded the streets leading to the railroad station, only to be turned back by soldiers' bayonets. The few trains that were available and able to move were reserved for the president and other government officials, the treasury, and military personnel.

Confusion, panic, and fear reigned in many of the hospitals. The convalescent patients and every patient who could walk or hobble left to flee the invading army and avoid capture. "Beds in which paralyzed, rheumatic, and helpless patients had laid for months were empty," one nurse noted as she walked through an almost empty ward. "The miracles of the New Testament had been re-enacted. The lame, the halt, and the blind had been cured."

In the evening, the character of the crowds and the city changed. Saloons and gambling halls began to empty their customers, many of them drunk, into the streets. A slave dealer with fifty slaves, finding no possible way to evacuate them, turned them loose to run free. When guards at the state penitentiary fled, the prisoners broke free and began to roam the city at will. Law and order had completely collapsed. Only a local defense brigade was left to maintain the law. Some of the brigade were busy burning records while others were deployed to guard the railroad depot. Still others had been ordered to burn all of the tobacco and cotton that could not be removed from the warehouses along the riverfront. It was indeed a night to be remembered for a long time.

Despite the chaos in the city and at the station, preparation for the departure of the presidential train had been well organized. The train for Danville was scheduled to leave at 7 P.M., but when Jefferson Davis did not show up then, its departure was delayed. The cabinet members were becoming uneasy, worrying that something might have happened to Davis. At 11 P.M., Davis arrived. He and Breckinridge had been waiting and hoping for "better news" from Lee, messages that never came. As soon as Davis arrived, the train pulled out. Looking northward across the dark waters of the James River, the fugitives had their last glimpse of Richmond. From a distance, the doomed Capitol had a peaceful appearance. Davis and his colleagues, although facing an uncertain future, were spared the sights and sounds of the city's destruction at the hands of its own people.

In the meantime, in the interest of public safety the city council had appointed a committee in each ward to see that all liquor was destroyed. Casks and barrels were rolled to the curbs, where they were broken open and the contents allowed to run off into the gutters. People gathered immediately; some scooped up what they could in buckets, while others simply drank from the gutters. Soon many were drunk, an out-of-control mob roaming the dark streets plundering warehouses, commissaries, private shops, stores, and offices throughout the commercial district.

In the early morning hours, a more ominous element was added to the chaos—fire. The soft night sky became pink, then turned a bright red. The fire started at a warehouse at Thirteenth and Cary, where 10,000 hogsheads of tobacco had been set on fire. At first the fire was modest, but suddenly the flames bellowed skyward as if shot from a huge blowtorch. A breeze from the southeast fanned the flames to nearby buildings; soon the fire was out of control and spreading through the business district. The flames soared higher and higher, widening their path until it seemed as if the red-hot sea would engulf the whole city. Richmond's citizens watched helplessly as the fire spread, for there was no fire department to fight it—and someone had sabotaged the fire-fighting equipment by cutting the hoses.

Just before daylight, the fire had spread to the arsenal on the northern slopes of Shockoe Hill. Suddenly a large powder magazine was detonated. The blast shook the city, shattering windows, rocking buildings, and knocking people in the streets to the pavement. Many citizens were behind locked doors at home, but all were wide awake, terrified by the events of the night and fearful of what was to come when the new day dawned.

Richmond was now an inferno of flames, noise, smoke, and trembling earth. The roaring fire moved from the riverfront, destroying the two railroad depots, banks, flour and paper mills, warehouses, and hundreds of stores and homes. An area of more than thirty square blocks was a solid wall of flame. Men and women climbed onto their rooftops to sweep hot cinders into the street in a desperate effort to save their homes. In some cases, families were trapped in their houses and burned to death; others were forced to jump from their windows to the fire in the streets below. In house fires alone, seventeen people died. The exact death toll for that night is not known. The area today is still referred to as the "burnt district."

Late in the night, Mayo's Bridge began to burn after thousands of retreating soldiers and civilians had crossed to the south bank of the river. Confederate Major General Richard Ewell and his troops crossed the bridge despite the flames of freshly set fires. Major General Joseph Kershaw's South Carolina

The White House of the Confederacy: Jefferson Davis's house

division were the last individuals to cross the bridge safely. When all his division had crossed, Kershaw called to one of his command: "All over. Good-bye. Blow her to hell."

The next morning, a large crowd gathered in front of the government commissary warehouse. These were some of the people hardest hit by inflation and food shortages. They had survived the winter on diets of pea soup, dried beans and apples, and a little rice. The warehouse doors were opened, and clerks began distributing the remaining supplies. At first the distribution was orderly, but then some drunks joined the crowd and trouble began. Barrels of hams, bacon, flour, molasses, sugar, coffee, and tea were rolled into the streets, their contents scattered on the cobblestones. Fights broke out over the food, and the crowd turned into a mob. Then they swarmed into other sections of the city, looting and burning. The frenzied rabble roared on unchecked.

The Confederate capital, abandoned now by Rebel officials and its armed defenders, was completely chaotic. Many civilians had fled along the northern bank of the James River, vying with retreating troops for places on the road. Distraught and weary, many of the retreating soldiers and civilians cursed the president, expressing the views of many others who had begun to blame him for the conditions they now faced.

General Robert E. Lee's house

Early in the morning of April 3, General Grant, in pursuit of Lee, sent Major General Godfrey Weitzel with the forces left behind to occupy Richmond, establish guards, and preserve order. The infantry, about 12,000 officers and men strong, formed into two columns and moved toward Richmond. At about 6:30 A.M., they encountered Mayor Mayo and a few of the city officials in an old carriage. Mayor Mayo officially surrendered the city to Major General Weitzel, requesting that Weitzel take possession of Richmond with an organized force to restore order and protect the women, children, and property.

Major Atherton Stevens accepted the surrender for Major General Weitzel, then continued on into the city. The first official act of the Union troops was to pull down the Confederate flag from the Capitol's roof and replace it with a flag of their own. Having no federal flag with them, the soldiers ran up two of their cavalry guidons while a band played the "Star-Spangled Banner." The first sight of Union troops as they reached the center of the city would always be remembered by its witnesses: "They gaped in wonder at the splendidly equipped army . . . the beautiful sunlight flashed everywhere from Yankee bayonets." Crowds of freed slaves rushed into the streets, sometimes falling on their knees, hailing the soldiers—many of whom were black themselves—as their deliverers, at times almost halting their columns. A seemingly endless column of exultant troops entered Richmond. Although the fall of the capital after four devastating years of war was hardly unexpected, its residents nevertheless were stunned. Many were deep in grief, and those ministers who still remained became a source of comfort for them.

"I never knew of anything more painful and touching than that . . . when the Litany was sobbed out by the whole congregation," wrote Constance Cary, a young Richmond woman. She continued: "I then, with a tremendous struggle for self-control, stood up in the corner of the pew and sang along. At the words, 'Thou Savior see'st the tears I shed,' there was again a great burst of crying and sobbing all over the church. I wanted to break down dreadfully, but I held on and carried the hymn to the end. When the rector prayed for 'the sick and wounded soldiers and all in distress of mind and body,' there was a brief pause, filled with a sound of weeping all over the church. He then gave out the hymn. . . . There was no organ and a voice that started the hymn broke down in tears. Another took it up, and failed likewise."

In the defenseless city, families of rebel leaders had been left to face the invading federal forces. One such person was Mary Custis Lee, the arthritic wife of General Lee. Although immobilized by arthritis and left alone with her daughter Agnes and a few black servants, Mrs. Lee never considered flight. Before the Confederate troops evacuated the city, two officers called on her at her house on Franklin Street and found her in good spirits. She would remain in the city, she said, come what may. The fire that swept the heart of the city during the night of April 2 roared down Franklin Street. It came as close as the roof of the house next door to Mrs. Lee's before it was extinguished. Across the street, a church burned to the ground. A women friend who called on Mrs. Lee a few hours later found her calmly knitting, as usual. She had sat in her chair most of the night and was unshaken by the fall of the capital. She still had faith in her husband's ability to turn the tide. "The end is not yet," she said. "Richmond is not the Confederacy."

For some devoted to the South, the fall of Richmond was a moment that went beyond sadness and despair. Watching from her window in agony, one woman asked herself, "Was it to this end that we have fought and starved and gone naked and cold, to this end that our homes were in ruins, our state devastated?"

When Major General Weitzel arrived at the capital, about 8:15 A.M. on April 3, he received Mayor Mayo's second surrender. Then the general devoted his entire attention to having his men put out the fire. By that time, the city was engulfed in flames and dense clouds of smoke. The business district had been completely destroyed, and advancing flames threatened to destroy the entire city.

The Federal infantry brigade, with the assistance of an engineering company, went into action to fight the fire. By midafternoon, the fire was under control, but the embers continued to smolder for days after. Once people were able to return to the burned-out area, the destruction was so complete that they could not locate their stores or homes; sometimes it was even difficult to find traces of their own street. About 700 buildings had been burned, leaving a black ruin from Main Street to the James River.

Some citizens of Richmond faced another fear—the fear that freed slaves would rise in bloody vengeance to annihilate Southern whites. With mostly women and children remaining in the city, this fear grew to epic proportions. Many believed that their only salvation now was to beg for protection from the Federal troops. Among the hundreds of women requesting guards to be posted at their homes was Agnes Lee, sent by her mother. Agnes explained that her mother was Mrs. Robert E. Lee and that she was an invalid and could not leave her home. A corporal and two privates of the 9th Vermont Cavalry were assigned to guard her house. An army ambulance was made available, ready to rescue Mrs. Lee if the flames should come closer.

The Federal soldiers sought to reassure all of Richmond's citizens that they would be protected. An officer told a frightened crowd, "We'll picket the city with a white brigade." He continued, "I assure you that there won't be a bit of molestation, ladies. Not a particle." An order was posted prohibiting anyone from being on the street after 9:00 P.M. Soldiers and civilians found on the street after that hour were to be arrested. By nightfall on April 3, peace had begun to settle over the city.

The stars shone down that night on the smouldering ruins of Richmond. Gaunt chimneys stood naked against the black velvet sky. A Federal officer, picking his way through the littered streets to inspect the guard, noted that the silence of death seemed to brood over the city. Occasionally a shell exploded somewhere in the ruins. Then it was quiet again. For Richmond the war was over.

Despite the ruins around them, Union troops would not be denied their celebrations. "An inspiring feature of the first evening of our occupation of the city was the music of the military bands," noted one of the Yankees present, "discoursing such patriotic airs as 'Yankee Doodle,' 'Hail Columbia,' 'The Star Spangled Banner,' etc.—airs that must have fallen rather oddly on the ears of citizens, after having listened four years to the music of treason." "For us, it was a requiem for buried hope," wrote one Richmond woman.

The next day dawned on a strange city—occupied Richmond. Those who ventured outside found that Federal troops in the streets and in their headquarters at city hall were well behaved. Ladies who were forced to ask for food were met with politeness. But the courtesy angered them; they would almost have preferred rudeness. Still, the troops filling the streets of Richmond were the enemy. Their presence evoked a conflict in Southern hearts, as expressed in the diary of fourteeen-year-old Frances Hunt. "The Yankees are behaving very well," she noted, "considering it is them."

With the arrival of Union troops, sutlers, who followed the army to sell their wares, immediately opened business in tents or rented stores. The currency was greenbacks only. Hundreds of blacks, enjoying their new freedom, were in the streets celebrating. Northern reporters, war artists, photographers, and even sightseers had come along with the Federal troops. Life had resumed in Richmond.

When news of Richmond's fall reached New York City, diarist George Templeton Strong ran to Trinity Church, where he convinced the sexton to have the chimes rung. Then he hurried down to Wall Street, where a large crowd had gathered to listen to speeches and sing patriotic songs. "Never before did I hear cheering that came straight from the heart," Strong reflected. As the news spread throughout the North, similar celebrations were held. For the Union, it seemed certain that the war would soon be over.

In the meantime, after touring Petersburg, Lincoln decided to visit Richmond. Before reaching Richmond, he observed Confederate prisoners of war (POWs) being transported to prison. "They were in pitiable condition, ragged and thin," remarked Lincoln's bodyguard. "They looked half starved." Lincoln looked at the prisoners and said, "Poor fellows. It's a hard lot. Poor fellows . . . " His face was pitying and sorrowful," the man remembered. "All the happiness had gone."

About midmorning, Lincoln arrived at Richmond by boat. His son Tad, Admiral David Porter, and William Crook, a White House guard were with him, accompanied by one dozen armed sailors. As they walked through the streets, they were met by throngs of former slaves. "God bless you, sir!" said one, taking off his cap and bowing. "Hurrah! Hurrah! President Lincoln has come! President Lincoln has come!" rang through the streets. Their deliverer had come. Black people pressed around the president all along the route. They came from all directions, running, shouting, cheering, and dancing with delight. The men threw up their hats; the women waved their bonnets and handkerchiefs, clapped their hands, and shouted, "Glory to God! Glory! Glory! Glory!" and rendered all the praise to God. After long years of waiting, the freed slaves had met their great benefactor.

The walk was long, and the president rested along the way. Lincoln and his contingent struggled on with a large crowd in front of them and an equally dense crowd of blacks following behind. Finally they reached Jefferson Davis's mansion. President Lincoln was shown into the reception room. He made a tour of the mansion, seated himself in Davis's chair, and seemed interested in everything. When news of Lincoln's violation of the Davis mansion reached

Judith McGuire, a Richmond resident, it greatly upset her. "Our President's house! Ah, it is a bitter pill! I would that the dear old house, with all its associations so sacred to Southerners, so sweet to us as a family, had shared in the general conflagration. . . . Oh, how gladly would I have seen it burn!"

2   The Stillness at Appomattox

O N the night of April 1, 1865, when Robert E. Lee lay down to take a few hours' rest at Edge Hill, the Federal artillery could be heard all along the line. For almost four years, Lee had faced that artillery and the great Union army behind it, but never had he been in such a desperate situation as he was that night.

The winter of 1864–65 had been as harsh a one for Lee's men at Petersburg as the one Washington's army had faced at Valley Forge in 1777. There never was enough to eat. By February 1865, Confederate soldiers were living on a daily ration of only a pint of cornmeal and two spoonfuls of sugar. On occasion, if they were lucky, they received a scrap of fatty bacon along with their regular ration. Men became so weak that it was difficult for them to work for any length of time, let alone to fight. They would start digging a trench, but gasp for breath and feel faint after less than an hour of work. Private John Casler knew how desperate a person could get when on the verge of starvation. Assigned to bury dead Yankees, he searched their pockets for food before rolling them into the grave. "I have been so hungry," he said, "that I have cut the blood off from [hardtack] crackers and eaten them."

Nakedness went along with hunger. Thousand of Lee's soldiers went barefoot, leaving bloody footprints in the snow. The uniforms of the few men who had them had become threadbare rags. Lookouts from a Union outpost had a clear view of the Confederate's plight. They were a sorry sight, a Yankee wrote: "I could not help comparing them to women with cloaks, shawls, double bustles, and hoops, as they had thrown over their shoulders blankets and tents which flapped in the wind." Whenever Lee rode through the camps, soldiers called out: "General Lee, I am hungry." There was no disrespect or anger in their voices; they knew he was doing the best he could for them. But even Lee was helpless, given the lack of support by the Confederate government. By this time, the government was on the verge of collapse and paralyzed by defeat.

Lee's Army of Northern Virginia was losing an average of a hundred men a day through desertion. The Southern soldiers had not run out of courage; they still fought as hard as ever until the moment of desertion. For growing numbers of Rebels, it was clear that no amount of sacrifice would change the outcome of the war. The war was lost, the Confederacy collapsing. Those who remained did so not because they expected to win, but from a sense of duty to their comrades and their flag.

For Grant and the Army of the Potomac, the conditions were completely different. Except for the danger the troops faced on the front line, they spent a comfortable winter. Grant's army never went barefoot or were hungry. Rear-area camps were safe, snug, and warm. Northerners went all out to see that their men had a merry Christmas. Each soldier received a boxed dinner containing turkey, stuffing, cranberry sauce, and mince pie. Soldiers welcomed in the New Year with band concerts and sing-alongs. Some men were even visited by their wives. General Grant lived in a house with his wife, while his children attended a private school in New Jersey. The North grew steadily stronger, while the South was on the verge of total collapse.

On March 25, Lee had made an effort to break through the Federal trenches at Fort Stedman but had failed and suffered heavy losses. Now Sheridan, with the Union cavalry, was joining Grant from the Shenandoah Valley. Sheridan was threatening Lee's right and preparing to cut him off from the Southside Railroad. Lee did not have sufficient cavalry to meet the stronger Union thrust. Before retiring that night, Lee had received reports that Sheridan had smashed on April 1 a Confederate force under Major General George Pickett at a road junction called Five Forks. Details were few, but disaster was facing his army.

Before daylight on April 2, General A. P. Hill arrived at Lee's headquarters.

Soon after his arrival, Lieutenant General James Longstreet came. He had been summoned with part of his small corps to help Pickett at Five Forks. While Lee was explaining the disposition of Longstreet's men, a staff officer interrupted the meeting with the news that the Union troops had overrun the Confederate trenches. The officers sprang up, Longstreet and A. P. Hill hurrying off to their troops. It was the last time Lee would see Hill alive.

Heading southward with a courier on the Boydton Plank Road, Hill spotted two Federal soldiers in the trees ahead. "We must take them," snapped Hill, drawing his revolver. The Union soldiers from the 138th Pennsylvania took cover and leveled their rifles. "If you fire, you'll be swept to hell," shouted Hill's courier. Then bluffing, he said, "Our men are here—Surrender!" Hill repeated the cry: "Surrender!" The answer came in the form of a bullet, which pierced Hill's heart. He was dead before he hit the ground. Hill's courier, C. W. Tucker, rode back to headquarters and reported the tragedy to Lee. Lee's eyes filled with tears. "He is at rest now," Lee murmured, "and we who are left are the ones to suffer."

Lee soon ascertained that Petersburg could not be held. If Petersburg was abandoned, Richmond would also fall; but Lee had no other choice. Swiftly and grimly he gave the necessary first orders. A young officer close to Lee that day wrote later: "Self-contained and serene, he acted as one who was conscious of having accomplished that which was possible in the line of duty, and who was undisturbed by the adverse conditions in which he found himself. There was no apparent excitement and no sign of apprehension as he issued his orders for the retreat of his sadly reduced army and the relinquishment of the position so long and successfully held against the greatly superior force opposed to him. . . . It was a striking illustration of Christian fortitude, the result of a habitual endeavor to faithfully perform the duties of one's station and of unquestioning trust in the decrees of an all-wise Creator. . . ."

That night Petersburg was abandoned by all the troops who had defended the line from the Appomattox River to the point where the enemy had broken through. The thin Confederate brigades were withdrawn, and nearly all the artillery was removed. Lee rode on Traveller and had little to say. Afterward he confessed that his heart ached at the thought of leaving the women and children of Petersburg to the mercy of Union troops. The Confederates left so quietly that the enemy was unaware of their movements until the next morning—Lee had gained a head start in his attempt to escape from Grant.

If Lee was lucky and met with no delay, he hoped to keep ahead of Grant's army. He planned to bring together all the Confederate troops in the area so they could be in reach of a railroad line from which they could receive supplies. The column from Petersburg was to move west until it reached Amelia Court House. There they would be joined by troops retreating from Richmond. Together they would move down the railroad tracks toward Danville. Somewhere south of the city, General Joseph Johnston with the remnants of his army would join Lee.

On April 3, General Grant and his troops marched into Petersburg uncontested. The streets along the riverfront were crowded with Confederate soldiers struggling to get away. Grant showed compassion; he could have wreaked havoc on the stragglers with his artillery, but he elected to let them get away. "I had not the heart," he explained later, "to turn the artillery upon such a mass of defeated and fleeing men. Besides I hope to capture them soon."

The first day out of Petersburg, Lee stopped for dinner at Clover Hill, the plantation home of young Kate Cox. Cox tried to reassure Lee that victory was still possible: "We shall still gain our cause; you will join General Johnston and together you will be victorious." "Whatever happens," Lee responded, "know this—that no men ever fought better than those who have stood by me."

As Lee passed his soldiers on the road that day, he found them cheerful and not exhausted by their march. They were hungry because most of them had not eaten since they had left Petersburg. The men were accustomed to being hungry, but they were expecting to be fed when they reached Amelia. The first to reach the quiet little village was Longstreet, accompanied by the remnants of A. P. Hill's corps, now under the command of Major General Henry Heth. Major General John Gordon's corps was close behind. But to their surprise, no supply train was at the station, and none were reported to be on their way. To add to the problem, the residents scarcely had enough food for themselves. Lee was aghast; in the most desperate retreat of the war, his army was without even the barest essentials. Lee's only recourse was to halt the army and send wagons out into the countryside to borrow, beg, or buy from the farmers. While waiting for the wagons to return, Lee's army would lose the advantage of their earlier march. As quickly as possible, Lee sent a message to Danville indicating the serious nature of his position and requesting rations. An appeal was made to the farmers for food and wagons. The men waited hungrily and wondered why provisions had not been sent. Lee could not answer. He did not know.

During the night of the fourth and the morning of the fifth, the army wagons returned, but very little food had been collected. The farms had been stripped already, but this wasn't the only bad news; the enemy was catching up. No more time could be lost. If the army waited, the Federals could cut off the railroad and the Confederate's supply line from Danville—the army would starve. Although the troops were weakened by their lack of food, Lee was forced to give the order for his army to move out. Lee wanted to move down the railroad tracks in hopes of keeping ahead of the Federal troops and of meeting any trains that could be sent from Danville. By 1 P.M. on the fifth, Longstreet's troops were on the move, using a road parallel to the railroad line. The troops from Richmond had arrived at Amelia and pursued the same route.

The absence of food made it even more imperative that the Confederates' push westward continue at a rapid pace. "I know that the men and animals are much exhausted," noted Lee in a message to General Gordon, "but it was necessary to tax their strength." The soldiers understood their desperate situation. One wrote in his diary, "It is now a race for life or death."

The federal troops were equally aware of what was at stake. They outran their own wagon trains in anticipation of following up their victory. As Grant reported, "They preferred marching without rations to running a possible risk of letting the enemy elude them." Major General George Crook's cavalry and Brigadier General Charles Griffin's V Corps reached Jetersville, directly in Lee's path, on the afternoon of April 4. Lee knew that the Union cavalry and infantry were waiting for him at Jetersville and that if they attempted to smash through, Grant's superior forces would certainly overwhelm his depleted army. Lee's only hope was to avoid engagement and move around the Federals. His men must have food, and soon.

Lee waited until darkness to make his move. The night march turned into a nightmare. His men had eaten their last rations at midday on April 3; it was now sixty hours since they had last eaten. The feebler of his soldiers began to drop by the roadside, unable to continue. Some wandered off to look for food and never returned. Obedient to duty, most of the men continued to follow orders. They stumbled along in the dark, through heavy rain, hardly conscious of what was happening. Many had lost track of all time and were unable to remember afterward where they had been or what they had done. Captain McHenry Howard of Curtis Lee's staff recalled, "Every expedient was resorted to in order to obtain something to eat, however scanty, with total disregard of the ordinary rules of discipline and respect for private property."

An earlier attack on the Confederate wagons had left the route blocked with wreckage; the surviving vehicles returned on the same road being used by the infantry, adding to the confusion and slowing their retreat even more. Horses and mules broke down, forcing the wagons carrying the remaining scraps of food to be abandoned. "We stopped for what was supposed to be the midday meal," one officer recalled. "The midday was there, but the meal was not."

On April 6, Lee rode with the troops of the I Corps who were leading the retreat. Lee chose to lead. If the army was to escape, it had to be pushed steadily on. He must be where he could make speedy decisions if the route had to be changed. Lee's veterans responded to his presence. Tired as they were, the troops marched on until they reached the Southside Railroad at Rice Station. Lee halted the column there until divisions in the rear caught up.

The Union soldiers in pursuit found the roads littered with discarded weapons, blanket rolls, and artillery pieces. The roads were also filled with stragglers, deserters, and men who had no strength to go on or who could no longer stay awake. Prisoners poured into the Federal lines by the thousands. It was the beginning of the end for the Army of Northern Virginia.

Before Lee moved on, he received more bad news from Colonel Charles Venable, one of his staff officers. The Federals, Venable reported, had captured all of the Confederate wagons near Sayler's Creek. "What has become of the troops behind Longstreet?" Lee asked. Venable had heard nothing. Lee ordered Major General William Mahone to move his division back toward Sayler's Creek in order to salvage what he could from the fiasco. Lee went with them. When he arrived, he was aghast, as Mahone said later. Lee saw below him his troops retreating, "a harmless mob, with the massive columns of the enemy moving orderly on." Lee straightened himself and exclaimed, "My God! Has the army dissolved?" A moment later he took a battle flag and rode out to rally his men.

Lee's efforts to rally his men went unheeded—after a brief, futile battle, most of Lieutenant General Richard Anderson's and Lieutenant General Richard Ewell's troops surrendered. Anderson and his division commanders managed to escape, but Ewell and seven other generals were taken prisoner along with 7,000 men. Part of General Gordon's men also fell victim to Union forces when they took the wrong road and wandered into enemy lines. In the two phases of the Battle of Sayler's Creek, a third of Lee's army was captured.

That night Sheridan sent an exultant message to Grant detailing the victory at Sayler's Creek: "If the thing is pressed, I think Lee will surrender." Grant relayed Sheridan's message to Lincoln and received an immediate response: "Let the thing be pressed." Thus the frantic chase went on, the Confederates staggering through the night, and the Federals taking time to eat and sleep before resuming pursuit.

With those of his men who still had strength enough to march, Lee moved westward again that night. On April 7, they reached the town of Farmville. There, at last, food was waiting for them, having been sent from Lynchburg on the Southside Railroad. The leading troops received the first food they had had in four days. The soldiers took their rations and moved to the north of the Appomattox River. There they thought they would be safe to cook their food and catch some sleep.

Peace for them was not to be. As the half-starved Confederates were cooking their meat, Lee received news that one of the bridges that was believed to have been burned was still accessible to the enemy. Now the Union troops had found it and were in close pursuit. The Confederates had to grab up their uncooked food and run for their lives. Many of the men were forced to leave without getting anything to eat. The starving army, with no opportunity to rest, had to retreat once more.

By the evening of April 7, Lee's army had been severely reduced in size. He had with him only the most resolute of his soldiers. Many of the bravest had dropped from exhaustion. Other devoted men had dragged themselves along but had thrown away the rifles that they no longer had the strength to carry. A few who could no longer walk were forced to surrender. Starved horses were breaking down along with the men. The road leading to Lynchburg was littered with wagons and dying animals. When possible, the wagons were set afire to prevent them from falling into the hands of the enemy.

That evening General Grant stayed at the Prince Edward Hotel in Farmville, where Lee had stayed the night before. He sat on the hotel porch and watched the VI Corps come into town. As they marched through the streets, they seemed to have renewed vigor, appearing to have as much energy as they did on the first day of their toilsome march. Colonel Horace Porter, who was present at the scene, reported, "Then was witnessed one of the most inspiring scenes of the campaign. Bonfires were lighted on sides of the street . . . ; cheers arose from their throats, already hoarse with shouts of victory; bands played, banners waved and muskets were swung in the air. . . .The night march had become a grand review, with Grant as the reviewing officer."

Grant enjoyed the celebration, but he was also deeply thoughtful. He had recently heard of remarks from the captured Confederate general, Richard Ewell, who was depressed and thought their cause was lost. Ewell believed they should have surrendered earlier, while there was still a chance to ask for concessions. If Ewell felt this way, Grant reasoned that Robert E. Lee might have the same feeling.

That evening Grant sent a message to Lee: "The results of the last week must convince you of the hopelessness of further resistance of the Army of Northern Virginia in this struggle. I feel that it is so, and regard it my duty to shift from myself the responsibility of any effusion of blood, by asking of you the surrender of the part of the C. S. Army known as the Army of Northern Virginia."

When Lee received the dispatch, he said nothing, but handed it to Longstreet. After reading it, Lonstreet summed up their shared attitude in two words: "Not yet." The army was not yet ready to surrender. As long as he had a choice, Lee felt there was still a flicker of hope.

Saying nothing to Longstreet, Lee replied to Grant: "Genl: I have read your note of this date. Though not entertaining the opinion you express of the hopelessness of further resistance on the part of the Army of Northern Virginia—I reciprocate your desire to avoid useless effusion of blood, and therefore before considering your proposition, ask the terms you will offer on the condition of its surrender."

Although weary and burdened with the loss of much of his army, Lee was outwardly calm and appeared confident that his army would escape Grant and join Johnston in the successful continuation of the war. Supplies had arrived from Lynchburg by rail at Appomattox Station, twenty-five miles west of Farm-ville, and were waiting there without adequate protection. First, the Confeder-ates would have to disengage from the attacking Federals and get a safe dis-tance away; then, after resting, they would move on to Appomattox Court House, a village two miles northeast of the railway station.

The conditions on the morning of April 8 brought confidence to Lee and his men. There was still hope that they would escape the trap the Union army was trying to spring. The march that morning was not hindered by Union attacks; scarcely a shot was heard. But part of Grant's infantry was close behind them, and another part of his army was moving westward, parallel to and south of the Confederate army. If the parallel column marched faster than Lee's army, they could cut off his retreat.

The hopelessness of their situation caused several of Lee's principal officers to decide that—in order to lighten his responsibility and soften the pain of defeat—it was time to talk with him about negotiating a peace. The Reverend General Pendleton was their spokesman. When Pendleton found Lee, he was taking advantage of the tranquillity to lie down on the ground to rest. Lee lis-tened in silence and when Pendleton finished, he sat up and responded with "some harshness of manner." Lee did not like such unsolicited suggestions from his officers. Lee did not tell Pendleton that he had already commenced nego-tiations with Grant. As Brigadier General Edward Porter Alexander observed, "I believe that General Lee took no one into his confidence as to his intention, or to his correspondence with General Grant. . . ." "Oh, I trust it has not come to that, General," Lee responded. "We have yet too many bold men to think of laying down our arms. They fight with great spirit . . . the condition of demanding unconditional surrender—a proposal to which I will never listen."

Before long, a courier brought Grant's response to Lee's inquiry about pos-sible terms of surrender. Grant's only condition was "that the men and officers surrendered shall be disqualified from taking up arms again against the gov-ernment of the United States until properly exchanged." This was a far more generous offer than Lee had expected from "Unconditional Surrender" Grant.

That evening Lee and his generals could see the painful evidence of their situation. Although Lee's pursuers, the II and VI Corps, were still ten miles to the east, the red glow of enemy campfires to the south indicated that Major General Edward Ord's divisions, marching on a parallel road, had caught up with them. To the west, Sheridan's cavalry was waiting to cut off Lee's move-ment in that direction. Lee summoned his top commanders to a meeting at his camp. Quietly he reviewed their predicament. A Federal force was undoubted-ly ahead of them, cutting them off from Lynchburg. Lee's dignity in this extreme situation was reported by General Gordon: "We knew by our own aching hearts that his was breaking. Yet he commanded himself, and stood calmly facing and discussing the long-dreaded inevitable." Somehow, Lee still held out hope. If their route was blocked by cavalry alone, without the support of infantry, Lee's army still might be able to break through and reach Lynchburg. It was decided that Gordon would attack westward with the support of Fitzhugh Lee's cavalry.

That evening, having still not heard from Lee, Grant rode into that night's makeshift headquarters and greeted General Meade with a friendly "Old Fellow." Grant was suffering from a severe headache and resting on a sofa when a message from Lee arrived. At first Grant's aides were reluctant to disturb him, hoping he had fallen asleep. When Grant heard the door open, he immediately called for the note. The dispatch was Lee's response to his surrender terms. Grant was disappointed by his response: "I did not intend to propose the surrender of the Army of Northern Virginia," Lee wrote. "To be frank I do not think the emergency has arisen to call for the surrender of this army." Lee asked to meet with Grant the next morning at ten, not to negotiate surrender, but to see how "your proposal may affect the Confederate State forces under my command." After receiving the note, Grant lay down again, hoping to relieve his throbbing headache.

After sleeping just a couple of hours, at three in the morning, Lee began to dress in his finest uniform. When asked later in the morning why he had done this, Lee replied, "I have probably to be General Grant's prisoner and I thought I must make my best appearance."

It was Palm Sunday, with a blue cloudless sky, and the warm air had the smell of spring. If it hadn't been for the dire situation in which he found himself, Lee would have been attending a Sunday service. But at eight o'clock an officer reported to him with a message from General Gordon: "Tell General Lee I have fought my corps to a frazzle, and I fear I can do nothing unless I am heavily supported by Longstreet's corps." Longstreet could not help; his small force was facing Union troops who were closing from the rear. To the report of this situation, Lee listened in silence. To the east of Lee's army, the Federal II Corps resumed its advance. Sheridan and his cavalry prepared to attack Gordon on his left. Lee's two corps would soon be fighting back to back. Lee's situation was described by one of Ord's soldiers: "He couldn't go back, he couldn't go forward, and he couldn't go sideways."After hearing of the gravity of his position, Lee said: "Then there is nothing left for me to do but go and see General Grant, and I would rather die a thousand deaths." Lee's officers were overwhelmed with grief. "Oh, General, what will history say of the surrender of the Army in the field?" "I know they will say hard things of us," Lee said. He continued: "They will not understand how we were overwhelmed by numbers. But that is not the question, Colonel: The question is, is it right to surrender this Army. If it is right, then I will take all the responsibility."

For a moment, Lee's strength faltered. "How easily I could be rid of this, and be at rest! I have only to ride along the line and all will be over!" He paused and gained grip of his emotions: "But it is our duty to live. What will become of the women and children of the South if we are not here to protect them?"

Lee talked with Longstreet and Major General Mahone, and they believed he should surrender. General Porter Alexander said he thought the army should be scattered and take to the woods and reorganize later. Lee thought the number was too small to accomplish anything. He said: "General, you and I as Christian men have no right to consider how this would affect us. We must consider the effect on the country as a whole. Already it is demoralized by the four years of war. If I took your advice, then men would be without rations and under no control of officers. They would become mere bands of marauders, and the enemy's cavalry would pursue them . . . the only dignified course for me would be to go to General Grant and surrender myself and take the consequences of my acts."

At the start of the greatest day of his life, Grant told Horace Porter, his aide, that the best thing that could happen to him that day would be for the pain of his headache to clear. It was still torturing him; but he turned down an ambulance, mounted Cincinnati, and rode off, hoping that the morning air might help relieve the throbbing in his head. Grant had no intention of meeting with Lee until Lee was ready to surrender his army. In the meantime, Lee rode out to the point on the Richmond road where he expected to meet Grant at ten, only to receive Grant's note that he was not coming. With his military position worsening by the hour, Lee could no longer hope for terms that did not involve admission of defeat. With great sadness, he agreed to surrender. When his message reached the Union lines, General Meade was notified and he ordered a truce. "General," said Longstreet, "unless he offers us honorable terms, come back and let us fight it out."

The two armies faced each other at long range; the firing slackened and almost stopped. This was not the first time the armies had paused to look at each other across an empty field, each side sizing up the other before going to war with the enemy. Now they were taking their last look. The Confederate battle flags were about to fly for the last time. The Confederate soldiers would leave nothing behind but stars and the memories. The men who looked across the battlefield were tired and hungry. The only thoughts on their minds were of weariness and hunger and the single hope that they might live through the next half hour.

Off toward the south, Sheridan had his cavalry in line, mounted and ready to hit the Rebels' flank. To the west, the Federal infantry was poised to attack the Confederates from the front. Major General Joshua Chamberlain moved his men into position, as ordered by Sheridan. All of Ord's and Griffin's men were in line now, coming up on higher ground where they could see the whole field.

They could see the Confederate line draw back from in front of them, crowned with its red battle flags. The sunlight gleamed brightly off the metal and the flags for a last haunting moment. Then Sheridan's bugles sounded, and all of his brigades wheeled and swung into line, every saber raised, every rider tense. In just a moment, infantry and cavalry would drive in on the battle-worn and greatly outnumbered Confederate lines and destroy them in a last savage encounter. Out of the Rebel line came a lone rider, a young officer in a gray uniform, galloping madly, a staff in his hand with a white flag fluttering at the end of it. He rode up to Chamberlain's lines and was taken off to see Sheridan. The Federals watched while the Rebels stacked their muskets as if they never expected to fight again.

All up and down the lines, the men stared, unable to believe the hour they had waited for so long was actually at hand. There was a truce, and word was passed that Lee was going to meet with Grant in a small village that lay now between the two lines—the belief was that Lee was going to surrender. It was April 9, Palm Sunday. They would all live to see Easter, and with the guns silenced, it might be easier to comprehend the mystery and the promise of the day.

One of General Ord's soldiers wrote about the event: "We should have gone wild with joy, then and there; and yet," he said, "somehow we did not. Later there would be frenzied cheering and crying and rejoicing, but now. . . , for some reason, the men sat on the ground and looked across at the Confederate army and found themselves feeling as they had never dreamed that the moment of victory would make them feel. . . . I remember how we sat there and pitied and sympathized with these courageous Southern men who had fought for four long and dreary years all so stubbornly, so bravely, and so well and now, whipped, beaten, completely used up, were fully at our mercy—it was pitiful, sad, hard, and seemed to us altogether too bad."

When Grant received Lee's request to meet with him to discuss "the surrender of his army," he was elated. "I was still suffering with the sick headache; but the moment I saw the note I was cured," Grant recalled. He immediately dictated a reply to Lee explaining his location and saying he would meet with him as soon as possible.

With a Union officer, a member of his own staff and a courier, Lee rode into the village of Appomattox Court House. Lee asked Colonel Charles Marshall to ride ahead and arrange for a meeting place. The two-story frame dwelling of Wilmer McLean was selected. By the strangest of chances, McLean had moved from Manassas after the battle and had come to Appomattox to escape all contact with war.

Lee rode into the yard of the McLean house, where he dismounted, climbed the steps, went into the parlor, and took a seat. He remained there for half an hour until Grant arrived. Grant made his way across the porch and entered, followed by a number of his staff officers and by Generals Ord and Sheridan. Lee stood up and the two generals shook hands.

The men were a study in contrasts. Lee was tall, white-bearded, and dignified, wearing his best uniform and finest sword. Grant was slight and slouched, with brown hair and red whiskers. His three-starred shoulder straps were sewn on a mud-spattered sack coat. Grant's field glasses were slung across his shoulder, but he wore no sword.

At Grant's request, several more Union officers were invited into the crowded parlor. Those who could find a chair sat; the others stood against the wall. "What General Lee's feelings were I do not know," Grant later wrote. "As a man of much dignity with an impassable face, it was impossible to say whether he felt inwardly glad that the end had finally come, or felt sad over the result, and was too manly to show it. Whatever his feelings, they were entirely concealed from my observation."

Grant was motivated by a desire to make the ordeal for Lee as easy as possible. He wanted to end the fighting in a spirit of amity. On that April Sunday, Grant probably believed that his victory reunited the nation and was deeply moved by the humiliation forced upon his opponent. As he prepared to discuss the surrender, Grant was seized by a sense of sadness. After receiving Lee's earlier note, he had been jubilant, but now he found his mood had changed. Grant later said, "I felt anything rather than rejoicing at the downfall of a foe, who had fought so long so valiantly." Grant was also embarrassed by his careless dress. "I was afraid," he confessed, "Lee might think I meant to show him studied discourtesy by so coming."

It was difficult for Grant to come to the point of their meeting. He talked about other things, including old army days and their service in Mexico. But Lee brought him back to the purpose of their meeting. "I suppose, General Grant," he said, "that the object of our present meeting is fully understood. I asked to see you to ascertain upon what terms you would receive the surrender of my army."

Grant's reply must have lifted an enormous burden from Lee. Without a change in his tone, Grant answered that the terms were those he proposed in his letter—"that is, the officers and men surrendered to be paroled and disqualified from taking up arms until properly exchanged, and all arms, ammunition, and supplies to be delivered up as captured property." Lee replied: "Those are the conditions I expected would be proposed."

Lee suggested that Grant write out the terms, and Grant began to write rapidly in pencil in his order book. He paused for a moment and took a long look at Lee's sword. As Grant explained later, he then thought it would bring a needless humiliation on Lee's officers to give up their swords, baggage, and horses. Continuing, he wrote: "The arms, artillery, and public property to be stacked and turned over. . . . This will not embrace the side arms of the officers, nor his private horses and baggage . . . each officer and man shall be allowed to return to their homes not to be disturbed by United States authority as long as they observe their paroles and laws in force where they reside."

When Lee read the terms, he was touched by Grant's act of generosity. "This will have a very happy effect upon my army," he said. Lee hesitated a moment and then forced himself to say, "There is one other thing I would like to mention. The cavalry and artillerists own their own horses in our army . . . I would like to understand whether these men will be permitted to retain their horses." Grant told Lee that the terms as written did not allow for this, but then reconsidered. "I will instruct the officers I shall appoint to receive the paroles to let all the men who claim to own a horse or mule to take their animals home with them to work their little farms."

"This will have the best possible effect upon the men," Lee said. "It will be very gratifying and will do much toward conciliating our people." After the papers were signed, Lee mentioned that he had more than one thousand Federal prisoners whom he wished to return to Grant. They had been forced to share the meager Confederate rations, and they, like his army, were on the verge of starvation. Again Grant was generous. "I will take steps at once to have your army supplied with rations," Grant said.

Lee shook hands with General Grant, bowed to the others, left the room with Colonel Marshall, and mounted his horse. Without a word, Grant removed his hat. The rest of the Federal officers did the same. Lee raised his hat in return and slowly rode away. He seemed oblivious to the Federal soldiers in the McLean yard, who rose respectfully at his appearance.

Meanwhile, the Federal camps were erupting with joy. General Meade, hero of Gettysburg, who had been sick for the past week, mounted a horse and took off down the road at a gallop. Waving his hat and shouting at the top of his voice, he cried, "It's all over, boys! Lee's surrendered! It's all over!" Men shouted until they could shout no longer. Artillerymen fired salutes. Grant sent word to have it stopped. "The Confederates were now our prisoners and we did not want to exult in their downfall. The war is over. The Rebels are our countrymen again," Grant said.

The early halt in the fighting that day had led some of the Confederate soldiers to suspect that a surrender was being arranged. Most of the higher officers knew this was true. Most Confederates were unwilling to admit even to themselves the possibility of such a thing. When the troops saw Lee coming up the road, they went to meet him. They crowded around the general and started to cheer him, and then when they saw the agony on his face, they sensed the reason for it and choked their cheer. "General," some of them asked, "are we surrendered?" As they spoke, they crowded around him and took off their hats. Lee removed his hat and bowed, but he could not reply. Still the question came, "General, General, are we surrendered?" Lee stopped his horse and in shaken tones, struggling with his emotions, he said, "Men we have fought the war together, and I have done the best I could for you. You will all be paroled and go to your homes until exchanged." He tried to say more, but all he could force from his trembling lips was "Good-bye."

Lee's misery made the soldiers forget their own. They crowded even closer around him. Some reached out to touch his arm, his uniform, or his boots, trying to comfort him as best they could. "General, we'll fight yet. General, say the word and we'll go in and fight 'em yet." When he rode back to his tent, they followed him there. They appealed to him to continue the fight and lead them once more against the enemy. One soldier held out his arm to him: "I love you just as well as ever, General Lee." When he reached his tent, he stopped to make a brief speech: "Boys, I have done the best I could for you. Go home now, and if you make as good citizens as you have soldiers, you will do well, and I shall always be proud of you. Good-bye and God bless you all." Lieutenant George Mills, who was present, later wrote: "He seemed so full that he could say no more." Lee disappeared into his tent.

Lee had another option that day, which, to the lasting good fortune of his countrymen, he did not exercise. Instead of surrendering, he might have told his troops to scatter, to take to the hills, and to carry on guerrilla warfare as long as there were Yankees in the South. There were generals in the army who hoped he would do this, and the federal government would have had great difficulty putting down a rebellion of this type. The results of such action would have been tragic for both Northerners and Southerners of the day—and for their descendants. There would have been repeated atrocities, brutality, and enduring hatred, which would have created a wound beyond which the nation could not heal. Lee realized the consequences of making the wrong decision. He was the first to speak for reconciliation. He and his men had been fighting for an accepted place in the family of nations. When the fight was finally lost, Lee encouraged his men to forget their hatred, return home, become good citizens, and make the best of what still remained for them.

That night, after things quieted down, Lee asked Colonel Marshall to prepare an order, a farewell address, to his troops. After a few changes, Lee had copies made for the corps commanders and officers of the general staff. It thanked his army for their devotion and courage and reminded them that they were to remain at home until they were exchanged for Federal prisoners. This became known as the famous General Order Number 9.

After four years of arduous service, marked by unsurpassed courage and fortitude, the Army of Northern Virginia has been compelled to yield to overwhelming numbers and resources. I need not tell the brave survivors of so many hard fought battles, who have remained steadfast to the last, that I have consented to the result from no distrust of them. But feeling that valor and devotion could accomplish nothing that would compensate for the loss that must have attended the continuance of the contest, I determined to avoid the useless sacrifice of those whose past service have endeared them to their countrymen. By the terms of the agreement, officers and men can return to their homes and remain until exchanged. You will take with you the satisfaction that proceeds from the consciousness of duty faithfully performed, and I earnestly pray that a Merciful God will extend to you His blessings and protection. With an increasing admiration of your constancy and devotion to your country, and a grateful remembrance of your kind and generous considerations for myself, I bid you all an affectionate farewell.

Grant too was anxious to see the war followed by a good peace. He told Lee to have his men lay down their arms and go home; and into the terms of the surrender, he wrote the binding pledge that if they did this and lived up to the formal articles of parole, they would not be disturbed by the federal authority. This pledge had far-reaching importance because there were many men in the North who wanted to see leading Confederates hanged. What Grant had written and signed made it difficult to hang Lee and his cohorts. If Lee's decision spared the country the horror of continued guerrilla warfare, Grant's decision helped to avoid reprisals and hangings by the victorious Northerners. Between the two, these noble soldiers served their country well on that Palm Sunday, 1865.

As a tribute to the fallen Confederates, the Union troops remained silent. They were as splendid in victory as brave men could be in considering the feelings of a defeated adversary. But the commanders insisted that a formal surrender be made. The Northern people must have evidence that the rebel army had laid down its arms and flags in front of a federal line.

On the morning of April 12, the official surrender of the Army of Northern Virginia took place. General Joshua Chamberlain, hero at Gettysburg and Medal of Honor recipient, was honored with the command of the ceremonies. He aligned his troops on both sides of the road leading through Appomattox. There were no bands and no drums, just the shuffling sound of tramping feet. "On they come," wrote Chamberlain, "with the old swinging route step and swaying battle flags." General John Gordon led the column; behind him was the Stonewall Brigade, now thinned to scarcely two hundred men. All the Confederate units had been greatly reduced in size, so that their crimson battle flags were "crowded so thick, by thinning out of men," said Chamberlain, "that the whole column seemed crowned with red."

As the column neared the double line of Union soldiers, Gordon heard a spoken order and the clatter of hundreds of muskets being raised in salute.

Gordon responded by raising his sword to acknowledge the Union tribute. Gordon shouted a command and the advancing Confederates shifted to shoulder arms, returning the salute. "It was," said Chamberlain, "honor answering honor." Many of the veterans wept. "On our part," Chamberlain wrote, "not a sound of trumpet nor roll of drum; not a cheer, nor motion of men standing again at the order, but an awed stillness rather, and breath-holding, as if it were the passing of the dead."

After the exchange of salutes, the Confederates fixed their bayonets and stacked their muskets. Then, Chamberlain wrote "lastly—reluctantly, with agony of expression—they fold their flags, battle-worn and torn, blood stained, heart-holding colors, and lay them down." "This was the most painful part of the ordeal," said a former Confederate veteran. "We did not even look into each other's faces."

It was nearly 4:00 P.M. when the last Confederate troops finished stacking their arms and folding their regimental flags. One Union soldier remembered, "The Army of Northern Virginia, the pride of the Confederacy, the invincible, upon which their hopes and faith had been reposed, had disappeared forever, existing thenceforth in memory only." The remainder of the Confederate Army, some 175,000 soldiers under arms, were scattered throughout the South at various locations.

On May 26, General Kirby Smith sent his top subordinate, Major General John Bankhead Magruder, to surrender the last of these Confederate forces. The war was declared officially over by presidential decree in May of 1865, but most people considered it over when Lee surrendered on April 9 at Appomattox.

3   Reconstructing the South

TWELVE YEARS OF PAIN

O N the evening of April 9, 1865, President Lincoln received a telegram from General Grant: "GENERAL LEE SURRENDERED THE ARMY OF NORTHERN VIRGINIA THIS AFTERNOON." The next day the entire country had the news. Bells rang, bands played, flags and banners flew everywhere. A crowd gathered outside the White House. To the cheers of the crowd, "Tad" Lincoln, the president's twelve-year-old son, appeared at the window happily waving a captured Confederate flag.

Unfortunately, this happy mood did not last long. Five days later, on the evening of Good Friday, Abraham Lincoln and his wife, Mary Todd Lincoln, attended a comedy at Ford's Theater in Washington. Suddenly the rejoicing turned to grief as once more the telegraph clicked out momentous news—this time the news was of grave importance—the assassination of the president. During the play, John Wilkes Booth, a prominent actor, gained entrance to the president's box and shot him in the head. The shot proved fatal. Jumping to the stage, Booth shouted, "Sic semper tyrannis (thus always to tyrants)." In the process, he broke his leg but was able to hobble out a rear door and make good his escape before anyone could stop him.

Booth had plotted for months to kidnap Lincoln and hold him hostage for concessions from the Union. To help in his mad scheme, he recruited several drifters, Rebel spies, and Confederate deserters. With the fall of Richmond and Lee's surrender, Booth changed his plans and decided to kill the president instead. Also involved in the plot would be the murder of Vice President Andrew Johnson and Secretary of State William Seward. The accomplice assigned to assassinate Johnson lost his nerve and did not carry out his part of the plot; Seward suffered serious stabbing wounds, but survived. Only the president was dead. On April 26, Union troops tracked down the Maryland-born Booth and shot him to death in a burning barn in Virginia. Eager to avenge the fallen president, the government acted quickly. A military court convicted Booth's eight accomplices of collusion in the assassination. Four were hanged, and the others were sentenced to long jail terms. In two cases, some believe a miscarriage of justice occurred. Mary Surratt, keeper of the boarding house where the plot originated, was believed to be involved. Involved or not, she was to pay with her life. Dr. Samuel Mudd, who treated Booth's broken leg, was at most an accessory after the fact. He was found guilty, but later pardoned in 1869 when he performed acts of courage during a malaria outbreak while in prison. The convictions of Mary Surratt and Dr. Mudd were partly the product of postassassination hysteria and the clamors for revenge.

John Wilkes Booth's assassination of Lincoln was one of the greatest tragedies in American history. Confused motives crowded Booth's mind; by removing Lincoln, he in some way thought he was helping the defeated South. He had not, of course, helped the South at all; he had in fact hurt it. The assassination of the North's great war leader at the moment of victory aroused a display of mass emotion, scarcely equaled before or since in the United States. A special funeral train carried Lincoln's body home to Springfield, Illinois, across a mourning country—"through day and night," in Walt Whitman's words, "with a great cloud darkening the land."

The death of Lincoln evoked both deep grief and savage anger. Many in the North assumed that Jefferson Davis and other Southern leaders had instigated the crime. Secretary of War Edwin Stanton, supplying the press with official information, fanned their wild suspicions. He announced that evidence had been found to indicate the crime was the result of a conspiracy "planned and set on foot by rebels." The cry went up that the South must be punished. By this single act, Booth had damaged the hopes of the entire nation for an easy reconstruction. Booth had killed the one man who might have provided the leadership needed so badly at this time in history.

President Abraham Lincoln

On April 15, 1865, Andrew Johnson took the oath as president of a nation in shock and mourning. The murder of the president on Good Friday seemed to be more than a coincidence. For black people especially, Lincoln's death at the moment of victory over slavery made him a Christ-like figure. Anger as well as sorrow marked the Northern mood in the weeks that followed. There were cries of vengeance against not only the conspirators but all Confederate leaders. Such cries seemed to be contrary to the teachings of Christ, to whom Lincoln was now being compared. This anger also seemed to be contrary to the mood of Lincoln's second inaugural address: "With malice towards none; with charity for all; with firmness in the right, as God gives us to see the right, let us strive . . . to bind up the nation's wounds [and to achieve] a just, and a lasting peace among ourselves and all nations."

Everyone in Washington, Stanton most of all, was under great pressure during the weeks following the assassination. Although Lee had surrendered, Jefferson Davis and his cabinet still remained at large, moving southward. At every stop, Davis exhorted his people to fight on. Even after General Johnston surrendered, Davis spoke of moving the government to the trans-Mississippi states and carrying on the war. To the Union government, it appeared that guerrilla warfare might go on for years, but most Southerners had had enough. Lee's example was stronger than Davis's rallying cries. On May 10, Union cavalry captured Jefferson Davis and his entourage in Georgia. General Edmund Kirby Smith surrendered the trans-Mississippi army on May 26. The war was over, but the problems of peace still lay ahead.

For more than a week, three of the great armies of the United States, 200,000 strong, had been gathering around Washington, D.C., preparing for what would become known as the Grand Review. The feelings among the soldiers were mixed. One Connecticut boy recalled that "time hung heavily with the men as every hour kept them from home seemed to be endless." First Lieutenant James Merrill of the 7th Rhode Island looked forward to the review with pride and was anxious to have his unit make the best possible impression. "I remember that I kept awake most all night in order that the boys might be well groomed for parade."

The Grand Review was held on May 23–24, 1865, in a pageantry of power before the army was demobilized. "This was a great event," a Massachusetts soldier declared. The city was crowded with visitors from all over the country who had come to witness the review. Sidewalks, windows, parks, and every available space was filled with people anxious to honor their returning veterans.

It had been decided that on the first day, veterans of the Eastern theater, the Army of the Potomac, would march, while the honors on May 24 were given to Sherman's western armies. Major General George Gordon Meade, his staff, and an escort from the 1st Massachusetts Cavalry led the way on the first day. Behind them came file after file, first the cavalry, then the infantry, with artillery units sandwiched in between foot-soldier regiments. The long lines wound their way to the White House and the reviewing stand of notables, including President Andrew Johnson and General Grant. Lieutenant J. Howard West of the 209th Pennsylvania thought that the "most impressive sight . . . was the cheering of the school children. . . .They displayed their patriotism by standing hour after hour in the dust and hot sun, as the troops filed by. Thousands of flags and handkerchiefs were constantly in motion." The full procession took more than six hours to file past the reviewing stand.

At 9:00 A.M. on May 24, Sherman's men stepped off. "Flags, banners, and streamers everywhere swelled to the breeze," one Illinois veteran recalled, "as far as the eye could reach on every street and bayonets gleaming in the sunlight as troops went filing by." The band played "Marching Through Georgia." Sherman later remembered this day as "the happiest and most satisfactory moment of my life."

After the Grand Review, the victorious veterans scattered quickly to their homes. At the end of the war, the federal government had over one million men under arms. The way in which these men were quickly demobilized and returned to their homes and productive jobs was a miracle of American efficiency. The War Department had to break up each army, select from it men from various parts of the country, and arrange for each of them to be sent on their way. The government was obliged to do more than get the troops home. Before being discharged, the men had to be held long enough for their army history to be taken. When the men were finally free to go, the government had to be sure that transportation was provided and that each man had money in his pocket and a good feeling toward the government he had served.

A long series of orders were issued to reduce the size of the army. In rapid succession, they followed each other: Recruits, patients in hospitals, officers, and men whose terms expired before May 31. The troops with Meade and Sherman whose terms were to end before September 30 were all to be disbanded. For some men, this sudden demobilization produced a feeling of insecurity and fear. Four years of fighting, of experiencing defeat and victory, had hardened them into warriors who loved their trade. They had been dissatisfied at times, but the passion for danger and adventure had become a part of their way of life. Many of them had gone into the army as boys—the dangers and suffering they had experienced had turned them into men. They had learned to live off the land, pillaging and confiscating what they needed as a right of war. But now the war was over and they no longer could take a chicken or a loaf of bread for which they had not paid. For these men, becoming a civilian again would be a difficult adjustment.

In nine months, 800,000 volunteers had been returned to their homes. By November 1866, only 65,000 men remained in an army that eighteen months earlier had numbered more than a million. Most of the soldiers seemed to readjust quickly to civilian life, apparently without the social and psychological problems that have plagued so many veterans of recent wars.

But there were some problems. It took time to reorganize and reassign the Regular Army. Until that could happen, trained volunteer units had to be kept in uniform to patrol the Mexican and Canadian borders and the Great Plains, where troubles were looming with American Indian tribes. Few volunteers wanted to remain in the army after the fighting was over, and morale problems became serious. Some units mutinied and had to be forcibly disciplined. Desertions became widespread. There was growing discontent among the soldiers at being sent further south when, as they supposed, the war was over. In the South, they were met with resentment, distrust, and hostility. This led to numerous desertions from squads and platoons. On several occasions, nearly the whole command was called out at night to prevent the threatened desertions of companies and of a regiment. Even the more highly motivated volunteer officers were anxious to be released from the army. There was also fear among the men that by the time they were discharged, all the good jobs would be taken. One field commander complained to General Grant that his officers were afraid that "everybody at home will have got the start on them in business."

Others worried about the transition from the military to civilian life. "I have almost a dread of being a citizen, of trying to be sharp, and of trying to make money," one of Sherman's veterans admitted. "I don't think I dread the work. I don't remember shirking any work I ever attempted, but I am sure that civil life will go sorely against the grain for a time."

Finally the Yankee boys came home. An Indiana veteran wrote in his diary on the morning after his arrival that it was the first time he had slept in a bed since he left home. An Illinois comrade complained that the bed was "too soft to sleep in. For a long time, I preferred to sleep and to sit on the floor." For a returning Pennsylvania officer, the first night home with his wife was a spiritual one. "We so earnestly prayed together," he remembered, "and sought divine help to let the dead past hide its gloomy spots."

Among the shocks awaiting homebound Northern soldiers, especially those who had been away the longest, was that wages had risen forty-three percent during the course of the war, while the cost of living had increased at a rate of three times that. Nevertheless, the Northern soldier's return was relatively smooth, thanks to the strength of the Northern economy.

Most of the returning Union veterans slipped back into their old familiar niches or found new ones with a minimum of trouble and confusion. In the fall of 1865, Leander Stillwell returned to his home in the village of Otteville, Illinois. He had fought all over Arkansas and Tennessee, receiving his baptism of fire at Shiloh and nearly losing his life at Wilkinson's Pike. His parents welcomed him home, and the next morning he was out in the field, cutting and shucking corn.

For many Northern veterans returning home after Appomattox, the transition to civilian life was quick and easy. The killing was over, and for some, it seemed almost as if it had never happened. For Leander Stillwell and some others, it was as if they had taken up where they had left off. Yet Stillwell and thousands of others had changed in ways they hardly understood. Union and Confederate soldiers had fought in 10,455 major and minor engagements and suffered more than a million casualties. Aside from the 260,000 Confederate dead, 360,000 Union soldiers had died. Another 280,000 Union veterans had returned home with wounds of varying severity, not counting the hidden casualties of the war—those mentally disabled or so debilitated physically that their health would remain precarious the rest of their lives.

Inevitably, a few weak spots and some pockets of unemployment appeared, particularly in cities. While many men returned to former jobs or similar trades, four years had witnessed numerous changes in business, and often old-time jobs were no longer open. Furthermore, many of the youngest veterans had never been gainfully employed before the war, so jobs had to be found for them. Many returned to work on farms, while the more venturesome set out for the West.

Some returning veterans were unable to return to their former occupations because of various disabilities received during the war. In some areas, employers were reluctant or refused to hire one-armed or one-legged men, or rejected disabled veterans altogether. The Pension Act of 1864 (revised from 1862) provided pensions for veterans disabled by wounds or disease contracted while in the line of duty. But no pension was provided for those who had merely served in the Union forces.

The majority of enlisted men seemed to have little trouble adjusting to postwar life. They were young, single, and adaptable. Most had not committed themselves to a single trade or locality. Very often the veterans received preferential treatment, which most believed they deserved, often at the expense of men who had not served.

Officers of high rank, especially former West Pointers, found a world of opportunity awaiting them in both national and local politics, in federal jobs, in engineering or railroad operations, and in construction work of all kinds. Many veterans continued to serve in the Regular Army. In general, the people at home wished to support the returning soldiers even after the glitter had worn thin and become tarnished.

The problems facing returning Confederate veterans were numerous. The war-torn South had a long, hard path to travel before economic restoration and readjustment to peace would be complete. Conditions varied widely from Texas to Virginia, and the political aspects of Reconstruction were naturally affected by numerous economic difficulties.

"The most terrible part of the war is now to come," wrote a Georgia girl in her diary shortly after Appomattox. "The props that held society up are broken. Everything is in a state of disorganization and tumult. We have no currency, no law save the primitive code that Might makes right. We are in a transition state from war to subjugation, and it is far worse than was the transition from peace to war. The suspense and anxiety in which we live are terrible."

For Southern veterans, there was no waiting to be mustered out; a man's parole was his discharge, and he started home as soon as he received it. Unlike the Union soldiers, who returned home at federal expense and were given mustering-out pay, Confederate soldiers had to make their way home as best they could, often having to beg their way with nothing to exchange for food except the unwelcomed news of Appomattox.

The government that had enlisted and supported these men was no more—its officials were on the run or dead, its constitution void, its currency worthless. Most Confederate veterans had no money. Whatever money their generals had been able to get hold of was divided among them, but it was the merest pittance. When General Joseph E. Johnston saw that surrender was inevitable, he secured money to pay his men and officers a dollar apiece. Lee's men had received nothing. Only a small number of Kirby Smith's troops received any money after they surrendered.

Penniless as they were, nothing but walking, working, or stealing their way home had been left to the defeated Confederate veterans. But the U.S. government had wisely and justly come to their relief. General Grant set the stage for this movement by allowing Lee's men to keep their horses. He also allowed his own quartermasters to turn over to the Confederates whatever horses and mules they could spare. Johnston's army fared a little better. They were allowed to keep their animals, and arrangements were made for those who lived beyond the Mississippi to receive transportation by water to some Southern ports. The same arrangements were made for General Richard Taylor's army.

As the Rebels made their way home, they quickly learned the tricks of passage. "Too many together could not fare so well, so we thought it advisable to travel in less numbers so that people would not dread to feed us as we came along," recalled a North Carolina soldier. When returning veterans traveled in pairs, they were seldom refused food. A young boy in North Carolina never forgot the sad procession of returning veterans passing through his town: "Some were halt and lame, and some with one arm or one eye. Four years before, these brave men with high hopes went forth to reap the glories and victories of war. They had braved battles and left many of their comrades slain on the bloody field. They came home discouraged by defeat and found the country impoverished by the long and fruitless struggle." The Confederate veterans returned to a land much different from the one they had left. Sidney Andrews, a New England journalist who traveled to the South shortly after the war, reported his impressions. He saw Charleston as "a city of ruins, of desolation, of vacant houses, of widowed women, of rotting wharves, of deserted warehouses, of weed-wild gardens, of miles of grass grown streets, of acres of pitiful and voiceful bareness." His view of Columbia was much the same: "It is now a wilderness of ruins. Its heart is but a mass of blackened chimneys and crumbling walls."

Another visitor to the South, John Trowbridge, found farmers plowing among corpses, homeless families sheltering in hovels, and impoverished women searching the battlefields for old bullets and scrap metal to sell. Hogs rooted among the graves, and dead horses and mules lay rotting in the sun because there were no shovels with which to bury them.

The South suffered from more than just the loss of property and wealth. A former slave from Georgia recalled: "The master had three boys to go to war, but there wasn't one come home. All the children he had was killed. Master, he lost all his money, and the house soon begun dropping away to nothing. Us Negroes one by one left the old place, and the last time I seed the home plantation I was standing on a hill. I looked back on it through a patch of scrub pine, and it looked so lonely. . . . There were four crosses in the graveyard on the side lawn where he was setting. The fourth one was his wife."

The war had laid waste to the bravest of Southern youth. Thousands of graves told the story of the grim toll on a generation of young men. Many of the dead had been interred hastily near where they had fallen, the remains often subjected to the ravages of animals or the weather. Shortly after the war, John Trowbridge, visiting the Wilderness battlefield, observed the graves of four

Confederates: "The graves were shallow, and the settling of the earth over the bodies had the left feet of one of the poor fellows sticking out." Uncertainty about the location of dead relatives increased the pain of loss in countless Southern households.

Many Southerners lost everything, but they did not lose their spunk. A militant ex-Confederate told a reporter, "We have no government. We are aliens and foreigners, and will never have our souls so degraded as to have anything whatsoever to do with such a government."

Once back home, things didn't improve for the disbanded soldier. He was met with destruction and living conditions close to starvation. Richmond was in such condition that business could not be carried on. Before operations could resume, its ruins had to be cleared away and the city rebuilt. The same scenes, with variations, could be seen in the rural areas. A Northern traveler marveled at the destruction created by Sherman's march through South Carolina. There were "many miles like a broad black streak of ruin and desolation—the fences all gone; lonesome smokestacks, surrounded by dark heaps of ashes and cinders, marking the spots where human habitations had stood." For many Southerners, the problem was not how to live comfortably, but how to live at all.

Though the North could expect to get back to normalcy quickly, the story was very different in the South. Virtually every family—North and South had been touched by the war through the loss of a relative or friend, and for decades afterward, veterans who were missing an arm or leg were a familiar sight. But the South suffered more—the proportion of its population killed or wounded was much greater. It lost twenty-five percent of its white male population during the war. As Mary Chesnut, the South Carolinian diarist, pointed out in her *Diary from Dixie*, Southern women had to look at male beauty in a different way because whole men hardly existed any more. Many women in the South remained unwed because so few men returned from the war that there were not enough to go round.

Many Southerners still owned land and personal property but were unable to dispose of it. With the loss of manpower formerly provided by slaves, many landowners were left with large estates that they could not farm. In some cases, former slaves stayed on the farms and plantations to work the land, not for cash, but for a share of the crop. For the most part, except when they had been dealt with severely or in an unkindly manner, the emancipated slaves accepted employment with their former owners.

Small farmers who had not owned slaves suffered as well as large landowners. Their livestock was gone, their fields depleted, and their homes often in ashes. They had only their will to survive to carry them through this dark period in their lives. The story of their self-control in spite of adversity, their courage, and their effort to recover forms one of the finest chapters of heroism in American history.

The direct physical damages of the war were appallingly evident, but not so apparent were the losses in personal investments. Southerners who had invested in Confederate and state bonds saw their savings disappear. When the slaves were freed, former slaveholders lost $2 billion. A special cotton tax imposed by the federal government took an additional $68 million from the Southern economy.

Southern whites, although not then aware of it, were part of a unique historical episode. They were the only Americans ever defeated in war and the only Americans ever subjected to government imposed from the outside. The experience would have an important effect upon their psyche and North-South relationships for generations.

Even before the fall of the Confederacy and immediately following, thousands of ex-Rebels had voluntarily banished themselves from their native land. Now without homes or country or any predictable future, these Southerners fled to Latin America, Canada, and Great Britain. Some even went to nations in Europe and the Near East. Moving individually and in groups, they were former public officials, generals and soldiers, senators, statesmen, and farmers. All were disenfranchised. All had lost property or careers by supporting the Southern cause. All were faced with fear and uncertainty. In an effort to reconstruct their lives, the men, over 10,000 in all, took part in the largest movement of expatriates in American history.

Some of the exiles left for their own personal safety. Secretary of War John Breckinridge, Secretary of State Judah Benjamin, Generals Robert Toombs and Louis Wigfall, and others fled. They feared that federal indictments for treason against them might result in a death sentence if they were brought to trial. They were forced to remain in exile until they were granted a pardon or amnesty. Other Confederates, mostly military and state officials, left rather than submit to the humiliation of living under federal rule. Generals Jubal Early and Joseph Shelby, and Isham Harris (former governor of Tennessee) remained unreconstructed for years, exiling themselves out of bitterness. A few others simply sought new thrills in other lands. The great majority of the expatriates, however, left because they had to, or so they thought. Their homes and farms destroyed, unable to rebuild their fortunes under the supposed tyranny of Reconstruction, they tried to start a new life in another country.

When the war ended, a rapid influx of Confederates swelled the exile ranks in Canada. Other Confederates established the best-known refuge for expatriates, Mexico. Well over a thousand Southerners moved to Mexico in three years following the war. The most spectacular party of exiles was led by General Joseph Shelby of Missouri. Refusing to surrender, Shelby gathered the remnant of his Iron Brigade for a march south into Mexico. Others, including several generals, joined him on the way; by the time they reached Eagle Pass on the Rio Grande, he had a small army. The company crossed into Mexico on

July 4, 1865, burying their battle flags with their lost hopes in the muddy waters of the Rio Grande.

Further to the south, Confederates settled in sparsely populated areas of Central America. The most popular choices for a new home, Honduras and British Honduras, offered cheap land, pleasant climate, and beautiful scenery. In the vast expanse of Brazil lay the most successful of the colonization experiments. A legion of 4,000 expatriates moved there. Because slavery was permitted in Brazil, it had widespread appeal for many Southerners.

Never before had so many Americans left their homes and families to escape humiliation and supposed loss of freedom. By 1869–1870, hundreds of exiled Southerners were returning home. At home, many Southerners condemned the mass exile of their neighbors. Lee, for example, felt that he could not desert the South in its hour of need. "I must abide her fortunes," he wrote, "and share her fate." The loss of Southerners who elected to leave the country was felt in the South as those remaining struggled to recover from the devastation of the war.

The experience of war had a mystical dimension about it. The physical hardship was part of it; the terror and exultation and comradeship of battle; the bearing of wounds; the feeling of survival, almost always with some scar or mutilation. The men who had fought—both North and South—and survived knew something about themselves that peacetime could never teach. They had reached some limit of endurance and gone beyond it. They had experienced the horrors of war and come out alive. They knew things that they would not talk about, things to be shared only with those who had gone through the same fire. It was not just that they had experienced the unspeakable. They had trusted their lives to the God of battle in the name of preserving their country, their cause, and their comrades.

The idealism that had driven many men into the army was noticeably lacking among the returning veterans: "I am not the same man," Oliver Wendell Holmes Jr. told his parents as he left the army to begin a career in law. By his own admission, he had changed from a crusader to a pragmatist. Like many others in the North, his sense of purpose had been replaced with an increased respect for power.

The society to which Union soldiers returned was as different for them as the one to which Confederate soldiers had returned. The war had helped turn the North into an industrial society whose potential was unleashed by the coming of peace. Steel, oil, gold and silver mining, and railroad construction all expanded to an unprecedented level. The Industrial Revolution would lead to modern America and change the way Americans would live and think. Congressman William Kelly of Pennsylvania recalled that after the war, "The American people woke each morning to feel that there were great duties before them." There were "mines to be opened, forges and furnaces to erect, new houses to be built: Our wealth grew as it had never grown." Such was not the case in the South, which was wracked by physical devastation and social change. Fears of this sort were expressed by a young Southern woman who wrote that "the most terrible part of the war is now to come." For Southern blacks, there was the promise and also the peril of freedom. In 1865, the South faced many problems, some of them financial ones. The South was all but bankrupt. The collapse of Confederate bonds and currency wiped out the savings of many individuals and the endowments of colleges, churches, and other institutions. Little money circulated and interest rates soared; many commodities were exchanged by bartering. "The only money here," a Charlestonian reported, "is in the hands of Northern exchange brokers and bankers . . . men entirely unknown to us."

Material losses in the South were enormous. The Confederate states owed $712 million in war debts and had lost untold millions in the destruction of property, livestock, crops, industrial plants, and transportation. It would take more than twenty-five years to replace livestock and to return farm production to its prewar levels.

The railroad system of the South had been badly destroyed and almost ceased to exist. Rails were wrapped around trees, cross ties burned, freight and passenger cars wrecked, and bridges destroyed. Mills and factories were dismantled or burned to the ground. The collapse of the Confederate monetary and credit system wiped out private savings and forced banks to close. People were forced to make a living any way they could. Landowners who had never held a job before took positions as clerks and farmhands.

Loathing of the North was widespread and unrelenting in the South. A Savannah woman taught her children never to use the word *Yankee* without the epithets *hateful* and *thieving*. There were more moderate voices, of course, and some even saw emancipation as liberation from the responsibility and guilt of owning slaves. Most Southerners remained not only bitter about Yankees but resentful and fearful of the emancipated slaves.

Now that the war was over, the country faced the problems of rebuilding the South and restoring the Union. On the basic problems of reconstruction virtually everyone, North and South, agreed. Somehow the seceded states had to be brought back into a proper relationship with the rest of the Union; somehow the war-torn economy of the South had to be rebuilt; somehow the newly freed blacks' rights had to be protected; and somehow a feeling of loyalty to the nation must be restored among white Southerners. Such were the problems. It was only about the solutions that disagreement arose.

To help the newly freed African Americans realize some of the benefits of emancipation, Congress created the Freedmen's Bureau in March of 1865. The purpose of the bureau was to distribute food and clothing to needy Southerners, provide shelter when necessary, establish schools, and find jobs for both blacks and whites. The head of the bureau was Oliver Otis Howard, who had served under Sherman during his March to the Sea. He was an astute man and

Ward in the Carver General Hospital, Washington, D.C.

good at managing people, but many of his subordinates were inefficient, corrupt, and careless with public funds. Some white Southerners came to regard the bureau as a tool of the Republican party, not engaged in working for relief and rehabilitation, but in bringing benefits to blacks at the expense of white Southerners.

The bureau's critics repeated this theme again and again. For their part, blacks sought the assistance of the bureau. From their view, the bureau was often attuned to the planters' interests more than their own. On occasion, freedmen requested the removal of hostile officials, recommending the appointment of others known to be sympathetic to their aspirations. For the same reason that Southern whites demanded the removal of the bureau, most blacks remained loyal to it. In 1866, President Johnson sent generals Joseph Steedman and Joseph Fullerton on an inspection tour of the South. Johnson hoped to receive enough complaints to discredit the agency, but in city after city, blacks rallied to the bureau's support.

Many white Southerners feared that blacks were planning to murder them, and there was a deep reluctance to accept the reality of emancipation. Mary Chesnut recorded in her diary a story about a planter who had returned to his plantation at the end of the war only to be told by his former slaves, "We own this land now: Put it out of your head that it will ever be yours again."

For African Americans, emancipation was filled with hope and enormous difficulty. They responded to the news of emancipation with outbursts of joy and celebration. "I guess we must have celebrated Emancipation about twelve times in Harnett County. Every time a bunch of Northern soldiers would come through they would tell us we was free and we'd begin celebrating. Before we would get through somebody else would tell us to go back to work, and we would go," said Ambrose Douglas, a former North Carolina slave. "Some of us wanted to join up with the army, but didn't know who was going to win and didn't take no chances."

A persistent rumor in black communities was that freed slaves were to share in the division of their former master's land. Merchants sold them little red, white, and blue sticks that were to be used to stake out the land they claimed as their own. This dream of owning "40 acres and a mule" became a reality for some. By June of 1865, the federal government had relocated nearly 10,000 families on half a million acres of land abandoned by planters who had fled Union armies. Moreover, the powerful Republicans were threatening to "strip the proud nobility" in the South "of their bloated estates," and to redistribute the land.

Some blacks took their first opportunity to travel. For months after Appomattox, thousands of former slaves wandered the roads in a restless migration. Some were hoping to find family members; others were looking for jobs, schools, or government food and clothing.

Few blacks had the education, skills, or experience to cope with their sudden freedom. Almost ninety-seven percent were illiterate; many had never eaten with utensils or used money. Some blacks made ends meet by trading stolen goods to unscrupulous white merchants who gave them food, trinkets, and liquor. African Americans who went to work were often exploited by both their employers and the merchants from whom they purchased items at exorbitant prices. "It came so sudden on them they wasn't prepared for it. Just think of whole droves of people, that had always been kept so close, and hardly ever left the plantation before, turned loose all at once, with nothing in the world but what they had on their backs, and often little enough of that; men, women, and children that had left their homes when they found out they were free, walking along the road with nowhere to go," said Parke Johnston, a former Virginia slave.

Despite the grim reality of desolation and poverty, the South's economic recovery would involve more than rebuilding farms that had been destroyed and reconstructing bridges and railroads. An entire social order had been swept away and a new one constructed. For blacks and whites alike, the war's end ushered in "the perpetual trouble that belongs to a time of social change."

Southern planters emerged from the Civil War in a state of shock. Their prosperity and their own survival as a class had depended, as a Georgia newspaper said, upon "one single condition, the ability of the planter to command labor." Their class had been devastated physically, economically, and psychologically. Thousands of wealthy young men had gone off to war, only to die in battle. The loss of the planters' slaves and life savings wiped out the inheritance of generations. Bitter and demoralized, many planters sold their land and left the region, hoping to begin anew in the North or in Europe, or to establish themselves as planters in Mexico or Brazil.

For those planters who remained, the end of slavery ushered in a period of adjustment to new forms of race and class relations—and a new way of organizing labor. The first change was in the paternalistic behavior of prewar planters. A sense of obligation based on mastership over slave, paternalism had no place in a social order in which labor relations were mediated in impersonal markets and blacks aggressively pressed for autonomy and equality. "The law which freed the Negro," a Southern editor wrote in 1865, "at the same time freed the master of all obligations springing out of the relations of master and slave, except those of kindness, cease mutually to exist."

Kindness proved to be a rare item in the aftermath of the war and emancipation. Planters often evicted blacks too old or infirm to work from their plantations. The freedmen no longer enjoyed the rights they once had as slaves— clothing, housing, access to garden plots. "Some think," reported a bureau agent, "that the only difference between freedom and slavery was then the Negroes were obligated to work for nothing; now they have to pay for what they used to have for nothing." Or, rather, for their back-breaking labor. Dealing with their former slaves, now freedmen, was difficult for many planters. "It seems humiliating to be compelled to bargain and haggle with our own servants about wages," wrote Fanny Andrews, the daughter of a Georgia planter.

Southern blacks had entered Reconstruction with great optimism and determination. Many blacks knew their rights, but not all knew how to defend them. The tension between Southern whites and blacks, who now enjoyed a position of power but were ill prepared to exercise it, simmered for a time, but eventually would turn into violence.

Even as the Freedmen's Bureau did its work, there was much evidence that some Southerners were undermining its purpose. They believed that somehow the former ways of doing things could be revived. Ex-Confederates were elected to high positions, and the state legislatures, beginning in Mississippi, began to pass laws known as "black codes." These codes, designed to control and restrict the economic and social activities of blacks, were modeled on the old slave codes. The black codes extended a number of rights to freed blacks, including the right to hold property, make contracts, and sue in court, while denying them important civil rights. Among these were the right to serve on juries, testify in court against whites, carry firearms, or organize and attend meetings without whites present. In some states, blacks could be arrested and fined as vagrants if they had no visible means of support, and then be hired out by local sheriffs to work until they had earned enough money to pay the fine.

Many white Southerners found it difficult to accept the dissolution of their old way of life. In their minds, they constantly relived the past and mourned their young men sacrificed in the Lost Cause. Many Northerners, on the other hand, would never view the South as anything other than the land of treason. Busy erecting monuments to their war dead, Northerners were constantly reminded of the price they had paid to save the Union. They measured the cost in dollars too—billions of them.

The political fate of the South had been a concern of Lincoln and the federal government almost from the time the war began. Lincoln's initial experiment with reconstruction came early in the war in his dealings with border states. In both Maryland and Kentucky, he learned that Federal troops were needed to maintain Unionist governments. In Missouri, after Governor Claiborne Jackson joined the Confederates, Federal commanders reassembled the Missouri convention. Then they declared all state offices vacant and filled them and the governorship with those who would support the Union. Lincoln's early view of Reconstruction involved replacing state governors and providing military support to maintain peace and order. While Lincoln was alive, however, his views on Reconstruction were constantly changing. By 1863, his plan would be much more conciliatory.

Abraham Lincoln had believed this task to be the responsibility of the president. On December 8, 1863, he had used his power as commander in chief to issue a proclamation outlining a policy of conciliation toward the South. Lincoln had maintained that because a state could not leave the Union, they had never been lost; they were merely not in their proper relation to the Union. Lincoln's plan called for amnesty to all Confederates who would take an oath of loyalty to the United States. For a state to be restored to the Union, at least ten percent of those who had voted in 1860 would have to take the oath. Finally, when the state accepted emancipation, the political reconstruction would be complete.

At the same time Lincoln was presenting his Ten-Percent Plan, many Republicans were arguing that the task of reconstruction was a function of Congress. Some Republicans in Congress had already been critical of Lincoln's conducting of the war and supported a harsher policy toward the states that had

Ruins of Hood's ammunition train near Atlanta, Georgia, 1864

formerly been a part of the Confederacy. The issue was more than a choice between the president and Congress; it was also a choice between a lenient or a harsh treatment of the South.

The most ardent advocates of a harsh reconstruction process were the Radical Republicans. In the House, their leader was Thaddeus Stevens of Pennsylvania. The Radical Republicans in the Senate were led by Benjamin Wade, Charles Sumner, and Zachariah Chandler. The Radicals advocated that leaders of the Confederacy be excluded from political life, that some Southern whites be disenfranchised, and that the property of rich Rebels be confiscated and distributed among the freedmen. They also believed that blacks should be allowed to vote. When Abraham Lincoln was assassinated in April 1865, his successor was Andrew Johnson, the former senator from Tennessee. At first the Radical Republicans looked upon Johnson as one who would support their position. In the early months of his presidency, Johnson was satisfied that Reconstruction was going along smoothly. All the former Confederate states except Texas had met the conditions first set down by Lincoln and modified only slightly by

Johnson. The new president sent Grant on a fact-finding trip through the South. After five days, Grant returned and reported that Southerners were accepting the defeat. He advised that the fate of blacks be left to the "thinking people of the South."

Johnson had executed his Reconstruction plan during the summer of 1865, when Congress was not in session. When the legislatures convened in December, they found representatives from eight Southern states demanding admission to Congress. The identities of some of these men shocked the Republicans. Among them were many prominent Confederates, including a senator from Georgia, Alexander H. Stephens, the late Confederate vice president. Eight months earlier, many of these men had been in arms against the Union. The Republican majority angrily denied admission to all of these delegates. Congress appointed a joint committee of both houses to advise on the development of a restoration program.

Johnson's attempt at Reconstruction angered Congress. It seemed to Radical Republicans that Johnson was giving away the victory won by the North. "The Republic can not be lost," ranted Senator Charles Sumner of Massachusetts, "but the President has done much to lose it." Johnson's generous terms, the Radicals believed, encouraged many of the people in the South to think they could live as they had before the war.

The Thirteenth Amendment, which abolished slavery everywhere in the United States, went into effect just as Congress was convening in December. Determined to continue their work on behalf of black Americans, the Republicans saw Johnson as a major obstacle. Their frustration mounted when, in February 1866, the president vetoed a bill extending the life of the Freedmen's Bureau. In April, Congress passed a Civil Rights Act, but Johnson again vetoed it. When Congress promptly passed the bill over his veto, the struggle was on. The confrontation between Johnson and Congress made 1866 the critical year of Reconstruction. When the Fourteenth Amendment was submitted to the states for ratification, President Johnson let it be known that he hoped the amendment would be rejected. All of the former Confederate states, except Tennessee, followed Johnson's advice. When Kentucky and Delaware joined them, the amendment was not ratified. Congress rang with indignation. One Radical predicted what lay ahead for the South: "They would not cooperate with us in rebuilding what they destroyed. We must remove the rubbish and rebuild from the bottom." The Radicals resolved to proceed on their own, ignoring the president and attacking him whenever possible.

In the election of 1866, the Radical Republicans won a sweeping victory, putting them in the position of taking over Reconstruction. In March 1867, Congress passed, over Johnson's veto, a series of bills that continued their plan of Reconstruction. Under the Reconstruction Act of 1867, the South was divid-

The Hollywood Cemetery in Richmond, Virginia, 1865

ed into five military districts, each with its own military commander. These commanders were to prepare the states in their district for self-government by enrolling all male voters, both white and black. By the end of 1868, seven states had taken the steps required to be readmitted to the Union. By 1870, all of the states had been restored to the Union.

In 1867, the Radicals were at the height of their power and in their triumphant hour, they reached out for still more control of the government. Because they controlled Congress, they considered that branch the central power of the government. "Congress," said Thaddeus Stevens, "was sovereign. No government official, from the President and Chief Justice down, can do any act which is not prescribed and directed by the legislative power."

Despite the passage of the Reconstruction Act, President Johnson still had power to block the Radicals' plans. As a result, Congress passed several laws designed to reduce his powers. The Radicals warned Johnson that they would watch him carefully to see that he carried out their Reconstruction policies.

When Johnson decided to test the constitutionality of the laws, the Radicals at last had a clear opening to attack him. In March 1868, the House of Representatives brought impeachment charges against Johnson for "high crimes and misdemeanors."

The trial began on March 13, 1868, and was an ordeal for both Johnson and the nation. Hanging in the balance was the future of the American government. The Radicals were attempting to shift the balance of power among the three branches of the government in favor of Congress. When the trial concluded, Johnson was acquitted, but for the rest of his term, Johnson was no more than a prisoner in his office. In less than a year, he would depart the scene; Johnson would not run for reelection.

From 1868 until Reconstruction ended in 1877, a number of African Americans were elected to office in the South. The Reconstruction governments were the target of much criticism. Stories of corruption and extravagance were widespread. The dishonesty and corruption in government were not just limited to the South, but its effects were felt more there. Many of the officeholders in the Radical-controlled Southern state governments had moved to the South from the North after the war. These Northerners were commonly referred to as "carpetbaggers," a word derived from their supposed practice of bringing with them their worldly possessions, crammed into a cheap carpetbag. Southerners who sided with the Union were called "scalawags," a term that can be traced to the town of Scalloway in the Shetland Islands, known for its scrubby cattle. It signified something mean, shabby, or venomous. Both terms created highly emotional responses and had an important influence on attitudes in both the North and South. Both carpetbaggers and scalawags were thought to be growing fat by taking advantage of the prostrate South.

The realities, however, were considerably different. Although some carpetbaggers were opportunists, many idealists also came south, hoping to improve its economy and encourage understanding and tolerance between races. Some went south as teachers, clergymen, officers of the Freedmen's Bureau, or agents of various benevolent societies providing aid to former slaves. They were well educated; nearly two-thirds of those who were elected to state legislatures were professionals. In addition, they often brought much-needed capital to the South.

Scalawags often have been described as unscrupulous opportunists who crawled up out of the lowest levels of Southern society to seek power and financial reward. Some scalawags fitted the description exactly, but most of them were upper-class whites—planters and businessmen who had opposed black suffrage primarily for economic reasons. Now that the black vote had been realized, these men thought the pragmatic thing was to accept it. They believed they needed to control the blacks, and if they had to join the Republicans to do that, they would. From the beginning, both carpetbaggers and scalawags played an important part in the seats of Republican power. Of the 76 most prominent Republican officeholders in Alabama between 1870 and 1875, seven were blacks, 24 were carpetbaggers, and 45 were scalawags.

Opposition to Republican policies was keen in the South. Sometimes it was secret; sometimes it was out in the open. Whites who took part in the Reconstruction governments were often jeered, even by neighbors and old friends. Beginning in 1867, many white Southerners began to form organizations to frighten and bring pressure on black voters and officeholders and their white supporters. The best known of the antiblack organizations was the Ku Klux Klan. The Klan's goal was the restoration of white control over blacks. They tried to rid the region of all those who opposed this purpose. Klansmen rode at night, dressed in white robes and hoods, first trying to frighten away enemies, then using violence if that did not work.

When the warning failed, the Klan resorted to violence, crippling beatings, or execution by shooting or hanging. "The aim," said a Klan paper in Alabama, "was to kill or drive away leading Negroes and only let the humble and submissive to remain." The Klan held frequent rallies and marches with 500 or more of its members taking part. It soon counted many leading landowners among its Grand Dragons and had sufficient rank-and-file strength to mount a parade of 1500 Klansmen in Huntsville, Alabama.

The rise of the Klan and other hate groups in the South resulted in further efforts by Congress to protect African Americans' voting rights. In February 1869, Congress proposed another amendment to the Constitution. The Fifteenth Amendment, ratified in 1870, provided that suffrage could not be denied to any citizen because of "race, color, or previous condition of servitude." Congress added approval of this amendment to the list of steps that states had to take to rejoin the Union.

As the 1868 presidential election approached, the Radicals nominated Ulysses S. Grant as their candidate for the office. Grant's majority in the electoral college was overwhelming, but his popular margin was only 300,000. His victory was assured by the 700,000 African Americans voters who went to the polls for the first time in the South. In 1872, Grant won a second term.

Between 1868 and 1871, a wave of Klan violence swept over the South. State officials tried with varying degrees of success to suppress the Klan. When they were unable to stop the Klan's violence, they asked for help from the federal government. Congress enacted the Ku Klux Klan Act in April 1871. This law provided severe penalties for violations of the Fourteenth and Fifteenth amendments. It authorized the president to use martial law where the rights of blacks were endangered. It gave federal courts, rather than state courts, jurisdiction over cases arising under this legislation. In 1872, for the first time since the Civil War, peace reigned in the former Confederacy.

Despite the Grant administration's effective response to Klan terrorism, the North's commitment to Reconstruction waned during the 1870s. Many Radical leaders, including Thaddeus Stevens, who died in 1868, had passed from the scene. Within the party, their place was taken by politicians less committed to the idea of equal rights for blacks. Many Northerners thought the South should be able to solve its own problems without interference from Washington.

Other factors weakened the North's support for Reconstruction. In 1873, the country plunged into a severe economic depression. Republicans had more important problems to solve, so they were in no mood to devote further attention to the South. It was clear that the North was retreating from Reconstruction. For the first time since before the Civil War, the Democrats swept the election of 1874 and would control the House of Representatives. By the mid-1870s, supporters of Reconstruction were on the defensive and Reconstruction was all but over.

Long before the end of Grant's second term, it was apparent that the program of Radical Reconstruction was doomed. The majority of Northern people turned against it. The Democrats, of course, had always opposed the Radicals. After the economic depression of 1873, renewed public interest was not in Reconstruction, but in legislation that would effect economic stability; thus, the Democratic party was able to make great gains in the North. Equally important, an increasing number of Northern Republicans began to oppose the continuation of the Radical program. From the beginning, government reformers had been dubious about the carpetbag regimes of the South. The scandals exposed during the Grant administration made it difficult for them to continue to describe the Democratic party as "common sewer and loathsome receptacle" and themselves as the "best elements in our national life." By 1870, the fear that white Southerners might attempt to re-enslave blacks had been eliminated.

On March 5, 1877, Rutherford B. Hayes was inaugurated president. Recognizing that Radical Reconstruction had been a failure, Hayes proceeded to withdraw federal troops from the South, and he would appoint a Southern ex-Whig to his cabinet. For all practical purposes, the Reconstruction period had ended.

The Reconstruction period was one of the most controversial eras in American history. During the twelve years after the Civil War, basic changes took place that would alter the course of life in America. Writers have often labeled the Reconstruction period as the "Tragic Era" or the "Age of Hate," but it is also important to remember that the treatment given the South after the war was one of the mildest punishments ever inflicted after an unsuccessful civil war. The North required of the South recognition of three general positions. First, the doctrine of secession was to be renounced and the Union recognized.

Second, the institution of slavery was destroyed forever. And third, it was tacitly recognized that the prewar Southern leadership in national politics was to be replaced by that in the North.

To many white Southerners, these conditions seemed severe and oppressive, but when measured against the crushing reparations, the mass deportation of peoples, and the genocide that followed later wars, it was relatively mild. With the exception of Major Henry Wirz, commander of the notorious Andersonville prison, who was hanged, no Confederate was executed for war crimes. Only a few Southern political leaders were imprisoned for their part in the rebellion, and except for Jefferson Davis, their release was prompt. Although slavery was abolished, there was no mass confiscation of property of ex-Confederates. Despite the addition of the Fourteenth and Fifteenth amendments to the Constitution, the caste system of blacks and whites remained essentially the same.

The Civil War and Reconstruction are the epic drama of American history. Some idealists believed the end of the war would issue in a new age and the final fulfillment of the promise of America; both the hopes and the promises had to be deferred. Instead of an era of Christian brotherhood, of equality, of freedom for all without regard to class or race, the country entered into an age of widespread inequality and social and racial injustice. The last American Indians were driven from the plains and mountains of the West and moved onto reservations, buried in an avalanche of white settlers moving relentlessly westward. The nation did, however, emerge from the war with "a saved and strengthened Union, the abolition of slavery, and an invigorated consciousness of national power." It was into this world that the gallant heroes of the war returned.

4 $\quad$ Noble Hero of Peace

ROBERT E. LEE

ON Saturday afternoon, April 15, General Robert E. Lee returned to Richmond. It was just six days after he had surrendered the Army of Northern Virginia to General Grant at Appomattox Court House. There was no advance word of the general's visit; the citizens of Richmond were surprised when Lee, accompanied by five aides, rode over the pontoon bridge from Manchester. All permanent spans across the James River had been burned the night of the evacuation. Richmond still smelled of smoke and charred timbers.

One of Lee's aides, Colonel Walter H. Taylor, noted, "The general quietly proceeded to the house on Franklin Street then occupied by his family." According to William Merriam, a correspondent for the *New York Herald*, an immense crowd that had learned of Lee's arrival was present: "He was greeted with cheers upon cheers." Even the occupation Union officers raised their caps as a sign of respect. "Lee turned into Cary Street," wrote a resident. "He was riding Traveller and looked neither to the right nor left, but straight ahead. The streets were filled with debris . . . and it was difficult to make your way through." When word spread that Lee had arrived in Richmond, there was an instant wild chase after him and his party. As the crowd gathered, the cheers grew louder. The acclaim came in waves, again and again, and each time Lee doffed his hat.

When Lee reached his house, a crowd barred his way to his door, as "so many as could get near his person shook him heartily by the hand," according to the *New York Herald*. "Men in blue," an eyewitness said, "were as numerous as those of the Confederate gray seeking the privilege." Somehow Lee was able to back up the steps on the house and through the door.

Lee was not allowed to relax for long. He was resting in his front parlor when a friend entered bearing unanticipated news: President Lincoln had been assassinated. Lee was deeply shocked. He stared at the floor and then exclaimed, "This is the hardest blow the South has yet received."

For Lee, the road to Appomattox began in Arlington, Virginia, on the night of April 19, 1861, when he resigned from the U.S. Army. The decision, like every decision in his life, was deeply rooted in the history of his family and his nation.

Lee was born on January 19, 1807, into Virginia aristocracy, the combination of two of the state's most venerated families—the Lees and the Carters. Two of his uncles had signed the Declaration of Independence. Lee's father, Henry "Light-Horse Harry" Lee, served in the Revolution, in the Continental Congress, for three terms as governor of Virginia, and for one term in Congress. He was a close friend and confidant of George Washington, eulogizing him as "first in war, first in peace, and first in the hearts of his countrymen." Robert's mother was Anne Hill Carter, Henry Lee's second wife. Members of the Carter family had a long history of service to their communities.

Henry Lee's early years were filled with promise, perhaps even an opportunity to become president, but then his fortunes changed. His later years were spent in land speculation and other bad investments that left him penniless. In 1810, financial ruin sent Henry Lee to debtor's prison. The family was forced to leave Stratford Hall and moved to a small house on Cameron Street in Alexandria. Robert was three at the time. In 1813, his father abandoned his family and went to the British West Indies. On the way home in 1818, Light-Horse Harry died on Cumberland Island, Georgia. In some way, he had made a failure of his life, but Mrs. Lee always spoke of him in terms of love and respect and taught her children to do the same. In Robert's eyes, his father was always a hero of the Revolutionary War, the companion of Washington.

In the absence of her husband, Anne Carter was left alone to care for five children and their finances, training, and education. Self-denial, self-control, and the strictest economy in all financial matters were part of the code of honor she taught them from infancy. Throughout his childhood, Lee was a model son, caring for his invalid mother in the absence of his father. She taught him the Christian tenets of duty, honor, and country. In 1825, his belief in these teachings resulted in his appointment to the U.S. Military Academy at West Point.

Lee survived the four-year program without a single demerit, attaining the coveted cadet rank of adjutant and graduating second in his class. He attended the military academy at a time when a number of future leaders on both sides of the Civil War were there. He quickly made friends with fellow Virginian Joseph Johnston. Outside of his class, Lee looked with awe at the magnificent adjutant of the cadet corps, Albert Sidney Johnston, and the thin Mississippian, Jefferson Davis. Perhaps Lee's admiration of Davis was inspired by the contrast in their personalities. Whereas Davis was carefree, often flaunting the rules of the academy, Lee was a model cadet, exhibiting great self-control.

Lee was a studious young man who felt the need to restore the family's name. This desire compelled him to do his best in all that he did; his record at West Point, during the Civil War and after, illustrated his belief in duty and honor. Success usually brings with it the jealousy of others, but not in Lee's case. "I doubt if he ever excited envy in any man," wrote a fellow cadet. "All of his accomplishments and alluring virtues appeared natural to him, and he was free from anxiety, distrust and awkwardness that attend a sense of inferiority."

Lee's excellent West Point record enabled him to enter the Engineer Corps, an elite branch of the army that attracted the brightest officers. Lee loved the corps; his work appealed to his sense of order and creativity. But his duties were frequently grueling and unglamorous. His first assignment took him to marshy Cookspur, Georgia, where—as an engineer second in command—he worked to prepare the foundation for a coastal fort. Later he would assist Captain Andrew Talcott in constructing another coastal fort at Monroe, Virginia.

As he commenced his military career, Lieutenant Lee began to court Mary Anna Randolph Custis. She was the daughter of George Washington Parke Custis, the adopted son of the first president. Although her parents were fond of their daughter's suitor, her father was reluctant to have her marry a soldier. George Custis finally came around and gave his approval. The young couple were married at Arlington on June 30, 1831. The Lees had seven children, four daughters and three sons. Over the next thirty-nine years, Lee was a devoted husband and father.

Much to Lee's dismay, his duties as a soldier always took him away from his family. He served in a variety of engineering tasks. Among his assignments was one at St. Louis. There the Mississippi River threatened to move away from the levee, creating a real economic hardship for the city. Lee's creative plan redirected the water flow and eliminated the sediment deposits that had menaced the harbor. A valuable benefit to Lee for his service as an engineer was to develop his sense of terrain and topography of land. Such insights served him well during the Civil War.

In the spring of 1846, Lee welcomed the chance to see active service during the Mexican War. Lee was a captain and faced battle for the first time in his life. He had been in the army for twenty-one years and never faced an enemy or heard a hostile shot. Lee distinguished himself during the war, where he served on the staff of fellow Virginian, General Winfield Scott. As a captain, Lee was responsible for several courageous personal reconnaissance missions, which produced intelligence leading to American victories. During that time, the military had no medals for bravery, but officers were given brevet promotions for brave acts during the war. Captain Lee received three of these brevets during the war with Mexico, being promoted to major, lieutenant colonel, and finally to colonel. Lee also had won the confidence of his brother officers and their superiors and above all General Scott, in whose eyes he was a paragon of military virtue. Scott described Lee as the "very best soldier I ever saw in the field." The Mexican War brought Lee more than rank and glory—it gave him the training he would need for the far greater trials that lay in the future.

On the other hand, however, his Mexican War experience may have given Lee an erroneous impression of what could be accomplished by daring, perhaps rash, frontal assaults. He actively participated in such successful attacks, but they were against poorly trained infantry armed with muzzle-loading muskets. At Cerro Gordo and the Mexican fortress of Chapultepec, the Americans attacked successfully with low casualties. There was to be little resemblance between those victorious charges and the deadly, disastrous frontal assaults of the Civil War.

After the excitement of the Mexican War, the next ten years were comparatively tame. Lee returned to his former job of constructing coastal forts. He welcomed the opportunity to settle down with his family and friends. In 1852, he was assigned to West Point as the new superintendent. This assignment was considered a plum, and most soldiers would have rejoiced at the opportunity, but not Lee. He would have preferred active service or service near Arlington to take care of his family and their estate. Nevertheless, he approached the assignment as he did all others, with his best effort. Only the ninth man to have held the position, he oversaw the extension of the academy's program of study from four to five years, encouraged the study of military strategy, and improved the quality of the cadets by weeding out the lazy and incompetent.

While at West Point, Lee underwent a change in his religious fervor, developing a deeper dependence on God. As a child he had been baptized in the Episcopal Church, but was never confirmed. It was during the Mexican War that he began his reformation. Now that he was in charge of some of the nation's finest young men, he felt he should confess his faith and ally himself with the church. Side by side with two of his daughters, he was confirmed on July 17, 1853. Lee's alliance with his God would remain first in his heart his entire life. Lee's faith continued to grow until during the Civil War, he sincerely believed that Providence had ordered everything and that man had only to do what was right and leave the rest to God.

In March 1855, Congress authorized the formation of four new regiments. Lee was appointed second in command and brevet (temporary) lieutenant colonel of the 2nd Cavalry Regiment. After more than a quarter of a century in the Engineer Corps, Lee was finally joining a combat unit. This was a major shift in his career, and one that he welcomed. For the next several years, he spent most of his active service in the wilds of central and western Texas.

In October 1857, Lee's father-in-law died, leaving his family in debt, a complicated will to handle, and a run-down estate. The family was "land poor," owning a great deal of property but no money for its upkeep. Lee took a leave from his army duties to go home to Arlington and settle the estate. The job facing him required a lot of time; he had to make repairs on Arlington and make the farm self-supporting again to pay off the debts. Because of these demands, his leave had to be extended for nearly two years. What was more depressing, Lee found that in his absence, Mary had become physically impaired with painful arthritis and had great difficulty walking. Most of the children were away in the army or at boarding school. It was a dark time for Lee, and he began to reconsider his life, seriously thinking about resigning from the army. Lee's thoughts about the army were common in a profession that offered little but drabness and routine. Promotions came slowly or not at all, and many officers were forced to resign in pursuit of more lucrative civilian careers. Lee eventually decided to stay on, but it took him thirty years of service to reach the permanent rank of colonel.

At fifty-four years of age, Lee could look back on a long, dutiful career. He had proved himself a capable engineer, a clever administrator, a brave soldier, a respected leader of young men, and a devoted husband and father. In 1861, people looked to Lee for his opinion on matters threatening the nation. Lee was opposed to slavery, strongly pro-Union, and against civil war; but above all, he remained loyal to Virginia.

Lee had listened to hundreds of arguments over slavery and states' rights. He himself had little use for either. Lee acknowledged that "slavery as an institution, is a moral and political evil," but he had owned at least four women slaves, part of his mother's bequest to him. As late as 1852, he owned a manservant. His wife also owned slaves that she had inherited from her father. Crucial to Lee's views were his perception that whites were superior to blacks. In rationalizing his ownership of slaves, he wrote that "blacks were immeasurably better off here than in Africa, morally, socially, and physically. . . . How long their subjugation may be necessary is known and ordered by a wise Merciful Providence."

In holding these beliefs, Lee was much in step with most Southerners of the time. He accepted no responsibility for acting on his belief that slavery was "a moral and political evil." On December 29, 1863, in accordance with his father-in-law's will, Lee set free all of the slaves owned by him. To be sure, Lee was a limited emancipator because he was only following the Custis will.

After Lincoln's election, Lee denounced the secessionist fever that was sweeping the Deep South: "Secession is nothing but revolution." "Still," he concluded sadly, "a Union that can only be maintained by swords and bayonets, and in which strife and civil war are to take the place of brotherly love and kindness, has no charm for me. . . ."

In April 1862, Lincoln was prepared to offer Lee the field command of the armies of the United States, with the rank of major general. One day after Virginia seceded, Lee resigned his commission, and to General Scott he wrote a regretful note that included the line, "Save in defense of my native state, I never again will draw my sword." Mrs. Lee understood and approved of her husband's resignation: "My husband has wept tears of blood over the war, but as a man of honor and a Virginian, he must follow the destiny of his state."

During the early days of the war, Lee realized that the South would fight a defensive war and that Virginia would become the major battlefield of the war. He accepted a commission as a commander of Virginia's troops and a brigadier general in the Confederate army. He remained in a relatively obscure position during the first year of the war until his West Point classmate Joseph E. Johnston was severely wounded at the Battle of Seven Pines. In June 1862, Lee was placed in command of what was soon to become the legendary Army of Northern Virginia.

Lee initiated the Seven Days' Campaign on June 25, 1862, and he had soon pushed the Union army from the outskirts of Richmond. By August, Lee and his army were positioned to do battle at Manassas, Virginia, where he defeated the Union army for the second time before invading Maryland. In just a short time, Lee had completely changed the Confederate military situation in the east. In June, the entire Union army had been poised to attack Richmond; by September, Lee was in a position to threaten Washington, D.C.

In September 1862, Lee's army fought to a stalemate at Antietam. In December, Lee was able to conclude the 1862 campaign with a major victory over Ambrose Burnside's Union forces at Fredericksburg, Virginia. In reflecting on his army's victory, Lee said: "It is well that war is so terrible. We should grow too fond of it."

Climaxing Lee's six months of command, his army of 75,000 had blocked the advance of 130,000 Federals, causing more than 12,500 Union casualties and losing only 5,000 of his own troops. General Johnston himself conceded that Lee was more fit to command, adding, "The shot that struck me down is the very best that has been fired for the Southern cause yet." Realizing that he did not have Jefferson Davis's confidence—but that Lee did—Johnston believed that his removal was for the good of the army.

In the spring of 1863, Union army commander Joseph Hooker would feel the terrible swift sword of Lee and his fleet subordinate, General Thomas "Stonewall" Jackson, at Chancellorsville. A great deal of Lee's success came from his ability as a battlefield commander and his willingness to take risks. There is no greater example of Lee's classic tactics than in this battle. His army was outnumbered more than two to one, and yet he still divided his forces to face the enemy on his front. A rapid flanking movement by Jackson caught the unprepared Union soldiers by surprise, and a rout developed when Jackson attacked. But the victory was a costly one. Jackson was wounded by friendly fire while conducting a reconnaissance of the enemy lines. In an attempt to save Jackson's life, doctors had to remove his shattered left arm. Lee was hopeful that Jackson would recover and be back at his side soon. On May 6, he sent Jackson his "affectionate regards" and urged him to "come back as soon as he could." Lee said of Jackson's wound: "He has lost his left arm, but I have lost my right arm." On May 10, Jackson babbled of battles and charges and victories and then, quietly and distinctly, he said, "Let us pass over the river, and rest under the shade of the trees." When he died, so did the Confederate's chance for success.

Following Chancellorsville and Jackson's death, Lee organized his 75,000-man army from two infantry corps of four divisions each to three corps, each having three divisions. The I Corps was commanded by Lieutenant General James Longstreet, the II Corps by Lieutenant General Richard Ewell, and the III Corps by General A. P. Hill. Neither Ewell nor Hill had worked directly under Lee's command, and neither had Stonewall Jackson's ability to lead in combat. Lee and Jackson had been a team. Lee came to rely heavily on Jackson's ability to act on his own without very explicit instructions from him. Lee's failure to adjust his style in dealing with his two new corps commanders would prove to be troublesome and even disastrous at Gettysburg.

The victory at Chancellorsville cleared the way for another Confederate invasion of the North. Confusion within the Union army, combined with their losses in earlier battles, gave Lee the opportunity he was hoping for—a chance to destroy the Union army once and for all. Within weeks of his victory at Chancellorsville, Lee was on the move again. This time he advanced into Pennsylvania. On July 1, 1863, the fighting began north and west of Gettysburg. Lee had not planned to fight there, but part of his advanced troops strayed into the town of Gettysburg. There was a skirmish: Each side threw in reinforcements, and the battle of Gettysburg was on.

When Lee encountered the enemy at Gettysburg, he did not have General J. E. B. Stuart with him. Utilizing the confusing and discretionary orders Lee had given him, Stuart had engaged in a meaningless frolic behind enemy lines and did not rejoin the army until the end of the second day of the battle. By that time, Stuart was of little use to Lee. Without Stuart to tell him the location and size of the Union force, Lee was forced to operate in the dark. This alone was reason enough not to engage the enemy at that time. Events, however, happened so quickly that Lee was drawn into into a battle he did not wish to fight. Longstreet advised Lee not to engage the enemy there; but after an initial advantage, he decided to stay and fight.

Lee ordered Ewell to take the high ground "if he found it practicable, but to avoid a general engagement until the arrival of the other divisions of the army." Ewell's hesitancy in doing so proved disastrous. Lee's failure to take full advantage of his temporary superiority and to issue definitive attack orders to Ewell allowed the Union army to gain control of the high ground for the battle.

On the second day, July 2, Lee ordered Longstreet to attack the left flank of the Union army. In doing so, Lee ignored Longstreet's advice to move south of Gettysburg, seek a strong defensive position, and await a Union attack. Longstreet argued that General Meade would be compelled to attack any Confederate force placed between them and Washington, setting up a similar situation that they had enjoyed at Fredericksburg. Longstreet had learned the Civil War's major lesson—frontal attacks are costly and often not successful. Lee's response to him was, "If the enemy is there tomorrow, we must attack him."

After two days of fighting, the Yankees still held a commanding position on Cemetery Ridge and Little and Big Round Tops. Again ignoring Longstreet's advice and pleas, Lee made a final effort to drive the Federals from the ridge. He believed if he put strong artillery against the Union lines, followed by a charge at the center, he could break the line. Major General George E. Pickett's fine Virginia troops, a part of Longstreet's I Corps, were chosen to lead the principal charge.

At one o'clock, the Confederate artillery opened up on the Union front. The Yankees returned the fire. Then, when the guns were silent, General Pickett prepared his division for a desperate charge. Over the field, into the range of the Union artillery, and then onward until they could hear the whine of rifle bullets, the Confederates moved. Soon they were stumbling and falling dead, or crying out in anguish when they were hit. They pressed on until the line disappeared in dust and smoke. For a few minutes, the rebel yell could be heard above the fire of thousands of rifles and scores of cannon. And then it died down. Back toward the Confederate lines, the survivors of the charge streamed. The charge had failed. The Union line had held. Lee had attempted the impossible and failed.

Lee rode out to rally and cheer the devastated troops as they fell back. "All will come right in the end," he told them; "we'll talk it over afterward; but in the meantime, all good men must rally." Soon he saw Pickett and rode over to him. "General Pickett," Lee said, "place your division in rear of the hill, and be ready to repel the advance of the enemy should they follow up their advantage." Pickett was frantic. "General Lee," he cried, "I have no division now, Armistead is down, Garnett is down and Kemper is mortally wounded." "Come, General Pickett," Lee answered, "this has been my fight and upon my shoulders rests the blame." In the same spirit, he spoke to General Cadmus Marcellus Wilcox, whose brigade had been shattered. "Never mind, General," Lee replied, "all this has been my fault—it is I who have lost this fight, and you must help me out of it the best way you can."

The loss to the Army of Northern Virginia at Gettysburg was devastating. Of the 75,000 engaged, 22,600 were killed or wounded. Union losses were high too; of the 83,300 troops, 17,700 were casualties. The loss of Confederate field-grade officers would be felt for the duration of the war. Pickett's division was hit especially hard. Pickett would lose his three brigade commanders. Brigadier General Lewis Armistead, after being captured, would die two days later in a Union hospital. Brigadier General Richard Garnett's body would never be recovered. Brigadier General James Kemper was severely wounded and captured. When his wounds healed, he was exchanged for a Union officer in September.

Late in the evening, Lee went wearily back to camp. "General," said one of his officers, "this has been a hard day on you." He paused, reflected, and then spoke out: "I never saw troops behave more magnificently than Pickett's Division of Virginia did today in that grand charge upon the enemy." Again he paused and added, "Too bad, too bad! Oh, too bad!"

On July 4, Lee started his wagontrains for the Potomac. As the army retreated, Lee might have said that he had been misled into battle, blaming Stuart who had not returned until the second day of the battle and after the armies were already engaged. Lee might have blamed Ewell and Longstreet for their hesitation at critical times during the battle. But, as the army's leader, he was to blame. He would not attempt to put the blame on others when he felt it was rightly his. To Longstreet, he admitted, "It's all my fault. I thought my men were invincible."

Lee had gambled for high stakes and lost. After Gettysburg, he was never able to gain the offensive again. When Grant took over command of the Army of the Potomac and crossed the Rapidan River in May 1864, Lee's army had to move back into entrenched positions to resist the heavily reinforced and

Robert E. Lee in 1865

experienced Union army. This proved to be the beginning of the end for the Confederacy.

Lee's army fought brilliantly for nearly two years after Gettysburg, but they were faced with overpowering adversities. The Army of Northern Virginia had been thinned by heavy battle losses and desertions, with no chance for reinforcements. The soldiers who were left, "Lee's Miserables," as they called themselves in grim jest, had very little with which to fight. Thousands were barefoot, and all were without overcoats, blankets, or warm clothes for the biting winter. Food, too, was in short supply. Sometimes companies would go for several days at a time on nothing but hardtack and a bit of salt pork. Lee shared their privations, living in a tent in the open without heat or other comforts and eating dinners of potato and salt pork.

It was Grant's inability to admit defeat that spelled trouble for Lee. When Lee had whipped McClellan, Pope, Burnside, and Hooker, they had accepted the verdict of the battle and retreated. But Grant didn't wage war that way. He was, as Lee once said regretfully, "not a retreating man." Grant would smash at

Lee and be hurled back; then he would pull his army together and, instead of retreating, file away to the south and attack again. Lee had never met an opponent like that. Lee's army fought a series of savage battles—Spotsylvania, the Bloody Angle, and Cold Harbor. Each time Grant struck, Lee had his army in position to repel his attacks, but Grant stayed in the field and kept right on going.

Even with the war going against him, Lee could still call upon an endless reserve of compassion and was able to express sympathy to Confederate General Wade Hampton, who had lost his son in battle: "I grieve with you at the death of your gallant son. So young, so brave, so true. I know how much you must suffer. . . . We must labor on in the course before us, but for him I trust in rest and peace, for I believe our Merciful God takes us when it is best for us to go. He is now safe from all harm and evil. . . . May God support you under your great affliction and give you strength to bear the trials He may impose upon you." Sadly, Lee must have written many letters similar to this one.

With the war entering its last phase, Grant's army settled down at Petersburg and prepared to wear down Lee by sheer weight of numbers. As for Lee, his army was melting away by desertion, disease, and death. "The struggle is to keep the army fed and clothed," Lee wrote. "Only fifteen in one regiment had shoes, and bacon is issued only once in a few days." The courage of the Army of Northern Virginia continued, but their strength did not. Lee's army was now reduced to 40,000 and stretched to the breaking point. In February 1865, a new danger appeared. Sherman had completed his March to the Sea, taking Savannah and then turning north. Within a few weeks, Sherman would be joining Grant. Then Lee would face an army three or four times the size of his.

Lee made one last desperate attempt on March 25 to break Grant's lines at Fort Stedman, east of Petersburg, but failed. This meant giving up Richmond—a city he had defended so heroically for three bitter years. On April 2, the retreat began. With Grant snapping at his heels, two courses were open to Lee. He could disperse his army and try to rally a new one to fight a guerrilla war in the mountains and valleys of the West. Or he could surrender. "I would rather die a thousand deaths," Lee said about surrender. But he chose the course he thought was best for his soldiers and the people of the South. Clearly it would be wrong to condemn his people to years of guerrilla warfare. And so, with heavy heart, he wrote to Grant that he would discuss the terms of surrender. The two met at a brick house in the village of Appomattox Court House.

On the afternoon of April 9, 1865, Lee waited half an hour for Grant in the parlor of Wilmer McLean's house at Appomattox. His thoughts may have flashed back to scenes of the Army of Northern Virginia lying hungry, exhausted in the fields near Appomattox. A great many things were on his mind, but chief among those had to be that all three of his sons had been reported missing. Perhaps he looked back upon all that had taken place in the four previous years and asked himself how he came to be at Appomattox. Above all, he must have felt a tremendous sadness. Lee wanted to spare his army any useless bloodshed. He was a man who would have taken advantage of any military option available, but there were no more options.

When Grant arrived, he was in the uniform of a private, his trousers spattered with mud, tucked inside his boots. He wore no sword or spurs, nothing to show that he was the commander in chief except his shoulder straps with their golden stars. Despite his dress, the rough-appearing Union commander was a gentleman. He did not ask for Lee's sword. His terms were generous. He sent rations to the starving Confederates and ordered the Union soldiers to refrain from cheering or firing volleys to celebrate their victory. "The war is over," he said. "The rebels are again our countrymen, and the best way of showing our rejoicing will be to abstain from such demonstrations."

So ended the Army of Northern Virginia. Lee had taken it when it was beaten and disorganized and shaped it into one of the greatest fighting forces in history. He had led it to victory and finally to defeat. Now he bid it farewell. As he sat astride Traveller, his men crowded around him, many with tears streaming down their cheeks, not cheering, but saluting the leader who had never failed them. Then he turned and rode off. Now Lee had one duty—to help reunite the country.

Lee did not attend the formal ceremony of surrender on the morning of April 12, 1865; he remained in camp until his men had returned. Then with a few of his officers, Lee rode home. Word of his coming traveled faster than he did, and all along the way people ran to see him and bring him food. On April 14, he stopped to spend the night at his brother's farm. The house was crowded and Lee did not want to inconvenience any of his brother's guests. He insisted on spending the night in his old tent, which he pitched on the lawn.

The next morning, Lee rode through the rain into Richmond. Much of the once-proud capital of the Confederacy now looked like a cemetery of destroyed homes, factories, and shops. Above the Capitol waved the symbol of the occupied city's defeat—the Stars and Stripes of the Union flag. Despite the rain, Southerners and Northerners alike turned out to stare in awe at Lee and to greet him with cheers and tears. At last Lee came to 707 East Franklin Street, the home his wife had set up during the war. He bowed to the crowd, then went inside, and took off his sword for the last time.

Once Lee was home, he had no other place to go. His home at Arlington was gone, confiscated by federal authorities for nonpayment of taxes. Its spacious lawns now held the graves of thousands of Northern soldiers. "I am looking for some quiet place in the woods," he wrote, "where I can procure shelter and my daily bread if permitted by the victor."

Robert E. Lee had reason to be concerned about his future. President Abraham Lincoln had been murdered on April 14 by John Wilkes Booth. The assassination only increased the North's desire for vengence and a hard peace. When Jefferson Davis was captured, he was placed in prison. In June, Lee was indicted for treason. Lee asked Grant to help him. The terms of his parole at Appomattox stated that he would not "be disturbed by the United States authority." Grant agreed to help and threatened to resign from the army if federal authorities arrested Lee. President Johnson suspended Lee's prosecution, and he was never arrested or brought to trial, nor during his lifetime, was his citizenship restored.

Lee's personal example after the war would be taken as the South's social model of how to live in its defeat. Southerners regarded Lee's honor as their own, Colonel Charles Marshall would say in eulogizing him. If Lee agreed to terms of surrender, then Southerners felt bound by them too. Lee disliked public ceremony but understood that attention would be continually upon him. This imposed a special burden of self-control and leadership. From the very beginning, men submitted to his command because he was one of those rare men who is in command of himself. Indeed, Lee was a model of propriety not only for the South, but for the nation as a whole. Americans continued to expect much from him and he did not let them down.

Knowing the eyes of the South were on him for direction, Lee acted accordingly. A few weeks after the surrender, as Lee sat one Sunday in St. Paul's Episcopal Church in Richmond, a black man rose and approached the altar rail for communion. This was a great surprise and shock to the communicants and others present. Blacks were expected to wait until all whites had left the rail before they were allowed to step forward. Dr. Minnegerode, the pastor, was openly embarrassed and appeared not to know what to do. Lee, rising in his usual dignified manner, walked to the rail and knelt down near the black man to partake of the communion. Others in the congregation followed him, and the service continued.

On another occasion, Jubal Early wrote to Lee from his self-imposed exile in Mexico to say, "I hate Yankees this day worse than I have ever done and my hatred is increasing every day." Lee responded: "We shall have to be patient and suffer for a while at least; and all controversy, I think, will only serve to prolong angry and bitter feelings, and postpone the period when reason and charity may resume their way."

In applying for citizenship, Lee established a precedent that greatly influenced other Southerners. Captain George Wise, a son of Confederate General Harry Wise, protested to Lee that he did not think the terms of the parole obliged him to take the oath of allegiance, and he would rather leave the country than do so. Lee quietly told him, "Do not leave Virginia. Our Country needs her young men now." Captain Wise signed the oath. When his father heard of what his son had done, he said, "You have disgraced the family!" When his son told him that General Lee had advised him to do so, he said, "Oh, that alters the case. Whatever General Lee says is all right; I don't care what it is." Thousands of Southerners felt the same way.

Nothing could be greater than the veneration and love that the people and soldiers had shown Lee through the war. But it was after the war that the affection seemed more than ever a consecrated one. The name given to him in the army, "Ole Marse" Robert, shows the tenderness with which he was regarded. After the war ended, all of these feelings were intensified by the added one of sympathy. He could go nowhere without being greeted with demonstrations of love and admiration. Lee indeed became one of the symbols of the Lost Cause.

Wherever Lee went, he was admired and treated with respect. On one occasion, when he entered a large dining room at a Southern resort hotel, 500 guests rose and stood in respectful silence. He was grander in defeat, living proof of the superiority of Southern gentlemanly values. He, himself, was not exalted in overcoming defeat—he was heartbroken by it. "Why do you look so sad?" asked a girl who saw him not long after Appomattox. "Why shouldn't I?" Lee answered: "My cause is dead. I am homeless—I have nothing on earth." Yet he continued to live a life that inspired the South to forget their hate and once more become Americans.

A short time after the surrender at Appomattox, Lee was offered several homes in which to live. Lee's family was of English origin. Now relatives and other admirers had offered him the opportunity to come to England and share the luxury of their homes with them. But he positively declined to expatriate himself, thanking them and saying: "No, I will not forsake my people in their extremity; what they endure, I will endure, and I am ready to break my last crust with them." He refused to leave Virginia. Nothing ever gave him greater pleasure than to see the personal efforts of his people to overcome the disasters of the war.

Lee was eager to get away from Richmond and settle down to the simple life of a farmer. "I wish to get Mrs. Lee out of the city as soon as practical," he said. Lee was able to find such a retreat in a small cottage called Derwent on the estate of Mrs. Elizabeth Randolph Cooke. In late June, the General, Mrs. Lee, his daughters, and his son, Custis, went to spend the remainder of the summer. There he was to receive the summons that was to determine the future course of his life.

Lee had been besieged with many attractive financial offers since his surrender. He was offered $50,000 a year to go to New York to head a firm being organized to promote trade with the South. An insurance company offered him $25,000 a year to act as its president. Another company proposed to pay him $10,000 a year merely for the use of his name. Lee's sense of personal honor would not permit him to accept any of these efforts to capitalize on his fame. "My name is not for sale at any price," he said. Nor did he hesitate to say no when an admiring British nobleman offered him an estate, with an annual income of $15,000.

When homes and financial offers were being made to Lee, his eldest daughter said to one of the trustees of Washington College, "Why don't they propose to my father some place in which he can work? For he will never accept the gratuity of a home." The remark was brought to the attention of the trustees of the college. Washington College was founded before the American Revolution and had received a large endowment from Washington himself—it was the first institute of any kind that bore Washington's name. The college had educated some of the most prominent men of Virginia. Its buildings were greatly in need of repair, its professors and students scattered, and its resources crippled by the war. The war had taken its toll on the institution.

At the next board meeting, a proposal was made to elect Robert E. Lee to serve as president of the college. If he accepted the position, the board believed that students and funding would follow. The board liked the idea and voted to offer Lee the position. A representative from the college was sent to Derwent to see whether Lee would accept. They had little hope, however, that a man of his stature would come to their college.

Lee considered the college's offer for three weeks. He had no educational background beyond his tenure as superintendent of West Point, over ten years before. He was still under indictment for treason, and his past might bring harm to the college. Worse, his health had begun to decline, and he wasn't sure if he could perform more than administrative duties. Yet he saw this as a good opportunity to work with young people, and the cause of Southern education had a strong appeal to him. "If I thought I could be of any benefit to our noble youth, I would not hestitate to give my service," he told a friend. He finally accepted the position, subject to the condition that he would not be responsible for teaching, which might jeopardize his health. Perhaps Lee's decision to accept the offer from Washington College was influenced by his close family relations with, and his admiration for, George Washington. Undoubtedly, he had also heard favorable reports from Stonewall Jackson about the town of Lexington, where Jackson had lived while teaching at Virginia Military Institute. The position paid a meager yearly salary of $1,500, provided a house for Lee, and included a yearly bonus based on the amount of tuition collected. The trustees were elated at Lee's acceptance, and he was officially installed as president in mid-September 1865.

Washington College was located in the small town of Lexington, Virginia. Lee's first entry into the town was observed by Professor James J. White, who taught Greek at the college and had served in the Confederate army. "The first appearance of General Lee in our streets was thoroughly characteristic. . . . Nobody in the town knew he was coming." This was as he wished it, for it was his desire to shun demonstrations.

Lee quickly established rapport and built a kind of devotion with his new associates the same way he had done with his wartime staff. His silence as well as his spoken word improved their morale. Trustees, faculty, and townspeople supported General Lee in efforts that quickly gave the college a vigor it probably had never known before. Only fifty students registered on opening day, but others soon came. Young men continued to arrive all through the first session until the enrollment reached 146. Three members were added to the faculty. Gifts were generous and encouraged hope that the college would have a sufficient endowment to implement the program modernizations recommended by Lee.

Lee immediately embarked on his duties as college president and helped to revise the curriculum to reflect the South's need for men who could rebuild it. Metallurgy, engineering, physics, and other practical skills were emphasized along with modern languages (French, German, Italian, and Spanish). In this way, Lee began the transformation of Washington College from a nineteenth-century classical academy to a twentieth-century university. He wrote letters to solicit financial assistance and letters to encourage students to resume their studies after spending years in the war. One veteran told him that he was impatient to make up for the time he had lost in the army. Lee cut him off sharply. "Mister Humphreys!" he snapped. "However long you live and whatever you accomplish, you will find that the time you spent in the Confederate army was the most profitably spent portion of your life. Never again speak of having wasted time in the army."

At Lexington, Lee adopted a rigid routine. Rising early he washed, dressed, and walked to the college. When the chapel service began at 7:45 A.M., he was invariably in his seat, having already said his private prayers. At eight he went to his office and started to work. He had no clerk or secretary, so he had to handle every routine matter himself. In addition to his correspondence, planning, and administering, Lee supervised all activities related to the buildings and grounds and to the outlay of any money. He also visited classes regularly during recitation periods and oversaw final examinations.

Lee was unsparing of himself. He was constantly in his office, always available to all callers, faculty, parents, and students alike. His time seemed as flexible as the demand made on it. No letter was unanswered; no effort of courtesy was too insignificant. Students were inspired and amazed by the president's familiarity with their scholastic standing, outside behavior, home life, and athletic achievements. When a request was made of a student to appear before him, the student knew that he would be treated with justice, courtesy, and gentleness. "His sense of personal duty was also expanded into a warm solicitude for all who associated with him," one of Lee's faculty later stated. "To the faculty, he was an elder brother, beloved and revered, and full of tender sympathy. To the students, he was a father, in reproof. Their welfare and their conduct and character as gentlemen were his chief concern." Lee thought it was the responsibility of the college not merely to educate the intellect but to make Christian gentlemen. The moral and religious character of the students was more important in his eyes than their intellectual progress. He would not tolerate dishonesty or meanness.

Lee set a goal for himself to know every student—and the academic record and problems of student. He never lectured these students or preached to them at chapel, but he tried to get them to live according to a few spiritual laws, which he knew from his own experience as sound. "As a general principle," he told a professor, "you should not force young men to do their duty, but let them do it voluntarily and thereby develop their character."

Lee had discovered the charms of liberal education and that there could be discipline without regimentation. Twenty-six months after Appomattox, the soldier of thirty-nine years' service was telling the faculty, "Make no needless rules." Lee believed that discipline can best be safely trusted when it is based on honor and the self-respect of students themselves. Although Lee believed in following rules, he could stretch or even disregard rules if he thought vital principles were involved. He tried to keep the framework of responsibilities simple enough to be understood and obeyed by all. When a student asked him for a copy of the school's rules, Lee replied: "We have only one rule here—to act like a gentleman at all times."

This was the spirit in which Lee approached Lexington and his position as school president. This was no small feat, changing from a military to a civilian life when he was approaching sixty. He did it all without whining or despairing. By Christmas 1865, Lee's routine had been firmly established, and the college was functioning and growing. The Lee family was together now under one roof, surrounded by people who loved and respected them. The Christmas of 1865 was a good one for Lee—he had his family with him; he had a job where he was needed; and he had the opportunity to fight for a difficult and honorable cause—the restoration of the South.

Lee continued to hear from ex-Confederates, who consulted him for advice. When General Beauregard wrote to him, Lee responded with the need for reconciliation and peace. "I need not tell you," he wrote, "that true patriotism sometimes requires men to act exactly contrary, at one period, to that which it does at another, and the motive which impels them—the desire to do right—is precisely the same. . . . History is full of illustrations of this." As an example, he used George Washington as one who had served the King of England

and at a later date served the Continental Congress of America against him. "He [Washington] had not been branded by the world with reproach for this, but his course has been applauded."

To the widow of a Confederate soldier, Lee spoke frankly, "Madam, do not train up your children in hostility to the government of the United States. Remember, we are all one country now. Dismiss from your mind all sectional feelings and bring them up to be Americans."

By the end of the second session, the enrollment at Washington College had grown to 399 students. To advance the college, Lee had to continue his hard work and adhere to an exact schedule. He always attended chapel in the morning, then went to his office or elsewhere on the campus until noon. In the afternoon, he usually took a ride on Traveller, his companion since 1861. He went to bed early because he believed that "one hour's sleep before midnight is worth two after that time."

In November 1867, a Richmond grand jury ordered Lee to testify during the legal proceedings against Jefferson Davis. The prosecution attempted to get Lee to admit that he had conducted military operations that were ordered by Davis. Lee, however, refused to be drawn. "I am responsible for what I did," he declared frankly, "and cannot now recall any important movement I made which I would not have had I acted entirely on my own responsibility."

As a result of his appearance at the grand jury, radical newspapers and magazines attacked Lee and the college. He traveled little for fear that he would bring harm to his friends. He wrote, "I hesitate to darken with my shadow, the doors of those I love best lest I should bring upon them misfortune."

When his son, Rooney Lee, was to be married, the general was invited to attend the wedding. Rooney's wife-to-be, Miss Tabb Bolling, lived in Petersburg, and the wedding was scheduled to take place there. Lee was reluctant to attend the ceremonies; some of his saddest memories of the war had been associated with Petersburg. He wasn't certain if the residents would welcome him there, but finally consented to attend after his son came in person to Lexington to see him.

On the afternoon of November 28, 1867, the ordeal Lee had dreaded began. He went to Petersburg by train, the first time he had returned since he was forced to evacuate the city. The town held unhappy memories for him. He said of his visit: "My old feelings returned to me as I passed well-remembered spots and recalled the ravages of the hostile shells." Much to his surprise, Lee was welcomed by an enthusiastic crowd. Station and street windows of a nearby hotel were all jammed. Instant cheers arose. The experience opened Lee's eyes. The brave old town had put the war behind them. Everywhere Lee found people smiling, his old soldiers working and the children welcoming him with laughter. On his return to Lexington, he wrote his son of the delight he found in Petersburg: "A load of sorrow which had been pressing upon me for years was lifted from my heart." In the renewed life of his people, Lee lived anew.

Lee was known to have an excellent memory. While president of Washington College, he learned the names of virtually all the inhabitants in the town and the names, latest grades, and disciplinary history of the college's 400-plus students. Lee had planned to write a book after Appomattox to explain the war. He said he would undertake the project not to vindicate himself but to let the world know what "my poor boys, with their small numbers and scant resources, succeeded in accomplishing." Although Lee never forgot the project—he referred to it in letters until his death—his duties at the college consumed all his time and energy.

Lee's postwar policy was "silence and patience." Only those things that would help reconcile the country or would contribute to the restoration of the South were worth doing. When asked why he refused to talk about the war or become politically involved, he answered: "I am anxious to do as little harm as possible. I deem it wisest to remain silent."

During his years at Lexington, Lee's faith seemed to grow. Religion meant more than ever to him. In addition to attending chapel exercises every morning at college, he took an active part in advancing the little Episcopal church. At home, General Lee always had prayers before breakfast.

In the fall of 1870, the new session at Washington College began, the sixth since Lee became its president. He attended the opening exercises and met students and faculty in the usual manner. Those who knew him well could see that he was failing in body. To others, he seemed merely an old man, although he was not more than 63. His hair was white. He who had been the most erect of men now stooped slightly. His end was near and he knew it.

Quietly he did his duty until the 28th of September. That afternoon Lee went through the rain to a vestry meeting where he presided for more than three hours in the chilly auditorium. His last official act, before adjourning the meeting, was to contribute the sum needed to raise the salary of the rector to a new figure that had been set. From the church, Lee walked home in the rain. He took off his cape and went into the dining room. "You look chilly," Mrs. Lee said, but Lee responded that he was warmly clothed. Lee took his usual place at the head of the table and started to say grace. He tried to speak, but could make no sounds. His wife, Mary, remembered the look of resignation on his face. Doctors examined him later that evening and diagnosed his problem as a blood clot in his brain. At Lee's command, death had come to men in gray and to even more in blue. When it came for him, he faced it as he believed a soldier should. After a week of stoical, heartrending silence, he sank into delirium.

Word of Lee's illness spread throughout the country. Messages and offers of help poured in, but he was beyond all help. When one of his doctors tried to arouse him by saying that it had been a long time since Traveller had been out of the stable and was in need of exercise, he got no reply. The fast-sinking Lee merely shook his head and closed his eyes. He knew that he would never ride again or even see his beloved horse.

During that last morning, Lee's mind returned to the battlefield. "Tell Hill he must come," he said audibly and then lapsed into unconsciousness. In his dreams, he may have been bringing his last campaign to a close. Finally he said, "Strike the tent." After that he sank into a silence that was never broken. At 9:30 A.M. on October 12, he crossed over the river to rest where his companions in arms had preceded him. Mary spoke of her husband at his death: "I have never so truly felt the purity of his character as now, when I have nothing left me but its memory. A memory which I know will be cherished in many hearts besides mine."

Word of Lee's death spread quickly. The *New York Tribune*, which had been hostile toward the South during the war, described Lexington in its mourning: "the town [is] overwhelmed with grief. . . . At the hotels, by the headstone, in the schools, on the streets, everywhere, the only topic of conversation is the death of General Lee. All classes of the community seem to be affected, even the colored people, who walk along in silence with sorrowful countenance and mourn the loss of 'Good ole Marse Robert.' Every house in town seemed to be draped with the emblems of mourning. . . . The students of Washington College, of which Lee was president, held a meeting this morning. . . . Many of the students were affected to tears. They seemed to have had for General Lee the affection of children for a father."

Funeral services were held in Lexington and were attended by thousands— not just Southerners, but Americans. He was buried in a vault under the chapel on campus. Looking back, Lee had said, "I did only what my duty demanded. I could have taken no other course without dishonor, and if it all were to be done over again, I should act in precisely the same manner."

In 1871, the trustees of Washington College voted to change the college's name to Washington and Lee. The two men who had so much in common were thus forever linked.

In 1875, a larger-than-life figure of Lee, lying as if asleep on a draped couch, was completed. The recumbent statue was placed in the Lee Memorial Chapel on the campus of Washington and Lee College.

Clearly Robert E. Lee had his faults as both a person and a general. Although Lee was opposed to slavery on moral grounds, he did little to speak out against it. Both he and his wife owned slaves. As a general, he has to at least share the blame for the Confederate defeat at Gettysburg. There are those who believe Lee should have ended the war as early as June 1864, when his diminished forces were tied down by Grant at Richmond and Petersburg and before Sherman reached Atlanta in September. For five months more after Lincoln's reelection, up until the last hours at Appomattox, Lee continued the futile struggle. The result was continued death and destruction throughout the South. But there was another side to Lee, the "Noble Hero of Peace."

After the war, Lee was a model of gracious defeat. That attitude would win him admirers among friends and foes alike. He did not spend his last years in bitter regret. Instead, as president of Washington College, he taught young Southern men the skills they needed to build a new life and future. He appealed to the defeated South to put aside its hatred and bitterness and join him in becoming a model citizen. Lee's manners and code of ethics far outshone those of the people around him. His deep religious faith let him accept the disappointment and hardships of his life. Few public figures in any age have left such an enduring legacy of national respect and affection. And seldom has any military commander so infused his troops with the love and esteem displayed toward Lee by his army. Despite the passage of time and ever-changing popular culture, Robert E. Lee remains the foremost Southern hero.

Robert E. Lee's life has been described with words such as *gentleman, honor,* and *duty.* In legend, he is defined so completely by the use of these words that in Virginia they still tell the story of a little boy who came home from Sunday school and said, "Mama, I'm confused. Was General Lee in the Old Testament or the New?"

5   *Good General, Poor President*

ULYSSES S. GRANT

HE was 5 feet 8 inches tall and weighed only 135 pounds; he had light brown hair and beard and clear blue eyes. He had failed in every enterprise he had attempted. When he was a young man working in his father's leather-tanning business, the townspeople gave him the name "Useless." As a lieutenant in 1854, he had to resign from the army to avoid a court-martial. The governor of Illinois would remember him simply as "plain, very plain." It was said of the unimposing little man that men obeyed him simply because he expected it. No one could possibly have predicted that he would one day became the savior of the Union and the eighteenth president of the United States.

One of Grant's closest friends, William Tecumseh Sherman, said of him: "I knew him as a cadet at West Point, as a lieutenant of the 4th Infantry, as a citizen of St. Louis, and as a growing general all through the bloody Civil War. Yet to me he is a mystery, and I believe he is a mystery to himself." He is the great mystery of the Civil War. Nothing in Grant's background suggested he would become the Union hero of the war. He had little interest in a military career, confessing: "The truth is I am more a farmer than a soldier. I take little or no interest in military affairs. I never went into the army without regret and never retired without pleasure."

Grant was a mystery because his abilities came to the forefront when emergencies arose. Once on the battlefield, faced with a life-or-death situation, the real Grant emerged. His was a uniquely American story. He was the boy who through virtue, courage, and luck rose from obscurity to the highest position in America.

He was born Hiram Ulysses Grant on April 27, 1822, in the village of Point Pleasant, Ohio. Grant's father, Jesse, was an enterprising tanner who had left Kentucky at the age of twenty-one because, as he said, "I would not own slaves and I would not live where there were slaves." Grant's mother was a farmer's daughter, quietly strong and direct. Grant later said, "I never saw my mother cry." In 1832, the Grants moved to Georgetown, Ohio, where Ulysses was to spend his boyhood. He was one of six children whose early lives were free of both hardship and luxury. "Useless" Grant, as some liked to call him, farmed, hauled wood, helped his father at the tannery, and gained a reputation for being able to ride and break horses.

Grant was not much like his father, who was outgoing and aggressive. Ulysses was more like his mother, quiet and determined. This quality of determination played an important part in his success during the Civil War. Early on, Grant seemed more at home with animals than with people. He loved horses, a passion he had all his life: "I love to train young colts. When old age comes on, I expect to derive my chief pleasure from holding a colt's leading line in my hand and watching him run around the training horse ring."

Ulysses' father decided early that his son had little potential. Nothing Ulysses did, or would ever do, quite pleased Jesse Grant. His approach toward his son reflected this feeling. When Ulysses was eight, Jesse sent him to a neighbor with careful instructions on how to bargain for a certain colt. Young Grant wanted the colt so badly he went up to the man and blurted: "Papa said I may offer you twenty dollars, but if you won't take that, I am to offer twenty-two and a half, and if you won't take that, to give you twenty-five." The story quickly circulated around Georgetown, and a lot of people had a good laugh—at young Grant's expense.

At age eighteen, Ulysses went away to boarding school at Maysville, Kentucky. When he returned, his father told him he would go to the United States

Military Academy at West Point. His father believed the academy would provide Ulysses with a solid education in engineering. After Ulysses had spent a few years in the army, Jesse's plan called for his son to resign his commission and go to work in the private sector. At first, Ulysses balked at his father's decision, but in a short time, he capitulated; in 1839, he entered West Point.

Upon his arrival at the academy, Grant found that the congressman who had signed his appointment papers had inadvertently written his name as Ulysses S. Grant. Grant informed the adjutant that his name was incorrectly listed on the roster. The adjutant replied that as the appointment was in the name of Ulysses S. Grant, that was who he was and that was who he was going to remain, at least as long as he was in the army. And so it was; Hiram Ulysses Grant became Ulysses Simpson Grant.

Ulysses had nothing against West Point except a fear of failing out. Once enrolled, he soon realized he could cope with the situation, and his fear of disgrace subsided. It was here that his classmates saddled him with the nickname "Uncle Sam," based on his initials. Soon it became just plain Sam Grant.

As a cadet, Grant received numerous demerits for slovenly dress, unsoldierly bearing, and tardiness. He was not a man for dancing or social etiquette, but preferred going off to a local pub for off-limit drinking. Promoted to sergeant in his third year, he confessed that the higher rank was "too much" for him, and he willingly served his senior year as a private. At first, Grant was a reluctant soldier and said: "A military life had no charm for me, and I had not the faintest idea of staying in the army." Soon Grant learned to admire the academy as the "most beautiful place I have ever seen," and he saw it as providing for his future security. "If a man graduates here, he is safe for life, let him go where he will."

Grant put in a decent, undistinguished tenure at the academy, graduating in 1843 and standing twenty-first in a class of thirty-nine. His modest record made him ineligible for both the prestigious Engineer Corps and the artillery. His attempt at joining the cavalry failed, and he was assigned as a second lieutenant in the 4th Infantry Regiment.

Before reporting to his first assignment, Grant took a brief leave of absence and traveled to his family's new home in Bethel, Ohio. As he passed through Cincinnati, he was embarrassed by a young boy on the street who gaped at him and jeered, "Soldier! Will you work? No sur-eee; I'll sell my shirt first!" To add insult to injury, when he reached Bethel, a local livery hand marched around the village streets in a homemade caricature of Grant's uniform. "The joke," Grant later wrote, "was a huge one in the mind of many people, and was much enjoyed by them; but I did not appreciate it so highly." From then on, Grant had a distaste for military uniforms; even when he became general in chief of all the Federal armies, he wore a private's blouse with his rank insignia stitched on it.

In the 1840s, the question of slavery dominated political discussion. Southwestern Ohio had been involved in the slavery issue from the days of Grant's childhood. By the time Grant was an adult, he had strong views on the subject. He saw the use of other human beings as property for the evil it was, but because of his shyness, he seldom discussed the issue. Grant never argued anything with anyone. Other than formal debate, he saw all argument as a waste of time and a way of creating bad feelings. "He never had a personal controversy with man or boy in his life," said his father, who always seemed to relish one.

In 1843, Grant was assigned to Jefferson Barracks, outside St. Louis, Missouri. It was during this time that he met and courted seventeen-year-old Julia Dent. Julia was the light of her father's existence. From the moment of her birth, Julia was her father's favorite. On one of her birthdays, he gave her a slave of her own who became known as "Black Julia." Julia was happy with the gift and to the day she died, never thought there was anything wrong with owning a slave. Julia and her family never used the word *slave*, instead preferring to call them servants.

Julia was five feet tall, plump, had dark brown hair pulled into a bun, and was strabismus (cross-eyed) in her right eye. Appearances aside, she was full of life, strong-willed, and optimistic. Julia was the antithesis of Grant's mother, but very much like his father. Her warmth and sociability broke down his shyness and hypersensitivity.

Although there was a shortage of young unmarried women in the West, Julia was not particularly sought after. She had a quick wit and few illusions about her physical charm. Within a short time, Grant had fallen in love with Julia and decided he wanted to marry her.

In April 1844, Grant obtained a three-week leave before departing for Ohio. One evening he removed his West Point class ring and offered it to Julia. She did not react in the way he had hoped. "Oh, no," she said. "Mama would never approve of my accepting a gift from a gentleman." Grant was disappointed and hurt. The ring stayed on his finger and in a few days, he boarded the steamer that would take him upriver to Cincinnati. But Grant, true to form, didn't give up.

Four years later, on August 22, 1848, Grant married Julia. Their union was a strong one and gave both a solid base upon which to build their lives. She gave him a sense of stability he never had known from his own family. The marriage produced four children; the oldest, Fred, had close ties with his father. At age eleven, Fred accompanied Grant through several Civil War campaigns and later followed his father's example and attended West Point.

In May 1845, the United States annexed Texas, and Grant's regiment was moved to Corpus Christi. Their mission, Grant wrote, "was to provoke a fight but it was essential that Mexico commence it." It was doubtful if Congress would declare war unless American troops were attacked first. The U.S. Army advanced south to the Rio Grande in order to extend Texan soil to that point. The move had the desired effect. In May 1846, the Mexicans attacked, and the war was on.

Grant was opposed to the war with Mexico, but there was nothing he could do. "With a soldier, the flag is paramount," he explained to a journalist more than thirty years later. "I know the struggle I had with my conscience during the Mexican War. I have never altogether forgiven myself for going into that. I had very strong opinions on the subject. I don't think there was ever a more wicked war. . . . I had not moral courage enough to resign. . . . I considered my supreme duty was to my flag."

In March 1847, an American force under Major General Winfield Scott launched an attack against Veracruz, capturing it and then moving against Mexico City. Grant's 4th Infantry went with Scott, and Grant participated in the climactic battle for the Mexican capital. Grant's single great moment came in this campaign. With a small party of men, he dragged a howitzer into a church belfry and fired on Mexicans defending the San Cosme city gate. The exploit affected the outcome of the battle, and Grant was given recognition for his efforts and mentioned in Scott's dispatches.

Like Lincoln, Grant was thoroughly opposed to the war with Mexico; his heart went out to the ragged and starving Mexicans. It was this side of Grant that is not often remembered. Despite his vicious Civil War title, "Butcher," he was opposed to the cruelty of hunting and found bullfighting "sickening." It was he, also, who preferred to sit out in the cold, drenching rain at Shiloh rather than in a warm tent where he might see the blood of his soldiers in surgery. "I never went into battle willingly or with enthusiasm," he would later state.

When the war ended, Grant was stationed at Sacket Harbor, New York, where he and his wife spent the first four years of their marriage. Then in 1852, Grant's regiment was transferred to the Pacific Coast. The boredom and loneliness of peacetime garrison life pushed Grant into a state of depression, and he began to drink. In April 1854, Grant, then a commissioned captain, was discovered drunk in public by his commanding officer, who promptly demanded that Grant either resign or stand trial. Fearing a scandal and the heartbreak a trial would bring to Julia, Grant chose to resign. After leaving the army, nothing seemed to go right for Grant. He returned to his family and tried to support them in a variety of jobs, none of them successful. He was unsuccessful as a real estate agent and collector of overdue accounts. He tried farming and worked mainly by himself. When he had to hire field hands, he preferred freedmen to slaves, often working alongside them in the field. To the disgust of neighboring farmers, he paid his freedmen more than the current rate for black farmhands. Although Julia owned four slaves, Grant made it clear to his wife and family that he was "opposed to slavery as an institution." He told his wife's slaves that it was his ambition to give them their freedom "as soon as I am able."

When things continued to go badly for him, Grant was forced in desperation to appeal for help from his father. His father provided assistance by setting him up in his family's leather business. There Grant was able to eke out a living, but barely. What saved him, and so many other men of his generation, was the outbreak of the Civil War.

When President Lincoln issued his call for 75,000 Union volunteers, Grant promptly offered to drill a company of Galena volunteers. In June 1861, he was appointed a colonel to lead the 21st Illinois Volunteers. In August he was named a brigadier general in charge of troops in southern Illinois and southeastern Missouri. Early in 1862, Grant's star began its incredible rise. He captured Confederate-held Fort Henry on the Tennessee River, then Fort Donelson on the Cumberland, pushing the enemy back to Tennessee. When Grant insisted that the Confederates surrender "unconditionally," he earned a new nickname: Ulysses S. Grant became "Unconditional Surrender" Grant. President Lincoln was jubilant; he showed his appreciation by naming Grant a major general.

The capture of Fort Donelson was the first sizable, decisive Union victory of the war. News reports informed the public that Grant smoked cigars, so well-wishers mailed him crate-loads of pungent stogies. The report was erroneous: Grant smoked a pipe, but switched to cigars after finding himself swamped with them.

Two months later, Grant's reputation suffered a setback. In April 1862, Grant's troops were camped at Pittsburgh Landing on the Tennessee River in Tennessee, near a little church known as Shiloh. While Grant was preparing to move his army, he was surprised by a Confederate attack in the early morning. The army was just beginning to stir, still yawning and trying to wake when the attack came. Grant was on the verge of losing his entire army; he ordered a counterattack. Cries from the wounded filled the air, and for two days, the intense battle raged on. Grant managed to halt the Confederate assault and to prevent them from winning the battle, but the price was high. The heavy casualties horrified both the North and South. Grant's losses came to 13,000 killed, wounded, and missing; the Confederates' losses were close to 12,000 men. As a result of his heavy losses, Grant gained a new reputation and nickname, "Butcher." Many who had praised Grant a few weeks earlier now clamored for his removal.

Rumors and whispers had followed Grant for years, ever since he resigned from the army in 1854. He drank, people said, and seemed to drink not for conviviality, but just to get drunk. Grant suffered from migraine headaches and was often forced to take time out. These attacks were believed to be the result of heavy drinking. Before Shiloh, the newspapers had kept the stories and rumors largely to themselves. Now they were blaming the heavy Union losses on Grant's drinking and he was damned in newspapers and congressional mailbags across the North. President Lincoln, however, could see beyond the losses and rumors. "I can't spare this man," Lincoln said. "He fights." Grant felt bad about the losses and even considered resigning, but his friend General Sherman talked him out of it.

Grant continued his tenacious drive and siege against the Confederate stronghold on the Mississippi River at Vicksburg. During the campaign, Grant broke away from his own supply and communication lines as he fought through a large part of Mississippi, something unheard of in military strategy. His army was able to live off the land, an approach used by Sherman a year later when marching through Georgia. On July 4, 1863, Grant took Vicksburg. Five days later, he took Port Hudson, securing Union control of the entire Mississippi. In late November, in the Battle of Chattanooga, Grant, then commander of the Union armies of the West, drove the Confederate forces out of Tennessee and opened the road to Georgia.

Lincoln was delighted to find a general who would fight and who was not afraid to make sacrifices to reach his objectives. On March 9, 1864, a grateful Lincoln named Grant a lieutenant general and three days later placed him in charge of all Union armies. Grant soon faced the greatest challenge of his military career—he was pitted against one of the best generals of the day, Robert E. Lee.

After assuming the general command, Grant divided the task of winning the war. It was decided that Grant would pursue Lee in an attempt to destroy the Army of Northern Virginia. Meanwhile Sherman, who now commanded western forces, would attempt to eliminate Joseph Johnston's army, which was defending Atlanta. These plans were a major change in the North's strategy to win the war. Previous campaigns had all aimed at the capture of strategic geographical points. This new strategy, however, had as its main objective the pursuit and destruction of the enemy's armies.

After crossing the Rapidan River, Grant planned to attack Lee. He expected to push his troops quickly through the hundred square miles of dense timber known as the Wilderness and strike Lee's flank. If anything went wrong, Grant could easily find himself fighting a battle in the same terrain as General Hooker had at the Battle of Chancellorsville. Once the battle began, dozens of small fires were started by sparks dropping from the barrels of rifled muskets. Soon the men on both sides found themselves fighting in clouds of smoke. Being shot was bad enough, but being burned to death was even worse.

When the battle began to go against Grant, one of his officers, on the verge of panic, informed Grant that he thought he knew what Lee was going to do.

With this, Grant's patience snapped: "I am heartily tired of hearing about what Lee is going to do. . . . Go back to your command and try to think what we are going to do ourselves."

Again Grant suffered heavy losses, but he quickly demonstrated how different he was from his predecessors. Many of the earlier commanders of the Army of the Potomac had retreated to their Potomac River base after suffering losses such as those sustained by Grant. But Grant stated that he "propose[d] to fight it out on this line if it takes all summer."

The spring campaign of 1864 was a costly one for the Army of the Potomac. From the Wilderness to Spotsylvania to Cold Harbor, Grant continued to attack Lee. At Cold Harbor, Grant made an unsuccessful frontal assault. He followed this with another attack, an attack that he would regret the rest of his life. Before the attack, his troops pinned their names on their uniforms so that their bodies could be identified later. They had a sense of impending death as they made their second charge against tremendous odds. This assault was nearly as disastrous as Pickett's charge at Gettysburg. The Union suffered nearly 7,000 casualties against only 1,500 for the Confederates.

After Cold Harbor, Grant's reputation as the Butcher returned. It is a reputation that has been exaggerated over the years, but it is undeserved. In the three years prior to 1864, the Union armies in Virginia suffered more than 100,000 casualties and achieved nothing. In the six months after Grant took command, he took Lee out of the war by containing him at Petersburg and placing the city under siege. Grant's casualties were 60,000—a high count, but he had something to show for his losses. The battle between Lee and Grant was developing into a fight to the death. Grant had a larger number of men and could sustain losses better than Lee. It was simply a matter of time before Grant would find a vulnerable spot in Lee's defense.

Grant's strategy to keep moving south and applying continuous pressure on Lee had worked. Grant had broken the siege at Petersburg; Sherman had burned his way to Atlanta; and Philip Sheridan had laid waste to the Shenandoah Valley, the Confederate breadbasket.

On April 2, Lee's divisions pulled out of Richmond and Petersburg. They converged at Amelia Court House on the Richmond-Danville railroad, hoping to find rations. What they found instead was Sheridan's cavalry blocking the road south. Lee had no choice but to swing his army to the west toward Farmville. This destroyed all hopes that Lee had of joining Joseph Johnston's army further south; he was forced to continue westward toward Appomattox Court House. Lee had to seek surrender terms.

On the evening of April 7, when Grant reached Farmville, he wrote a note to Lee advising him of the hopelessness of further resistance. After dinner, Grant stood on a hotel porch, smoking and talking with his aides. Dozens of regi-

Ulysses S. Grant in 1864

ments marched passed the hotel where he was staying. When they realized the man standing on the porch puffing a cigar was Grant, they broke into cheers. The cheers continued until all the regiments had passed. Then Grant threw his last cigar butt into the street and went to bed, hoping to relieve the throbbing in his head.

On April 9, Grant and Lee met at Appomattox to discuss the terms of surrender. It was one of the great moments in the war, a beginning of the nation's reconciliation—the meeting of two great men. It was charged with emotion and a study in contrasts. Their dress was as different as their backgrounds. Lee, manor born, was handsomely dressed in a brand new uniform, red sash, shining boots, and magnificent sword in a golden scabbard. Grant, the son of a tanner, arrived travel-stained from two days in the saddle, in muddy boots with his pants tucked into the tops, and wearing a private's blouse and lieutenant general's stars. Before the war, Lee had met with repeated success; Grant had experienced numerous failures and embarrassments. Now the situations were reversed. It was Grant who held the upper hand; Lee who must rely on his mercy. Yet Grant claimed it was he who was self-conscious, fearing Lee might have been insulted by his appearance.

At Appomattox, Grant demonstrated his humanity. He was in a position to humiliate his enemies if he wanted to, but he did not. Grant himself had experienced failure and defeat. Now Lee had suffered defeat; Grant could empathize with him. He recalled, "I felt like anything rather than rejoicing at the downfall of a foe who had fought so long and valiantly and had suffered so much for a cause, though that cause was, I believe, one of the worst for which a people ever fought."

Even though he was known as "Unconditional Surrender" Grant, he gave Lee very generous terms, allowing Confederate officers to keep their sidearms and permitting all who owned their horses to take them for spring planting. Grant also shared his army's rations with the starving enemy troops. He allowed Lee to leave Appomattox with his dignity and his sword. But he had done more than that—in the terms of the surrender, he had written that officers and men were to sign paroles and then go home, "not to be disturbed by the United States authority so long as they observe their paroles and the laws in force where they reside."

Grant realized that the war would soon be over and it was time to begin work on the peace. The war had aroused much hatred and bitterness, especially among those who had done no fighting. Grant knew that powerful men in Washington were talking angrily of treason and wanting to see leading Confederates jailed or hanged. Grant's terms had made that difficult. He had pledged his word at Appomattox. Grant had both the will and power to see that the agreement was carried out. There would be no jailings or hangings. Grant would see to that.

As they rode away from the McLean house, one of Grant's aides reminded him that he should inform Lincoln of Lee's surrender. Grant scribbled a short telegram to Secretary of War Stanton: "Gen. Lee surrendered the Army of Northern Virginia this afternoon."

Back at his headquarters, Grant's staff welcomed him and he could see something like worship in their eyes. He had to deflate their feelings to bring them and himself down to earth. "More of Grant's luck," he remarked wryly. Every success he had accomplished in the past four years had been ridiculed by his detractors and Lee's admirers as luck. Grant joined the scoffers and mockers, laughing at himself, at them, and at glory itself. Then he sat down and started writing dispatches.

The surrender at Appomattox is enshrined in American history as the great sacrament of reconciliation. Differences were overcome and the nation made whole in that meeting. In their differences, Lee and Grant were the perfect celebrants of the mass of reunification. Robert E. Lee taught his countrymen that good things can result from losing a war. Grant, as the magnanimous victor, by his terms of surrender did much to help bring the country together again. No matter how much fault might be found with Grant for his presidency, people could always look back and be restored by this hour of his undoubted greatness—his finest hour.

Victory over Lee propelled Grant into the limelight and placed him on a pedestal. Grant received great honor for his military accomplishments, which moved him into realms that it would have been best for him not to have entered. Grant was a soldier; he was not prepared to be a politician.

No one ever mistook the authority Grant wielded as a commander during the war; he literally held the power of life and death over thousands of men. Possessing great power almost always changes the person who has it, but it cannot relieve him of his own temperament, weaknesses, and humanity—and his past. These stayed with Grant as he gave orders and conducted the operations of the war.

Grant possessed his full share of quirks and eccentricities. He detested the sight of blood; when he ate red meat, it had to be well done, almost burnt, so that there was no trace of blood remaining. He was completely tone deaf and found the sound of music little more than an irritant. He had difficulty telling one tune from another and once remarked that he knew exactly two songs: one of them was "Yankee Doodle;" the other wasn't. He had a sense of humor and enjoyed hearing a good story, but in repose, he usually wore an expression of quiet seriousness.

In some respects, Grant was a lonely man who needed the reassuring presence of his family. He also needed the company of men who respected him and with whom he felt at ease. Whenever possible during the Civil War, he liked to have his wife, Julia, live with him in camp. She had to leave his side during the Vicksburg campaign, but Grant was accompanied by his twelve-year-old son, Fred. His personal staff consisted of midwesterners who shared Grant's background and outlook.

Grant made little display of religion, and some observers thought him to be an atheist or an agnostic. Actually, he was a Methodist and had been raised in a strict religious atmosphere. In his adult years, he was not a regular churchgoer until he became president, but some of his last letters to his family indicate a belief in God and the hereafter.

Some believed Grant to be a prude. He never exposed any part of his body; he always bathed in a closed tent, with all flaps tied. His associates stood outside naked in front of their tents and had their orderlies douse them with buckets of water. Grant very rarely swore, and abstained from obscenities. Although he did not object to others doing so, he did not contribute to the "parlor stories" usually swapped at the evening campfires.

Loyalty was an important part of Grant's personal code—loyalty to those above him and those junior to him. During the war, Grant was loyal to General Henry Halleck even when he received unfair treatment from his superior. He supported subordinates whom he suspected of working to undercut him, as long as they appeared to be devoted to the common cause of winning the war. It was this loyalty to his appointees that led to the corruption and scandal during his presidential administration. Grant's admiration for Sheridan ran beyond all bounds. His praise was so extravagant that it tended to defeat itself. Ten years after the war, Grant told Senator George Hoar that he believed Sheridan to have "no superior as a general, either living or dead, and perhaps not an equal."

The stories about Grant's drinking have been greatly exaggerated. Grant did drink occasionally, but usually quite moderately. Whether he ever got drunk remains controversial. The evidence suggests that on at least two occasions, he did. In the years after his death, a smattering of accounts emerged that seemed to confirm stories of his occasional intoxication. In 1887, Sherman wrote a friend concerning some of these reports: "We all knew at the time that General Grant would occasionally drink too much," and went on to say Grant's drinking did not really mean very much. From a military standpoint, Grant's drinking never adversely influenced his professional judgment, and he probably did not drink at times when major decisions had to be made.

After Appomattox, the victorious North exulted, and Grant's name shone second only to Lincoln's. Even the South hailed Grant for his considerate and kind terms at Appomattox. Wherever the General went, he was mobbed by crowds. When Grant returned to Washington, Lincoln received him with deep emotion, inviting the Grants to join him and Mrs. Lincoln at Ford's Theater. Grant accepted the invitation, but Julia, who didn't get along with Mrs. Lincoln, decided that they should not go, offering the excuse that she wanted to get back to her children. It was a fateful decision because Grant's name was also on the assassins' list. On the way to New Jersey, Grant learned of Lincoln's assassination and returned to the capital. "It would be impossible for me," he wrote, "to describe the feeling that overcame me at the news."

With Lincoln's death, Vice President Andrew Johnson became president. Initially, Johnson appeared certain to impose a harsh peace on the defeated South. Blaming the rich and powerful Southerners for the Civil War, Johnson told Grant he intended to hang those who had served as general officers in the Confederacy, starting with Robert E. Lee. Grant said that was out of the question. Under the agreement made at Appomattox, those officers who had sworn oath to the United States and been paroled were exempt from punishment. "When can these men be tried?" asked Johnson. "Never," Grant said, "so long as they do not violate their paroles." Grant threatened to resign if Johnson tried to carry out his plan. If Grant resigned, Johnson knew he would be swept right out of the White House.

The president backed down. He made several gestures to appease Grant, giving his son Fred an appointment to West Point and making Jesse Grant postmaster of Covington, Kentucky. He also gave Grant a fourth star and the title of "General of the Army."

In a short time, Johnson's feelings toward the South changed. He showed sympathy for the Southern people and instituted a surprisingly mild policy of Reconstruction. The policy was so mild that many Republicans felt that it practically overturned the verdict of the war. This and other actions soon brought Johnson into conflict with the Republican-controlled Congress. Grant found himself caught in the crossfire. At first he supported Johnson, but as time went on, he became more reluctant to back him in his battles with Congress. When Congress passed severe Reconstruction policies, Johnson decided to take the issue to the people, along with some of the war heroes to bolster his presence and to bring out the crowd. It was a disaster. Grant wrote to Julia: "I have never been so tired of anything before as I have been with political speeches of Mr. Johnson."

In the 1866 Congressional election, the Radical Republicans strengthened their position and were able to pass several bills restricting presidential power. The most significant of these was the Tenure of Office Act, which required senatorial consent for the removal of any official whose appointment had required Senate confirmation. Johnson considered the act an outrage and also believed it unconstitutional. To secure a Supreme Court ruling, Johnson needed to create a test case. To that end, he suspended Secretary of War Stanton. Johnson told Grant in advance of his intention and asked the general to serve as interim secretary of war, hoping that Grant's great popularity would help him win the coming political battle with Congress. Grant reluctantly agreed.

While serving as interim secretary of war, Grant's support for Johnson soon grew lukewarm—perhaps because he himself was being considered a candidate for president and he needed the Republican support. In January 1868, he vacated the office when he learned that the Senate had refused to confirm Stanton's dismissal. Johnson was furious, feeling he had been betrayed by Grant. Grant's departure helped pave the way for Johnson's impeachment a month later. The president attempted to portray Grant as a vacillating liar who had committed a breach of faith. Grant responded that he would not defy the will of the Senate and had never promised Johnson that he would.

For the first time in America's history, a president was placed on trial before the Senate for "high crimes and misdemeanors." If convicted of the charges against him, which essentially involved the violation of the Tenure of Office Act, Johnson would be removed from office. When the Senate failed to get the required two-thirds vote necessary to remove Johnson from office, the Radicals' position within the party was weakened.

In early 1868, Grant considered running for president, a move that seemed at odds with his personality. This apparent change was brought on by his damaged relationship with Andrew Johnson and by the acclaim that greeted him as he traveled about the country. He later justified his entry into politics by saying that he owed the Republican party a debt that could not be denied. But behind his growing interest in the presidency was the desire to ensure that the results of the war could be secured. Grant was convinced that a Democratic presidency would mean an appeasement of the South and make a mockery of the Union's sacrifice. The Republicans nominated Grant as their party's presidential candidate. His Democratic opponent was Horatio Seymour. Grant easily won the election.

The bitterness between Johnson and Grant was never as great as it was made out to be in the newspapers, but on the morning of Grant's inauguration, Johnson chose not to attend the ceremony, instead calling his cabinet to a meeting. In an effort to appear gracious, Grant pulled up to the White House, but he was told that Johnson was too busy to be disturbed. Johnson vacated the mansion while Grant took the oath of office.

"The office," said Grant in his inaugural address, "has come to me unsought; I commence its duties untrammeled . . . I shall on all subjects have a policy to recommend, but none to enforce against the will of the people. . . ." The new president advocated prompt payment of the nation's war debt of $400 million and a sounder national credit. Grant urged fairer treatment of American Indians and a continuation of Reconstruction.

When Grant took office, he inherited a failing Reconstruction, but he hoped there was still time to make it work. In 1868, Congress had passed the Fourteenth Amendment, which forced the courts to recognize that African Americans had rights. These rights, however, did not include the right to vote. The Fifteenth Amendment, which was being considered in Congress when Grant became president, would give African Americans that right. In 1865, Grant had favored allowing only those who were literate to vote. By 1869, he had changed his mind and wanted to enfranchise African Americans, most of whom could not read or write. Now Grant believed the last chance to save Reconstruction was to give blacks the right to vote.

On March 30, 1870, Grant signed the Fifteenth Amendment into law. The army fired a hundred-gun salute, and tens of thousands of people paraded by torchlight down Pennsylvania Avenue. Grant acknowledged the crowd and told them he had no doubt that the rights guaranteed by the Fifteenth Amendment would be used wisely. In his message to Congress, Grant called the amendment "the most important event that has occurred since the nation came into life."

The new legislation, however, was fundamentally flawed. It did not ban the use of literacy tests, property ownership, or educational requirements as a way of determining who would be allowed to vote. Congress nevertheless passed, with Grant's support, an enforcement act in May 1870. The act prohibited any use of force, bribery, or intimidation to deprive people of their right to vote.

The last of the enforcement acts, which Grant signed into law in April 1871, was aimed specifically at the Ku Klux Klan. For the first time, the federal government could punish criminal acts made against individuals. A few years earlier, such a step would have been considered impossible. By 1872, the Klan had been shattered. The twentieth-century version of the Klan is a re-creation, with no links to the original one. Breaking the KKK was Grant's greatest contribution to Reconstruction.

President Grant presided over the United States at the beginning of an era of growth and optimism, creativity and shame. No one wanted the federal government meddling in their affairs, unless the intervention took the form of railroad subsidies, grants of free public land, a protective tariff to stem foreign competition, or defense against American Indians as settlers moved west. In Grant, the movers of American society had just the man they wanted to preside over their pursuit of wealth. Grant was easy prey for their intentions. He had a narrow interpretation of executive power, one designed to please congressional bosses. They governed the nation through control of patronage and federal disbursements. The hope that Grant's administration would provide an inspired, reforming government died when he announced his cabinet appointments, most of whom were personal friends. The American people expected a great deal from their hero who had won the Civil War when Grant became president. Unfortunately for Grant, his leadership style, which had been so effective with the military, was destined to be a failure in politics.

Grant's presidency was plagued with corruption and scandal. As far back as 1863, Grant's friend Sherman had warned him to avoid the political chicanery of Washington, describing the capital as a nest of thieves. Grant did not have the requisite ability to be president. He had a very poor grasp of political theory, and he frequently demonstrated almost no real understanding of the American constitutional system. In many respects, he saw his job as one of administration rather than true executive leadership. His understanding of practical politics was no better. Grant acted as if he were still a general who needed only to give orders.

One scandal broke when Secretary of Treasury Benjamin Bristow uncovered a fraud in which a large group of distillers, in collusion with government agents, were permitting the sale of untaxed liquor. The Whiskey Ring involved Grant's chief secretary, General Orville Babcock. Babcock had been taking large sums of money and expensive gifts for allowing the operation. Grant himself accepted a valuable team of horses complete with harness, though he was unaware of what was happening. The same could not be said of Babcock.

When Grant first heard of the conspiracy, he said: "Let no guilty man escape." As the evidence became more conclusive, Babcock requested a court-martial as a military officer rather than face a civil court. When the court-martial convened, President Grant provided a deposition as a character witness in Babcock's behalf. This voluntary testimony by the president was so favorable that no jury would have convicted him.

Although Grant was not directly involved in the scandals, many Republicans resented the whole direction his administration was taking. Some were disgusted at the excesses and expense of Reconstruction and thought the time had come to end military rule in the South. Some objected to Grant's failure to press tariff reductions. Still others condemned his association with ruthless and greedy party bosses. By the election of 1872, the opposition to Grant had become so strong that his chief critics left the party and created their own organization. Despite the split in the party, Grant was still able to win reelection to a second term by defeating Horace Greeley.

Grant displayed very poor judgment in the selection of his closest advisers. Often they were old army cronies with no more political savvy than he possessed himself. They indulged in bribe-taking, influence-peddling, and just plain corruption. Grant removed them only when public pressure was so great that he had no other choice. Although Grant himself was never accused of wrongdoing, as a president he is considered a failure. By 1876, the country had had enough of Grant. He left office in 1877 after two terms.

After the war, great work, energy, and imagination were required to stabilize the nation's economy. Grant's two terms as president were not without accomplishment. In addition to his efforts at Reconstruction, Grant was the first president to insist on a humane policy for Native Americans. With his direction and under the guidance of Secretary of State Hamilton Fish, the principle of international arbitration was established for the first time.

When Grant left the White House, he and Julia embarked on a two-year tour of the world. Although the Grants traveled as private citizens, they were welcomed everywhere. Everyone wanted to see the great American hero, and Grant rose to the occasion. They met and dined with Queen Victoria at Windsor Castle and with Otto von Bismarck, the Prussian Chancellor whose statesmanship produced modern Germany. Wherever the Grants went—Europe, Egypt, the Holy Land, Siam, and Japan—dignitaries and large crowds turned out to meet them.

In August 1879, Grant and Julia returned to the United States, landing in San Francisco and making a leisurely four-month trip back to Philadelphia. Grant's popularity was such that he was nearly nominated for president a third time in 1880. The following year, he settled in New York City. A fund of $100,000, raised by twenty friends—including A. J. Drexel and J. P. Morgan—allowed him to buy a mansion there. William H. Vanderbilt lent Grant $150,000 to found a brokerage firm, Grant and Ward. Again Grant met with failure. In mid-1884, the firm suddenly failed, and Grant was left penniless and humiliated. Although Vanderbilt would gladly have written off the debt, the proud Grants turned all their property over to him.

Again Grant faced financial hardship. Now he was about to face a more serious problem, one that would take his life. He began to have stabbing pain in his throat. He demanded and received the truth from his doctor—he had cancer, and he was going to die. Congress restored him to the rank and full pay of a general, but he needed more money to pay his mounting bills. A generous offer was made by an admirer of his, the famous Mark Twain, to publish his memoirs. As a friend, Twain wanted to see that Grant received the most lucrative advance and the highest royalties possible.

Throughout the autumn and winter of 1884 and the spring of 1885, the dying Grant labored on his memoirs, much of which was done in longhand. He scrawled his story across hundreds of sheets of paper. As his illness grew worse and he tired more easily, he dictated to a stenographer. Finally the advancing cancer choked off his voice, and he went back to writing the manuscript himself. Doctor-prescribed cocaine and morphine helped to relieve his pain, but the medication clouded his mind, making his task all the more difficult.

The book when completed filled two volumes—1,200 printed pages—and covered Grant's life from his childhood in Ohio to the end of the Civil War. There is no evidence that he intended to incorporate the eight years of his presidency in his memoirs. In the process of writing, he survived at least one crisis when his physicians thought he would probably die. He rallied and pressed forward to finish his task; his family's future welfare depended on it. As the pain in his throat increased, Grant communicated more and more by writing notes on pads or on small slips of paper.

Grant left New York in June 1885 to die in a place he did not know and in someone else's house. In the city, the summer's heat was oppressive, and Grant had been offered the use of a summer cottage at Mount McGregor, a few miles from Saratoga Springs, New York. He traveled to Saratoga Springs in Vanderbilt's private railroad car, but had to make the remainder of the trip over rough roads by carriage. His trip to Mount McGregor was such an ordeal it seemed unlikely that Grant would survive it. But again he rallied. He couldn't die yet; he hadn't finished his memoirs.

A few days after reaching Mount McGregor, Grant wrote to his wife: "I had an idea that I could live until the fall . . . I see that the time is approaching more rapidly." He told her that he preferred to be buried at West Point, but she would not be allowed to join him there when she died. So he left it for her to choose his burial site. Meanwhile, Julia decided that her husband and family needed the comfort of religion to see them through the death watch. Grant had never been baptized. Julia asked the Reverend John Newman, pastor of the Methodist Church in Washington, to come and baptize him, but Grant refused. Newman waited until Grant had one of his fainting spells and then baptized him anyway. Grant refused to take communion. He would have to be conscious to do that.

On July 16, 1885, Grant completed his 295,000-word *Personal Memoirs of U. S. Grant*, which would earn $450,000 for Julia and his family. The two-volume edition sold 300,000 copies in its first printing, making it one of the most successful books of the nineteenth century. Grant's personal memoirs were much like Grant himself: simple, unpretentious, yet brilliant. Many consider them the finest memoirs ever written in America. Mark Twain said, "It's a book I wish I had written." Grant closed his memoirs with the statement: "I feel that we are on the eve of a new era when there is to be a great harmony between the Federal and the Confederate. . . . Let us have peace."

Just seven days after completing his memoirs, on July 23, with his family, physicians, and his trusted servant by his bedside, Grant died. It was 8:08 in the morning. To commemorate the moment, Fred Grant stopped the parlor clock.

Without the writing of the book to occupy him, Grant had succumbed quietly to the ravages of his disease. The same stubbornness that helped Grant to prevail, despite the many setbacks throughout his life, had bolstered his resolve to stay alive to complete his memoirs. With his story told, he surrendered to death with courage and grace. Grant was buried on New York's Riverside Drive in a funeral that rivaled Lincoln's tribute. Four words are engraved on his tomb: "Let us have peace." As Lincoln's favorite general, Grant had won peace for a nation. Now he had earned it for himself.

6   The Man Without a Country

JEFFERSON DAVIS

EVEN at the very end, with the Confederacy and the South in ruins, Confederate President Jefferson Davis refused to acknowledge defeat and discard his vision of an independent Southern nation. On May 2, 1865, Davis presided over what would be his final war council, held in a borrowed house in the small town of Abbeville, South Carolina. Richmond, once the proud capital of the Confederacy, was now gutted by fire and occupied by Federal troops. After four years of determined resistance, Robert E. Lee and his Army of Northern Virginia had surrendered and disbanded. In North Carolina, General Johnston and his army had also laid down their arms; in Mobile, Alabama, General Richard Taylor was preparing to do the same. The war was clearly lost, but Jefferson Davis was not yet ready to give up.

President Davis and the Confederate cabinet had evacuated Richmond, fleeing into the Deep South. Davis, his entourage, and a military escort had retreated to Danville, Virginia, then south to Charlotte, North Carolina, and finally to Abbeville. There, hoping to plan a strategy for carrying on the war from west of the Mississippi, Davis assembled his last war council: Secretary of War John Breckinridge, General Braxton Bragg, and five brigadier generals.

Faced with the reality of defeat, Davis was still determined to do all in his power to keep the Confederacy alive. Refusing to give up and admit defeat was characteristic of President Davis. Revered by many Southerners, reviled by some, he was a forceful, determined leader motivated by a remarkable reserve of energy and self-confidence. His opponents viewed him as stubborn, dogmatic, and inflexible and accused him of mishandling the war. Supporters saw him as a man of high character who faced a very difficult task, who had directed the new nation through the Civil War with skill and tireless devotion.

Over forty men have been president of the United States, but only one man was president of the Confederate States of America. He was Jefferson Davis, born in Kentucky only a short distance from the birthplace of his archfoe Abraham Lincoln. Unlike Lincoln, whose reputation shone in the light of Northern victory, Davis's reputation has been shadowed by his views on slavery. He had the further misfortune of being labeled a traitor. Nevertheless, this sullen man gave the Confederacy a leadership that brought it to the brink of victory.

Jefferson Davis was born on June 3, 1808, in a humble log cabin in Kentucky, but his family moved to Mississippi when he was still a child. He was named after Thomas Jefferson, the author of the Declaration of Independence. Jefferson's mother, Jane Davis, had already given birth to nine children in twenty-three years. She was forty-six when Jefferson was born and her husband, Samuel Davis, was just over fifty. Jefferson's father had served in the Revolutionary War and was given government land to start a farm. After several moves, Samuel finally made his home in Mississippi. As Davis put it, he wanted "higher and healthier" land, where he could grow cotton. He found it in the southwest corner of the Mississippi Territory. There Samuel grew cotton, the new boom crop of the Deep South, and built a large, verandahed house, which Jane named "Rosemont."

Jefferson Davis's early education was varied, but adequate. After two years at a Catholic boarding school, he returned to his father's plantation and attended a succession of local schools. In the spring of 1823, Davis entered Transylvania University in Kentucky, then considered the best school west of the Appalachians. It was there that Davis learned the art of public speaking. At the spring graduation, Davis was selected to speak. He titled his address "Friendship." The local newspaper reported that "Davis on Friendship made friends of his hearers."

Jefferson's older brother Joseph had a profound influence on him. Twenty-three years older than Jefferson, Joseph was a prosperous lawyer and planter who helped write Mississippi's state constitution. It was primarily through his efforts that Jefferson received an appointment to the United States Military Academy. Samuel and Joseph Davis secured the appointment without consulting Jefferson, but when presented with the opportunity, he embraced it, apparently because his father and brother seemed to want it. Jefferson had no military ambition at the time but had expected to become a lawyer after graduating from Transylvania like his successful brother.

In 1824, when Davis was sixteen years old, he entered West Point. He was an undistinguished student and received numerous demerits for a variety of petty offenses. During his "plebe," or freshman, year he was arrested, tried, and nearly expelled for visiting a tavern. The following year, he was arrested and confined to quarters for six weeks after attending an illegal Christmas party.

A cadet at the academy at the same time as Davis was Joseph Johnston. Davis and Johnston were both smitten with the local tavernkeeper's pretty daughter; they tried to settle their differences with their fists. Johnston, the heavier of the two, won the fight; the two men were at odds with each other from that day on.

In 1828, Davis graduated twenty-third in a class of thirty-two, a decidedly mediocre performance. His undistinguished showing was partly due to his passion for extracurricular reading on every conceivable subject. His checkered West Point career made his future look uncertain, but his years at the academy did affect his character and imbued him with a high sense of honor and duty.

Davis began his military career as a second lieutenant but was forced to spend most of his time in dreary garrison duty in Missouri and the old Northwest. Like his future nemesis, Abraham Lincoln, Davis was involved in the Black Hawk War in 1832. During his time in the army, he met Sarah Knox Taylor, the eighteen-year-old daughter of Colonel (and future president) Zachary Taylor. Taylor disapproved of the match, having vowed that none of his daughters should ever have to endure the hardships of an army life. In 1835, Davis resigned his commission to marry Sarah. Colonel Taylor grudgingly consented to the marriage, but neither he nor his wife attended the wedding.

The marriage was tragically brief. The couple settled on a Mississippi plantation, which Jefferson's brother Joseph had given to him. Within three months, Davis and Sarah both came down with malaria. Davis was in serious danger for over a month, but survived; Sarah did not. Jefferson took the loss of his young wife very hard and would feel responsible for her death the rest of his life. He spent the next couple of years in relative seclusion on his plantation, immersed in reading books: law books, literature, political tracts, and, above all, the U.S. Constitution, which he is said to have memorized.

Davis devoted himself to running the plantation and during that time, developed his beliefs on slavery. He was convinced of the fundamental inferiority of African Americans and considered himself responsible for the well-being of all his slaves. By the standards of the time, Davis treated his slaves leniently. They were educated, fed well, and rarely beaten. Discipline was handled by courts made up of slaves from his plantation. Rules governing their punishment allowed Davis to intercede only when he thought the punishment was too harsh. Under the guidelines, he could not increase the punishment. Unfortunately for Davis, he never fully understood what slavery was like elsewhere. His plantation's success, along with the relative contentment of his slaves, reinforced this belief. He thus had a false notion of slavery and never fully understood its evil.

From 1835 through 1843, Davis rarely left Brierfield, his plantation. The area of cleared land steadily increased, and his cotton crop grew year by year. Within five years, Davis owned forty slaves; by 1860, he owned more than a hundred. Davis ran Brierfield with the conscientious paternalism of an enlightened despot. He did not view slavery as a permanent condition for blacks but thought emancipation would require several generations and should be allowed to occur naturally. "The slave," he said, "must be made fit for freedom by education and discipline. . . ." Years later, upon Davis's death, one of his former slaves was asked how he felt about his old master. "I loved him," he said, "and I can say that every colored man he ever owned loved him."

In the years following Sarah's death, Davis paid little attention to politics. His brother finally convinced him that he should run for elected office. In 1844, he ran for Congress but lost the election. It was during this election year that he was introduced to Varina Howell, whom he married in 1845.

Like Sarah, Varina was young—just seventeen years old; Davis was thirty-five. Varina was well educated for a Southern woman. Her family was not wealthy but had acquired the aristocratic manners of the Natchez, Mississippi, society. Varina was a fascinating person: emotional, puritanical, proud, and generous—a woman of strong prejudices and a powerful personality. She was loyal and jealously possessive. Although not by nature unkind, she sometimes hurt people with her sharp wit. Varina made excellent company, having a lively sense of humor and loving a good laugh. Davis understood both her strengths and shortcomings. As she matured, Varina became strong and steady and influenced her husband, not only at home but also in his political decisions.

Jefferson and Varina Davis had a strong, sometimes volatile union that was frequently interrupted by tragedy. Their marriage produced six children. Only two daughters survived into adulthood; three of the boys died during childhood, the fourth at age nineteen.

A few months after his marriage, Davis won election to the House of Representatives. He and Varina left Brierfield and traveled to Washington D.C., where they would spend most of the next 15 years.

When the Mexican War erupted, Davis resigned from Congress to take an active role in the conflict. He was elected colonel of the 1st Mississippi Rifles and served in northern Mexico in the army of his former father-in-law, Zachary Taylor. Colonel Davis proved himself an able commander. His leadership was critical to the success of the American forces in the Battle of Monterrey. At Buena Vista, he displayed courage and leadership, receiving severe wounds; he returned to Mississippi to recover and was received as a hero.

After the war, Davis was elected to the United States Senate. The feelings of national unity that followed the war quickly faded in the face of growing conflict between the North and South. Davis's loyalty to the Union began to fade as well.

In 1851, Davis resigned from the Senate to run for the governorship of Mississippi, a campaign that he lost. Upon his election to the presidency, Franklin Pierce appointed Davis to the position of Secretary of War in his new cabinet. The innovative West Point graduate was soon busy improving the army's weapons and equipment. He doubled the army in the short period of two years. Davis has since been considered by many to be the finest secretary of war in the nation's history.

The issues of slavery and states' rights were consuming the nation, and in 1857, Davis returned to the Senate, where he remained until after his state seceded from the Union. As a senator from Mississippi, Davis followed the pattern of South Carolina senator John Calhoun in championing states' rights, slavery, and free trade. He believed that the measures he supported were essential to the security of his region and in accord with the founding principles of the nation. He was earnest in supporting his position, retaining the respect and even the friendship of many Northerners who opposed his views.

The Supreme Court became involved with the slavery issue. All past laws were ruled unconstitutional, and the Dred Scott decision of 1857 ruled that no African American could be a citizen of the United States. The South was overjoyed, but the new Republican party stood firmly against any expansion of slavery in the United States. Republicans like William Seward of New York and Abraham Lincoln of Illinois rode a rising wave of protest against the higher court's decision.

In 1860, Davis introduced several resolutions that took an uncompromising position on slavery. In them, he insisted that the interference by Northern states in the "domestic institution" of Southern states subverted the Constitution and imperiled the Union. He also believed that Congress did not have the power to prevent a citizen from emigrating into federal territory with his slave property and that Congress should ensure that this property be protected within the territory. Neither Davis nor anyone else expected the resolution to be adopted, but he hoped to influence the Democratic party's platform in the upcoming presidential election.

Davis's tactic worked well, but not the way he had hoped. It contributed heavily to the split in the Democratic party. The Northern wing nominated Stephen Douglas, while the Southern wing nominated John Breckinridge. A third faction nominated John Bell of Tennessee. Davis tried to get all three to withdraw in favor of a compromise candidate. Breckinridge and Bell agreed, but Douglas refused. He thought if he withdrew, most of his supporters would simply vote for Abraham Lincoln, the Republican nominee.

As it turned out, Lincoln won anyway. His election sent fear throughout the Deep South. "Fire-eaters," radical Southern rights advocates, urged that the South secede from the Union. South Carolina led the way. On December 20, before Lincoln took office, a specially elected state convention voted unanimously to leave the Union. On January 9, 1861, Davis's own state of Mississippi seceded. By February 1, the entire Deep South had left the Union.

For all his protests, Davis did not really want to see the South leave the Union. Davis was ordered by Mississippi to resign from the Senate. In a farewell speech to his colleagues in the Senate, described by his wife as "inexpressibly sad," he said, "I feel no hostility to you senators from the North. In the presence of God, I wish you all well."

When Davis returned to Mississippi, the governor appointed him a major general in charge of the state militia. But Davis held the rank for only a few days before receiving another, more important appointment. When the Confederate Provisional Congress met in Montgomery, Alabama, in February to form a new government, the delegates voted unanimously to elect Jefferson Davis as their president. Alexander Stephens of Georgia was selected as vice president. Davis would have preferred to serve the Confederacy in the army, but he accepted the presidency with good grace.

Varina did not like the idea of her husband becoming president. "I thought his genius was military," she later wrote, "but that as a party manager, he would not succeed. He did not know the arts of the politician and would not practice them if he understood, but he did know those of war." Her assessment would prove accurate. Davis had many things in his favor: a good education, strong intellect, and excellent background in military and government affairs. But he had serious flaws in personality and temperament, which in turn would flaw his performance as president of the Confederacy.

Davis spent the first six weeks of his presidency trying to deal diplomatically with Northern officials in Washington. He hoped the whole problem could be resolved diplomatically and peacefully. When Federal troops occupied Fort Sumter in Charleston Harbor, Davis, feeling this was an insult to the South, gave his soldiers the order to fire on Sumter. On April 14, Fort Sumter, out-manned and outgunned, surrendered. The following day, Lincoln ordered loyal states to provide 75,000 militia to put down the rebellion. At Virginia's invitation, the Confederate capital moved from Montgomery to Richmond. Southerners had made a nation and consummated it by force of arms.

The Confederacy's aim at the beginning of the war was simply to hold on to the de facto independence already obtained. There was no need to invade the North or dictate a peace treaty on the steps of the White House. All the Rebels had to do was continue the struggle long enough for the North to tire of the war and accept the fact of secession. In many respects, this aim was little different than that of the American colonies during the Revolution.

Davis ordered the first military draft in the history of the nation, a conscription act that required all males from eighteen to thirty-five to serve three years in the military. In addition to raising an army, the president of the Confederacy had to create a whole new breed of generals almost overnight. In so doing, he revealed one of the weakest facets of his leadership, a dependence upon old friends and cronies. Two of the worst examples of cronyism were the appointments of Leonidas Polk and Braxton Bragg.

Leonidas Polk was given command of the entire northern Mississippi area, one of the most vulnerable areas of the Confederacy. Polk and Davis had been friends at West Point, but immediately after graduation, Polk resigned his commission and never served a day in uniform. Instead, he became an Episcopal minister and later a bishop. The loss of the Mississippi River in 1862–1863 can largely be traced to mistakes made by the inexperienced Polk at the beginning of the war.

Braxton Bragg had impressed Davis in Mexico during the war. He had left the army in 1857 for the life of a Louisiana planter. Bragg was among the first West Pointers around which Davis organized the Confederate army. He was given command of the Army of Tennessee, but before long, the total army was in disarray. Davis himself went to Tennessee to try to settle the differences between feuding personalities, but was unsuccessful. Despite observing the confusion and disarray of the army, Davis failed to replace Bragg.

Davis's problems were not unique. President Lincoln was also plagued with incompetent and egotistical generals, but he had a different way of dealing with the problem. He allowed himself to be embarrassed, humiliated, slighted, and snubbed to keep the peace. Lincoln, unlike Davis, was willing to lose an argument if it would help him win the war. Once, Lincoln said he would be willing to hold McClellan's horse if he would only give him a victory.

Davis had successes too. It was he who promoted and supported Robert E. Lee, with whom he would form one of the greatest military partnerships of the war. Lee bears most of the credit for their close relationship; he could read

Davis very well, and he knew how to get along with him. Lee was not a person who suffered from insecurity and could afford to defer to Davis's need for deference and flattery. Davis gave Lee his full support, and Lee in turn gave Davis a string of victories.

In assembling his cabinet, Davis tried to include representatives from each state of the Confederacy. This well-intentioned gesture sacrificed talent and ability for geographical location. During the four-year history of the Confederacy, only two men—John Reagan and Stephen Mallory—maintained their appointments. There were four secretaries of state, four attorneys general, five secretaries of war, and two secretaries of the treasury.

Initially the Confederate Congress performed very well. The "fire-eaters" and radical secessionists had played their part in launching the government, but they were replaced by more moderate representatives. The Congress endorsed Davis' emergency war measures and appropriation requests as well as confirming his cabinet. By late 1861 the good rapport between Davis and Congress had deteriorated, and it continued to do so to the end of the war. Davis' insistence on having his own way and his inability to compromise contributed greatly to this break. The main point of disagreement grew out of Davis' new viewpoint on states' rights. As a wartime president, he found it necessary to increase the power of the central government in order to conduct the war. Many of the individual states did not want to relinquish their powers to the president.

Davis ran the war effort and the Confederacy from his wartime home, known as the Confederate White House, at Clay and 12th Streets in Richmond. Three stories high and handsomely furnished, it served as the president's home from July 1861 until April 1865. There, Davis pored over an endless stream of paperwork until his eyesight grew strained. He found it difficult to delegate work and responsibilities. Despite his self-imposed workload, Davis spent at least an hour with his family every day and rarely failed to attend worship services at St. Paul's Episcopal Church. When the weight of responsibility became almost unbearable for Davis, he would collapse on the sofa in his study, often declining dinner. As his wife later recalled, "I remained by his side, anxious and afraid to ask what was the trouble which so oppressed him." On these occasions, Varina would read to him, sometimes poetry, sometimes light fiction.

The conduct of military operations took more of Davis's attention than anything else. Preference and necessity for military matters both took a hand. The president had an affinity for military strategy, and he felt that if the Confederacy was defeated, nothing else mattered anyway. On occasion, he would travel to the fighting front, but he seldom interfered.

As president, Davis was usually decisive; he acted quickly to resolve problems as they developed. During a bread riot in Richmond in 1862, a crowd of several hundred women and children marched to the city's business district and demanded bread from the bakeries. The crowd quickly became a mob. Davis rushed to the scene and appealed to rioters to disperse. When they refused, he took all of the money from his pockets and threw it to the crowd. He told them they had to bear their share of the privations and that he would do what he could for them. Then he told the crowd that he would order arriving troops to fire upon them if they did not return to their homes.

With the help of a few trusted military advisers, including Robert E. Lee and Albert Sidney Johnston, Davis's long-time friend, the president mapped out the war strategy. Like Lee, Davis preferred to fight a defensive war, which would conserve the South's strength and force the North to attack Confederate strongholds.

The early victory at Manassas touched off a celebration throughout the South and convinced many delirious Southerners that it would soon be over. As the war heated up, it became apparent that the war would not be a short one. When the South's casualties increased and supplies decreased, Davis was hard-pressed to find ways of financing the war and keeping the ranks of the Confederate armies filled. As early as 1863, the Southern bid to become an independent slave nation had failed. The war the Southerners believed would be short had turned into a grueling bloodbath, and the South's determination and confidence began to wane. Lee's defeat at Gettysburg, coupled with the surrender of more than 30,000 Confederate troops to Grant at Vicksburg on July 4, 1863, ended whatever hope Davis had of gaining a negotiated peace. He called the twin Confederate defeats "the darkest hour of our political existence," which provoked another torrent of abuse from his critics.

Despite the huge losses suffered by the Confederates in 1863, Davis refused to call a halt to the war. He reasoned that the South had already survived the worst of the fighting, and the courage of his people would eventually carry them through to victory. The loss of life continued to grow as the war progressed. By mid-1863, the South had lost Mississippi, and Yankee soldiers had vandalized and destroyed Davis's house at Brierfield.

It was the president who bore much of the blame for the failed campaigns and the strain showed on Davis. A virus had blinded one of his eyes and badly inflamed the other. He also suffered from a digestive ailment called dyspepsia. Davis went into a protective shell, becoming obsessed with the details of troop movements and supply reports. He slept and ate very little and stubbornly battled through his recurring bouts of pain and exhaustion.

Tragedy visited Davis even more directly. In the spring of 1864, Davis's young son Joseph was killed in a fall from the balcony of the Confederate White House. Davis was overwhelmed with grief, and when messengers brought him news of the war, he said, "I cannot do it. I cannot. I cannot." He went upstairs and spent all night with his son. The next day, he was back on the job, doing what he had to do as the Confederate president. Emotionally, his public front never changed. He always remained stern and was often called "the Sphinx of the Confederacy."

As the war continued, Davis's problems mounted; now the outcry came from the common people. Ordinary Southerners resented the loss of labor manpower, particularly among nonslaveholders, who had no one to work the land since all the able-bodied men had gone off to fight. Class resentment also surfaced. Wealthy families did not suffer to the same extent as those not as advantaged. As late as 1864, men of means were able to pay substitutes to take their place in the army. Poor men who enlisted individually were required to serve for three years; rich men could raise their own units, stocked with the sons of other rich men, and were required to serve for only twelve months.

By the fall of 1864, the Confederacy had been split into three parts. In Georgia, General Sherman had begun his March to the Sea, utilizing his concept of total war, burning and pillaging the countryside. Davis refused to make more than a halfhearted attempt to negotiate a peace settlement as long as Lincoln insisted that the abolition of slavery and reunification with the North be conditions of a truce. There was a strong public demand for peace at any price, but Davis was determined to preserve the honor of the South. In desperation, he proposed that slaves be inducted into the Confederate army. By the end of March, Grant was ready to break through the lines at Petersburg. If Petersburg fell, surely Richmond would have the same fate shortly after.

On March 31, Varina and her family left Richmond. They took with them nothing but their clothes. They were to go to Charlotte, North Carolina, first and if necessary to Abbeville, South Carolina. From there, Davis wanted her to go to the Florida coast and then to sail to Cuba or even Europe. It was a tearful farewell. To Varina, he said, "If I live, you can come to me when the struggle is ended, but I do not expect to survive." Varina believed him, thinking this was probably the last time they would see each other.

On April 2, 1865, the Confederate defenses at Petersburg collapsed, opening the way for the Union army to seize Richmond. Southern officials, troops, and civilians evacuated the city. Davis and his cabinet also fled, leaving behind a city in near riot. A fire began in the early hours of April 3 and raged out of control with no one to fight it. Shortly after sunrise, Federal troops occupied the smoldering city.

Davis had expected Richmond to fall eventually, but not as soon as it did. He and his cabinet and aides escaped to Danville, Virginia, that same evening. Danville had been carefully selected in advance because it could be defended by both Lee and Johnston, and it had good rail connections. Davis remained in Danville for a week, then on April 10, he learned that Lee had surrendered at Appomattox Court House the previous day. The news, Secretary of the Navy

Stephen Mallory wrote, "fell upon the ears of all like a fireball in the night." Later that evening, Davis and his cohorts left by train for Greensboro, North Carolina.

A wanted man now, Jefferson thought first of his family, from whom he had become separated in the chaos. As he traveled through North Carolina, Davis received a cool welcome. In Greensboro, all doors were closed to him and his government for fear of vengeance by federal troops if they found that they had harbored them. Finally, a member of Davis's staff found a bed for him in a small house.

Davis was still convinced that the Confederacy could win the war, but it was evident to everyone else that the Southern cause was lost. Still determined, Davis met with Beauregard and Johnston and indicated that he wanted them to keep fighting. Both men found the order utterly devoid of realism; in a second meeting the next day, Johnston bluntly informed Davis that "it would be the greatest of human crimes for us to attempt to continue the war." Davis turned to Beauregard and asked his opinion. Beauregard agreed with Johnston, and so did most of those present.

When Davis met with his Cabinet, the response was the same: Everyone present told him the fight was over. The hopelessness of the situation was underscored when a dispatch from Lee arrived officially announcing his surrender. After reading it, Davis passed it along and "silently wept bitter tears." R. E. Lee Jr., who was present, later wrote, "He seemed quite broken . . . by this tangible evidence of the loss of his army and the misfortune of its generals. All of us, respecting his great grief, silently withdrew."

Davis left the meeting depressed; now he was all alone. He was still bitter the next morning, but he took time to write a short letter to Varina: "Everything is dark. I have lingered on the road and labored to little purpose." He said he would try to join her if possible. Meanwhile, she should "prepare for the worst." His cabinet pressed him to leave Greensboro. They were all too exposed to remain there. The president and his entourage left for Charlotte on the evening of April 15. Federal cavalry had cut the railroad, so they went by horseback.On April 19, Davis learned of Lincoln's assassination and commented: "I certainly have no regard for Mr. Lincoln but there are a great many men whose end I would rather have heard than his. I fear it will be disastrous to our people, and I regret it deeply." For Davis, it was the calamity of a defeated cause. In speaking of Lincoln in kindly terms, Davis had mellowed, or perhaps he was only contrasting his feelings with those he had for the new president. On assuming power, Andrew Johnson had proclaimed Jefferson Davis an outlaw and accused him of being involved in Lincoln's murder. Johnson offered a big reward for Davis's capture. "$100,000 Reward in Gold," the proclamation read. Moreover, Johnson had told a Washington street crowd that he would hang Jefferson Davis and all the "diabolical" crew at Richmond if he ever got the chance.

Davis became a familiar sight on the streets of Charlotte in his gray suit and crepe-covered hat. "He alone, of all the vast crowd," said a soldier present, "seemed to retain the majesty and self-possession of his character." Davis said, "I cannot feel like a beaten man!"

Feeling very alone, Davis had no one to turn to but Varina, and he was not sure where she was. In her escape from Richmond, she had always been several days ahead of him. Varina had left Charlotte on April 13 when she heard rumors of an anticipated raid and moved to Abbeville, South Carolina. On April 26, Davis left Charlotte, riding south to find Varina.

Davis arrived in Abbeville early on May 2 to a warm welcome, only to find that Varina had left two days earlier. After the warm reception in Abbeville, Davis had renewed enthusiasm for continuing the fight. That afternoon, Davis called a meeting of his generals, the men commanding the remnants of the cavalry brigades composing his escort on the trip. The cause was not lost, he said: "Energy, courage and constancy might yet save all. . . . Even if the troops now with me be all that I can for the present rely on, three thousand brave men are enough for a nucleus around which the whole people will rally." Davis then asked for their suggestions on the future course of action for continuing the war. None could believe what they heard. There was a silence, the kind of silence Davis had heard before in recent cabinet meetings when he made similar comments. Again, those in attendance told him that the war was over and that a guerrilla war such as Davis proposed would lead to greater evils than it could justify. Emphatically, they all said they "would not fire another shot to continue hostilities." Painfully, Davis stood and without adjourning the meeting, started to leave but moved so feebly that he might have fallen had General Breckinridge not jumped up to assist him.

On May 5, Davis was united with his family. Varina begged him to leave her and "go swiftly alone." Davis took her advice, and on May 8, he and his party rode on ahead. But their progress was slowed by a heavy rain, allowing Varina's party to catch up. Davis decided to stay in camp for the night with Varina.

On the morning of May 10, the Davises were awoken by a rifle shot. Yankee cavalrymen surrounded the camp. In the darkness inside the tent, Davis reached for his overcoat, grabbing instead Varina's short-sleeved cloak. He barely had stepped outside when Varina rushed out and threw her black shawl over his head and shoulder. Thus the story was born that Davis had tried to elude capture by dressing as a woman. In time, the story of Davis's arrest was embellished and circulated, primarily to embarrass him, and the story persisted that Davis was trying to escape in his wife's hoopskirt. Davis anguished over what was termed his "ignominious surrender," deeply resenting that anyone believed him capable of an act so "unbecoming a soldier and a gentleman."

The war might be over, but the postwar battles were about to begin for Jefferson Davis. For him, the fight must go on. Already the taunting and teasing began. The jubilant captors sang the favorite lyric of the time, "We'll hang Jeff Davis from a sour apple tree," and spoke profanely in front of Varina and her children. Once Davis's captors learned about the reward, the soldiers became more insulting.

Weary and ill, Davis expected to be executed. Instead he was taken to Fort Monroe in southeastern Virginia and placed in solitary confinement under heavy guard. There he was to await his destiny. It turned out to be a long wait. The federal government was in a highly vindictive mood. A deranged actor, John Wilkes Booth, had assassinated President Lincoln, and Davis had been accused of complicity in the murder. The charge of being a part of the assassination was eventually dropped, but Davis still faced charges of treason against the United States.

Davis was imprisoned at Fort Monroe and placed under the supervision of Brigadier General Nelson Miles. With Washington's blessing, Miles had Davis placed in irons, but public outcry was so great that after five days they were removed. Davis was not permitted to leave his cell; all exercising must be done there. When he stripped to take a sponge bath, or when nature's call made it necessary for him to use the portable commode, he was not allowed any privacy. General Miles decided when Davis would be permitted to change his underwear. Fearful that Davis might attempt suicide for a time, Miles did not allow the prisoner to use a knife and fork when eating. Davis's health suffered as well. A light was kept burning inside his cell for twenty-fours a day. All guards were ordered not to speak to him, and his cell was inspected at fifteen-minute intervals. Not for a moment was he without a hostile gaze upon his slightest movement. A year went by before he was allowed to see his wife.

Other indignities befell the Confederate president. He received letters from newly freed slaves congratulating him on his confinement and their freedom and sending him worthless Confederate currency. The Northern press also spread the rumor that Davis had been captured, wearing not a shawl but a petticoat, and that he tried to escape in women's clothing. One editorial expressed it this way: "A peal of laughter goes ringing round the globe. Davis, with the blood of thousands of noble victims upon his soul, will go down to posterity cowering under a petticoat."

Davis's suffering, however, made him a hero in the South. He was more popular than when he had been president. Southerners began to see Davis as representing all that was the embodiment of the Lost Cause. Davis became a martyr, almost a Christ-like figure—the one who was paying for the sins of the

South. The impression of martyrdom was further reinforced by a gift from the Pope, a crown of thorns, which the Pope had made himself to signify Davis's suffering.

Gradually, the terms of Davis's confinement were relaxed. The light was removed, and Davis was permitted to walk in the courtyard and receive books and newspapers. Not until August was he allowed to write to Varina, and then on the condition that he discuss family matters only. It was not until April 1866 that Varina was allowed to visit him.

As the months dragged on, Washington was not sure what to do with Davis. Many of the high-ranking Confederates had been granted pardons, but Davis refused to ask for one. He wanted to go on trial to prove that secession had been legal; this issue had not been legally settled in court. The federal government did not want to risk a trial in Virginia to answer the question. There was the strong fear that a jury might find for Davis.

Varina, in the meantime, was working hard to secure her husband's release from prison. Pressure was also growing for his release from a group of wealthy Northerners, including Cornelius Vanderbilt, who offered to pay Davis's bail. Finally in May 1867, Andrew Johnson authorized the transfer of Jefferson Davis from Fort Monroe to the civil authorities to answer charges of treason. Davis arrived in Richmond on May 11 in response to a writ of habeas corpus. "I feel like an unhappy ghost visiting this much beloved city," he said.

As Davis's carriage moved through the streets of Richmond, a cry arose: "Hats off, Virginians!" together with the refrain "God bless you" as a "great concourse of people . . . a sea of heads," according to Varina, greeted her husband. The crowd was so large that the mounted police had to make room for the carriage. "The windows were crowded and even on the roofs people had climbed. Every head was bared. The ladies were shedding tears."

On May 13, Davis arrived in federal circuit court, which was located in the old customs house. The customs house was among the government buildings not damaged by fire; Davis's presidential offices had been there. He was championed by a battery of supporters led by newspaperman Horace Greeley, businessman Cornelius Vanderbilt, and a well-known New York lawyer, Charles O'Conor; none of these men had ever had a kind word to say about secession. With their persuasion, Judge C. Underwood agreed to release the prisoner on $100,000 bail. The bond was instantly signed by Greeley, Vanderbilt, and eight other prominent Northerners and Southerners.

At the order from the bench to discharge the prisoner, the suppressed feelings of the audience broke forth in every part of the hall; the clapping of hands, stamping of feet, and shouts of hundreds of throats "making the hall resound." After two years, Jefferson Davis was at last a free man. He didn't tarry long; that evening, he and Varina departed for New York and then Montreal. Never again would he appear as a prisoner in a court of law, nor would the amount of the bond ever be demanded. The hypothetical case of the *United States* v. *Jefferson Davis* had been, in effect, thrown out of court.

Immediately after being released, Davis was taken to the Spotswood Hotel. All along the way, the ex-Confederate president was saluted with the rebel yell. When his carriage reached the hotel entrance, a silence fell upon the crowd; they seemed too moved to shout. As Jefferson Davis rose to step down, one deep voice commanded, "Hats off, Virginians!" "Five thousand uncovered men," wrote an eyewitness, "did homage to him who had suffered for them." In an emotional silence, Davis descended and entered the hotel.

Davis was free now, but a man without a country. President Andrew Johnson had denied rights of citizenship to high-ranking Confederates. Neither Davis nor Lee regained his citizenship in his own lifetime; more than a hundred years passed before the American government finally voted to restore their civil rights—to Lee in 1976 and to Davis in 1977. After the Civil War, both men had done their part to persuade the South to accept defeat and to support the new Union.

After Davis was released from prison, his personal life was seldom happy. Disappointment and tragedy followed him most of the twenty-two years that remained to him. In frail health, he first traveled to Canada and then to Europe. In the fall of 1870, Robert E. Lee died. Lee's five years as a college president had enhanced his reputation, but only after his death was he considered among the top American heroes. Davis was invited to speak at a memorial service for Lee in Richmond. The Richmond audience responded to its first glimpse of Davis with a roar of approval, a warmth of feeling for him that he had never experienced before his imprisonment. The *Richmond Dispatch* reported the occurrence: "As Mr. Davis walked to the stand every person in the house rose to his feet, and there followed a storm of applause as seemed to shake the very foundations of the building, while cheer upon cheer was echoed from throats of veterans as they saluted one whom they delighted to honor."

Davis spoke of his friendship with Lee and praised his modesty: "I never in my life saw in him the slightest tendency to self-seeking." After a pause, the frail ex-president added, "Of the man, how shall I speak. . . . His moral qualities rose to the height of genius." Not even the most fervent members of the Lee Memorial Association could have hoped for a more favorable opening of this movement to enshrine Lee.

A friend found Davis a job as president of the Carolina Life Insurance Company in Memphis, Tennessee. He held the job there until the company went bankrupt during the Panic of 1873.

Shortly after, Davis returned to Mississippi and his plantation, which had been turned into a home for freed slaves. His plantation was overgrown and his house vandalized by federal troops. His father had never transferred the property title to Davis, but the plantation was generally acknowledged as his. Finally he achieved ownership of the property, but he soon discovered that the shifting river and chronic flooding had made the plantation unprofitable.

Davis was finally forced to accept the charity of an admirer, Sarah Dorsey, who invited him to live at Beauvoir, her estate near Biloxi. Mrs. Dorsey rented a cottage to him at a very nominal sum. She soon began to serve as Davis's secretary as he began to write his memoirs, *The Rise and Fall of the Confederate Government*. In his writings, he attempted to defend the South's right to secede and apologized to no one. Varina was very jealous of Mrs. Dorsey's close association with her husband and for a long time, refused to set foot on the property. It was not a sexual jealousy that upset Varina, but rather an intense resentment that another woman had taken her place as his confidant. Mrs. Dorsey eventually sold Davis's residence to him for a modest price. When she died in 1879, she willed him not only Beauvoir but her entire estate.

The last dozen years of Jefferson Davis's life may have been his happiest. He had always liked Mississippi's Gulf Coast. Davis found a sense of serenity and peace at Beauvoir that enabled him to enjoy his remaining years. Old friends, including some Yankees, came to visit; Davis proved to be a genial host. When he wasn't writing or entertaining, Davis would sit on the verandah and enjoy the sea breezes. The work on his history of the Confederacy gave him the opportunity to talk to old friends and recall memories. As the years passed, his book got longer and longer until it was finally published in two volumes. However, *The Rise and Fall of the Confederate Government* did not sell well initially. Northerners didn't care, and Southerners couldn't afford the stiff price. The book was a tiresome rehash of Davis's old arguments.

Immediately after the Civil War, Jefferson Davis had become the scapegoat for the country. In the North, he was blamed for helping to start the war; in the South, for losing it. Unable to blame the brave soldiers or generals like Lee, Southerners pointed their fingers at Davis. By 1880, however, the tide had turned. Southerners increasingly closed ranks behind their former leader. His incarceration at Fort Monroe had contributed greatly to this change in attitude and helped to ensure that he would be remembered as a martyr of what some Southerners referred to as the Lost Cause.

In the spring of 1886, the ex-Confederate president was invited to make a tour of the South. Reluctant to accept the invitation, Davis was finally convinced by the argument that it might be the last chance his youngest daughter, Winnie, would have to see the affection the South held for her father. Traveling in a special train car, the Davises reached Montgomery at 8 P.M. A drizzling rain did not dampen the spirited greetings of the 15,000 persons standing in the muddy streets. Cannon, fireworks, and cheers boomed through the night, and a band played "Dixie." Huge banners welcomed "Our Hero."

At ceremonies honoring him, Davis did not seem anxious to dispel the mood of conciliation. He spoke briefly, exalting the Confederate dead, "the spirit of Southern liberty," and Southern womanhood. His only note of discord came when he spoke of the Civil War as "that war which Christianity alone approved—a holy war for defense."

The next day he delivered a lengthy speech. As was usual for him, he defended a state's right to repel invasion. He concluded with a statement of conciliation: "Permit me to say though the memory of our glorious past must ever be dear to us, duty points to the present and the future. Alabama having resumed her place in the Union, be yours to fulfill all the obligations devolving upon all good citizens seeking to restore the General Government to its pristine purity and, as best you may, to promote the welfare and happiness of your common country."

On the morning of April 30, the Davis party left Montgomery for Atlanta. In Atlanta, Davis was cheered by a crowd estimated to be 50,000 in number. The *Atlanta Constitution* reported that visitors from Southern and Northern states had arrived for the festivities. Just before Davis spoke, ex-Confederate General James Longstreet suddenly rode up to the speakers' stand. Longstreet had suffered charges of turning scalawag after the war and had earned Davis's enmity as well as that of many other Southerners. Longstreet mounted the platform, approached Davis, and embraced him emotionally.

Davis continued his tour to Savannah, where he received another prolonged ovation. Invigorated by the continued outpouring of affection, Davis again stressed his belief that state sovereignty had always been the basis for his defense of Southern secession. Such comments were bound to be upsetting to the North. After the Savannah speech, Davis tried to soften his remarks by saying that he did not equate state sovereignty with war. The clarification did little to quiet the criticism. Many of Davis's comments were printed out of context and in a few instances were misquoted. The *Chicago Tribune* described his speech as a "disloyal harangue." The *New York Tribune* called him an "unrepentant old villain and Union-hater."

Davis's tour had revived Southern emotions better left buried. Many Americans feared that Davis's speeches would retard progress that had been made toward healing the wounds left by the war. Although some damage had been done, in time the furor subsided.

Davis lived well into his eighty-first year. He continued to make speeches on numerous public occasions. Sometimes conciliatory, he was more often defiant. "Nothing fills me with deeper sadness, "he said, "than to see a Southern man apologizing for the defense we made of our inheritance." Long after most prominent ex-Confederates had regained their citizenship, Davis refused even to apply. He remained to the end a man without a country.

On December 6, 1889, the unrepentant Confederate died of bronchitis in New Orleans; he had caught a cold when he made his last visit to his beloved

Brierfield. His body laid in state in the city hall, as mourners came from all over the South to pay their final respects. It was believed that at least 50,000 people filed past his flag-draped casket. In May 1893, his body was moved from the grave in New Orleans to Hollywood Cemetery in Richmond.

Despite Davis's unpardonable position on slavery, he possessed some admirable qualities. He was generous to the needy, loyal to his friends, and devoted to his family. His letters to his wife and children are marked by exceptional warmth and tenderness. Unfortunately for him, few people outside his family were aware of these fine features. People were greatly impressed by his appearance and demeanor. He wasn't considered handsome, because of the hollowness of his cheeks and the sharpness of his features. Davis's character and personality were commonplace. But his military bearing, dignity, courtesy, poise, and self-assurance commanded attention and respect. What set him apart from others was the exaggerated degree to which he possessed these characteristics. Whereas others might be dedicated, he was committed. Whereas others were enthusiastic, Davis was passionate. Whereas others were determined, he was resolute.

For better or worse, there were two faces to Jefferson Davis, and it was when these faces approached the extremes that his personality baffled those around him. The strong loyalty he held for his friends made him susceptible to cronyism and manipulation. The bravery he had displayed during the Mexican War often led to combativeness and an instinct to fight first and think later. His determination and dedication easily turned to obstinacy. When Davis found a good general, as with Lee, he stood by him even in the face of criticism; unfortunately, when he found a weak general such as Braxton Bragg, he stood by him too. He was thorough in almost everything he did, down to the smallest detail, a fault that took up too much of his time.

Few men suffered more than Davis had. One of the greatest sorrows of his life was the loss of all four of his sons. He often showed compassion for others, hesitating to inflict pain on them when the health of the Confederacy depended on it. For a man who was frequently violent, he was remarkably patient at times. Few Southerners treated their slaves in such a humane way, yet he retained a fundamental position that blacks were inferior to whites. Davis was generous in granting accolades to others, but more grudging than most men in his insistence on having the last word in an argument.

The man who was selected to lead the Confederacy brought with him the accumulated traits and attitudes of fifty-three years of living in the South. In hindsight, Davis was probably not the right man for the job.

The myth that the South could not have won its independence regardless of anything Davis might have done is one that continues to persist. So much during the war was decided by such a small margin—the result, at least indirectly, of decisions made by Davis. This is not to say that Davis alone bears the responsibility for the South's defeat. The poor performance by some Confederate generals and the excellent leadership by Union generals like Grant and Sherman certainly played important roles in the outcome of the war.

Jefferson Davis remained a die-hard Confederate to the end. Although finally accepting the reality of the Union, he never apologized for either secession or slavery. Just before his death he said, "Were the thing to be done over again, I would do as I then did. Disappointments have not changed my conviction."

7   A Beleaguered President

ANDREW JOHNSON

IT was an actor's bullet that gave the country its new president. Everyone was asking what kind of man he was. People didn't know quite what to expect of their new president, Andrew Johnson. He was almost the same age as Abraham Lincoln and like the old rail-splitter, he had risen from a background of poverty.

Andrew Johnson once said: "I have grappled with the gaunt and haggard monster called hunger"—and he had. Like his hero Andrew Jackson, Johnson grew up wanting many of the necessities of life. When he achieved high office, he never forgot his humble beginning. Even in the White House, he and his wife, Eliza, preferred to think of themselves as just plain folks from Tennessee. Johnson developed into a tough and courageous political leader. His opponents thought of him as mule-headed and cantankerous. Johnson insisted that he always acted out of principle.

Andrew Johnson was born on December 29, 1808, in North Carolina. Neither of his parents could read or write, but somehow he learned to read and later his wife taught him to write. When he was three, his father died; his mother remarried, but his circumstances were no better than before. When he was thirteen, his mother signed him over as a tailor's apprentice. He left the apprenticeship and then moved to Greeneville, an east Tennessee village located in a valley surrounded by hills.

He went to work in George Boyle's tailor shop. When he was not busy stitching and sewing, Andrew was able to meet some of the townspeople. Among these was Eliza McCardle, the daughter of a local shoemaker. According to the story commonly accepted in Greeneville, it was love at first sight for Eliza. When Johnson first arrived in town, she is supposed to have told her friends, "There goes the man I am going to marry." Although the story may be fiction, there is no question that the two fell in love. Eliza was attractive and had a better-than-average education. She was modest, retiring, and generally "regarded as a model woman by all who knew her." When Andrew was seventeen, he married sixteen-year-old Eliza. They had five children.

Although Andrew and Eliza were married for fifty years, not much is known about their relationship. For most of Eliza's life, she was an invalid, suffering from consumption. Johnson was frequently away from home, but because of her condition, Eliza was not able to go with him. People who knew them believed that their marriage was a happy one. Although their temperaments were different—he was passionate and aggressive and she, calm and retiring—friends agreed that they were a perfect married couple. Eliza was solicitous of her husband's comfort; he was always considerate of her feelings.

Johnson's political career began in Greeneville, Tennessee. He had once been a tailor, but when he spoke at political meetings, he found he had a special talent. He had no difficulty captivating and holding an audience's attention. Eliza, determined that her husband should amount to something, encouraged him to continue to educate himself. Soon his tailor shop became the gathering place for the discussion of politics, and at the age of twenty-one, Johnson was elected alderman. This was followed by a two-year term as mayor and a stint as a state legislator. All this time, he was developing his skill as a stump speaker, and in 1843 he was elected as a Democrat to the United States House of Representatives.

A Jacksonian Democrat and self-proclaimed champion of the common people, Johnson never lost his fierce plebeian pride. "Some day I will show the stuck-up aristocrats who is running the country," he had vowed early in his Tennessee career. "A cheap purse-proud set they are, not half as good as the man who earned his bread by the sweat of his brow."

Andrew Johnson was a good congressman, industrious and dedicated to the needs of working people. He pressed for economy in government, opposed high tariffs that would raise the cost of living, and supported a homestead act that would provide land for settlers. When a general increase in salaries for government employees was suggested, he insisted that laborers share in the benefits. Conscious of his lack of formal education, he drove himself to study, to read omnivorously, and to gather information that would be helpful in his debate in Congress. He practiced his elocution and held his own in an age of brilliant orators. A *New York Times* reporter wrote that in his speeches, Johnson "cut and slashed right and left, tore big wounds and left something behind to fester and remember. His phraseology may be uncouth, but he talks strong thoughts and carefully culled facts in quick succession."

An admirer of Thomas Jefferson and Andrew Jackson, Johnson was a Democrat, but by no means always a faithful party man. The needs of the people, as he saw them, always came first. His independent posture frequently irritated Democrats as well as Whigs, and he was often the victim of bipartisan attacks. Although he antagonized his Southern colleagues in Congress, he continued to please his constituency. He was reelected four times. Unable to defeat him at the polls, the Tennessee Whigs gerrymandered his district out of existence. The strategy promptly backfired when Johnson returned home and was elected governor of the state. Once in office, Johnson established the first public school system in Tennessee, placing the needs of the working people over those of the slaveowning aristocracy. Johnson once said: "Let the mechanic and the laborer make our laws, rather than the idle and vicious aristocrats." Johnson was always proud of his ability as a tailor. As governor of Tennessee, he sewed a suit for the governor of Kentucky; the Kentucky governor, a former blacksmith, sent Johnson a handmade shovel and fireplace tongs in return.

As governor, Johnson was successful in advertising himself and his ideas. He was able to divest control of the party from his conservative opponents, while prostrating the opposition. It was a record of which he could be proud and provided him with entry into national politics. In 1857, the state legislature named him to the U.S Senate. "I have," he said, "reached the summit of my ambition."

Although Tennessee was a slave state, Johnson did not favor slavery. His dislike of slavery was not on moral grounds but the consequent devaluation of the white laborer. He accepted slavery as a fact of life, a local institution peculiar to the state and beyond the province of Congress. In 1860, the Tennessee delegation to the Democratic National Convention gave Johnson its favorite-son vote for vice president. The slim chance Johnson had of being a part of the ticket was nullified when the Southern states withdrew over the slavery issue and nominated John C. Breckinridge to oppose the regular Democrats' choice, Stephen Douglas. Johnson campaigned for Breckinridge because of his pro-Union position. Because of the split in the Democratic party, Lincoln was elected president. Although secession had not been an election issue in

Tennessee or elsewhere, the crisis of the Union was at hand. Johnson would soon be forced to make the most difficult choice of his life.

Between Lincoln's election and inauguration, Andrew Johnson, alone among Southern congressmen and senators, called on Congress to prevent secession. In the process he pledged himself —"my blood, my existence"—to save the Union. In the North he was acclaimed a hero; in the South he was hanged in effigy. After Lincoln's inauguration, Johnson hurried back to Tennessee, disregarding threats on his life and narrowly escaping a lynch mob, to try to prevent his state from seceding. Once while he was speaking in a church in Kingsport, Tennessee, a hostile audience tried to shout him down. Johnson took a pistol from his pocket, laid it on the pulpit, and calmly continued his speech. Despite his efforts, Tennessee voted to join the Confederacy. Johnson was the only Southern senator not to leave the federal government. As a result, he was branded a traitor and had to flee to Kentucky.

Like most Unionists, Johnson's family were turned out of their homes. His two oldest sons joined the Union army. In September 1862, Eliza Johnson, who had remained in Tennessee after it seceded, received the Confederate government's permission to cross into Union territory to rejoin her husband. The grueling trip left her in poor health for the rest of her life.

In 1862, Grant took Nashville and part of western Tennessee. President Lincoln appointed Johnson as military governor of the occupied portion of Tennessee "to provide . . . peace and security to the loyal inhabitants of the state until they shall be able to establish a civil government to conform with the Constitution." Johnson held the office for three years amid great physical peril. Johnson accepted the assignment; but it was not until late in 1863, when all of Tennessee had been cleared of Confederate troops, that he could begin to establish a civilian government. As military governor, Andrew Johnson gave amnesty to Confederates who swore loyalty to the Union, and he supported an amendment to the state constitution outlawing slavery.

In the summer of 1864, delegates to the National Union Convention—the Republicans and Democrats—selected Andrew Johnson as the president's running mate. Johnson, a Southerner, a former slaveowner, and a Democrat, was placed on the presidential ticket with Lincoln to attract the votes of other Democrats. By choosing a candidate from Tennessee, Lincoln felt he could strengthen his position with the reconstructed Southern states and hoped their votes could ensure the outcome of the election. From Lincoln's standpoint, Johnson was a perfect running mate. In general, the selection of Andrew Johnson was well received in the North. The *New York Times* called the nomination "eminently fit to be made," emphasizing the importance to the Union party of the War Democrats, as the combination of Republicans and War Democrats now called itself. Lincoln and Johnson went on to victory in November, but some

Northerners attacked the modest background of the two candidates. According to an editorial in a New York newspaper, "the age of statesmen is gone. The age of rail-splitters and tailors . . . has succeeded."

After the victorious election, Johnson returned to Tennessee to continue his Reconstruction plan. By the end of February 1865, the job was complete. In March, Johnson returned to Washington to take the oath of office. Ill and exhausted from the trip, Johnson sat waiting for the ceremonies to begin. He said he did not feel well and asked for a stimulant. Some brandy was sent for and he had several sizable drinks. The delay and the heat of the stuffy Senate chambers gave the brandy time to act. When he was called upon to speak, he slurred his words and spoke irrationally as the assembly and Lincoln looked on. Although Johnson was not a frequent drinker, in gossip and press, he became "Andy the Sot." Lincoln defended him, but the label as a person with a drinking problem remained.

Little more than a month after his inauguration, and less than a week after Appomattox, President Lincoln was assassinated by John Wilkes Booth. Lincoln's assassination—and his own sudden succession to the presidency—left Johnson stunned. After being sworn in, the new president told Lincoln's cabinet, "I feel incompetent to perform duties so important and responsible as those which have been so unexpectedly thrown upon me."

Johnson's accession to the presidency was to have fateful consequences for the freedmen, their former masters, and for the country as a whole. Many thought that Johnson would simply follow Lincoln's plan for Reconstruction. Nothing was further from the truth. Lincoln's Ten-Percent Plan for amnesty and Reconstruction was a wartime measure, designed to encourage the seceded states to return to the Union. What Lincoln might have done in times of peace is largely an unanswered question. Johnson's Reconstruction policy, however, still lay in the future. For several weeks, Johnson took particular care not to commit himself to any specific program.

In Congress, the Radical Republicans were strong advocates of a harsh Reconstruction. Thaddeus Stevens of Pennsylvania was their leader in the House; in the Senate, they were led by Benjamin Wade of Ohio, the idealist Charles Sumner of Massachusetts, and Zachariah Chandler from Michigan. The Radicals urged that the leaders of the Confederacy be excluded from political life, that many of the Southern whites be disenfranchised, that the property of rich Rebels be confiscated and distributed among the freedmen, and that their suffrage be placed in "loyal" Negroes' hands. Although the Radicals argued that the Confederate states had lost their constitutional rights, most Republicans were not ready to go that far. Instead, the party leaders talked about the doctrine or "forfeited rights." By seceding, the states had lost or forfeited some of their rights. They should be kept out of the Union until they properly repented. How much repentance was needed depended on the spirit demonstrated by Southerners and on the leadership of the man who succeeded Lincoln as president—Andrew Johnson.

On the evening after Lincoln's death, Senator Benjamin Wade of Ohio, a leading Radical, strode into Johnson's suite at Washington's Kirkwood House, grasped Johnson by the hand, and declared: "Mr. Johnson, I thank God that you are here. Lincoln had too much of the milk of human kindness to deal with these damned rebels. Now they will be dealt with according to their deserts."

No inheritor of the presidential title assumed the office under more difficult conditions than Andrew Johnson. He took the oath of office on the morning of April 15 in the parlor of the Kirkwood House. The secretary of the treasury wrote that Johnson was "grief stricken like the rest, and he seemed to be oppressed by the suddenness of the call upon him to become President . . . but he was nevertheless calm and self-possessed."

Andrew Johnson was in almost every way unfit to be president, especially in the dark and dangerous crisis of Reconstruction. He was a staunch states' rights advocate who had always fought measures to increase federal power. Johnson was willing to concede that some blacks should have the right to vote, but he insisted that under the Constitution, the privilege should be bestowed only by the states. A self-proclaimed spokesman for the poor white farmers of the South, he condemned the old planter aristocracy but believed African Americans should play no role in Reconstruction. Essentially, Johnson was an honorable man, but he was not a politician. He could not compromise; hence, he could not lead. At times he was paranoid. Suspicious and secretive, he saw plots to destroy him on every hand.

Andrew and Eliza allowed Mary Todd Lincoln all the time she needed to leave the White House. President Johnson moved into the White House in May; the rest of the family—including Eliza, two sons, two daughters, a son-in-law, and five grandchildren—moved in gradually. Eliza stayed out of sight in the White House. By that time she was a semi-invalid, suffering from tuberculosis. She did not like public life at all and would have preferred returning home, but she felt she belonged with her family. Johnson's daughter, Martha Patterson, assumed White House duties for her mother. Then 36, Martha was married to David Patterson, a senator from Tennessee. She ran the White House with a firm and confident hand, free of the severe criticism that Mary Lincoln had attracted. Once again, under Martha's guidance, the mansion became the prime attraction for Washington's society. Martha brought two cows that grazed on the White House lawn. Early every morning, Martha was up to attend the dairy before breakfast.

As president, Johnson had his chance to show the Southern aristocrats, whom he blamed for secession, who was in charge. He investigated the possibilities of indicting leading Confederates for treason and confiscating their property under the 1862 Confiscation Act.

On the day of Lincoln's death, the Radical Republicans met in caucus and, remembering Johnson's consistent opposition to Southern aristocratic leadership, agreed that Johnson's accession to the presidency "would prove a god-send to the country." They felt he too would favor a harsh peace in which land would be confiscated, Confederate sympathizers disenfranchised, and white suffrage limited, while blacks would enjoy full rights to vote.

At first Johnson seemed to justify the Radicals' faith. On April 17, General William Tecumseh Sherman met with Confederate General Joseph Johnston for the surrender of Johnston's army. Recalling the policy of conciliation that Lincoln had explained to him in a meeting just a few weeks before, Sherman offered astoundingly lenient terms. They provided not only for the surrender of all remaining Confederate forces, with the men permitted to keep their weapons, but for the readmission of the Confederate states to the Union, with full rights of citizenship and no prosecution.

When the news reached Washington, authorities were aghast and angry. Stanton even suggested treasonous motives on Sherman's part. In his first major test, the new president held firm. Sherman was forced to renege on the terms he had offered Johnston. On April 26, General Johnston was required to sign a surrender document similar to the one given Robert E. Lee at Appomattox.

In April of 1865, Johnson spoke menacingly about crimes of treason, but by September, his viewpoint had changed to one of forgiveness. The president never forgot that he was a Southerner. He had no more love for the Radical Yankees than did other Southerners. His experiences during the summer and fall of 1865 convinced him that Southern whites, including ex-Confederates, were his real friends. They praised his policy and flattered his ego, while Radical Republicans criticized him openly and spoke ill of him in private.

The White House was thronged day after day with requests for pardon. Johnson felt a deep sense of gratification when members of the haughty Southern ruling class, whom he had once vowed to show "who is running the country," humbly confessed that they had been wrong when they seceded from the Union. Johnson said, "I remember the taunts, the jeers, the scowls with which I was treated." He was happy, he said, "to have lived to see the realization of my predictions and the fatal error of those whom I vainly essayed to save from the results of secession."

As the postassassination furor subsided, Johnson's mood toward the defeated South softened. He gave no more speeches classifying treason as an odious crime. The joyous Northern celebration of victory and the grim reports of the destitute in the South convinced Johnson that a more lenient policy should be adopted. He was not alone in his opinion. "We want true union and concord in the quickest possible time," declared the influential *Springfield Republican* in June 1865.

It didn't take the Radicals long to discover they had misjudged Johnson's view on Reconstruction. Johnson meant to continue Lincoln's magnanimous policy. Reconstruction of the South, he felt, should be based on faith in its people; if reasonable terms were offered to Southerners, Johnson reasoned, they would carry them out.

Johnson's dealings with Congress were dismal. Reconstructing the South after the Civil War was the main issue during his administration. Clearly, Lincoln's earlier plan did not involve social and political change beyond the abolition of slavery. Lincoln assumed that many Southern whites, especially former members of the Whig party—to which he himself had belonged before the slavery issue destroyed it in the 1850s and which had included reluctant secessionists—would be eager to step forward to accept his lenient terms. In 1864, Lincoln attempted to implement his reconstruction plan. Radicals became convinced that his Ten-Percent Plan was too lenient to rebels and did little to protect African Americans' rights. Although Lincoln and the Radicals differed over Reconstruction, they were able to work together to pass the Thirteenth Amendment. This amendment irrevocably abolished slavery throughout the nation, including those border states where the Emancipation Proclamation had not applied.

Congress also passed, and Lincoln signed, a bill creating the Freedmen's Bureau, an agency empowered to protect the legal rights of former slaves and to provide them with education and medical care. Although Lincoln's plans for Reconstruction were lenient to whites, he did not abandon concern for the rights of blacks. In his last speech, just a few days before his assassination, the president endorsed the idea of limited black suffrage for the reconstructed South. He singled out former blacks who had served in the military and those with some education as being most deserving of the right to vote. This was the first time any American president had called for granting African Americans the right to vote. It illustrated the flexibility and capacity for growth that always had been the hallmark of Lincoln's leadership. These were qualities, unfortunately, his successor lacked.

Johnson was opposed to the Republican's vision of the freedmen's place in society. During the war, the federal government turned the war into a crusade to free the slaves. Johnson's comment when he heard this was: "Damn the Negroes! I am fighting these traitorous aristocrats, their masters." In 1866, a delegation of blacks headed by Frederick Douglass visited the White House to urge that suffrage be a condition of Reconstruction. Johnson listened to their arguments and afterward remarked to his secretary: "Those damned sons of bitches thought they had me in a trap! I know that damned Douglass; he's just like any nigger, and he would sooner cut a white man's throat than not."

Although Johnson initially seemed to agree with Radicals on the need to punish rebels, his fundamental convictions clashed with their ideology in other important aspects. A Jacksonian Democrat to the core, Johnson was suspicious of banks, corporations, bondholders, and New England. He opposed the Whig-Republican policy of using government to promote economic development. He disliked both the plantation aristocracy and the corrupt leaders of the commercial industrial economy emerging in the Northeast.

Radical Republicans criticized Johnson's plan of Reconstruction for ignoring the rights of former slaves. But most Northerners believed the policy deserved a chance to succeed. In May 1865, Johnson announced his plan. It included pardoning all Southern whites except the main leaders and wealthy supporters of the Confederacy. The defeated states were to form new governments, abolish slavery, and take a loyalty oath to the nation before being admitted to the Union. Under this plan, the states would determine the role of blacks.

Johnson's plan quickly ran into trouble. The new state governments passed black codes, packages of laws designed to keep control over blacks. In addition, many of the newly elected representatives and senators from the Southern states, who appeared when Congress reconvened, had been Confederate officials or sympathizers. When Congress assembled in December, Johnson announced that with the loyal governments functioning in all Southern states, Reconstruction was over. Radical Republicans became more estranged from Johnson and called for the repeal of these governments. They insisted on the establishment of new ones, with former Confederates excluded from power and black men granted the right to vote. Moderates joined with the Radicals and refused to seat the Southerners newly elected to Congress. They appointed a joint committee to investigate the progress of Reconstruction.

Early in 1866, both houses of Congress passed two laws. The first extended the life of the Freedmen's Bureau. The second was a Civil Rights Bill, which guaranteed the principle of equality before the law regardless of race. To the surprise of Congress, Johnson vetoed both bills. These bills, he said, threatened to centralize power in the federal government and deprived the states of their authority to regulate their own affairs. Johnson was firm on his position and offered no opportunity for compromise with Congress. His vetoes made a complete breach between Congress and the president inevitable.

Enraged, the Radical press called the president an "insolent, drunken brute" and circulated rumors that he had been involved in Lincoln's assassination, that he maintained a harem of harlots, and that he was scheming with Southern Rebels to usurp Northern power. Thaddeus Stevens said that he was an "alien enemy, a citizen of a foreign state . . . and therefore not now legally President."

In April 1866, the Civil Rights Bill became the first major law in American history to be passed over a presidential veto. In June, Congress approved the

Fourteenth Amendment, which broadened the federal government's power to protect the rights of all Americans. The congressional policy of guaranteeing civil rights for blacks became the central issue of the political campaign of 1866. Congress demanded that in order to regain their seats in the House and Senate, the Southern states must ratify the amendments. Johnson denounced the proposal and embarked on a speaking tour of the North to urge voters to elect congressmen who would support his Reconstruction plan. The tour was a failure because the hot-tempered Johnson sometimes exchanged insults with angry crowds. The president made wild accusations that the Radicals were plotting to assassinate him. His behavior further undermined public support for his policies.

In the fall, Republicans opposed to Johnson's policies won a sweeping victory. Congress now moved to implement its own plan of Reconstruction. In March 1867, over Johnson's veto, Congress adopted the Reconstruction Act, which divided the South into five military districts. Only after the new governments ratified the Fourteenth Amendment would the Southern states be readmitted to the Union. This began the period in American history referred to as Congressional or Radical Reconstruction, which lasted until the fall of the Republican party in 1877.

The conflict between President Johnson and Congress did not end with the passage of the Reconstruction acts. In 1867, Congress adopted the Tenure of Office Act, which prevented the president from removing certain officeholders, including cabinet members, without approval of the Senate. Both acts of Congress were an attempt to restrict Johnson's executive powers and to find an excuse to impeach him if he did not abide by the laws. It was Johnson himself who gave the Radicals the opportunity to impeach him. On August 5, convinced that Secretary of War Stanton's pro-Radical views presented too much conflict, Johnson asked for his resignation. When Stanton refused to resign, Johnson suspended him, appointing in his place General Grant.

A bill to impeach President Johnson failed in December of 1867. The year 1868 was an election year, and General Grant began to look like a presidential candidate. In January, when the Senate insisted that Stanton be reinstated, Grant quickly withdrew. Grant's withdrawal angered Johnson, but he would not back down. Tenure of Office Act or not, Johnson believed he had a constitutional right to remove Stanton. He appointed Major General Lorenzo Thomas to replace Stanton. Stanton refused to leave and swore out a warrant for Thomas's arrest, charging him with seizing his office. President Johnson hoped that the Supreme Court would back him up. "Very well, that is the place I want it," Johnson said, "in the courts." But the Supreme Court chose not to hear the case. Instead, on February 24, the House of Representatives voted 126 to 47 to impeach the president. "Resolved: that Andrew Johnson be impeached of high crimes and misdemeanors." So began the impeachment resolution passed by the House of Representatives. Andrew Johnson became the first and, at that time, the only president to be impeached.

Under the Constitution of the United States the sole power of impeachment belongs to the House of Representatives, which functions as a grand jury. The Senate has the responsibility for conducting the trial once the House has indicted. Conviction requires a two-thirds majority vote of the Senators. On March 5, Chief Justice Salmon Chase took his seat on the Senate rostrum. Nine charges were placed against the president. The first eight articles of impeachment charged Johnson with "intent and conspiracy" to violate the Constitution and the Tenure of Office Act. The ninth article dealt with the violation of the Army Appropriation Act. Later, two more articles were added. If convicted by a Senate vote, Johnson would be removed from office. Because Johnson had no vice president, the acting president, or president pro tempore of the Senate, Radical Republican Benjamin Wade, would become president.

The trial began on March 13, 1868. Johnson stayed away from the Senate, leaving his defense in the hands of his lawyers. So many people wanted to attend the impeachment hearings that the Senate had to print up tickets. The lucky few who managed to get into the Senate gallery witnessed a heated legal duel. For more than two months, the president's lawyers argued with the prosecution, which was led by two Radicals from the House, Benjamin Butler and Thaddeus Stevens.

On May 16, the Senate voted on one of the more serious charges. To convict Johnson would require 36 votes, a two-thirds majority of the Senate. Before the vote, seven Republican senators who had initially favored conviction changed their minds. When Senator Edmund Ross of Kansas voted "not guilty," the chance for conviction on any of the other charges collapsed. Ten days later, Johnson was acquitted of two other articles of impeachment. Leaving the eight remaining articles forever in limbo, Justice Chase adjourned the Court sine die (without fixing a date for a future meeting). Johnson received word of his victory with tears of joy. When Eliza, who had stood by her husband during the ordeal, heard the news, she quietly told William Crook, the president's bodyguard, "I knew he would be acquitted. I knew it."

By one vote, Andrew Johnson escaped becoming the only president to be removed from office by means of impeachment. The vote saved the power and prestige of the presidency. Conceding defeat, Stanton resigned to resume the practice of law in Washington. In failing health by the time the president came to trial, Thaddeus Stevens, Johnson's nemesis, died shortly after the acquittal. The Pennsylvania legislator, crushed by the court's failure to convict Johnson on impeachment charges, slumped into a mental and physical decline. Unable to accept the defeat, he had muttered to his friends that if Johnson could not be removed by law, there was "Brutus's dagger." By provisions of his will, Stevens was buried in an African American cemetery in Lancaster.

Johnson had hoped to receive the Democratic nomination for president in 1868, but he didn't. Instead, Governor Horatio Seymour of New York was selected. Grant's role in the Stanton controversy led the Republicans to see him as an ally. In May, he won the party's nomination for the presidency, with Speaker of the House Schuyler Colfax as his running mate. Grant accepted the nomination and went on to victory in the election. Grant's personal popularity contributed to his victory, as did the fact that many Democrats had been less than enthusiastic supporters of the Union during the war.

On Christmas day, Johnson proclaimed a complete pardon for all Southerners who had taken part in the Civil War. It was his last official act. Johnson's proclamation showed his desire to end the sectional bitterness that had divided the nation during the Civil War. Johnson, however, did not forgive Grant for having sold out to the Radical Republicans.

With Grant safely elected, Johnson appeared before Congress to give his last annual message. His warning was prophetic: "The attempt to place the white population under the domination of persons of color in the South . . . has prevented the cooperation between the two races so essential to the success of the industrial enterprise." Already the Ku Klux Klan were riding, and the seeds of lasting hatred had been sown.

Johnson was still so bitter about the way Grant had treated him that he was unwilling to participate in Grant's inauguration. "Grant," as Secretary Gideon Wells put it, "we knew to be untruthful, faithless and false, a dissembler and deliberate deceiver." Johnson also prevented his cabinet members from attending the inauguration as well. "The truth is," wrote Wells, "Grant is elected by illegal votes and fraudulent and unconstitutional practices." It was too much to witness the triumph of "this ignorant, vulgar man."

When Secretary Wells said good-bye to the Johnson family, he recorded his thoughts in his diary: "No better persons have occupied the Executive Mansion and I part with them . . . with sincere regret. Of the President . . . he was faithful to the Constitution."

Johnson managed to fire one last parting shot before he left Washington. In a farewell address to the American people, he once more sought to justify himself. He continued to take pride in his accomplishments as president. Among those, he reminded the people, were disbanding an army of nearly a million men and preserving the peace. He declared that his sole ambition had been "to restore the Union of the State, faithfully to execute the office of President and, to the best of my ability, preserve, protect, and defend the Constitution." After once more attacking the Reconstruction of Congress, Johnson concluded with, "Forgetting the past, let us return to the principles of the government, and, unfurling the banner of our country, inscribe upon it, in ineffaceable characters, 'The Constitution of the Union, one and inseparable.'"

Johnson was now out of office for the first time since 1839, but his retirement from the presidency did not mean that he would withdraw from politics as well. His first opportunity to test the water came on a trip to Lynchburg, Virginia. There he received a grand welcome. Responding to their enthusiasm, he expressed his gratification at the evident popular approval of his actions. In Charlottesville, Virginia, he again was met by a friendly crowd. There, he admonished the young people to study and stand by the Constitution, stressing his devotion to the basic law of the land.

When he reached Tennessee, his reception was even warmer. In Greeneville, on the same spot where eight years earlier banners had been displayed reading "Traitor, Traitor" and he had been hanged in effigy was a large flag with the inscription "Welcome Home." After a welcoming speech by Thomas A. R. Nelson, a longtime supporter, Johnson responded. He said he was glad to be home and asserted that he had no further ambitions for public office. Judging from his later actions, this was probably just a case of polite modesty.

Despite the battles while he was president and his statement at Greeneville, Johnson never lost his appetite for politics. He was much too ambitious and restless, to say nothing of his desire to be vindicated for his policies and his administration. He didn't have to wait long to attempt his comeback.

In 1869, the circumstances for him to reenter politics seemed favorable, a chance, as he saw it, to redeem himself. He campaigned vigorously for a seat in the House of Representatives, attacking Jefferson Davis to please conservative Republicans and Grant to win the moderate Democrats. In a close balloting, Johnson lost. It was his first defeat since 1837. He ran unsuccessfully again in 1872; but in 1874, when the controversies of Reconstruction were beginning to cool, Johnson won a Senate seat.

When Johnson moved back to Washington in 1875 to serve in the Senate, he moved into a hotel. A friend observed that Johnson's new lodgings weren't as grand as the White House. "No," the former president replied, "but they were more comfortable." In March, Johnson attended a special session of Congress. He was nervous when he entered the chamber. From the galleries came a great burst of applause, and he found his desk covered with flowers. When the senators, even those who had judged him guilty, came to him to shake his hand, he shook hands with all of them.

When Andrew Johnson came home in the spring of 1875, he had every reason to take a vacation and relax. He had achieved his goal of making a remarkable comeback. He needed time out because of his failing health. But Johnson's time for rest and relaxation was short. While visiting his daughter's home in Tennessee, Johnson suffered a stroke. On July 31, he died. A steady stream of visitors paid their last respects. He was laid to rest on a hilltop outside Greeneville.

News of the former president's passing took the country by surprise. President Grant issued a proclamation announcing the death of the "last survivor of his honored predecessors." The White House and government departments were draped in black. In commemorating the fallen leader, the newspapers reflected their owners' prejudices. Northern papers tended to stress Johnson's loyalty during the war; Southern journals emphasized his service to the South after the war. Even Republican papers praised him for his inflexible honesty. The *London Times* commented that his career, with his rise from poverty and ignorance, illustrated both the strengths and weaknesses of the American system. All agreed that Johnson's course had been extraordinary.

With Johnson's passing, the question was, How would he be remembered? Johnson was from Tennessee, a slaveholding state, and from a social class held in contempt by the planter aristocracy. His association with plantation owners left him with feelings of resentment and hostility toward them and any other economically powerful group. There was no indication that Johnson had sympathy for the conditions of black people, but he was opposed to slavery. Some have even labeled him a racist. Because the Union was of great importance to him, it is not surprising that he felt the preservation of the Constitution was his most solemn obligation. To Johnson, this meant protecting states' rights, which in turn meant restoring the Confederate states to the Union with all their rights as states intact. He believed that the Radical Republicans were set on destroying the Constitution and that it was his patriotic duty to fight to preserve it.

Johnson's behavior was more complicated. Even his friend Gideon Wells, generally not critical of him, took note of his secretiveness and indecision. Johnson was always willing to listen patiently to his cabinet members but often made the most critical decisions without consulting anyone. There was clearly a touch of madness in Johnson's actions, a reckless spirit that drove him to excesses and hasty words and actions. He lacked tact and was deliberately abrasive and forthright. He believed his adversaries were wicked men bent on destroying him, and so he missed no opportunity to strike out viciously at them.

It was only fitting that Andrew Johnson's last request for his burial should be honored: "Pillow my head with the Constitution of my country." He was wrapped in a large American flag, with his head upon his copy of the Constitution.

8   Lee's Scapegoat Lieutenant

JAMES LONGSTREET

CONFEDERATE Lieutenant General James Longstreet, commander of the I Corps of the Army of Northern Virginia, rode onto the Gettysburg battlefield on the afternoon of July 1, 1863. As he arrived, infantry units were advancing through the streets of Gettysburg. The Confederates had gained a decisive victory, with the possibility of greater gains before nightfall. Dismounting, Longstreet approached General Lee. For several minutes, he observed the ground east and south of the town, where the Union troops were rallying. Their position appeared to be strong. Utilizing his experience, his brief survey of the field, and his tactical preference, Longstreet concluded that assaults on the enemy position should be avoided. He lowered his field glasses and turned toward Lee—thus, the greatest controversy of Gettysburg and perhaps of the Civil War had begun.

Few figures from the American Civil War have generated more controversy than James Longstreet. Once referred to by Robert E. Lee as "my old war-horse," he stood arraigned, in his own words, "before the world as the person and the only one responsible for the loss of the cause." He had fought many battles on the battlefield, but never had he encountered a more formidable enemy than his own people. For more than a century, he has been the South's most controversial soldier. History would be a tenacious foe, its long shadow extending across time and distance. Many people blamed General James Longstreet for the Confederate loss at Gettysburg and the loss of the war that followed. Cast as a scapegoat, Longstreet would spend the rest of his life defending his record.

James Longstreet was of Dutch lineage, born in his paternal grandparents' home in Edgefield District, South Carolina, on January 8, 1821. He was the third child of James and Mary Ann Dent Longstreet. The Longstreets owned a cotton plantation in the Piedmont section of northeastern Georgia. Both of his parents belonged to families whose ancestry in America dated from colonial times. Mary Ann Dent counted among her kinfolk Supreme Court Chief Justice John Marshall.

Young James, called Pete by his family, spoke often of a military career. He dreamed of glory on the battlefield and read books about Alexander the Great, Caesar, Napoleon, and George Washington. When he was nine years old, his father took him to live with his uncle in Augusta, Georgia, so he could attend the state's finest preparatory school, the Richmond County Academy. He would spend half his childhood with his Aunt Frances and Uncle Augustus.

Augustus was a talented, well-educated man with a good sense of humor. He had served in the state legislature and in 1821 was appointed as judge on the Supreme Court of Georgia. Young James would spend the next eight years on his uncle's plantation. Augustus's family, which included his two daughters, would welcome Pete as a member of the family. Much of the personality and character that young James was to acquire came from his aunt and uncle.

On October 7, 1830, young James entered the Richmond County Academy. The academy had a good reputation for its curriculum and strict discipline code. At the academy, students studied mathematics, grammar, composition, Latin, Greek, and oratory. Breach of conduct brought stern punishment. Young James was not fond of school. Like many other boys of his age, he preferred the outdoors and physical activities to those that required his intellect. He never seemed to adapt to his studies, as his grades reflected. By the time he left for West Point in 1838, he had reached his adult height of six feet two inches on a powerful frame.

In 1833 James suffered a personal tragedy when his father died during a cholera epidemic. Pete continued to live with his aunt and uncle, and in 1837

Augustus was able to secure an appointment for him to West Point. In June 1838, he left for the academy, traveling to New York and the career he had sought since he was a young boy.

The academic demands at West Point challenged Longstreet from the very beginning, and he struggled in the classroom the entire four years. In his memoirs, he admitted that he "had more interest in the school of the soldier, horsemanship, sword exercise, and the game of football than in academic courses." In most subjects, he ranked near the bottom of the class; only in the courses devoted to military science did he do better. Longstreet's highest ranking was in the course on infantry tactics; he stood next to last in ethics. By any measure, Longstreet was a poor student. His disciplinary record was little better than his academic record. When he graduated in 1842, he ranked fifty-fourth in a class of fifty-six.

Longstreet was popular with his fellow students. His leadership in pranks, his sense of humor, and his open disregard for academy rules made him a favorite companion with his classmates. The friendships he made at West Point endured for a long time. Among his friends, whom he would serve with and against during the Civil War, were George Thomas, William Rosecrans, John Pope, Harvey Hill, and Lafayette McLaws. Among the class of 1843, Longstreet found his best friend—Ulysses S. Grant. Grant, also a reluctant cadet, admitted in his memoirs that a "military life had no charms for me" and that he did not expect to remain in the army after graduating from the academy. Longstreet described Grant as "of noble, generous heart, a lovable character, a valued friend." Although the two would fight on opposite sides during the Civil War, their friendship never wavered.

Longstreet's first assignment was one of the best posts in the army—Jefferson Barracks outside St. Louis. He commented, "I was fortunate in the assignment to Jefferson Barracks, for in those days the young officers were usually sent off among the Indians, or as near the borders as they could find habitable places." At Jefferson Barracks, Lieutenant Longstreet met Louise Garland, the daughter of his post commander, Colonel John Garland. Louise was slender, petite, and quite attractive, with high cheekbones and black hair. It did not take long for them to fall in love. They were married on March 8, 1848, and would have ten children, but only five survived childhood. Two died in infancy and three during a scarlet fever epidemic that raged through Richmond in 1862. But Longstreet had little time to grieve for his lost children or to worry over the prolonged illness of his eldest son, for Union troops had begun moving en masse to the Virginia Peninsula near the beginning of the war.

For two years, he endured the monotony of drilling, training, and inspecting that were common to peacetime army life. Longstreet left Jefferson Barracks in fall of 1844. Following tours of duty in Louisiana and Florida, he joined the

8th Infantry in Texas. During this time, a border dispute sparked the Mexican War.

On April 23, 1846, Mexico declared war on the United States. Longstreet fought at Palo Alto, Resaca de la Palma, and Monterrey under General Zachary Taylor before his regiment joined General Winfield Scott's army in the campaign against Mexico City. He distinguished himself at the Battle of Cherubusco and again at Chapultepec. When the 8th Infantry stormed Chapultepec, Longstreet carried the flag. As they went over the fortress wall, he was wounded, shot in the leg and knocked down. He handed the flag to George Pickett, who then carried it across the wall. Pickett would later command a division in Longstreet's Corps. On September 14, 1847, the Americans entered Mexico City, ending the war.

Longstreet's wound was painful and slow to heal. By early December, he was fit enough to return to duty. Unknown to Longstreet and his fellow officers, the Mexican War would serve as a training ground for the Civil War. Longstreet had learned a great deal about war: the difficulties of supply and transportation over rough terrain; the rising power of artillery and the declining effectiveness of smooth-bore muskets; the costliness of a frontal assault and the effectiveness of maneuvering a numerically smaller army. But more important for Longstreet, his physical stamina and skill and bravery under fire on the battlefield had been tested.

After returning to the States, Longstreet married Louise Garland. In May 1849, with his wife and newborn son, he traveled to San Antonio, Texas, to resume duties as an adjutant of the 8th Infantry. For the next twelve years, he would serve at various posts throughout the country, and his family would continue to increase. In 1858, Longstreet was appointed as paymaster and promoted to major.

After Republican Abraham Lincoln was elected president in November of 1860, South Carolina seceded from the Union in December. Six other Southern states soon followed. In February 1861, delegates from the seceded states met in Montgomery, Alabama, and formed the Confederate States of America. Years later James Longstreet remembered the fall and winter of 1860–1861 as a time of "painful suspense."

For Longstreet, the choice came early. When he learned that Lincoln had been elected president, he decided his allegiance belonged to the South. Although he did not embrace secession, in his mind he had little choice. He was a Southerner; his family were Southerners. It was, as he said later, a difficult choice, one shared by many Southerners in the army. But he didn't hesitate; in fact he acted with surprising haste.

In January, Longstreet offered his services to the Confederacy. On May 9, Longstreet submitted his letter of resignation: "I have the honor to tender my resignation as a Major of Paymaster in the Army of the United States." He accepted a lieutenant colonelcy in the Confederate army before his resignation from the U.S. Army. For nine days, he actually held commissions in both armies.

The first time Longstreet had worn gray was as a West Point cadet. Now he wore it in defense of his homeland. After serving the Union for twenty years, he rode off to fight for the South. Recalling the day that he left, he wrote: "It was a sad day when we took leave of lifetime comrades and gave up a service of twenty years. Neither Union officers nor their families made efforts to conceal feelings of deepest regret. When we drove out from the post, a number of officers rode with us, which only made the last farewell more trying. At every station old men, women and children assembled, clapping hands and waving handkerchiefs to cheer the passengers on to Richmond . . . laborers in the fields, white and black, stopped their plows to lift their hats and wave us on to a speedy travel."

When Longstreet reached Richmond he met with Jefferson Davis, who appointed him brigadier general in command of a brigade of Virginia troops stationed at Manassas Junction in northern Virginia. In July, he led his brigade in an engagement at Blackburn's Ford on Bull Run. When his troops started to fall back, Longstreet, amid fire from his own troops, rode among them, cigar in mouth, rallying and inspiring them to hold the line. A general who stood his ground and led his men from the front gave them the kind of confidence needed to put their fears aside and stand and fight. Moxley Sorrel, an aide-de-camp to Longstreet, elaborated on the general's demeanor under fire, stating: "[He] was then a most striking figure. About forty years of age, a soldier every inch, and very handsome, tall, and well proportioned. Strong and active, a superb horseman and with unsurpassed soldierly bearing." There were two important standards for an officer in the Civil War. The first focused on the care of his men at camp and in battle. The second was personal courage; officers had to demonstrate courage or they could not lead. General Longstreet excelled at both.

Longstreet was a prudent man, methodical and cautious by habit, blunt-spoken and stubborn in manner. Although he had a disregard for social graces, his personality was not unattractive. He was very strong, with a powerful chest and shoulders. Fearless and robust, Longstreet exuded a quality of reassurance. He possessed a hearty sense of humor and enjoyed exchanging stories with other men; when amused, he laughed loudly. Men of his type were strongly attracted to him, and he easily formed enduring friendships. One of his oldest friends was General Grant, whom he had known since his West Point days and who was married to his cousin.

On October 7, 1861, Longstreet was promoted to major general and given command of a division. While the army was in winter encampment, he spent time with his old army friends, playing cards, drinking, and reminiscing about their days on the frontier and in Mexico.

In March of 1862, the Confederate army under General Joseph E. Johnston abandoned its winter quarters and retreated south. A month later the Union Army of the Potomac, under the command of Major General George McClellan, began a movement up the peninsula between the York and James Rivers, just east of Richmond. On May 31, the first major battle of the spring campaign occurred at Seven Pines. Johnston assigned the main Confederate attack to Longstreet, who bungled the assault. Although he had spent the previous afternoon with Johnston mapping out the plan for an early morning attack, Longstreet misunderstood his orders. He led his division down the wrong road. As a result, the attack had to proceed without his division. In his report, he never offered an explanation for his error; instead, he blamed others, writing as if he had done nothing wrong.

As the battle progressed, both Johnston and Longstreet performed poorly. Johnston was unable to exercise control over events, and Longstreet, who actually conducted the battle, did it badly. His orders to subordinates had been unclear, causing confusion and not allowing the full force of his troops to be engaged at the same time. He further weakened the assault by dividing his six brigades. Longstreet had demonstrated that he was as unskillful at offensive tactics as he was skillful at defensive ones. Indeed, he had illustrated the essentially defensive character of his military talent.

Later in the day, Johnston was badly wounded, and on June 1, President Davis assigned General Robert E. Lee to command what became known as the Army of Northern Virginia. Longstreet took heart when the command of the army was given to Lee. Thereafter, Lee and Longstreet would be forever linked in history.

Longstreet won praise for his conduct during the Seven Days' campaign. The difference between his quick movements and Stonewall Jackson's sluggish ones did not go unnoticed. Within the army, his good reputation continued to grow, and his troops regarded him as a hard fighter.

Following the successful Seven Days' battles, Longstreet emerged as Lee's most reliable subordinate commander. Lee expressed his feelings about his new lieutenant in writing to Jefferson Davis: "Longstreet is a capital soldier and . . . I have confidence in him."

Lee and Longstreet became close friends. They pitched their headquarters tents near each other. They saw each other every day in the course of duty and were frequently guests at each other's camp for dinner and for conversation and companionship. Contrary to popular belief, Lee never developed a close friendship with Jackson anything like the one he had with Longstreet. Lee was able to relax more with Longstreet than with Jackson. Outwardly it seemed that Lee would have more in common with Jackson than with Longstreet because of their religious faith and sobriety. But Lee preferred the company of Longstreet because of his fun-loving, gregarious nature. Lee enjoyed the warm, relaxed atmosphere of Longstreet's camp, a place of laughter, jokes, and good spirits.

The first full year of the war, 1862, was a good year for Longstreet as a soldier. He followed up his strong performance at the Seven Days' battles with another excellent showing at Second Manassas. It was there that the Union Commander, General John Pope, walked into a trap and Longstreet's counterattack was decisive in the Confederate victory. The campaign and battle had been fashioned by Lee and was a strategic masterpiece. By a well-timed, well-executed turning movement, Lee had nearly crushed Pope's army before it and McClellan's troops could combine. Longstreet described the campaign as "clever and brilliant," giving the entire credit to Lee. Longstreet regarded it as an ideal blend of the strategic offense and the tactical defense. As the Army of Northern Virginia turned northward, James Longstreet remembered the plan that had worked so well at Second Manassas.

Shortly after Second Manassas, Lee decided to invade Maryland. He believed that a bold raid in the North would force a Federal withdrawal from Virginia and would hopefully encourage the secessionist movement in Maryland. He also hoped that a victory in the North would compel the European nations to recognize the Confederate states. Both Longstreet and Jackson supported Lee's plan to strike north but were opposed to dividing the army in order to capture the federal garrison at Harpers Ferry. Longstreet thought the plan to seize Harpers Ferry "a venture not worth the game," while Jackson urged that the army "should all be kept together."

Lee split the army despite the differences of opinion, with Jackson moving to Harpers Ferry while Longstreet remained near Sharpsburg, Maryland, seventeen miles north of Jackson's position. Lee had counted on moving swiftly to confuse his opponent, but Major General McClellan received a copy of Lee's plans, accidentally lost by a staff officer. Fortunately for Lee, McClellan was slow in reacting and was not able to take full advantage of Lee while his troops were so widely dispersed. After capturing Harpers Ferry, Jackson was able to reach Sharpsburg with most of his troops in time to take part in the action. Lee's army of 40,000 men repulsed a series of uncoordinated Federal attacks. Had McClellan made a strong effort to engage all of the troops available to him, he probably would have been able to crush Lee's smaller army.

The fighting at Antietam showed Longstreet at his best. The battle proved to be one crisis after another, with the thin Confederate line threatening to give way at a dozen different points. Confident and unperturbed, Longstreet committed his scant reserves. When they were depleted, he used his own presence at the front to bolster his weakening line in a display of courage that

Moxley Sorrel termed "magnificent." His efforts undoubtedly stimulated his men to greater action. A Virginia captain claimed that "Longstreet was one of the bravest men I ever saw on the field of battle."

Despite the vigorous efforts of Lee, Longstreet, and Jackson, the battle would have been lost had not A. P. Hill arrived late in the day with 2,000 troops that had been delayed at Harpers Ferry. Longstreet and Jackson had been correct in questioning the splitting of the army; Lee was fortunate to have survived the day. Antietam was scorched into the American conscience as the bloodiest day in American history. The casualties exceeded 24,000: 11,500 Confederates, 12,800 Federals. Over 3,700 soldiers lost their lives in combat that day.

Lee's stand at Antietam had jeopardized his army, but he had been confident that he could beat McClellan. Although McClellan eventually considered Antietam the highlight of his career, he missed the opportunity to destroy the Army of Northern Virginia. His attack had been piecemeal, and he had acted more like a spectator than the Army's commander. But Lee's retreat from Maryland had given Lincoln an opportunity to declare a major victory. Five days after the battle, on September 22, 1862, he issued the preliminary Emancipation Proclamation.

At Antietam, Longstreet showed his greatest strength as a tactical leader. His performance so impressed Lee that he bestowed the nickname "my old war-horse" on him. Lee rewarded both Longstreet and Jackson with promotions to lieutenant general and commands of recently authorized corps. Longstreet's promotion predated Jackson's by a day, making him the senior subordinate officer in the Army of Northern Virginia. Longstreet received the I Corps; Jackson, the II Corps.

As time moved on, Stonewall Jackson drew headlines and public adoration. Women begged for locks of his hair and buttons from his coat. But Lee chose Longstreet as his second in command. In the months that followed, Lee came to trust him more every day. Ironically, Longstreet at the same time began to doubt the wisdom of Lee's strategy and tactics.

By December 1862, James Longstreet had participated in five major campaigns. As a subordinate, he was not always free to choose a particular method of warfare; but if he had had a preference in a combat plan, it would be to allow the enemy to attack him at a position of his choosing and then counterattack. He felt the combination of defense and counterattack was the way the South should fight its battles, given their numerical inferiority.

On November 9, 1862, Major General Ambrose Burnside took command of the Union's Army of the Potomac. Burnside, who believed himself unfit for army command, moved swiftly to form an offensive plan. Within a few days, he decided to march to Fredericksburg, cross the Rappahannock on pontoons, and advance toward Richmond.

At Fredericksburg, Longstreet experienced his most satisfying moment as a commander. It was his kind of battle. He held a strong defensive position with artillery support. Longstreet took advantage of the topography to exploit a strong defensive position against superior numbers. Burnside's troops attacked on the cold misty morning of December 13, their major thrust coming against Longstreet's corps. Longstreet was confident that he could repulse the entire Federal attack from the strong position he held. The Union frontal attack was marked by courage and tenacity. By the end of the day, the ground in front of Longstreet's position was covered with dead and wounded Union troops. It was a perfect victory as far as he was concerned. That was how war should be waged: Pick your ground, let your enemy attack you, and then look for an opportunity to follow up your success. After the one-sided victory, Lee stated: "It is well that war is so terrible, lest we should grow too fond of it." Lee's casualties were light compared with Burnside's. Federal losses were more than twice those of the Confederates. J. E. B. Stuart, Lee's famous cavalry commander, wrote shortly afterward: "The victory won by us here is one of the neatest and cheapest of the war."

As the war progressed, Longstreet's ambition grew, and he experienced a rebirth of the "aspiration for military glory." With a growing delusion that his abilities were commensurate with his aspirations, he had convinced himself that he had a genius for high command. After the Battle of Fredericksburg, Longstreet tried in various ways to have himself detached from Lee's army. He felt the chance would never be given him to win the fame he deserved while he served under Lee—Stonewall Jackson stood in his way. Old Jack was getting all the publicity, and people were beginning to talk first of "Lee and Jackson" and then the rest of the army.

Early in 1863, Longstreet got his wish—his corps was deployed elsewhere, and he was not present for the Chancellorsville Campaign against General Joseph Hooker, the new Union commander. While separated, Longstreet corresponded with Lee, seeking his advice. After the war, Longstreet wrote that he and Lee often exchanged ideas. Lee, he said, welcomed his advice and often sought it.

Although Longstreet was not present at Chancellorsville in May, the battle was Lee's greatest victory—and a costly one. In addition to the 13,000 casualties the Army of Northern Virginia suffered, Lee lost his "right arm"—Stonewall Jackson. To replace him, Lee chose two men, creating a third corps and bringing more flexibility to his command structure. Richard Ewell and A. P. Hill were promoted to lieutenant general and assigned the II and III Corps, respectively.

Longstreet believed the fate of the Confederacy lay west of the Appalachians, and demanded immediate attention. He felt that reinforcements should be sent to the western front, but Lee opposed any concentration of forces that would weaken the Army of Northern Virginia. Instead, Lee favored an advance into Pennsylvania. In Pennsylvania, Lee could supply his troops at his enemy's expense. The move, he believed, would draw the Federals out of Virginia and perhaps North Carolina as well. Lee was able to win Longstreet's support of the plan, forcing him to temporarily forget about his interest in the West.

When Jackson died, Longstreet believed he would immediately fill his shoes. He had, however, incorrectly concluded that Jackson and Lee had been equal collaborators. Lee had welcomed suggestions from Jackson, but these were tactical in nature and made within the context of strategy developed by Lee himself. Jackson and Lee had shared a special intuitive understanding of each of their roles and both were comfortable with them. In contrast, Longstreet's short-term defensive thinking was antithetical to Lee's concept of war and he was, by demonstration, a limited soldier. In making his leap to corps commander, no small achievement, Longstreet had reached his fullest potential.

The campaign that followed was the most controversial of the war. Longstreet convinced himself that Lee had actually promised to fight, as he had suggested. In fact, Old Pete later contended that he had "consented" to the invasion only because Lee had promised to fight on the defensive. The use of the word *consented* by a corps commander shows the depth of Longstreet's delusion about the equality of collaboration. The campaign was marked with courage and valor breathtaking in today's context. It also stretched the friendship between Longstreet and Lee and brought into sharp focus the difference between their methods of generalship.

Unfortunately for Lee and the Confederate army, they stumbled into an unwanted battle at Gettysburg on the morning of July 1. Lee's cavalry commander, J. E. B. Stuart, had been given instructions to protect the army's flanks and to bring word if the Union army left Virginia. Exercising the discretion granted in his orders, Stuart had lost contact with Lee's army, passing completely around the Army of the Potomac. Because he hadn't heard from Stuart, Lee was denied crucial intelligence on the size and location of the Union army. In effect, Lee was going into battle without his "eyes"; thus he did not want a major engagement with the enemy until Stuart returned. Lee had given orders to avoid "a general engagement," but to no avail. Longstreet and Lee examined the ground south and east of Gettysburg and saw that the terrain favored the Federals, who were regrouping there. Longstreet suggested moving around the Federal's left flank and placing the Confederates between the Union army and Washington, D.C. With Lee's army so deep into Union territory, Longstreet reasoned that General Meade would have no choice but to attack a well-entrenched Confederate army.

When Longstreet reached Gettysburg, he believed he had already established his concept of Jacksonian collaboration with Lee. He had even deluded himself with the belief that he had imposed his idea of what strategy would be employed on the commanding general. He was deeply shocked and confused when Lee dismissed his suggestions during the first afternoon at Gettysburg. But he was stubborn. That night, while his troops were resting, Longstreet was making no plans for the early morning movement that Lee had requested. Rather, he was pondering ways of convincing Lee to follow his plan of action.

Lee was in no mood for a defensive campaign. His success on the first day had given him a taste of the prize he wanted, a great Confederate victory on Union soil. He reasoned, "The enemy is here, and if we do not whip him, he will whip us." Lee, believing he had the enemy on the run, became overconfident. He thought his men could do anything he asked. In every situation in the past, they had done just that. Lee also felt that his army could not sustain a prolonged entrenchment on enemy territory. He was convinced that a series of unexpected and well-timed attacks could crush the Army of the Potomac once and for all. On both July 2 and July 3, Longstreet reasserted his argument for a flanking movement. Each time, Lee rejected it. On the second day, Lee ordered coordinated assaults on both flanks of the Union army. Longstreet was to command the attack on the left flank. He stalled, playing for time, still trying to persuade Lee to do something other than what he had already ordered. When Longstreet didn't get his way, he sulked. As the time to attack drew near, General John Bell Hood, one of Longstreet's division commanders, requested permission several times to circle around and attack the Federals from the rear. Longstreet stubbornly denied these requests. If Lee wanted a frontal attack, that's what he would get. Longstreet could have used his prerogative as a corps commander to honor Hood's request, but he was going to do exactly as Lee had told him to prove him wrong. The attack was later than Lee had hoped, and the Federals had a chance to prepare for the assault. The attack failed, the troops coming within yards of capturing the strategically vital hill called Little Round Top.

The following day, Lee planned to attack the Union line with what has come to be known as "Pickett's Charge." Longstreet was strongly opposed to this attack. "I do not want to make this attack . . . I do not see how it can succeed," he told one of his subordinates. Longstreet told General Lee: "I have been a soldier all my life . . . there are no fifteen thousand men in the world that can go across that ground." Lee replied, "There is the enemy, and there I mean to attack him." Despondent, Longstreet recorded: "Never was I so depressed as upon that day. I thought that my men were to be sacrificed and that I should have to order them to make a hopeless charge."

Two hours before the attack, Confederate artillery opened up on the enemy position. During this bombardment, which drew a furious response from the Union guns on the opposite ridge, Longstreet showed himself at his most fearless. With the shells exploding all about him, he was observed by Brigadier General James Kemper of Pickett's Division: "Longstreet rode slowly and alone immediately in front of our entire line. . . . His bearing was to me the grandest moral spectacle of the war. I expected to see him fall every instant. Still he moved on, slowly and majestically, with an inspiring confidence, composure, self-possession, and repressed power in every movement and look, that fascinated me."

Just before the attack, Pickett came to Longstreet: "Shall I lead my division forward, sir?" "The effort to speak the order failed," Longstreet said, "and I could only indicate it by an affirmative bow." Pickett, confident of success, accepted the order, leaped on his horse, and rode to his command.

Pickett's three brigades spearheaded the charge across a mile of open field toward the center of the federal line on Cemetery Ridge. The Southerners were decimated by Union artillery and musket fire. Pickett tried valiantly to coordinate the ill-fated attack, but the task was impossible. Brigadier General Cadmus Marcellus Wilcox's brigade advanced in support of the attack, but there was little left to support. Seeing the futility of sacrificing more lives, Longstreet never gave the order for two other backup brigades to advance.

Following the withdrawal of what remained of Pickett's division, Lee accepted the failure of the attack. He ordered Pickett to reform his division. A dejected Pickett could only look up to his commander and reply, "Sir, I have no division left."

After Gettysburg and the end of the Confederacy two years later, Southerners fashioned their own interpretation of the battle; Gettysburg became the tantalizing what-if of the war. Lee became enshrined as the Southern hero, above blame, whereas for many Longstreet became the scapegoat, a former Confederate who joined the Republican party and accepted federal jobs. Politics and personal animosity fed the controversy, and Longstreet became known as the man who lost the war for the South. Gettysburg became the cornerstone of his critics' case. They believed that had he done his duty, had he not sulked and stalled, Lee would have achieved victory on July 2. Longstreet's conduct on that morning warranted criticism, but he was not the only one who failed at Gettysburg.

Colonel Edward Porter Alexander, who wrote extensively after the war, believed that Longstreet had been correct in his judgment at Gettysburg because "the Union position could never have been successfully assaulted." As for Longstreet's objections to Lee's attack plan, Alexander explained, "It is true that he obeyed reluctantly at Gettysburg, on the 2nd and on the 3rd, but it must be admitted that his judgment in both matters was sound and he owed it to Lee to be reluctant, for failure was inevitable, do it soon, or do it late, either day."

Seventy-five years after the war, at a reunion of veterans, a former officer in Pickett's division had his own opinion of Longstreet's performance at Gettysburg: "Longstreet opposed Pickett's charge, and the failure shows he was right. . . . We soldiers on the firing line knew there was no greater fighter in the whole Confederate army than Longstreet. I am proud that I fought under him here. I know that Longstreet did not fail Lee at Gettysburg or anywhere else. I'll defend him as long as I live."

In September, at his own request, Longstreet was sent with two divisions to report to General Braxton Bragg in Tennessee. His timely arrival and generalship assured a Confederate victory at Chickamauga, Georgia, on September 19 and 20. After the battle, the Confederates besieged Chattanooga, Tennessee. Longstreet became involved in a plot to have the unpopular Bragg removed from command. President Davis supported Bragg, but the effort failed. Longstreet was dispatched to Knoxville in an attempt to seize the city. He failed miserably, blaming others for an abortive attack, and prepared charges against subordinates. He even went so far as to tender his resignation from the army, but it was not accepted.

In April of 1864, Longstreet and his men rejoined Lee in Virginia. On May 6, during the second day of the Battle of the Wilderness, Longstreet was wounded by an accidental exchange of gunfire between two Confederate units. Longstreet reeled in his saddle, his right arm hanging limp at his side. He had been struck in the throat by a bullet that passed through his shoulder and severed nerves in his arm. Sorrel and two others lifted the general gently from the saddle and lay him against a tree. Bleeding profusely and nearly choking from his blood, Longstreet told Sorrel to report his wounding to Lee. Within minutes, Dr. Dorsey Cullen arrived to attend to him. Aides placed Longstreet on a stretcher and carried him to the rear. One of the officers covered his face with his hat. When the troops saw him, they feared he was dead. With his left hand, he lifted his hat, and "the burst of voices and the flying of hats in the air eased my pains somewhat." Longstreet had been wounded in a manner eerily reminiscent of Stonewall Jackson's mortal wound just a year earlier. When Lee heard that Longstreet had been wounded, a staff officer who was present said that Lee seemed almost overcome with emotion.

From the battlefield, Longstreet was taken to the home of a friend—Erasmus Taylor—at Meadow Farm, where his wounds were examined and treated. Eventually, he was moved to Augusta, Georgia, where he stayed with kinsfolk until he recovered. Longstreet lost the use of his right arm, and his once-clear voice became hoarse and raspy. By the time he returned to command, the war was winding down. Lee's army was close to collapse, but he would not surrender until the following spring at Appomattox.

Longstreet was with Lee to the very end. He made the trek from the defense of Petersburg and Richmond westward to Appomattox. When Lee left to meet with Grant, Longstreet said, "General, if he does not give us good terms, come back and let us fight it out." But the terms were generous and Lee surrendered.

At Appomattox, Longstreet was united with his old friend U. S. Grant. Grant offered his friend a cigar; their meeting was warm, with no bitterness, recriminations, nor judgments passed. They were still friends. Longstreet's feelings toward Grant had not changed during the four years of the war. In expressing his high opinion of his friend, Longstreet said that "General Grant was the truest as well as the bravest man who ever lived."

After the surrender, Lee bid farewell to the officers of the Army of Northern Virginia. T. J. Goree, one of Longstreet's officers, was standing next to him when Lee approached them. Lee warmly embraced Longstreet, then turned to Goree and, shaking his hand, said: "Captain, I am going to put my old War-horse under your charge. I want you to take good care of him."

Longstreet rode away from Appomattox with the idea of settling in Texas. He had been a soldier for more than a quarter of a century. He had been Lee's finest corps commander; some believed him better than Stonewall Jackson. Jackson had excelled at independent operations, while Longstreet was a better administrator and tactician. Longstreet's achievements as a Confederate general, however, were recast during the postwar years as he became the scapegoat for the Southern defeat.

Two months after parting with Lee at Appomattox, Longstreet traveled to Texas and then settled in New Orleans with his wife and family. He went into the cotton business in partnership with wartime friend William Miller Owen. Within two years, he was a successful businessman. He became president of the board of an insurance company and took an interest in large-scale railroad investments.

Longstreet made a speedy transition from military to civilian life, accepting defeat without bitterness. The tragic death of his three children, who died from scarlet fever during the war, seemed not to prey on his mind; if it did, his grief did not show. D. H. Hill, Longstreet's friend, described him in 1867 as "a genial, whole-souled fellow, full of fun and frolic." No one would have guessed that within two years Longstreet would soon become one of the South's most controversial figures.

In late October 1865, Longstreet went to Washington to meet with his good friend General in Chief Ulysses S. Grant and Secretary of War Edwin Stanton to secure a pardon from the government. Grant agreed to write a letter to President Johnson recommending a pardon for him. When Longstreet met with Johnson, the president refused, saying, "There are three persons of the South who can never receive amnesty: Mr. Davis, General Lee, and yourself. You have given the Union cause too much trouble." Like Lee, who applied earlier, Longstreet had neither amnesty nor political rights.

As a businessman and citizen, Longstreet watched the turmoil and controversy brought about by Reconstruction. The country was divided over the political rights of ex-Confederates and the civil and political status of freed blacks. In the election of 1866, the electorate repudiated the policy of Johnson, giving control of Congress to the Radical Republicans. In 1867, the Radicals passed Reconstruction acts that divided the former Confederate states into five military districts. The acts required each state to adopt a new constitution, allowing blacks to vote, and to ratify the Fourteenth Amendment, granting citizenship to black Americans.

Southerners reacted to these measures in various ways, but always in a heated manner. Longstreet urged "moderation, forbearance, and submission." He was quoted in a newspaper on March 18, 1867: "We are a conquered people. Southerners must recognize the fact 'fairly and squarely,' with but one course left for wise men to pursue, and that is to accept the terms that are now offered by the conquerors." Other former Rebel officers and politicians echoed his sentiments. Local Republican politicians flattered him with praise, hoping to lure him into the party. Longstreet concluded that the best solution for the South was to cooperate with the Republican party in order to use the Reconstruction acts to preserve the South and to control the black vote. "My politics is to save the little that is left of us, and to go to work to improve that little as best we can," he said.

On June 8, the *New Orleans Times* published a letter by Longstreet in which he openly gave his support and willingness to cooperate with the Black Republicans, as many Southerners referred to them. He had been warned against writing such a letter by his friends. John Bell Hood told him, "They will crucify you!" His uncle, Augustus Longstreet, also advised against it, saying, "It will ruin you, son, if you publish it." Undeterred by their warnings, Longstreet sent his letter to the *Times* anyway.

His words were carried across the country in many newspapers. The Northern papers generally praised the contents, while Southern papers vilified both him and his ideas. Southerners saw Longstreet's cooperation with the party that had freed the slaves and destroyed large portions of the South as traitorous. The criticism and death threats he received surprised him. He wrote to Lee seeking his endorsement, but his former commander refused to involve himself in public political disputes. Twenty-five years later, Longstreet still did not fully understand the problem he had caused for himself by his letter. In his memoirs, he dated the attacks on him from the publication of the letter.

Longstreet's political naivete cost him friends and business. He moved his family to the North to escape the furor. In June 1868, Congress restored political rights to a number of Confederates, including Longstreet. During the fall, Longstreet endorsed Grant's campaign for president. Six days after Grant was inaugurated as president, he nominated Longstreet for the position of surveyor of customs for the port of New Orleans. Newspapers accused Longstreet of putting self-interest over principle, calling him a scalawag, a Southerner who sold out the South for power and money doled out by Republicans. Even his old friend and fellow general Harvey Hill disapproved of Longstreet's actions: "Our scalawag is the local leper of the community. Unlike the carpetbagger [a Northerner], [Longstreet] is a native, which is so much the worst."

In 1871–1872, Longstreet became involved in another Republican political controversy. As a reward for his support, Longstreet was commissioned as a major general of the Louisiana state militia. Longstreet was also named president of the newly organized New Orleans and Northeastern Railroad. He now held three important positions with an estimated annual income in excess of $10,000. By the summer of 1872, Longstreet was regarded in Louisiana as a strong Radical Republican.

Longstreet's image continued to plummet as a result of the outbreak of violence in Louisiana. In September 1874, the Crescent City White League attempted to overthrow the governor's administration by force. As head of the militia, Longstreet led the state's largely black troops against the insurgents, many of whom were Confederate veterans. In the battle that followed, Longstreet was wounded and captured by his enemies. This experience must have been the most humiliating of his life. Order was finally restored when Federal troops intervened.

After Lee's death in 1870, former army officers began accusing Longstreet of failing Lee at Gettysburg. Longstreet responded in anger, criticizing Lee and losing even more support. Lee, he said in an 1893 interview, characteristically became "too pugnacious" when on the offensive and had "outgeneraled himself" at Gettysburg.

The first public criticism of Longstreet in 1872, by Jubal Early and Reverend William Pendleton, was a defense of Lee. Any attack on Lee at that time was considered unchivalrous, and it was resented even more when Longstreet did it. Longstreet had committed the cardinal sin of turning Republican. To criticize Lee now was asking to be ostracized and subjected to severe criticism himself. The high-ranking and highly placed former Confederate officers who attacked Longstreet in print concentrated on his failure at Gettysburg, quickly making him the villain of the battle. Longstreet fought back, declaring Lee had failed at Gettysburg because he had refused to listen to him. He even went so far as to imply that had Lee followed his advice, Longstreet himself would have been the hero of Gettysburg.

Much of Longstreet's time and energy during the 1870s were devoted to defending himself in a war of words. At the same time, Lee's devotees were in the process of enshrining his memory. Jubal Early, one of Lee's lieutenant generals, and Reverend John William Jones, a former brigadier general, corresponded widely with former Confederates. Thanks to their efforts, a distinct anti-Longstreet cult emerged which consisted of Jubal Early; Lee's former chief of artillery William Pendleton; William Jones; Lee's nephew Fitzhugh Lee; and Lee's former staff officers, Charles Venable, Walter Taylor, Armistead Long, and Charles Marshall. They were supported by Braxton Bragg, William Johnston, Cadmus Marcellus Wilcox, Wade Hampton, and eventually Jefferson Davis. It was their opinion that the blame for Gettysburg, and thus the loss of the war, rested on Longstreet and his corps alone. They sought to discredit everything Longstreet wrote in his defense as soon as it was published. Sometimes they even made statements that Lee's own battle report did not support. Marshall combed Lee's surviving papers for materials to use against Longstreet, but reported to Early that there was no evidence that Lee had blamed Longstreet for anything. In fact, Lee always spoke well of his old war-horse.

After the war, Longstreet's relationship with General Lee had been cordial. When he moved to New Orleans to begin his business career, he wrote to Lee often, much in the terms of one keeping in touch with a parent. To no other Confederate companion did Lee give more generous praise. Writing in 1866, Lee showed his feelings toward Longstreet: "If you become as good a merchant as you were a soldier I shall be content. No one will then excel you, and no one can wish you more success or more happiness than I. My interest and affection for you will never cease, and my prayers are always offered for your prosperity."

Longstreet had proved to be his own worst enemy, turning Lee's staff officers against him by the letters and article that he had sent to the press. They particularly resented the implication that he had been the brains behind Lee's defeat of McClellan.

In 1875, Longstreet's brother, William, urged him to move to Gainesville, Georgia, where he lived. Some residents objected to Longstreet's decision to make his home there, but that didn't stop him. While Louise and the children remained in Gainesville, Longstreet traveled extensively on business and political activities. No longer holding a politically connected job, in 1876 Longstreet approached newly elected Republican President Rutherford B. Hayes, hoping to receive an appointment to a government position. But not until 1878 did he receive one. Appointed deputy collector of internal revenue, his salary of six dollars a day was considerably less than he had made at most of his previous jobs. In 1879, he secured the position of postmaster of Gainesville, a job that gave him a modest steady income.

Longstreet's participation in Republican politics continued to provide personal gain for him. In May 1880, President Hayes appointed him United States minister to Turkey. In 1881, he was recalled by the government, and the new president, James Garfield, nominated him to a four-year term as U.S. marshal for Georgia. His term as marshal was marred by charges of incompetence. The Democrats used this situation as an issue in the presidential campaign of 1884.

The politics of the campaign doomed Longstreet; when Chester Arthur was elected president, he requested that Longstreet resign. With a Democrat in the White House for the first time in twenty-four years, Longstreet had no prospects of another political job. He operated the Piedmont Hotel for the next few years, and for the first time, he seemed to enjoy peace and freedom from controversy.

On December 29, 1889, his wife for over forty years died. She had borne him ten children, five of whom had died. She had endured the months of separation from her husband and followed him wherever duty or desire led him. To soothe his personal grief, Longstreet immersed himself in the writing of his memoirs. His goal in writing a book, he said, was "to illustrate the valor of the Confederate soldier." *From Manassas to Appomattox*, a 690-page work, was published in 1896 by J. B. Lippincott Company of Philadelphia. As expected, the book engendered both praise and censure. His detractors especially condemned him for his criticism of Lee. In the book, he states that, in his opinion, Lee was not a master of the art of war. On balance, the work enjoyed a good reception and is still considered one of the classic memoirs of the war.

As the years passed, Longstreet became increasingly involved in veterans' activities. He visited battlefields and helped with the marking of unit locations. He was a frequent speaker at national parks and attended the dedication ceremonies of Grant's Tomb. Even though Longstreet had offended and angered many Southerners after the war, Confederate veterans who had served under him retained their respect and admiration for him. When he made public appearances, they cheered him and offered the rebel yell. Such responses deeply pleased and gratified Longstreet.

"Old men get lonely and must have company," Longstreet once remarked to his children. To their dismay, he married Helen Dortch on September 8, 1897. She was thirty-four years old. Although she and Longstreet's children never got along with each other, Helen was a devoted wife to her husband. Outliving her husband by fifty-eight years, Helen became his most ardent defender after his death. During World War II, she worked on the assembly line in one of the defense factories. She died in 1962.

Longstreet canvassed for Republican William McKinley during the presidential campaign of 1896. McKinley rewarded Longstreet by appointing him the U.S. commissioner of railroads. Longstreet's predecessor was Wade Hampton, the former Confederate cavalry general and a bitter political foe of his. Hampton was so incensed by being replaced that he refused to assist Longstreet during the transition.

By 1903, Longstreet was afflicted with an illness that doctors were unable to identify. He also suffered from rheumatism and was so deaf that he had to use a hearing aid. In the autumn of 1903, Longstreet traveled to Chicago for x-ray treatment of a cancerous right eye. His health continued to deteriorate, his weight dropping from 200 pounds to 135. On the morning of January 2,

1904, he visited his daughter in Gainesville and became gravely ill with pneumonia. The end came quickly—at 5 o'clock in the evening he died, just six days short of his eighty-third birthday.

When Longstreet died, he was still a man vilified by former friends and comrades. Before his death, he told Union General Daniel Sickles that Gettysburg "was the sorest and saddest reflection of my life for many years." Longstreet grieved not for what might have been during those three days in July but for what had been—the terrible price that he had foreseen. Controversy over who was responsible for the loss at Gettysburg still continues today.

On January 6, Longstreet's body was laid to rest. State and local dignitaries, militia units, and Confederate veterans participated in the funeral service. As the pallbearers prepared to lower his casket, a Confederate veteran walked to the grave. Silently, he placed part of his uniform and his enlistment papers on the lid of the coffin, and then stepped back. His comrades understood.

Longstreet had many great qualities, but he never lived up to his potential. He dreamed of fame and high position, seeking them by any means and at anyone's expense. He was discontent with serving under Lee, considering himself the better man and always seeking independent command. As Lee's key subordinate, Longstreet's record rivaled Jackson's, but he never reached the heights he sought. In the South, there are a number of monuments to the heroic images of Robert E. Lee, Stonewall Jackson, and many lesser commanders, but only recently was a memorial erected to James Longstreet, Lee's scapegoat lieutenant.

9   *Statesman of the Sword*

WILLIAM TECUMSEH SHERMAN

NOVEMBER 16, 1864, dawned clear and crisp, signaling the coming of winter. The fires from the previous night had all but burned out, but smoke still poured from the ruined city and clung to the surrounding countryside of Atlanta. Union General William Tecumseh Sherman rode with the XIV Corps as the last of the Federal soldiers headed from Atlanta. The South had just lost one of its most productive manufacturing centers and an important rail junction, severely weakening the Southern Confederacy. Sherman hoped the destruction of Atlanta would destroy the South's will to resist.

The March to the Sea had begun, and the era of civilized warfare in which battles involved only contending armies had abruptly ended. Sherman sensed the future's presence: "The day was extremely beautiful . . . and an unusual feeling of something to come, vague and undefined, still full of venture and intense interest. . . . There was a devil-may-care feeling pervading officers and men that made me feel the full load of responsibility, for success would be accepted as a matter of course, whereas, should we fail, the 'march' would be adjudged the wild adventure of a crazy fool."

The weight of responsibility was indeed upon Sherman, but this was no "wild adventure of a crazy fool." Months of thought and preparation had preceded the army's departure from Atlanta. In fact Sherman had spent his life preparing for just this opportunity and a chance to prove himself.

Sherman's father, Charles R. Sherman, was born in Norwalk, Connecticut, in 1788. Charles was well educated in the liberal arts, attended Dartmouth College, and practiced law in his father's office. In 1810, he married Mary Holt, a graduate of a female seminary in Poughkeepsie, New York, and the daughter of a successful Norwalk merchant. To provide for his family, Charles rode the circuit from 1817 to 1829, first as a lawyer and then as a justice of Ohio's Supreme Court.

Although Charles was regularly away from his home in Lancaster, Ohio, he was home enough to father eleven children. It was on February 8, 1820, that the sixth Sherman child was born—Tecumseh. Cump, as his brothers and sisters quickly called him, bore the name of the Shawnee Indian leader, whom Charles admired for his courage and military prowess.

Cump Sherman spent the first years of his life in a comfortable home with his brothers and sisters, an affectionate mother, and a domineering grandmother. Sherman's memories of his father were sparse, but one event did stick in his mind. He recalled his father catching him in the stable crib and ordering him out. When his father turned his back, he jumped back in the crib again. He was ordered out again, but this time his father's tone was more demanding. Sherman, taking umbrage at the tone of his father's voice, decided to run away from home. He packed his clothes and went off to live with a close friend. His father did not try to stop him or to find him. After a short time, he quietly returned home on his own but was chagrined at his father's apparent unconcern.

In June 1829, while on the circuit, Charles developed a high fever and died a few days later. Charles Sherman left his family only the house, its furnishings, and some bank stock worth about $200 a year; most of his earnings had regularly gone to pay off debts he had accrued from earlier financial difficulties. His father had been a tax collector, but all of the money he collected lost its value with the introduction of the American dollar. As his brother John Sherman later expressed it, their father had "left his family poor in everything but friends." Fortunately, these friends stepped forward, taking in the children and making provisions for them. Sherman went to live with his next-door neighbor, Thomas Ewing.

His father's sudden death and the financial difficulties that resulted were pivotal events in Sherman's life. These difficulties led to the breakup of his family. Throughout his life, Sherman worried about remaining solvent, fearing that he would become destitute and his family would suffer the way his father's had. But young Sherman had been fortunate; his foster parent, Thomas Ewing, was a leading citizen of early Lancaster. He was renowned for his intellect, strength, professional success, and happy family life. Sherman grew to admire and respect his foster father. The Ewings had four children of their own and were raising two nieces and a nephew. Thomas Ewing's wife, Maria, was a devout Catholic, and she insisted on having Sherman baptized.

Father Dominic Young baptized Sherman in the front parlor of the Ewing home. Sherman's mother gave her permission for him to be baptized but did not attend the ceremony. The priest had a problem when it came to a name for the boy. Father Young insisted that the candidate add a good Christian name to his American Indian one. Because the event occurred on June 28, St. William's Day, the priest baptized him "William Tecumseh."

Although Thomas Ewing was away from home often, serving in the U.S. Senate, he tried hard to see that Sherman was reared in the same fashion as his own children. He made sure that he received a good education. Young Sherman did well but had a normal youngster's ambivalence toward school. He preferred play and even work to school. Thomas Ewing made Sherman an equal member of his family, but despite such acceptance, he never called the Ewings "mother" or "father"; they always remained "Mr." and "Mrs." He openly admired Ewing but experienced some ambivalence toward him as Ewing grew more successful each year. Young Sherman longed for his family to be like the Ewings. As a result, he was angry and frustrated. As he grew older, he wanted to make certain that his family did not experience such hardship.

Young Sherman was a good student and a fine athlete. Between 1835 and 1836, he devoted most of his time to studying French and mathematics, two subjects particularly important at a military academy. In 1836, Sherman's military career began. At the age of sixteen, he was appointed to West Point by Senator Ewing. There is no indication that he desired such a career, but he embarked on it simply from a sense of obligation to his foster father.

At the military academy, Sherman was a good student but a sloppy soldier. He accumulated so many demerits for discipline and infractions of the dress code that he finished sixth in a class of forty-three, rather than fourth as he was entitled by his academic record.

One of Sherman's courses was on moral philosophy, which included the reading of James Kent's *Commentaries on American Law*. Kent wrote that war eliminated all morality and during a civil war, he argued that "the central government had to defend the laws of the union by force of arms or be disgraced." Sherman's later actions reflected these ideas.

After Sherman graduated in 1840, his army service took him from New York to San Francisco and then from Pittsburgh to New Orleans, but gave him no opportunity for combat experience other than a few skirmishes in Florida with the Seminole Indians. During the Mexican War, when so many West Pointers were gaining fame and rank on the battlefield, Sherman was on routine duty in Pennsylvania and California. Thirteen years after graduating from West Point, he was merely a captain in the Commissary Department with no foreseeable opportunity for improvement for the future.

In an earlier letter to Hugh Ewing, his foster brother, Sherman had written, "I have often regretted that your father did not actually, instead of sending me to West Point, set me at some useful trade or business." Sherman was expressing a feeling held by many middle-class people of his time. The peacetime army was an almost shameful occupation, while commercial life was looked upon with esteem.

In 1850, Sherman married his foster father's daughter, Ellen Ewing. Together they had eight children. Although his marriage strengthened his ties to the Ewing family, it also increased the pressure on him to prove himself worthy of such an alliance. On January 28, 1851, Ellen delivered the first of four children, a girl baptized Maria, who quickly became known as Minnie. Early in June 1854, Ellen gave birth to their first boy, William (Willy). Sherman saw the children as joyous additions to his family, but also as an additional check on his economic freedom. His meager army salary was not sufficient to support Ellen and their children in appropriate style, so he was forced to accept financial assistance from his foster father.

Sherman took a six-month leave from the army to accept a job offer from a former army friend to manage a bank in San Francisco. A short time later, thinking he could make a fortune in banking and real estate, he resigned his commission. For a while, he was able to support his family and provide many of the fine things in life for them, including a large house. When a recession hit California, his bank was closed. As a result, in the summer of 1857, Sherman found himself unemployed and in debt. He blamed himself for this dismal outcome but managed to pay off most of his debts by selling all of his property.

At that point, Sherman contemplated reentering the army, but only at a rank higher than when he had left. Again his family came to his aid. This time Ewing's oldest son, Thomas Jr., asked him to join his law firm in Leavenworth, Kansas Territory. Sherman was admitted to the bar "on the grounds of general intelligence and reputation." Clients were few, and he lost his only case. Again a failure, he returned to his family in 1859. "I look upon myself," he wrote to Ellen before leaving Kansas, "as a dead cock in the pit."

As unfortunate as he was in business, Sherman was lucky in having good friends. One of them, Major Don Carlos Buell, told him of the position of superintendent of a newly established Louisiana Seminary Academy (present-day Louisiana State University) that was available. With the recommendation of two army buddies, P. G. T. Beauregard and Braxton Bragg, Sherman received the appointment. During the months that followed, he proved to be a capable administrator and a popular teacher. Sherman believed he had finally found his proper niche in life, but it did not last long.

On December 20, 1860, Sherman learned that South Carolina had seceded from the Union. The action brought Sherman to tears. He loved the South. Since his sixteenth year, his closest male friends had been Southerners. Of the twenty-five years since he had left home, practically all had been spent under the social influence of the South. At West Point, Southern ideals ruled. His stay in Florida and South Carolina, his four years as an intimate of Southern-born army officers in California, his six years representing Missouri bankers, and now his last year as superintendent of an academy in Louisiana had all left him with a favorable impression of the South.

The South had put its stamp on him. He was hoping to spend his life there and was in the process of building a house near Alexandria, Louisiana. His old army comrades, he knew, were preparing to follow South Carolina's lead. But Sherman could not go along; something was holding him back. It was not the slavery issue; he considered slavery the natural status for blacks. He was passionately devoted to the Union and regarded secession as a form of revolution and anarchy. Within three weeks, Sherman resigned. To the governor of Louisiana, he said: "I prefer to maintain all allegiance to the Constitution as long as a fragment of it survives."

Sherman returned to Washington. His brother, John Sherman, who was now a United States senator, introduced him to Abraham Lincoln. When Sherman offered his services to the Union, Lincoln informed him that his services were not needed because compromise would restore the Union peacefully. Sherman disagreed with Lincoln, predicting that a long, hard war would be needed to put down the Southern rebellion.

After the Confederates fired on Fort Sumter, Lincoln changed his viewpoint. In early June, at John's behest, the War Department offered Sherman a commission as colonel in the Regular Army. He believed, as other West Pointers did, that only trained and disciplined regulars could put down the rebellion. Sherman had a distrust of politicians, who he thought would make scapegoats of those generals who might fail through no fault of their own. In fact he had no love for democracy itself, which he equated to mob rule; he preferred a monarchy or dictatorship.

Sherman was assigned to a brigade of volunteers under General Irvin McDowell's command. He took a dim view of these raw recruits, many of whom were ninety-day enlistees who couldn't wait to go home. "With regulars," he wrote to his wife, "I would have no doubt, but these volunteers are subject to stampedes." On July 21, at Bull Run, Sherman's prediction came true. Yet he performed well, especially since this was the first battle in which he had ever been engaged. Following the Union collapse, Sherman kept his brigade in reasonably good order while it retreated from the field. Finally, on reaching Washington, Sherman rallied and reorganized his troops to defend the capital should the Confederates attempt to follow up their victory.

Late in August, Sherman was promoted to brigadier general and transferred to Kentucky. He was delighted, not only with the promotion, but with his transfer. He believed that the war would be won in the West and reputations could be made there; however, he still feared the unreliability of the volunteers and the unrealistic attitude of the government. For the time, he preferred to serve in a subordinate role, not wanting to be held responsible should they fail. "Not till I see daylight ahead," he confided to Ellen, "do I want to lead."

The War Department responded to his unusual request by assigning him second in command to Brigadier General Robert Anderson who was in charge of the Department of the Cumberland. Within a month, Anderson fell ill and asked to be relieved. As a result, Sherman was thrust into exactly the position he had tried to avoid—top commander in a vital theater of the war.

Fearing attack by Confederate General Albert Sidney Johnston, Sherman asked to be reinforced. Instead of sending reinforcements, Washington urged him to liberate East Tennessee. This response convinced him that he was being deliberately sacrificed. He wrote to Ellen saying that to do this would be madness. "The idea of going down in History with a fame such as this threatens me," he said, "nearly makes me crazy, indeed I may be so now."

People who observed Sherman in his quarters at a Louisville hotel concluded that he was demented. Tall and thin and always looking like he needed to shave and comb his hair, he spent hours pacing back and forth, smoking cigars, head bent forward, eyes darting about but seeing nothing. No one seemed to know when he slept.

Secretary of War Simon Cameron met with Sherman to discuss the assignment of troops. Upon hearing Sherman's outlandish request for at least 66,000 men for a defensive strategy and at least 200,000 men for offensive fighting, Cameron replied that such numbers were simply unavailable. Soon after his meeting, Cameron told a reporter that the general was "unbalanced and that it would not be wise to leave him in command." Cameron soon replaced him with his old friend Brigadier General Don Carlos Buell. In the process, Sherman was labeled by the newspapers as being "unbalanced and not fit for command." From then on, Sherman would have a strong dislike for the press. Sherman became more despondent, writing to Ellen, "I am almost crazy."

Upon General Buell's arrival, Sherman reported to Major General Henry Halleck in St. Louis. Halleck, who was a friend of Sherman's, ignored the reports about his instability. Halleck assigned Sherman to central Missouri to take command of Union forces there. After evaluating the situation, Sherman reported to Halleck that the Confederate forces were too strong to be beaten, all this despite other reports that they were too weak to pose a problem. Halleck immediately ordered Sherman back to St. Louis and declared him unfit for duty, giving him a twenty-six-day leave.

The newspapers again attacked Sherman with the headlines: "General William T. Sherman Insane," asserting that he was "stark mad." Sherman was totally crushed and again felt he had failed and disgraced himself. Sherman wrote to John Ewing, "I am so sensible now of my disgrace . . . that I do think I would have committed suicide were it not for my children. I do not think I can be entrusted with a command."

On December 23, Halleck assigned Sherman to the Union base at Benton Barracks near St. Louis, placing him in charge of recruiting, training, and logistics. In February 1862, Sherman was given an independent command at Cairo, Illinois, serving under Grant. Halleck, who could have ruined Sherman's career, instead had helped him increase his confidence. It was then that Sherman enjoyed his first victory. The lesson was valuable; it had given him the confidence that he could lead. He was back in action. Starting in 1862, a very special relationship would develop between Grant and Sherman, one that was useful to Grant but absolutely essential to Sherman.

Halleck had recognized Sherman's talent for strategic planning. Sherman proved to be a great help to Grant, planning the attacks on Forts Henry and Donelson. The two men quickly developed a strong bond of friendship and mutual admiration. War seemed to give Sherman purpose where before there had been none. He seemed to evolve, finding that the one thing he was good at was leading men in battle—a trait not too valuable in peacetime. Before the war, he had been a good student, had applied himself well, and had worked hard; but he had not been successful. It was only the coming of the war that Sherman came into his own. As a military innovator, he became a major prophet of modern warfare, introducing the concept of total war in America.

Under Grant, Sherman commanded brilliantly at the battle of Shiloh. Although his division was made up of raw recruits, his troops were among the most effective and disciplined of the entire line of battle. Sherman's division held the extreme Union right. When attacked, his men held their position. Sherman's calmness, even cheerfulness, under fire helped to keep them there. One newspaper correspondent wrote that his "unusually hot nerves" seemed to be soothed by combat. For several hours, his division checked fierce Confederate charges, inflicting and suffering heavy losses. During the evening, Grant received reinforcements; in the morning, Grant counterattacked, driving the Confederates back to Corinth.

In Grant's report of the battle, he singled out Sherman for "special mention" for having "displayed great judgment and skill in the management of his men." General Halleck also praised Sherman's efforts: "It was unanimous opinion here that Brig. Gen. W. T. Sherman saved the fortunes of the day on the 6th and contributed largely to the glorious victory on the 7th."

As a result of his success at Shiloh, Sherman was promoted to major general. To his credit, he made no claim to exceptional accomplishments at Shiloh, writing to his wife: "I received today the commission of Major General, but I know not why, it gives me far less emotion than my old commission as 1st Lieutenant of Artillery. The latter, I know I merited; this I doubt." Even so the promotion, the commendations from Grant and Halleck, and the praise from several newspapers restored Sherman's reputation and bolstered his self-confidence. Shiloh, for Sherman, was the turning point in his life.

Sherman continued to distinguish himself under Grant. Late in April, Grant began his campaign of maneuver, battle, and siege, which resulted on July 4 in the capture of Vicksburg and General John Pemberton's army. Sherman was instrumental in Grant's success. Now commanding the XV Corps, he kept Pemberton off balance by bluffing another attack on Vicksburg while Grant moved across the Arkansas and Mississippi Rivers south of the city. Then Sherman marched quickly to reinforce Grant, bringing badly needed supplies and transport. After several assaults and a siege, Vicksburg fell. Grant highly praised Sherman's performance in the Vicksburg operations. To his brother, John, Sherman wrote: "The share I have personally borne in all these events is one in which you may take pride for me." This was boasting, but it was true.

During the Vicksburg campaign, Sherman learned from Grant the importance of training his army to live off the land, enabling it to separate from his supply train and move more freely. This tactic Sherman would use to great advantage in Georgia and the Carolinas.

At the end of August 1863, during the lull after the victory at Vicksburg, Sherman sent for Ellen, Minnie, and Willy to join him at his camp. The reunion with Ellen must have been joyful, because she became pregnant during that time. And then, quite suddenly, disaster struck. Willy fell ill from typhoid fever and died shortly after. Sherman took the loss of his namesake hard, mourning his death deeply for a long time.

In October 1863, Grant became the top commander in the West. As a consequence, Sherman succeeded Grant as commander of the Army of the Tennessee. In March 1864, Grant became commander of the entire Union army and was promoted to the rank of lieutenant general. In announcing his promotion, Grant expressed thanks to Sherman and McPherson "as the men to whom, above all others, I feel indebted for whatever I have had of success." Sherman promptly replied, declaring that on the contrary, it was he who was obliged to Grant. When Grant made his headquarters in the East, he named

Sherman to succeed him as commander in the West. Sherman, the loyal subordinate, now was ready to become Sherman the conqueror.

Grant's plan for ending the war was to have Sherman move into Georgia against General Joseph Johnston's army while he attacked General Lee's Army of Northern Virginia. Sherman was to attempt to destroy the enemy's interior and inflict damage on the South's resources. Both Grant and Sherman were to attack simultaneously, keeping the pressure on both armies so that the Confederates could not move troops from one front to the other.

In May 1864, Sherman assembled an army of 100,000 men at Chattanooga, Tennessee, and began his invasion of Georgia. He was opposed by the crafty strategist General Joseph Johnston. To move swiftly, Sherman divided his army into three groups. Nearly all of his troops and officers were tough, seasoned veterans; however, their discipline off the battlefield was poor and in the months ahead, would grow worse. Despite this, Sherman felt he had one of the best armies in the world.

On May 2, two days after Grant advanced against Lee, Sherman began his offensive. By mid-June, Sherman believed Johnston's line was close to breaking. He decided to strike it head-on at Kennesaw Mountain. Against the advice of his officers, who were opposed to the attack, he ordered the Army of the Tennessee to attack anyway. His officers proved correct and the attack failed, leaving 2,500 of some of the North's best soldiers dead or wounded. Sherman wrote to Ellen two days later: "I begin to regard the death and mangling of a couple of thousand men as a small affair, a kind of morning dash."

As Johnston continued to retreat to Atlanta, President Jefferson Davis was convinced that he had no intention of holding Atlanta. On July 17, Davis replaced Johnston with General John Bell Hood. Hood was able to hold off Sherman for a while, but on September 1, Atlanta fell.

Hood marched his army toward Tennessee in the hope that Sherman would pursue him, interrupting his rampage through Georgia. Sherman was elated by the news of Hood's movement to Tennessee. "If he will go to the Ohio River, I will give him rations. My business is down south," he said. The people of Georgia felt they had been abandoned, left at the mercy of Sherman, whose cavalry had a free range of operation as much as one hundred miles south of Atlanta. Sherman split his army, sending a sizable force to deal with Hood while he embarked with 62,000 troops on his famous March to the Sea.

On November 15, the torch was put to Atlanta. This act brought up the curtain on Sherman's march to the sea and stunned the South with its heartlessness. Major Henry Witchcock observed: "Immense and raging fires light up the whole heaven. First, bursts of smoke, dense black volumes, then tongues of flame, then huge waves of fire roll up into the sky. Presently the skeletons of great warehouses stand out in relief against sheets of roaring, blazing, furious flames."

Sherman's March to the Sea was the result of his lifelong observation and study of warfare. "They [the Southerners] cannot be made to love us," Sherman said, "but they can be made to fear us." He came to see that the war was not just a battle between armies, but a campaign between societies. Rather than fight an army, he would attack the Southern mind. By marching his army through the center of the Confederacy, destroying the countryside as he went, he would show the people that their army could not protect them. This, Sherman felt, would break the South's will to fight and bring the war to an end.

Before Sherman started his march, he had to get both Lincoln and Grant's approval. Lincoln had concerns about whether his plan would help shorten the war. It was Grant's sense of trust in Sherman that convinced Lincoln and Secretary of War Stanton to give their approval. Sherman's planning for the march was meticulous and his eye for detail amazing. He obtained the census records for each county in Georgia and gathered information on where the food was produced. He used this information to plan his route. Attacking both civilian and military targets, Sherman wanted to destroy not only the South's will to win but also its means to fight.

The army marched with no information about where they were going. Only Sherman knew that their final destination was Savannah, 275 miles away. Facing virtually no military resistance, Sherman's army moved quickly and stealthily, foraging off the land and destroying everything in their way. Behind them was a trail of devastation sixty miles wide. With the abundance of food available, Sherman's order to "forage liberally" has been debated ever since. The vagueness of this order allowed his troops a great deal of latitude. The men ransacked houses along the way despite orders to the contrary, removing valuables, breaking dishes, smashing furniture, and stealing money they found. Their excuse was that they were "foraging liberally." Southerners charged that Sherman only winked at the abusers. They were doing exactly what he wanted them to do—terrorizing the countryside. In most cases, the soldiers were operating miles from their commanders' influence and supervision, and temptations were great. Many of the soldiers felt this was their opportunity to punish the South. The worst of Sherman's raiders were called "bummers." They wreaked havoc wherever they went, creating the image that dominates the popular conception of the March to the Sea.

Along with Sherman's army came hordes of freed blacks, rejoicing in their liberation from slavery. Their presence annoyed Sherman, who considered the Emancipation Proclamation a mistake. On December 21, Union troops entered the city of Savannah, and Sherman telegraphed Lincoln: "I beg to present to you a Christmas gift, the city of Savannah with 150 heavy guns, plenty of ammunition and 25,000 bales of cotton."

Lincoln replied with a letter that Sherman would treasure his whole life: "When you were leaving Atlanta for the Atlantic coast," Lincoln wrote, "I was anxious, if not fearful; but feeling that you were the better judge, . . . Now, the undertaking being a success, the honor is all yours . . . it is indeed a great success."

The extent to which houses and towns were burned during Sherman's March to the Sea has been greatly exaggerated. Among whites, there are no known murders, and there are only a few sketchy reports of rape. Some atrocities did occur, the victims being African Americans. Numerous blacks were physically abused by Union soldiers. The worst incident occurred on December 9, when General Jeff C. Davis marched his XIV Corps across the rain-swollen Ebenezer Creek near Savannah. After his troops had crossed, he had the pontoon bridges removed, leaving hundreds of frightened fugitive slaves on the opposite shore. Closely followed by Confederate cavalry and terrified of what the Rebel horsemen might do, hundreds of freedmen plunged into the water, hoping to swim across; many drowned. Even Sherman's hardened troops were offended by Davis's act of cruelty.

Sherman did little to protect the freed slaves on his march. His proslavery and racist views were well known. A Richmond newspaper quoted him as saying that slavery would survive the war and he would own slaves himself. When cautioned by Halleck to be careful about what he said about blacks, Sherman responded that "Military success, not protection of 'Sambo' was his main priority." To others who called for fair play for African Americans, his answer was, "The Negro should be a free man, but not part of any equality with whites . . . . Indeed it appears to me that the right of suffrage in our country should be abridged, rather than enlarged."

All in all, Sherman estimated the damage done to the state of Georgia and its military resources at $100 million. Of that total, at least $20 million worked to the Union's military advantage. The rest, he confessed, "is simple waste and destruction."

By the end of January 1865, Sherman had crossed into South Carolina. The mood of the men as they entered the state was described by a soldier: "The whole army is burning with an insatiable desire to wreak vengeance upon South Carolina. I almost tremble at her fate, but feel that she deserves all that seems in store for her." South Carolina did indeed have a great deal in store for it— what Sherman would call "minor depredations." A Pennsylvania soldier wrote that after his unit crossed into South Carolina, the division commander rode along the line of troops saying, "Boys, are you well supplied with matches as we are now in South Carolina?" At the end of the march, a soldier wrote, "We burnt every house, barn and mill that we passed."

Sherman's men devastated the countryside. He had ordered his troops to spare dwellings that were occupied and to be courteous to women but to take all provisions and forage they needed. In Georgia, few houses were burned; in

South Carolina, few escaped. Sherman, riding at the head of the column, was too intent upon the army's safety to worry about the conduct of his men.

In South Carolina, as during the March to the Sea, Sherman encountered little opposition. But when he entered North Carolina in early March 1865, he was confronted by Joseph Johnston. Grant ordered Sherman to move against Johnston to prevent him from joining up with Lee in Virginia, but this was not necessary when Lee surrendered.

Later reflecting on his campaign in Georgia, South Carolina, and North Carolina, Sherman thought that his wartime actions were justified. He did feel remorse for the way children felt about him. "They were taught to curse my name, and each night thousands knelt in prayer and beseeched the Almighty to consign me to perdition," he said.

While the Southerners may have hated Sherman, his men idolized him. To them he was known as "Uncle Billy." He would sit on a stump with some of the enlisted men, smoke a cigar, and exchange stories. This common approach endeared him to his men. Sherman was not a spit-and-polish soldier with a pretty sash and flashy sword. There was a bond between him and his men, and they respected him. Sherman was a hero to his men and to the nation.

At the beginning of April, Grant forced Lee out of Petersburg and Richmond, and on April 9, accepted his surrender at Appomattox. On April 14, Joseph Johnston, who saw no point in continuing in a war that was lost, asked Sherman for an armistice so they might discuss the surrender of his army. Northern jubilation that followed the news of Lee's capitulation and Johnston's surrender was suddenly stifled by the news of Lincoln's assassination. Sherman instructed the telegrapher to tell no one of the bad news until after he had met with Johnston. The two generals met in the little farmhouse of Mrs. James Bennett near Raleigh. Sherman showed Johnston the dispatch about Lincoln's assassination. Johnston was visibly moved; neither general knew what this event would ultimately mean. They agreed to meet again the next day with John C. Breckinridge, the Confederate secretary of war, joining the negotiations.

Sherman ordered all soldiers to their camps and issued a carefully worded announcement of the president's assassination. He stated clearly that the Confederate army had nothing to do with Lincoln's death. The Union troops were shocked. Some wanted vengeance and hoped the surrender negotiations would collapse. But Sherman maintained order and prevented his troops from attempting any reprisal measures.

The next day, thinking he was acting in the spirit of Lincoln's policy for Reconstruction, and attempting to satisfy Johnston as well, Sherman was more generous than Grant had been with Lee. He negotiated what amounted to a Reconstruction policy, something he had no authority to do. Under the terms, Confederate armies were to take their weapons to arsenals in their state capitals and promise to obey federal authority again. Existing state governments were to be recognized, and federal courts once again reestablished. The political rights of all individuals were to be guaranteed, and no one was to be punished for his role in the war as long as he obeyed the laws. Finally, "In general terms—the war to cease; [and] a general amnesty."

Sherman, who had vowed to "make war terrible" for the South—and had done so—now wanted to make peace as easy as he could. In the process, he entered into political matters beyond his realm of authority and unacceptable to the Radicals in Washington. Andrew Johnson, now president, had no choice but to repudiate Sherman's agreement with Johnston. Sherman half expected this response and was not offended. But he was incensed by the way Secretary of War Edwin Stanton and General Halleck, now chief of staff of the army, handled the affair. They implied that Sherman had betrayed the Union while seeking to make himself a military dictator.

Calling in reporters, Stanton accused Sherman of insubordination, stupidity, and treason. Headlines across the country echoed Stanton's condemnation. Sherman was outraged beyond measure. His soldiers were also angered by anyone who spoke unkindly of "Uncle Billy." To disrespect Sherman was to disrespect them. In Raleigh, the soldiers burned a collection of Northern newspapers that had been brought into town and threatened to burn the newspaper office. Sherman's western army had torn the South apart; now there was fear that it might march to Washington to do the same. To defuse the anger of Sherman and his men, the government decided to hold a "grand review" in Washington. It was decided that the eastern and western armies would march separately on successive days. The two-day event on May 23 and 24 turned out to be one of the greatest parades in American history.

Officially, Washington was still in mourning for the slain Lincoln. Many buildings were draped in black. Nevertheless, the government launched an all-out effort to create an atmosphere of celebration. For five days before the march, workers decked every public building with blue-and-white bunting. They built a pavilion and stands for military and government officials. Enormous crowds surged into the Capital.

On May 23, the eastern Army of the Potomac was given the privilege of marching first. This was Washington's own army, the men who had defended the city from oncoming Confederates in many desperate battles. At the head of the column rode General Meade, the hero of Gettysburg. It took seven hours for the army to pass the reviewing stand. Everyone agreed that the troops had given a splendid military performance. The *New York Times*, which had been so critical of Sherman's treaty with Johnston, assumed Meade's men would be much better received than Sherman's men. The paper predicted thin crowds for the next day's march.

Precisely at 9:00 A.M. on May 24, the Army of the Tennessee headed down Pennsylvania Avenue, marching before a crowd estimated at 200,000. At the head of the column was their leader, William Tecumseh Sherman. Within minutes, the westerners had won the hearts of the crowd, and the army received an overwhelming reception. As Sherman passed the presidential stand, he raised his sword in salute. One New York paper reported that the acclamation was "without precedent . . . Sherman was the idol of the day." This was the same man that the newspapers had called a traitor only ten days earlier.

After Sherman passed the reviewing stand, he dismounted and joined the other dignitaries on the stand. He embraced his wife and son Tom, shook hands with his father-in-law, Thomas Ewing, and with President Johnson and General Grant. When Secretary of War Stanton put out his hand, Sherman ignored it. "I declined it publicly," he wrote with grim satisfaction, "and the fact was universally noticed." Then he sat down to enjoy the parade. In retaliation for the way he had been treated, Sherman had snubbed Stanton, and harder to understand, broke with Halleck, the man who in 1861 had given him a second chance after his failure in Missouri.

As soon as the war was over, Sherman's attitude toward the South changed abruptly and completely. In his treatment of Johnston, he had proven to be more humane in his dealings than Grant had with Lee. Sherman had once loved the South and was now willing to hold out a hand of friendship to a fallen foe. In so doing, he followed Lincoln's conciliatory views. Later, in a letter, Sherman stated that persecuting the beaten South would be like slashing the crew of a sinking ship. He told President Andrew Johnson he would risk person and reputation to heal the wounds he had helped make.

Despite his destructive March to the Sea, Sherman proved his benevolent attitude toward the South by collecting money and supplies for the civilians of Atlanta. At Savannah, he had instituted a system of barter, which kept its people from starvation.

The time had come to leave Washington. Sherman had no political aspirations. He was a soldier, not a politician. On May 30, he issued a farewell to his troops: "Our work is done, and armed enemies no longer defy us . . . you have done all that men could do." He urged them to be good citizens. Sherman looked forward to peaceful days.

Sherman's tumultuous reception at the Grand Review and during a tour he and Ellen took in June demonstrated the nation's affection for and curiosity about him. When they reached New York, the crowds were so large that the police had difficulty controlling them. Soldiers and civilians applauded and serenaded them. It was an impressive sight—the hero lionized by a grateful nation publicly expressing its thanks.

But the nation wanted to do more for Sherman than shout and cheer. The citizens of Lancaster undertook a $100,000 testimonial fund drive throughout Ohio. Later, people in St. Louis raised money to buy him a $24,000 house and provided an additional $5,600 for his bank account. Still later, when Sherman became commanding general of the army, prominent businessmen bought him Grant's former home for $65,000, and Sherman banked an additional $37,000. These were enormous amounts of money; but Sherman, like other military figures, took it in stride as his just reward for his wartime effort.

Even in the South, where many Southerners were still upset by what Sherman had done to them in the war, they appreciated the lenient peace terms he had offered Johnston when he surrendered. When he visited the South in the postwar years, Sherman was always cordially received.

Sherman's fame extended beyond the North and South. His March to the Sea received wide publicity in Europe, where he was considered a great military leader. His fame gave him entree wherever he went. He met the European figures of the age, including kings and the Pope. Sherman enjoyed himself the ten months he traveled throughout Europe and Egypt. Everywhere he went he made a favorable impression.

With the Civil War over, Americans would return to their long-term plan of economic development and westward expansion. Vast new territories remained to be settled and linked with marketplaces of the East. The chief impediment to this objective was the buffalo-hunting American Indians of the Great Plains. Americans believed they would not be able to settle the West and build their railroads as long as the Indians stood in their way. The problem had to be solved while the railroads were being built. A postwar army of only 25,000 men was given the responsibility of working with railroads to make certain that the Indians did not impede their process. Grant went to Washington as commanding general of the army; Sherman was sent to St. Louis to serve as leader in the field and direct liaisons with the railroads. Sherman understood what his central focus was to be: "I regard the [rail] road as the most important element now in progress to facilitate the military interests of our Frontier." The army had to gain "absolute and unqualified control of the Indians."

The removal of the Indians would be a war of extermination if their removal could not be done by other means. Public opinion was divided between those in the West, who favored extermination of the Indians, and those in the East, who wanted to pacify them. Sherman never doubted that time was on his side. He felt he could neutralize the feelings of those in the East while attempting to eliminate the Indians. Underlying Sherman's strategy for removing the Indians was his belief that he was an "Agent of Progress" and the feeling that his enemy was a lesser race bound to lose in the harsh competition of history.

Sherman admitted he had "no doubt our people have committed grievous wrong to the Indians," but felt that "both races cannot use this country in common, and one or the other must withdraw. We cannot withdraw without check-ing the natural progress of Civilization." He believed the conquest of Ameri-can Indians was part of the natural law. "It is an inevitable conflict of races, one that must occur when a stronger is gradually displacing a weaker. . . . The Indi-ans are poor and proud. They are tempted . . . to steal. . . . To steal they some-times must kill. We in our turn cannot discriminate—all look alike and under the same pressure act alike, and to get the rascals, we are forced to include all."

Grant was in complete agreement with Sherman regarding the means and ends of his Indian policy, and gave him complete support. In 1868, when Grant went to the White House, he promoted Sherman to commanding general of the army. Sherman gave his replacement in the West, Phil Sheridan, full author-ization to carry on his policy of Indian extermination.

Sherman never used the term *extermination*, but he authorized Sheridan to kill as many men, women, and children as he felt necessary when they attacked the Indian villages. After 1868, Sherman lost interest in the Indian problem and turned it over completely to Sheridan. By May 1869, the last spike of the first transcontinental railroad was driven. Sherman was pleased that Sheridan was carrying out his Indian policy. When General Custer and a large part of his regiment were wiped out in July 1876, it did not concern Sherman greatly. Although regrettable, it had been only a temporary reversal. By 1879, Sherman was quoted as saying "order and peace covered the West as never before."

Sherman remained in the position of commanding general of the army for fifteen years, until his retirement. He considered his support of the railroads, contributing to the expansion of the West, and the elimination of the Plains Indians as his greatest accomplishments during that time. Considering his close relationship with Grant, his lengthy term in office, and his personal prestige, it is surprising how little Sherman was able to accomplish.

On one occasion, when Grant and Sherman were traveling together, Grant jokingly asked his friend what kind of hobby he planned to have now that the war was over. He had to have a hobby, Grant said, or the press would invent something for him. Grant planned to make a hobby of his horses. Jokingly, Sherman replied, "You may drive your fast horses, and I will kiss all the pret-ty girls. Ha! Ha! that shall be my fad."

During the postwar years, Sherman kissed every young woman he could. General W. B. Hazen's wife Mildred described Sherman's approach to women as "cunning." "He always made believe he [was] absent minded, and if a woman was young he made a habit of kissing her in an off-hand way every time he met her." Most women seemed only too happy to accept Sherman's attention. "I never saw a man so run after by womenkind in my life," a friend said. His wife did not seem to mind, joking on one occasion that she had no objection to his kissing young women, but she drew the line at widows. She wanted him to remember that she was the only love of his life, and she knew that he "was true" to her "in heart and soul."

But he was not always true to his wife and was not completely satisfied with her. Sherman wished for a wife who would share more of his life. Ellen was always preoccupied with her religion and showed no interest in his social life. Sherman knew many women, some very well. In his late life, he became good friends with young Mrs. Frances Cleveland, the wife of Grover Cleveland. The newspapers printed a story about their friendship, hinting that they were more than just friends. Ellen was concerned enough to send her husband a copy of the story and ask for an explanation. There was nothing to explain in that case, but there were two other young women in his life: the sculptor Vinnie Ream and Mary Audenreid, the widow of his deceased military aide. Correspondence between Vinnie and Sherman began in 1873, was steady for four years, and continued intermittently until his death. He told her to write to him often, because no one saw his mail and Ellen was away.

Sherman enjoyed an intense erotic affair with Vinnie. On April 19, 1873, he wrote to her: "My foolish little pet, I miss you more than I thought possible." After his departure for St. Louis in 1874, Sherman continued to visit her when he came to Washington, but the long-distance lovers drifted apart. In February 1875, two years after he first made love to Vinnie, Sherman wrote: "I often think of your studio and my precious moments there and wonder if you miss me." After he returned to Washington in 1876, Sherman visited Vinnie occasionally in the afternoon, but the intensity was gone. On May 28, 1878, when she married Lieutenant Richard Hoxie, a man more her age, the Shermans attended the wedding.

In the early 1880s, Sherman began an affair with another young woman, the wife of his aide, Joseph Audenreid. Mary Audenreid had no special relationship with Sherman until after her husband's death. Mary was in her mid-thirties and Sherman sixty years old when they began their affair. She was the daughter of a rich and socially prominent Philadelphia merchant. Six weeks after her husband's death, Sherman invited Mary to join the two-month-long West Coast tour he was going to take as part of President Hayes's party. Soon after, Sherman became both a father figure and lover for Mary. In August 1881, he expressed his mixed feeling in a letter: "You ought not to be alone—you must not be—for your nature demands a mate. . . . I value your attachment to me and hope to show you my appreciation by doing that which I would do for one of my own." He wanted her to marry again; but when suitors arrived, he was jealous. Soon he found himself deeply in love with Mary. As had been the case during his relationship with Vinnie Ream, his feelings for a much younger woman made him feel young and virile. Sherman even invited Mary into his home: "You can have the guest room right over my office and though somewhat jealous of my rights, I think I will let you have pretty free range of my sanctum"—his private dayroom and bedroom. He planned to bring his mistress to his bed right under his wife's nose, passing her off to outsiders as a friend of his wife and daughter.

Her visit did not go well; whether Ellen discovered or suspected her husband's sexual affair with Mary is not clear, but after the visit, she was not welcomed in their home again. To make things worse, Ellen discovered some of Mary's letters and destroyed them. Sherman was very upset when he learned of his wife's invasion of his privacy. He defended Mary, and then, to his consternation, heard nothing from her for months. After this, there seemed to be no further expressions of affection between the two.

Sherman made little effort to hide his flirtations with young women. His constant need for approval and Ellen's unwillingness to share his social life made him reach out to them. In the end, Sherman settled for flirtations and an occasional affair when he went out of town. Then he returned home to the security of Ellen and his family. In the outside world, he received the adulation he required; at home he had the steadiness of family life. He was going to maintain the best of both worlds, each supplying what he could not find in the other.

Being commanding general of the army was not easy for Sherman. When he gained the position in 1869, he found himself battling politicians in Washington and Indian agents in the West. Even his Civil War buddy, the new President U. S. Grant was not dependable, siding with his new political friends rather than his old army comrades. In the army itself, the independent staff bureaus opposed being placed under his command, preferring the greater latitude they had enjoyed under civilian authority. In the West, the Indians proved more of a problem than Sherman had expected, and he did not have the troops to deal with them as he desired.

Sherman believed that Grant would maintain the same relationship with him in peacetime as he had during the war, securing a stable place for his army in the postwar. Sherman watched with disappointment as Grant became more political and less supportive of the army. But he was even more upset by his policy toward the South. The mistake, Sherman said, was in putting the political power of the South in the hands of the "intelligent classes." Sherman walked away from all his political problems rather than facing them head-on. He viewed politicians as adversaries that he must tolerate, but not work with. He was absent from Washington regularly and neglected the political battles that were necessary if the army was to thrive.

When Rutherford Hayes took office in 1877, Sherman felt things would improve for the army; however, Congress was again pressuring him to reduce the army's size to below 25,000. Sherman argued that the army was needed to meet the country's responsibilities on the border, in the West against American Indians, in protecting public property, and against riots or rebellions. Sherman's battles with Congress continued. In many ways, Sherman tried to hang on to the old army rather than innovate. No matter what he tried, he could not achieve what he wanted—control of the army, free from political influence.

Sherman often talked of retiring when he became frustrated. What finally convinced him to leave the army, however, was Congress's willingness to let him retire at full pay and benefits for the rest of his life. In November 1883, Sherman turned the army over to Phil Sheridan. Sherman had no specific plans except to live in St. Louis free from the Washington politicians who had made his life so miserable. But Sherman was not to rest for long.

Some of Sherman's ineffectiveness as commanding general of the army can be attributed to his disinterest in the political process and politicians. Although Sherman had close ties to the Republicans—especially his brother, the senator, he avoided party affiliations, never voted after 1856, and often criticized some policies of both parties. As a result, both Democrats and Republicans censured and praised him. His reputation for being politically independent contributed to his popularity. Both parties spoke of nominating him to run for president. Perhaps no American so likely to be elected has rejected the prospect of the presidency so often as Sherman did. During the 1884 Republican convention, Sherman sent two telegrams to a friend among the delegates. The first read: "Please decline any nomination for me in language strong but courteous." The second, two days later, said: "I will not accept if nominated, and will not serve if elected." Sherman believed that the presidency destroyed those who held it. He knew that if he were a candidate, he and his family would come under fire because his wife and children were Roman Catholic.

Old soldiers and their welfare became one of Sherman's chief concerns. Veterans appeared at his door every day, usually in search of a handout. Sherman said that he gave about a third of his income to needy veterans. When marching in veteran parades, he always dressed in the plain blouse of a private with his four silver stars. It was to a veterans' group in 1880 that he made his remark, "War is hell. . . . War is usually made by civilians, bold and defiant in the beginning, but when the storm comes, they generally go below." The only office Sherman ever sought was that of president of the Army of the Tennessee veteran's organization, which he held from 1869 until his death.

Sherman opposed the Fourteenth Amendment, which assured African Americans the right to vote. The South respected and admired Sherman because of his outspoken opposition to the Fourteenth Amendment and what he believed was a harsh Reconstruction policy. However, their viewpoint changed with the publication of his memoirs in 1875. His two-volume work was a model of its kind, candid and outspoken, assessing the roles of individuals and governments alike. The books angered Jefferson Davis and a number of Federal generals, who challenged them as inaccurate and self-serving. Sherman dismissed their criticism of the work as disgruntled contemporaries. Southerners were outraged by Sherman's realistic account of his march and his description of the Confederacy as a "criminal and senseless conspiracy." But in the North, the memoirs were well received; there was an immediate move to have Sherman run for president.

Retirement brought major changes to Sherman's life, the most significant being freedom from politicians. Retirement did not, however, slow him down; he continued to live life to the fullest. When Grant died in 1885, Sherman became the leading survivor of the Union war effort. Everywhere he went he was a celebrity. He was sought after by various organizations to serve on boards or hold office. Sherman enjoyed the theater. He attended plays regularly throughout the postwar years, and the older he became, the more he seemed drawn to them. Sherman loved to ride horseback early in life, and later, in a buggy or carriage. He read a great deal and owned a large library. He had a general interest in history, and his favorite author was William Shakespeare.

By the time Sherman retired, his family had dispersed to half its previous size. Some of his children had married or were away at college. Two of his daughters remained at home, serving at social functions in place of his wife, Ellen. Ellen had complained of illnesses all her life, using them as excuses for not participating in her husband's social activities. By 1887, her health grew worse. Sherman hired a nurse to care for her, but it was difficult for him to accept that his wife was going to die. On November 28, as he was reading in his office, the nurse called to him that Ellen was dying. He ran upstairs, calling out in anguish, "Wait for me, Ellen, no one ever loved you as I loved you." It was too late; she was gone.

Generals William Tecumseh Sherman and Joseph E. Johnston both lived for a quarter of a century after the Civil War. Both wrote memoirs of their military experiences. Mutual respect led to a genuine friendship between the two. They corresponded and occasionally met with each other. At General Grant's funeral in New York, Sherman and Johnston stood side by side.

Sherman lived to be seventy-one years old. He had many ailments, but apparently his asthma finally caused his death on February 14, 1891. Sherman had asked that no one but his family should see his face when he died; but they felt that the veterans, with whom he identified so closely, should be allowed to show their last respects. On February 18, thousands viewed his remains. All of New York seemed to be mourning. Members of the Grand Army of the Republic—30,000 soldiers and veterans—many of them Sherman's, participated in the funeral. President Benjamin Harrison and former presidents Rutherford B. Hayes and Grover Cleveland were present, along with cabinet members, congressmen, senators, governors, and friends. Also among those present was Joseph Johnston, who had observed his eighty-fourth birthday on February 3.

General Johnston was an honorary pallbearer. It was a very cold day, following a winter rain. Johnston stood bareheaded as the other pallbearers carried the flag-draped coffin. A bystander, concerned about Johnston's health, urged him to put on his hat. Johnston replied: "If I were in his place and he were standing here in mine, he would not put on his hat." Johnston left New York with a severe cold that aggravated a bad heart condition. About a month later, on March 21, 1891, Johnston too was dead.

William Tecumseh Sherman chose his own epitaph, "Faithful and Honorable," and it was an accurate assessment of his life. He was true to his word, in both war and peace. He was genuine, never losing the sense of his true self. He was constant, devoted, trustworthy, and steadfast. He was not perfect, nor was he the brute of popular legend. He remained a soldier always; the Civil War was the defining moment of his life. He helped preserve the Union, and he was proud of it. Sherman was an appealing individual; soldiers, family, and friends idolized him. He impressed his contemporaries, influenced his age, and left his name for posterity.

10

Bold Retreater

JOSEPH E. JOHNSTON

ONE afternoon in May 1862, as the Battle of Seven Pines was nearing an end just a few miles east of Richmond, General Joseph Johnston rode out to Fair Oaks to check on the condition of the battle. It did not take him long to determine that his men would have to spend the night there, hoping to complete their victory in the morning. Giving his staff officer the necessary orders, he departed.

Suddenly, a bullet tore into Johnston's right shoulder. A moment later, he was hit by a shell fragment that knocked him from his horse. An aide ran over, picked him up, and carried him back to a safer spot. Johnston was unconscious and it seemed that he was dying. A few minutes later, a tall, gaunt man came over to check on the fallen general. The soldiers gathering around Johnston made way for the visitor, the president of the Confederacy, Jefferson Davis.

When Johnston opened his eyes, he was surprised to see the president. They had known each other since their days at West Point, nearly forty years earlier. But they had never been close, and recently they had hardly been friends. Even so, Johnston held up his hand for the president to take. Johnston said he didn't know the extent of his wound, but he thought the fragment had injured his spine.

Within a few minutes, Johnston discovered that he did not have his sword and pistols. "The sword," he exclaimed, "was the one worn by my father in the Revolutionary War, and I would not lose it for $10,000; will someone please go back and get it and the pistols for me." Several volunteered to do so. His aide, paying no attention to Union fire, returned to the spot where Johnston was hit and retrieved both sword and pistols. He hurried back to the general, who presented one of his pistols to him.

Although Johnston's wounds were serious, he was determined to recover, to fight again. He was a soldier every inch, a professional's professional. He had been wounded in battle before, and he had every reason to expect that he would receive other wounds; but wounds were of little consequence to him—the important thing was to serve.

Johnston was the most senior U.S. Army officer to resign his commission and join the Confederacy in 1861. He was the only general to command both of the Confederacy's principal field armies—the Army of Northern Virginia in 1861–1862 and the Army of Tennessee in 1864. He won the South's first victory, at Manassas in July 1861. Many of his contemporaries considered him the greatest Southern field commander of the war; others ranked him second only to Robert E. Lee. Both Ulysses S. Grant and William T. Sherman considered him the most skillful opponent they faced during the war. Yet, of all the generals who commanded major Confederate armies, Joseph E. Johnston remains the most ambiguous and controversial.

Johnston's military career aroused passionate debate even before the war was over. His partisans contended that he possessed the strategic and tactical ability necessary to be a successful field commander. His critics countered that he was more like a Confederate George McClellan—excellent at organizing, supplying, and raising the morale of an army, but unwilling or unable to fight successfully.

Joseph Johnston's father, Peter, had fought in the Revolutionary War under the command of General Henry "Light-Horse Harry" Lee. In the early 1800s, he became a judge, settling at Abingdon in southwest Virginia. Joseph's mother was Mary Valentine Wood, the niece of Patrick Henry. Peter and Mary's first child died in infancy, but then they were blessed with a succession of healthy children, all of them boys. Their seventh child, born on February 3, 1807, was christened Joseph Eggleston in honor of the man who had been Peter's squad commander during the war.

When the Johnstons moved to Abingdon, it was both a frontier town and a thriving center of nineteenth-century American culture. Young Joseph and his brothers grew up amid the contradictory influences of the Appalachian frontier and Abingdon society.

Young Joseph, like other boys of his age, enjoyed playing typical games around the countryside. His father was an ardent hunter whose sons naturally followed his interest. Several veterans of the Revolution lived in the area, and their stories of adventure excited the Johnston boys. They organized themselves into armies, emulating their heroes, and Joseph was one of the leaders. With a childhood of outdoor activities, Joseph became a fine horseman and a good marksman. These outdoor experiences contributed to the hardy constitution that helped Joseph to withstand the rigors of military campaigns and recover from the wounds he would receive as a soldier.

Joseph's father and mother were both interested in seeing that their children were well educated. Mrs. Johnston was a cultured woman, capable of instructing her children in the classics and inspiring them with a love of reading and learning. On cold nights, the family gathered around the fire, listening as one of the older boys read. It was then that Joseph was first introduced to the novels of Sir Walter Scott; he would retain an affection for Scott's writing throughout his life.

Joseph's mother gave him his earliest education, after which he attended the Abingdon Academy. He did well there, showing an interest in the classics, but his inclination continued to be toward the military. His father, noticing this, gave Joseph the sword he had carried through the Revolution. For the rest of his life, Joseph would cherish the sword as one of his prize possessions. Through a political friend, Joseph's father was able to secure for him an appointment to West Point. On the roster of new cadets from Virginia, along with Joseph's name, appeared that of Robert E. Lee, the son of Judge Johnston's Revolutionary War leader.

In June, the two young Virginians passed the entrance examination and became members of a class of 105 cadets. The two quickly became good friends. Years later, Johnston wrote of Lee: "We had the same intimate associates, who thought, as I did, that no other youth or man so united the qualities that win warm friendship and command high respect. For he was full of sympathy and kindness, genial and fond of gay conversation, and even of fun, that made him the most agreeable of companions."

Although Cadet Johnston was eager to be successful at West Point, he had to overcome one major handicap to maintain his scholastic average. For a period of time an "eye affection [sic]," probably retinitis pigmentosa, a hereditary and degenerative disease that causes night blindness, prohibited any serious night study. Johnston didn't, however, allow this problem to hinder his early interest in books. French, astronomy, military history, and biography were his favorite subjects and continued to be throughout his life. Johnston received his highest grade at West Point in conduct, a category that encompassed military bearing and behavior and was achieved by avoiding the kind of violations that earned demerits. Johnston was a good student, better than average, and his steady improvement over four years indicated that he was tenacious in pursuit of his studies.

West Point was not all academics, and its mission made leadership within the corps as important as a cadet's performance in the classroom. Johnston's sterling record made him a candidate for cadet officer. The summer before his final year, he was promoted to the rank of cadet lieutenant. Medical disability, however, related to his night blindness forced him to step down as cadet lieutenant when the school year began. His friend and rival, Robert E. Lee, was named to the most exalted of positions at the Academy—adjutant.

Despite this setback during his senior year, Johnston's four years at West Point were unquestionably a success. He earned few demerits, passed all his exams comfortably, and had the opportunity to exercise leadership. Graduating in 1829 and finishing thirteenth in a class of forty-six, he was commissioned as a second lieutenant in the artillery.

In 1830, the Regular Army had only four regiments of artillery, whose principal job was to man the guns of the coastal defense forts. As second lieutenant in Company C of the 4th U.S. Artillery, Johnston's duty was to serve as part of the garrison of Fort Columbus on Governor's Island in New York Harbor. His two-year stay there ended in late 1831, when his company was transferred to Fort Monroe in southeastern Virginia. In August, a house servant named Nat Turner had led a slave revolt that spread from plantation to plantation across the county, leaving sixty whites and scores of blacks dead; it was every slaveholder's nightmare. The immediate reaction was a plea for military protection. In response, Johnston's company was sent to reinforce Fort Monroe.

By the time Johnston arrived in Virginia, the crisis had ended. Turner had been captured and executed, but the planters still feared other insurrections. Like most well-to-do plantation owners, the Johnstons of Abingdon were slaveholders. Late in his life, Johnston would claim that he had regarded slavery as a moral and political evil since boyhood.

Johnston found his assignment at Fort Monroe one of the most pleasant. There he met up with his old friend Robert E. Lee. The two were unusual in their abstinence from both sex and drink. But they thoroughly enjoyed the friendship of fellow officers who were not as inhibited.

In May 1832, Chief Black Hawk of the Sac Indians violated an unfair treaty by returning across the Mississippi River to his tribe's ancestral hunting ground in Illinois. The local militia forces were unable to locate and capture the renegade chief and his followers. President Andrew Jackson ordered General Winfield Scott to raise an army of regulars to go to Illinois, capture the chief, and send him back across the Mississippi.

Johnston participated in the Black Hawk War; it was his first expedition against a hostile force. Johnston quickly learned that war was not all heroics and glamour. After four-and-a-half months in the field, he returned to Fort Monroe. His first experience had been a sobering one. Although he had traveled 2,000 miles and half his command had died from cholera, Johnston had never faced an enemy and never fired a shot in anger. Before Scott's army could catch up with Black Hawk's band, they had been annihilated by the Illinois militia in the Battle of Bad Axe. The war was over. Johnston's experience with war had consisted of a long trip under a cloud of pestilence. It could hardly have appealed to his sense of glory.

Trouble with the Seminoles in Florida from 1836 to 1837 gave Johnston his first experience in combat. He was sent to Florida as an aide to General Winfield Scott. After an unsuccessful campaign against the Seminoles, Scott had failed to satisfy his civilian superiors and was forced to face a court of inquiry. Johnston's career was not damaged, but the experience taught him that the military service was not free from politics. Scott was replaced and his successor, General Thomas S. Jesup, accomplished what Scott had not. With the signing of a peace treaty in 1837, Johnston resigned from the army with the intention of becoming an engineer.

Although he had recently been promoted to first lieutenant, Johnston's prospects at that time seemed uncertain. The low pay of an army officer had been a major consideration in his leaving the army. In the 1830s, a second lieutenant earned less than $800 a year—engineers could command as much as five times that amount in the civilian world. Only five months later, war resumed again with the Seminoles. Johnston volunteered to serve in a civilian capacity. In January 1838, he was caught in an ambush and took command when all the military leaders were wounded. "The coolness, courage and judgment he displayed at the most critical and trying emergency was the theme of praise with everyone who beheld him," a companion later reported.

The war in Florida sputtered on for several more years. One by one, small bands of Seminoles surrendered and were moved to the trans-Mississippi West. Johnston was not yet finished with the Seminoles; he would return again in 1842 to serve as assistant adjutant general. But in April 1838, he left the war behind and returned to the army as first lieutenant in the newly formed Corps of Topographical Engineers. In the same month, he was breveted to captain for his gallantry during the recent Everglades expedition. Johnston's brief civilian career had convinced him that his proper destiny was in the military after all.

When Johnston returned to the army, he was thirty-one years old and still single. He retained close ties with his family. His brother Charles died in 1832, leaving his two children without parents. Twelve-year-old Preston was adopted by his uncles, and Johnston offered himself as a surrogate father. He asked Preston "to regard me not as a formal old uncle, but as a brother." Their association became close, Johnston writing that his feelings were both "fatherly and brotherly." He took a father's pride in Preston's achievements and later encouraged him to enter West Point.

Surrogate parenthood was rewarding, but at thirty-one, Johnston was a prime candidate for marriage and a family of his own. While involved in a coastal survey, Joseph lost his heart to Lydia McLane of Baltimore. He had known her brother, Robert, also a West Point graduate in the Seminole War, and the two served together as engineers along the Canadian border. The McLanes were one of Delaware's prominent families. Lydia's father had served in both houses of Congress, as minister to England, and in Jackson's cabinet. Joseph and Lydia were married on July 10, 1845.

Lydia was not beautiful, but she fascinated both men and women by her grace and wit. The greatest disappointment of their long marriage was that they had no children. The void was filled somewhat by Joseph's nephew Preston, who had recently graduated from West Point. Lydia's frequent illness was a constant concern for Joseph; she had to make regular trips to hot springs and spas in pursuit of relief. Twenty years later, when Lydia's illness began to age her beyond her years, she worried that her husband would no longer find her attractive. He wrote to assure her that was not the case: "Do you really think that what you describe would affect your appearance to me? Do you know that I see your face with my heart, and that it is as lovely to me now—that it gives me as much happiness to look at it—as it did when you were eighteen?"

In 1846, when Johnston learned that the United States was at war with Mexico, he requested immediate assignment to that theater. He was thus ordered to join the invasion force commanded by General Winfield Scott as they prepared to advance on Mexico City. At first Johnston was assigned as an engineer—along with Robert E. Lee, Pierre G. T. Beauregard, George McClellan and other promising officers he would meet again during the Civil War. Once Scott had assembled his army, Johnston requested a combat command, which was granted and he was placed in command of a regiment known as the "voltigeurs."

The voltigeurs were a specially trained outfit of expert skirmishers who in Scott's army wore gray uniforms instead of the traditional blue. Johnston led his regiment on a reconnaissance in advance of the army. His mission was to advance until he made contact with the enemy and to hold the position until Scott could bring his main body into action. The voltigeurs encountered the Mexican Army under General Santa Anna, and during their initial brush with his troops, Johnston was wounded twice.

Johnston was badly hurt, but his wounds were not life threatening. In recognition of his bravery, he was breveted to lieutenant colonel. Johnston was able to recover from his wounds in time to lead his voltigeurs in the battles of Padierna, Contreras, Cherubusco, Molino del Rey, and Chapultepec. During their advance up the slopes of Chapultepec, Johnston was hit three times. Despite his wounds, he continued to lead his men forward. His bravery under fire was rewarded with a citation from General Scott: "Johnston is a great soldier, but has the unfortunate knack of getting himself shot in nearly every engagement."

During the war, Johnston was to suffer a severe loss. His nephew Preston was killed in action. For Johnston, the great tragedy of the war was Preston's death. In his heart, he had adopted Preston as his son. Johnston never fully recovered from the loss. More than forty years later, he reminded a friend how clever and winning Preston had been. "When Lee came to tell me of Preston's death," Johnston recalled, "he wept as he took my hand." Johnston ended his war in Mexico in military glory, but the loss of Preston plunged him into deep sorrow.

In 1848, Johnston came home to the dull routine of an engineer; but the thrill of combat remained fresh in his mind. He transferred to the cavalry in 1855 and two years later, when his friend McClellan left the army, Johnston also considered resigning. In a letter to McClellan he wrote: "There is no one left in the regiment or army to take your place. I wish I was young enough to resign too."

In 1858, Johnston was transferred to Washington. When the post of quartermaster general became available in 1860, he was considered along with Albert Sidney Johnston, Robert E. Lee, and Charles F. Smith. Joseph Johnston was selected, and he was promoted to brigadier general. He now outranked his contemporaries, and in time he hoped to become the army's senior officer. As quartermaster general, Johnston's principal responsibility was managing the supplies and accounts for the army, administering a budget of over $7 million. General Johnston carried out his assignment despite the controversy over secession. When Virginia left the Union in April 1861, Johnston had to make an important decision.

The crisis over secession caused Johnston a great deal of personal anguish. He was not a proponent of slavery, and he doubted that secession was a Constitutional right. But he did believe in the right of revolution as a natural principle of a free government as expressed in the Declaration of Independence. For all his agonizing, one thing was clear to him—his strongest loyalty was to Virginia. He would serve his state in any capacity that he could. If Virginia remained in the Union, so would he; if she left, Johnston would go with her.

Winfield Scott pleaded with Johnston to stay at his post. He even tried to get Johnston's wife, who had been born in Baltimore, to keep her husband from resigning. "[He] cannot stay in an army that is about to invade his native land,"

Lydia told Scott. Scott replied, "Then let him leave our army, but do not let him join theirs." Lydia Johnston had doubts of her own about the wisdom of her husband joining the Confederacy. She knew that Jefferson Davis, who had since become president of the Confederacy, disliked her husband. "[Davis] has power," she told her husband. "He will ruin you."

Johnston, however, felt obligated to defend his native Virginia, and submitted his resignation to General Scott. He left everything but his father's Revolutionary War sword behind him in Washington and headed for Richmond.

The trip south for Johnston was not a happy one. After thirty-five years of service in the United States Army, his leaving provided him no joy. The Johnstons arrived in Richmond on April 25. Johnston went immediately to see Governor John Letcher to offer his services. Letcher had already named Robert E. Lee major general in command of all of Virginia's troops. On Lee's advice, he offered Johnston the same rank, placing him in command of the forces around Richmond. Johnston accepted.

Johnston's personality and bearing made a strong impression on both officers and men. In short time he was able to bring order to his command. Keeping busy with the countless demands of his work helped distract him from his sadness.

When the Virginia convention met nearly two weeks later, they decided that the state should have only one major general; it would be Lee. Letcher offered Johnston a brigadier general's commission, but he turned it down. He instead accepted a brigadier's rank in the Confederate army. Johnston knew that the Confederate Congress planned to elevate brigadiers to full generals in the near future; he expected an automatic promotion to general as soon as the policy became effective.

Lydia Johnston left Richmond for Montgomery for safety reasons. One of her friends explained the reason for her move: "If one must be in a revolution . . . the center is more desirable than the circumference."

In May, Johnston met with Jefferson Davis to discuss his position in the Confederate army. For weeks, Davis had actively sought Johnston's presence. The new president needed a man with Johnston's accomplishments and talents for consultation and leadership. Johnston accepted a position in the field with orders appointing him commander at Harpers Ferry.

In this moment of crisis, Jefferson Davis anticipated great things from him, but Johnston never lived up to these expectations. Like his good friend McClellan, Johnston had a presence about him that impressed onlookers. He appeared every bit a soldier, even in civilian clothing. The fifty-four-year-old Johnston sported a grayish-white Van Dyke beard and, despite his slight frame, was deceptively powerful. Johnston carried himself well; he was graceful, elegant, and had a gentlemanly manner. Johnston exuded a magnetism that drew people to him, and he was quick to establish an intimate rapport with his troops. Johnston cared for his men, fulfilling their needs whenever possible and looking out for their welfare. In return, his soldiers loved him.

This charisma extended to the officer corps as well. Some of the best-known leaders of the Confederacy professed their friendship and esteem for Johnston. J. E. B. Stuart called him his best friend, and James Longstreet longed to return to service under him. Those who treated Johnston with dignity and respect found him to be warm and became his lifelong friend.

But Johnston had problems too, less visible flaws that inhibited his success at the highest levels. Johnston was by no means dysfunctional; rather, he lacked the capacity to grow to the level that both the war and Davis had expected. His problems surfaced in his first assignment. After two days at Harpers Ferry, Johnston's appraisal of the situation was that it could not be defended with the small force he had. He told the authorities in Richmond that he felt the town as "untenable by us at present against a strong enemy." It was his best judgment, he said, that the men under his command could be better used in defending the Shenandoah Valley. To stand and fight at Harpers Ferry might be a gallant act, he conceded, but at best his unit would be removed from the war, and that, he argued, would do no one any good.

Finally, after an exchange of correspondence with the War Department in Richmond, he was allowed to pull back to Winchester and occupy a position that would allow him to move with ease to prevent an invasion of the valley. Johnston's realistic evaluation of the situation at Harpers Ferry should have marked him as a commander with a good grasp of strategy; instead, he was considered by those in Richmond as a general who was reluctant to fight.

From the outset, the pattern was set. Johnston, a consummate realist, recommended actions he considered prudent for the safety of his command, a military policy that he believed should be adopted by the Confederacy for conducting the war. President Davis and the War Department held the opposite view, believing that every point of the Confederacy ought to be held. In one sense, it had to be that way. Davis's problems were complex, and Johnston was not in a position to fully understand them. It was not an easy task to weld a nation into a unit capable of fighting a war. Davis was forced to observe the rights of the states within the Confederacy. Each state wanted its territory protected and not occupied by enemy troops. Johnston, however, had little concern for such political matters. His professional standards required him to stick strictly to military considerations and the welfare of his men. Given the wide difference in their positions and their ideas of how the war should be fought, it was inevitable that Davis and Johnson would clash.

Johnston emerged as one of the early heroes of the Confederacy when he hurried his command from the Shenandoah Valley to Manassas. Although arriving on the field after the enemy was engaged, he was senior in command and directed his men toward the Federal attack in time to halt their advance at Henry House Hill. Confederate reinforcements later in the day gave the South its first major victory.

Shortly after nightfall, Davis met with Johnston for a briefing on the day's events. Davis urged a vigorous pursuit, but Johnston convinced him that prudence demanded a delay. Not long after the battle at Manassas, the relationship between Davis and Johnston began to show signs of strain. When Lee assigned an officer to Johnston's staff, Johnston refused to accept the man. Davis endorsed Johnston's written reply with a single word, "Insubordinate." A few days later, Johnston challenged another order from Lee. Because he outranked Lee, he said, "such orders I cannot regard, because they are illegal." Davis again noted on Johnston's reply, "Insubordinate."

The controversy over rank stemmed from a congressional law that created the grade of general and established rank. As the highest-ranking officer in the U.S. Army who had resigned, Johnston argued that he deserved the highest rank in the Confederate army, in accordance with the law. Davis interpreted the maze of regulations differently.

In addition to his conflict with Johnston, Davis also had clashes with Beauregard. It was less a disagreement over strategy than an irreconcilable conflict in personalities. Unlike Lincoln, who could shrug off a snub by McClellan, Davis was—as a Richmond editor wrote—"ready for any quarrel with any and everybody, at any time and all times." Davis settled his disputes with Beauregard simply by sending the general westward, out of the limelight. But Davis's problem with Johnston ran deeper, dating back—as rumor had it—to a dispute over a woman when they were both cadets at West Point.

Johnston was genial and generous with subordinates, but just as touchy as Davis when challenged. Because Johnston was so highly regarded by his fellow officers, Davis felt obliged to treat him more cautiously than he had Beauregard. Their differences were exacerbated when the president tried to settle the issue of rank. Davis nominated five soldiers for the rank of full general, placing Johnston fourth on the seniority list, despite the fact he had outranked all others in the prewar U.S. Army. Davis tried to explain his action on the grounds that Johnston had been a staff, not a line officer. It was obviously a poor excuse, for Davis had topped his list with General Samuel Cooper, who had also been a staff officer.

Johnston, of course, was disappointed and his pride was hurt. He wrote a nine-page letter to the president, protesting the attempt "to tarnish my fair name as a soldier and a man." Davis's reply was brief and scathing: "I have just received and read your letter of the 12th instant. Its language is, as you say, unusual; its arguments and statements utterly one sided, and its insinuations as unfounded as they are unbecoming."

Over the next few months, Davis and Johnston maintained a polite working relationship. But in the spring of 1862, another feud erupted. This time Johnston had acted against Davis's policy of defending Confederate territory whenever possible. Davis was shocked when he learned that Johnston had retreated from Manassas; worse yet, in his retreat, Johnston abandoned or destroyed quantities of equipment, food, and personal baggage. Johnston's retreat had been without Davis's authority. Now Davis ordered him to select a new position "as far in advance as consistent with your safety."

Johnston repeatedly and energetically advocated a strategy of concentration. He urged that troops be moved from the coastal positions and secondary theaters to achieve the critical mass needed for a decisive victory. To Johnston, territory was just that, space that could be abandoned and traded for time and the massing of troops until the enemy could be engaged in an all-out battle. Davis was aware that such a strategy was politically impossible. Congress would block any move that would leave areas of the Confederacy undefended, fearing it would demoralize its residents. Davis also realized that once Southern territory had been abandoned, it would be ruined for slavery; the possibility of forcing freed slaves back into the system would be virtually impossible.

During the Peninsula Campaign of May 1862, Johnston again repeated his familiar pattern of retreating, this time up the peninsula until Federal troops approached to within sight of Richmond—all without engaging in a single major battle. When Davis asked what Johnston's plans were to stop the Union advance, his only response was vague generalities. Despite Johnston's attitude, Davis was reluctant to relieve him. He believed Johnston had won the confidence of his men and that removing him would be bad for morale, particularly in the midst of an important campaign.

As the retreating Confederates reached the outskirts of Richmond, Davis placed pressure on Johnston to engage the enemy: "If you will not give battle, I will appoint someone to command who will." Under this threat, Johnston launched the attacks that resulted in the battles of Fair Oaks and Seven Pines. The audacity of the Confederate attacks drove the Union troops back. While Johnston was trying to figure out his next move, he was severely wounded and carried from the field.

Lee was appointed to take Johnston's place, and the fame of the Army of Northern Virginia began. Shortly after his appointment, Lee wrote a message to Mrs. Johnston: "The President has thought it necessary that I take his place. I wish I was able, or that his mantle had fallen on an abler man." When Johnston learned that Davis was sending reinforcements to Lee, he said: "Then, my wound was fortunate; it is concentration which I earnestly recommended, but had not the influence to effect. Lee had made them do for him what they would not do for me."

Johnston's wounds were severe, and he was unable to return to action for six months. During that time, Robert E. Lee was able to weld the army into one of the finest fighting machines ever commanded by an American.

While recovering from his wounds, Johnston became friends with Confederate Senator Louis T. Wigfall, who was prominent in the anti-Davis faction in Congress. As a result, Johnston became not only a factor in Confederate politics but also a player. Davis, who viewed all attacks on him as treasonous, now thought of Johnston as a political enemy whose motives were suspect. Johnston was doomed to be out of favor in Richmond for the rest of the war and to stay in Lee's shadow.

Davis's confidence in Johnston had been shaken somewhat by the general's apparent willingness to retreat right up through Richmond without a fight. But Davis still believed Johnston could be of value to the Confederacy. A month after Johnston was wounded, Davis wrote to Johnston's wife: "General J. E. Johnston is steadily and rapidly improving. I wish he was able to take the field. Despite the critics, who know military affairs by instinct, he is a good soldier . . . and could at this time render most valuable service." Davis was bombarded by politicians and generals with requests that Johnston be given overall command in the Western theater.

On November 12, 1862, Johnston reported himself fit for duty. It would take nearly a year for him to heal completely, and for some months to come, he lacked the stamina for active campaigning. But in November, he was given overall theater command of Confederate forces between the Applachian Mountains and the Mississippi River. From the beginning, Confederate forces in the West had taken one beating after another. Union General Ulysses S. Grant had defeated Generals Albert Sidney Johnston and Pierre G. T. Beauregard. Confederate Generals Braxton Bragg and Kirby Smith had led drives into eastern Kentucky, but by mid-October they had been driven back. The naming of Johnston was not the answer to the problems in the West, but the appointment was good politics and an excellent morale booster. Johnston was admired and respected by the citizens of the western states.

Johnston arrived in Chattanooga on December 4, 1862, to take up his command. Almost immediately, he became embroiled in a quarrel with Davis over the disposition of troops along the Mississippi. Johnston recognized that the river port of Vicksburg was strategically important to the Confederacy. He tried to get Davis to authorize the transfer of more troops to the Vicksburg area to join Pemberton's force. Davis refused. In the meantime, Grant had clearly committed his forces to the capture of Vicksburg. Johnston differed with the field commander General Pemberton, who against Johnston's advice withdrew his troops into Vicksburg.

When Grant attacked Vicksburg, Johnston, fearing Pemberton would be trapped, ordered him to evacuate the city and join him. But Pemberton believed that Vicksburg had to be held at all costs. With his small force, Johnston saw no profit in attacking Grant. Rather, Johnston watched while Pemberton lost his army and the city. Davis blamed Johnston for Pemberton's surrender, insisting that he had not done enough to break the siege. Johnston and Davis continued their feud in a series of public letters. When Johnston's wife advised her husband to resign, the General replied that he was not serving Davis but a people who had never been anything but kind to him.

The fall of Vicksburg had momentous consequences. It effectively ended Pemberton's career as a general (though he was exchanged within weeks) and brought the tension between Davis and Johnston to open hostility. The Confederacy had lost what Davis would call "the nailhead that held the South's two halves together." It was a tremendous blow to Southern morale and freed Grant's army for use elsewhere, turning the focus of the war in the West exclusively to Tennessee.

By the end of November, Grant had defeated Bragg at Chattanooga and had driven the Army of Tennessee back into Georgia. Bragg asked Davis to be relieved, and his request was granted. Davis offered the command to Lee, who declined. Finally, realizing there was no one else he could turn to, the president appointed Johnston as commander of the Army of Tennessee. Pleased with the appointment, Johnston delayed making the announcement of the change, because Bragg's wife was critically ill at the time and Johnston wanted to spare Bragg's feelings.

Johnston spent the winter of 1863–1864 refitting and reviving the army and preparing for the coming campaign against William T. Sherman. Because of his inferior numbers, Johnston's basic strategy was to use part of his army as a shield and then counterattack when the opportunity presented itself. As usual, Davis thought otherwise. Braxton Bragg, now Davis's chief military adviser, informed Johnston that Davis expected him to recapture Tennessee. Johnston felt his army was too weak to undertake such a venture, and he said so. But as the weeks went by, the pressure on Johnston mounted. Davis continued to emphasize his desire for a bold advance.

Johnston was not, as his critics maintained, afraid to fight. Rather, he saw no reason to expose the Army of Tennessee to senseless slaughter. Sooner or later, he knew Sherman would attack. Once he had defeated the Union force, a Confederate offensive might be possible. For the time being and until he received reinforcements, he would stay where he was.

Just as he did in the face of McClellan's army, Johnston intended to fight on the defensive, hoping for Sherman to make a mistake and leave an opening for a counterattack. Several times, Johnston planned to deliver a blow against Sherman, only to see the opportunity slip away. Davis grumbled, yet continued to send aid and support to Johnston, though he was growing increasingly impatient with Johnston's lack of aggression. Behind the scenes, Lieutenant General John Bell Hood, an ambitious corps commander in Johnston's army, had begun sending a stream of letters to the president, stating that the army was in top shape "and eager for the fray." Davis said nothing to Johnston of Hood's betrayal, nor did he question the truth of his reports, which merely reinforced what Davis suspected all along; Johnston had spurned the offensive. To investigate the situation, Davis sent Braxton Bragg. As a former army commander and a man beholden to Davis for his current position, Bragg could hardly act objectively. Bragg informed Davis that "I cannot learn that he has any more plan for the future than he had in the past." Davis had to act. He did not want to lose Atlanta, a major industrial center and a critical railroad junction vital to the Confederate war effort.

Removing Johnston from command was a decision over which Davis agonized. Despite his personal feelings about Johnston, he was reluctant to remove him. Yet Davis knew the vital importance of holding Atlanta. Had he been able to foresee that Johnston would give up mountainous northern Georgia and retreat to the gates of Atlanta without a major battle, Davis would have removed him earlier. Davis kept hoping that Johnston would find an appropriate place to stand and fight.

That was it. Davis had given Johnston one last opportunity to attack the enemy. The next evening, a message arrived for Johnston from the adjutant general: "Since you have failed to arrest the advance of the enemy to the vicinity of Atlanta . . . express no confidence that you can defeat or repel him, you are hereby relieved from command of the Army and Department of Tennessee." John Bell Hood was appointed to take Johnston's place.

The reactions to Johnston's removal were not favorable. "An universal gloom cast over the army," wrote Halsey Wigfall to his family. It was not because the men feared Hood's ability, but it came from their "love for and confidence in Johnston." As some of the units passed Johnston's headquarters, they lifted their hats. "There was no cheering! We simply passed silently, with heads uncovered," wrote Colonel J. C. Nisbet of the 66th Georgia. "Some of the officers broke ranks and grasped his hand, as the tears poured down their cheeks."

Before Johnston left that day, he received a note from a brigade commander who told him that his officers and men received news of his removal "in silence and deep sorrow. We feel that in parting with you as our commanding general our loss is irreparable, and that this army and our country loses one of its ablest, most zealous and patriotic defenders." So strong were the feelings of some of Johnston's men that there was fear that they might "throw down their muskets and quit." In their opinion, Johnston's leadership had enabled them to hold off an enemy superior in all but spirit. Dissatisfaction over the removal of Johnston also reached the general staff. Generals Hardee and Mackall asked to be relieved. Mackall, Johnston's chief of staff, received permission to leave the army within a week after Johnston's departure.

For five months, Johnston stayed at home, standing on the sidelines as the Confederate war effort fizzled out. The fall of Atlanta and the destruction of the Army of Tennessee under Hood in the Franklin-Nashville Campaign forced Davis to relieve Johnston of command. With Sherman preparing to move into the Carolinas, Davis once again called on Johnston, appointing him commander of the Army of Tennessee. Without adequate troops this time, Johnston faced overwhelming odds in trying to stop Sherman. Johnston was able to launch one last attack at Bentonville, North Carolina. The attack slowed part of Sherman's army and held his old adversary in check for two days until he was once again flanked. To the end of his life, Johnston always contended that he had won both the first and last Confederate victories.

Over the next few weeks, Johnston's only hope rested with Lee; he hoped, somehow, that the two armies would be able to link up and deal first with Sherman and then with Grant. The unification never happened. Lee surrendered at Appomattox on April 9.

After Lee's surrender, Johnston realized that the war was irrevocably lost. He met with Davis one final time during Davis's flight south, hoping to explain his intention to surrender to Sherman.

The meeting was held on the second-floor bedroom of a private home in Greensboro, North Carolina. In attendance were Davis's cabinet and General Beauregard. The president began by making a few conversational remarks and then turned to Johnston, saying: "I have requested you and General Beauregard, General Johnston, to join us this evening, that we may have the benefit of your views." Davis's opinion was that the situation was "terrible" but "not fatal." "I think we can whip the enemy if our people turn out." There was an awkward silence in the room as everyone waited for Johnston to respond. Johnston remained silent and had to be prompted by Davis: "We would like to have your views, General Johnston."

Then, in his "terse, concise, demonstrative way," Johnston began to speak. "My views, sir," he said, "are that our people are tired of war, feel themselves whipped, and will not fight. Our country is overrun, its military resources greatly diminished, while the enemy's military power and resources were never greater and may be increased to any extent desired. . . . My men are daily deserting in large numbers and are stealing my artillery teams to aid their escapes to their homes. Since Lee's surrender they regard the war as at an end. If I march out of North Carolina, her people will all leave my ranks. . . . My small force is melting away like snow before the sun, and I am hopeless of recruiting it." Davis did not look up while Johnston spoke, but sat quietly, "with his eyes fixed on a scrap of paper, which he was folding and unfolding abstractly."

Davis's head was still bowed even after Johnston had finished. There was absolute silence for what seemed like several minutes. Finally President Davis asked General Beauregard what his feelings were. "I concur in all General

Johnston has said," he replied. Davis asked the cabinet members their opinion. Only Judah Benjamin, loyal to the end, believed they should continue to fight. "Well, General Johnston," Davis said at last, "what do you propose?"

Johnston suggested that he be allowed to negotiate peace with Sherman. After a pause, Davis said, "Well sir, you can adopt this course, though I confess I am not sanguine as to the ultimate results." Davis dictated a letter and Johnston signed it. The letter was delivered to Sherman.

On April 17, Johnston met with Sherman in the home of James Bennett near Raleigh, North Carolina. Sherman drew a telegram from his pocket and passed it to Johnston; it contained the news of the assassination of President Lincoln two days earlier. After Johnston read it, he said, "It was the greatest possible calamity" that could befall the South, and he hoped that Sherman did not think that it was the result of a Southern plot. Sherman assured him he did not think the Confederate army had anything to do with it, but he would not say the same for Jefferson Davis. Johnston did not respond.

Sherman originally offered Johnston the same terms that Grant had offered Lee at Appomattox: The men would surrender their arms and go home on parole. The next day, Secretary of War John Breckinridge met with Sherman and Johnston. Sherman brought with him a memorandum proposing the dissolution of all Southern armies and the restoration and recognition of state governments. Johnston rode away from the James Bennett House, thinking he had signed the document that ended the war. But it was not to be.

A few days later, the offer was rescinded when Federal officials and the press learned of the generous offer made by Sherman. Johnston was not willing to ask his men to shed any more blood. Finally, on April 26, Johnston formally surrendered his army. For the rest of his life, Davis would consider Johnston's decision to surrender his army—when he was neither surrounded nor defeated—an act of treachery.

On May 2, 1865, Johnston said good-bye for the last time to the Army of Tennessee in a general order:

> *Comrades: In terminating our official relations I most earnestly exhort you to observe faithfully the terms of pacification agreed upon, and to discharge the obligations of good and peaceful citizens at your home as well as you have performed the duties of thorough soldiers in the field . . . with the admiration of people, won by the courage and noble devotion you have displayed in the long war. . . . I now part with you with deep regret, and bid you farewell with feelings of cordial friendship and with earnest wishes that you may have hereafter all the prosperity and happiness to be found in the world.*

Johnston's critics have often asserted that he was defensive-minded and that he was not aggressive enough, thinking too much about the possibility of defeat and the necessity of retreat. The official records show that his tactics were often dictated by the circumstances and not by a preference on his part. On several occasions, while still in command in Virginia, Johnston had pressed Davis for reinforcements to allow him to take the offensive, but Davis did not honor that request. Lee's operations in the summer and fall of 1862 coincided with Johnston's suggested strategy in the spring. There was, however, a difference between Johnston's and Lee's modes of operation. Whereas Johnston was willing to take the offensive, provided he was given the necessary strength, Lee was always willing to begin an offensive operation with what he had.

Although the war was over, for Joseph Johnston another one was just beginning. For the rest of his life, he would fight a rearguard action in defense of his reputation. He became obsessed with setting the record straight, and he could think of no better way than to discredit Jefferson Davis, his most prominent detractor. This became a personal tragedy for him. Johnston's legalistic excuses for the defeat of his army and his public attack of Davis, a man the South considered a martyr, ended up tarnishing his own reputation. His obsession brought him no satisfaction and embittered his remaining years. After his death, one of his friends wrote sadly of his behavior: "If General Johnston had never written anything . . . how much better it would have been."

Before Johnston took up the pen to justify his war record, he had to find work to make a living; his defense had to wait. For more than thirty-five years, he had made his way as a soldier. He took pride in his ability as an engineer, having pioneered railroad construction in Texas in the 1850s. When a position as president of the Mobile & Ohio Railroad became available, he sought the job. When the position went to someone else, he was despondent, saying, "I have had another defeat." As his wife's health continued to deteriorate, it became important for him to find work.

Johnston found temporary employment with the National Express and Transportation Company. When the company failed, he took another position as president of the Selma, Rome, & Dalton Railroad. He didn't enjoy the work, claiming he was bored. Finally, he found permanent employment in the insurance business. Recognizing the power of his name, a London insurance company invited him to become a manager of its southern department. He established Joseph E. Johnston & Company, agent for the Liverpool and London Globe Insurance Company, with headquarters in Savannah. Johnston offered former Confederate officers positions with the firm. Within four years, he was in charge of 120 agents in Georgia, Alabama, and Mississippi. This new security allowed him time to work on his memoirs.

Johnston wrote to former corps and division commanders, requesting that they send him any papers and information they might have about the war. In some cases, he wrote his recollections of particular events, requesting confirmation or correction. In one situation, he wrote to William Mackall, his former chief of staff, "Do you remember that Hood urged the abandoning of every position we held long before anybody else thought of it? If so, please state the fact with some fullness." When he didn't get the response he was hoping for, he made suggestions to Mackall: "I enclose a copy of your letter in relation to the Georgia campaign and beg you to reconsider certain parts of it." He was concerned that the exact words be used, writing: "Don't you think the word 'compelled' unnecessarily unfavorable?"

It was pretty clear that Johnston was trying to build a case against Hood. He had not forgotten Hood's underhanded correspondence to Davis nor Hood's role in having him replaced as commander of the Army of Tennessee. Johnston was also interested in gathering evidence showing that Jefferson Davis contributed heavily to the defeat of the Confederacy. But Davis was an unfortunate target. After spending two years in the Fort Monroe prison, he proved to be better as a martyr than as a president. During his incarceration, Davis's strongest critics forgave him; even his jailers developed respect for his courage. With this in mind, Wade Hampton wrote to Johnston in 1870, advising him not to pursue his feud with Davis. Hampton felt the feud would affect the unity necessary for the South to survive: "I feel sure no good could come in any way by any publication by you raising an issue on the point. Any controversy between Mr. Davis and yourself would jar upon the feelings of thousands who are friendly to both of you and would tend to throw discredit on our cause . . . Do not allow yourself to be drawn into any personal altercation." It was good advice, but it went unheeded.

Johnston's lengthy volume, entitled *Narrative of Military Operations Directed During the Late War Between the States*, appeared in 1874. It was essentially a brief against Jefferson Davis. Johnston was not a gifted writer, and his heavy reliance on official correspondence and legalistic arguments made the book very boring to read. It did not sell well; the publisher failed to make a profit. The poor reception of the book was a disappointment to Johnston. The book failed not only financially but also in its purpose. His argumentative tone betrayed his continuing resentment and bitterness. Davis wrote to his wife that "Johnston has more effectively than another could show his selfishness and his malignity." Unfortunately for Johnston, the book angered not only his targets—Davis, Bragg, and Hood—but also some of his friends.

Hood was quick to respond to Johnston's memoirs. In his official report, written during the war, Hood had insisted that Johnston had already destroyed the Army of Tennessee before he took command. Now Hood elaborated on the theme, claiming that Johnston's campaign had been nothing but a long series of errors of omission and commission. He stressed Johnston's reputation as a "retreating" general, stating that Johnston had allowed General Sherman to push him back one hundred miles in sixty-two days into the heart of the Confederacy without one major engagement. It was easier for Hood to attack Johnston than to defend his own record. What Hood had failed to include in his memoirs was that during Johnston's retreat, he had not made one mistake of which Sherman could take advantage.

Hood finished his book, entitled *Advance and Retreat* in 1879, but that same year, he and his wife both died suddenly. Just as the end of the war had prevented Johnston from responding to Hood's official report, now Hood's sudden death denied him the opportunity of responding to Hood's memoirs. At the same time, Jefferson Davis was writing his memoirs. *The Rise and Fall of the Confederate Government* was published in 1881. Davis refused to engage in mudslinging and devoted most of his effort to defending the legitimacy of secession and the rightness of the Southern cause. Thus, Davis had defeated Johnston again. This time, Davis's restraint in criticizing Johnston belied his claim that Davis's actions against him had been motivated throughout the war by animosity. A comparison of the two memoirs would suggest that all the animosity had been on Johnston's part.

Johnston continued to write articles to defend his actions during the war. He closed his series of articles by defending his conduct of the 1864 campaign: "Mr. Davis condemned me for not fighting. General Sherman's testimony and that of the Military Cemetery at Marietta refute the charge." It is ironic that Johnston's comrades in arms, Beauregard, Hood, Bragg, and Davis, were all offended by his public writing, while his former adversaries, especially Grant and Sherman, strongly supported him. Johnston was pleased to read in both Sherman's and Grant's memoirs that they respected him as a dangerous opponent but were critical of both Hood and Davis.

When comparing the behavior of Lee and Johnston after the war, there are clear differences. Lee adopted a dignified silence on questions concerning the war and accepted all responsibility for his actions. The South concluded that he was not responsible at all, and elevated him to sainthood after his death. To the contrary, Johnston's continued insistence that he was not at fault led many to assume he was probably guilty.

Like most professional army officers, Johnston had shown little interest in politics. Johnston's prominence caused his Richmond friends to consider him a good candidate to run for Congress. Astutely, they maneuvered other aspirants out of the contest until Johnston was the only Democratic candidate.

The spirited race caused Johnston's supporters to worry about finances. They did not want to discuss the matter with him, knowing that he believed a large expenditure of money was paramount to purchasing the seat and would resign his candidacy if this became an issue. A close friend called upon Mrs. Johnston and advised her of the financial situation. Not wanting to see her husband disappointed if he lost the election, she offered to cash some of her bonds to provide the needed money. "If he's beat, it will be simply disgraceful and shameful! It will kill him. He shan't be beat; you must not allow it. I will not permit it," she said. They quickly raised additional funds and did not need her bonds, so they were returned to her.

Johnston was elected, and when he took his seat in the 46th Congress in 1879, he found among its members a number of old Confederates. More important to him was the presence of two of his kin—his nephew, John Warfield Johnston, and his brother-in-law, Robert M. McLane. As a member of the House, Johnston served on the Military Affairs Committee and the Committee on Levees and Improvement of the Mississippi River. His chief interest seems to have been in improving the efficiency of the army and those matters affecting local Virginia problems. After his two-year term was up, Johnston did not consider running for reelection.

Soon after he left Congress, Johnston was involved in another controversy with Jefferson Davis. In a conversation with a reporter—Frank A. Burr—that he believed to be private and off the record, Johnston charged that Davis had failed to account for $2 million in gold, which the government had carried from Richmond in 1865. Shortly afterward, the *Philadelphia Press* carried the story in what was purported to be an interview by Burr with Johnston. Johnston immediately wrote a disclaimer, but it was neither firm nor explicit. Davis's supporters kept the episode alive to degrade Johnston in any way they could. Johnston's failure to make a strong denial of the reported accusation placed him in a position for more criticism.

The Democratic party finally won the White House in 1884 when Grover Cleveland was elected president. Johnston was seriously considered for a cabinet post and the position of secretary of war, even though he was a former Confederate general and now seventy-six years old. Johnston finally was appointed U.S. commissioner of railroads.

By the beginning of 1887, Lydia's health was poorer than ever. Despite her numerous trips to spas, there was no improvement. On February 22, 1887, at the age of sixty-five, she died. Her death devastated Johnston. For the rest of his life, he could not bring himself to write or speak her name. He compensated by working even harder.

Johnston lost his federal position in 1888 when President Cleveland left office. Retiring to his home in Washington, Johnston still had time to attend Confederate memorial ceremonies. At one ceremony in Georgia, Johnston was assigned to share an open carriage with Edmund Kirby Smith. The parade had just begun when a voice from the crowd shouted: "That's Johnston! That's Joe Johnston!" With that, hundreds of men burst from the crowd and surrounded his carriage, stretching out their hands to their old commander. Someone unhitched the horses, and members of the crowd pulled the carriage the length of the parade route, cheering wildly. The fact that his former troops continued to show their devotion for him brought tears to his eyes.

The very next month, Johnston was in Richmond helping to dedicate a huge equestrian statue of Robert E. Lee. By 1890, the shame of defeat had been replaced by pride. "I felt," one witness wrote, "as though I was assisting at a combined funeral and resurrection."

Funerals were a regular part of Johnston's life now. In 1885, he served as a pallbearer at Grant's funeral. Later in the year, he did the same for his old friend and wartime adversary George McClellan. In the winter of 1891, Johnston traveled to New York to attend Sherman's funeral.

Johnston's duty as a pallbearer was strictly honorary, but he stood bareheaded in the cold rain as the coffin was carried from Sherman's house to the caisson. "General," someone said, "please put on your hat. You might get sick." Johnston refused, saying, "If I were in his place and he were standing here in mine, he would not put on his hat."

This attitude was typical of Joseph Johnston's stubborn insistence on doing what he believed was right rather than what was expedient. He had behaved in this manner all his life, and although he was eighty-four and tired, he would not let his own concern for his health prevent him from paying his last respects to Sherman. Earlier, his close adherence to the principles of a strict professional had cost him glory, support by his superiors, and command of the Army of Tennessee. His belief in custom would also cost him his life; he caught cold that day, and he died five weeks later. Tradition and honor were not to be set aside, no matter what the cost. With Johnston, there could be no compromise.

Johnston's funeral was held the day after he died. All day long, a stream of callers arrived at his residence on Connecticut Avenue. William Rosecrans and John Schofield, each of whom had led troops against Johnston in the field, were among the first to call. After the funeral, Johnston's body was moved to the Greenmount Cemetery in Baltimore, where his wife is buried. Newspapers across the South and throughout the North paid tribute to his memory. It was the "knightly soldier and spotless gentleman" they remembered now. But the best tribute of all came from the men who served in the ranks of his armies. It was Sam Watkins, infantryman of the 1st Tennessee Regiment, who offered the most appropriate epitaph: "Such a man was Joseph Johnston and such his record. Farewell, old fellow! We privates loved you because you made us love ourselves."

11

Cavalry Chevalier

PHIL SHERIDAN

H E was an unimpressive little man, only five feet five inches tall, with a large bullet-shaped head. His coarse black hair looked, as someone said, like it had been painted on his head. Abraham Lincoln described Phil Sheridan as a "brown, chunky little chap, with a long body, short legs, not enough neck to hang him, and such long arms that if his ankles itch he can scratch them without stooping." All his life, until his feats on the battlefield, people looked down their noses at him. It was not until Ulysses S. Grant put the matter in proper perspective that Sheridan received the respect he deserved. When told that his protege was "rather a little fellow," Grant stated, "You will find him big enough for the purpose before we get through with him."

"Put your faith in the common soldier," Sheridan was fond of saying, "and he will never let you down." He knew, because he himself was a common soldier. Of all the Union's preeminent generals, including Grant and Sherman, Sheridan came farther—on less—than anyone.

Sheridan was born on March 6, 1831. He was the third of six children born to John and Mary Meenagh Sheridan, second cousins who had lived as tenant farmers on the Cherrymount estate in northern Ireland before immigrating to America. Hoping to improve their lot, the couple made their way to Albany, New York, where they were disappointed not to find the streets paved with gold. There was nothing in Albany for them; construction gangs, however, were hiring on the National Road, the thoroughfare extending from the Chesapeake Bay to the Mississippi. Somerset, Ohio, with its large Catholic population and location on the National Road, seemed a good place to put down roots. Therefore, John joined one of the construction crews there.

The exact location of Sheridan's birthplace remains a mystery. In his memoirs, he wrote that he was born in Albany, New York; but during his life, he also claimed both Boston and Somerset, Ohio, as his birthplace. Although not conclusive, there is some evidence that he may have been born in Ireland—or in the middle of the Atlantic during the family's crossing. Young Phil was raised mostly by his mother. She was quiet, devout, and patriotic. Phil saw very little of his father, who was always off somewhere working on a road, canal, or railroad project.

At the age of ten, Phil began attending the one-room schoolhouse in Somerset. It was a typical nineteenth-century frontier education, four years in length. Sheridan and his classmates attained a passing acquaintance with the English language and learned a little arithmetic. The rest, in the time-honored tradition of American education, was left to them. Their education was frequently interrupted by whippings; one teacher, when unable to identify a transgressor, would switch the entire class.

Phil's childhood was typical of the time and place for small-town America. He larked about, skipped school, stole apples, played tricks on his teachers, and teased the town tramp. Sheridan's small size and unconventional appearance made him a target of the town bullies. Some children respond to such abuse with clowning, or servility, but little Phil fought back. He learned that a quick, brutal assault usually overcame heavy odds, and before long, only newcomers risked igniting his explosive temper.

School was not the only ground for young Phil Sheridan's learning; Finch's Tavern on the town square proved more enlightening. There, tough-talking Conestoga wagon drivers met and exchanged stories in a style of their own. Their creative way with language was legendary, and Sheridan would honor their craft. Each Fourth of July, the area's one surviving Revolutionary War veteran was brought out for an appearance on the courthouse steps. Sheridan and his friends would follow him about, dreaming of glory in a war of their own.

Little Phil was too young to fight in Mexico, but his resolve to become a soldier was firmly set by the time the war was over. To be considered for West Point, he would have to be nominated by a member of Congress, but neither he nor his family were in a position to exert much political influence. He waited for a chance—and one came in 1848, when a young man who had been nominated failed the entrance examination. Sheridan wrote to his congressman asking for an appointment. The response came promptly: a warrant for the class of 1848.

For the next few months, Sheridan painstakingly studied for the entrance examination. Somerset's current schoolmaster, Mr. Clark, assisted him as a tutor. When Phil took the examination, he found it unexpectedly easy. He met the minimal standards, gave his age as eighteen years and one month, and enrolled as a provisional cadet.

Sheridan recognized his educational shortcomings, particularly in algebra and mathematics, and applied himself to his studies. He was fortunate to have for a roommate a scholarly New Yorker named Henry Slocum. At night, long after taps had signaled lights out, the two cadets would hang a blanket over their window and continue to study. Sheridan, like most midwesterners and Southerners, found himself at a disadvantage with cadets from the East when it came to the educational background they brought to the academy. Contrary to the popular idea that West Point was dominated by aristocratic Southerners, most of the faculty and highest-ranking cadets came from the Northeast, where better schooling gave them a head start in the academy's classroom.

Sheridan, who had all he could do to keep up his grades, was also something of an outcast among the more favored students. Not only was he short, unattractive, argumentative, and poor, he was also Irish Catholic—all traits that lent themselves to goading by his classmates. On September 9, 1851, he was involved in a fight with Cadet Sergeant William Terrill, a Virginian with an arrogant manner. A nearby officer stepped in and saved Sheridan from a thrashing at the hands of the larger cadet, but nothing could save him from his actions; he was suspended from West Point for a year.

Nine months later, Sheridan was back at West Point, but in the interim, his original class had graduated. Sheridan's months away from the academy didn't help his disposition; he received more demerits in his last year than during the previous three years. When he graduated, he ranked thirty-fourth in a class of fifty-two, higher than most people had expected.

Sheridan's low class ranking disqualified him from duty in the more prestigious branches of the army. He was assigned as a brevet second lieutenant in Company D, 1st Infantry Regiment, garrisoned at Fort Duncan, Texas. There, he developed two habits that were to stay with him for the rest of his military career—he studied the local ground, making maps where none were available, and he attempted to learn the local language.

In November 1854, Sheridan was promoted to second lieutenant and transferred to the 4th Infantry Regiment at Fort Reading, California. The frenzy of the gold rush of 1849 had played out by then, and pragmatic mining corporations had taken over. The West was being civilized. The major barrier to this process was the original inhabitants of the land, the Native Americans.

Despite the moral implications, young Sheridan had no difficulty in carrying out his duties in fighting Indians. His view in accomplishing the task was uncomplicated by any thoughts of justice or feelings of sympathy. "They were a pitiable lot," he said, "almost naked, hungry and cadaverous." Sheridan had little opportunity to test his military prowess against the Indians. The problems were minor, and the army's various expeditions turned out to be pointless. Sheridan was involved in a few small skirmishes, which gave him the opportunity to gain experience under fire. For the next five years, Sheridan's job was primarily the policing of an Indian reservation in western Oregon. He showed no signs of discontent, learning to speak Chinook, making maps, and staying ready for whatever his government might ask.

By the spring of 1861, Sheridan had been a second lieutenant for nearly eight years. He had commanded small numbers of men in battle, been wounded, seen men killed, and experienced both good and bad examples of how an army officer should conduct himself. In the process, he had impressed his superiors with his work ethic, ingenuity, and diplomacy. He was thirty years old and in the prime of health.

News of the firing on Fort Sumter and the Battle of Bull Run reached the West Coast. As the Union military efforts expanded in succeeding months, Sheridan was promoted to captain and anxiously awaited orders to proceed east on active service. Meanwhile, he prided himself that "my patriotism was untainted by politics." To him, the "preservation of the Union" was the sole issue, and the question of slavery did not concern him.

After the Union defeat at Manassas in September, Sheridan was assigned to the 13th U.S. Infantry, located in Missouri. His first assignment was to audit the books of Major General Halleck's successor, Major General John Fremont. As always, Sheridan did his best, first straightening out the enormous confusion left by Fremont, then untangling the snarled supply and transportation system. The year 1862 found Sheridan still deeply involved in inventories and supplies. Sheridan discovered he had been buying horses for the army that were stolen from Missouri farmers. He confiscated the horses, refusing to pay the thieves. General Samuel Curtis, who saw no reason to protect the interests of farmers who were Southern sympathizers, ordered Sheridan to make the payment. When he refused, Curtis threatened to have him court-martialed. Appealing to General Halleck, Sheridan was transferred out of Curtis's command.

As late as April 1862, a "forlorn and disheartened" Sheridan longed for an opportunity to see action, but was still buying horses. His chance finally came in May, when the governor of Michigan offered him a colonelcy of the volunteer 2nd Michigan Cavalry. After receiving permission from General Halleck to accept the position, Sheridan pinned on borrowed eagles and joined his command. If Sheridan wanted action, then he found it. In the next thirty-five days, he would lead his regiment in six skirmishes and one full-scale battle.

A few days later, on June 11, Sheridan's brigade commander was promoted and Sheridan took over the brigade. He immediately established rapport with his men. "I had striven unceasingly to have them well fed and clothed, had personally looked after the selection of their camps, and had maintained such discipline as to allay former irritation," he said. His care extended beyond physical needs: "Whenever my authority would permit I saved my command from needless sacrifices and unnecessary toil; therefore, when hard or daring work was to be done, I expected the heartiest response and always got it." Within a few weeks, he said, "I had gained not only their confidence as soldiers, but their esteem and love as men."

His first important command of the brigade was at Boonesville, Mississippi, during the Corinth, Mississippi, Campaign. After Shiloh, General Beauregard had pulled his badly mauled army back toward Corinth to await reinforcements and resupply his men. Grant had not mounted a pursuit, believing his troops were too exhausted. The capture of Corinth was left to General Halleck. During the campaign, Sheridan found himself under attack and outnumbered four to one. His response was to detach several companies to ride, hooting and hollering, into the Confederate rear while he led a frontal attack. The two Federal attacks came off simultaneously, and the Confederate force broke and ran.

It was not a large or important engagement, but it did showcase Sheridan as a potential leader of men. His case was put succinctly in a telegram sent shortly afterward to General Halleck, signed by no fewer than five brigadier generals. "Brigadiers scarce; good ones scarcer," it read. "The undersigned respectfully beg that you will obtain the promotion of Sheridan. He is worth his weight in gold."

For a short time, however, the only change made was to add other regiments to Sheridan's brigade. Soon Sheridan and his troops would be transferred to Louisville to help oppose Confederate forces there. Grant had just replaced Halleck as department commander when he learned of Sheridan's transfer. Not wanting to lose a good fighter, he called Sheridan to Corinth to meet with him. There, he tried to countermand the transfer orders, but Sheridan balked at the idea; he wanted to go where the action was. Sheridan got his way, but he left an unfavorable impression on Grant.

When Sheridan reported to the commanding general at Louisville, William Nelson asked him why he was not wearing the proper insignia of his rank. Sheridan tried to defend himself, but before he finished, Nelson explained that this was his way of announcing Sheridan's promotion to brigadier general. Sheridan, who had hoped the war would last long enough for him to become a major, was now a brigadier general and a division commander in the Army of the Ohio.

In October, during the battle at Perryville, Kentucky, Sheridan's division held the center. On the left flank was another newly appointed brigadier general, William Terrill, the Virginian Sheridan had fought at West Point. Terrill's decision to remain in the Federal army had caused him and his family a great deal of pain; his father had been so incensed at his son's action that he wrote to him: "Your name shall be stricken from the family records." Terrill had distinguished himself at Shiloh. Meanwhile, his brother James was making an equally brilliant career as colonel of a Confederate regiment, fighting in Virginia under Jubal Early. Earlier Sheridan and Terrill met, shook hands, and put away their past feud. Only hours later, Terrill was killed. Two years later, James Terrill died in the battle at Cold Harbor. After the war, the Terrill family reconsidered William's choice of sides. In remembrance of their fallen sons, they erected a memorial bearing the inscription: "God Alone Knows Which Was Right."

In writing about the Battle of Perryville, Sheridan called it "an example of lost opportunities." "Had a skillful and energetic advance of the Union troops been made, instead of wasting precious time in slow and unnecessary tactical maneuvers," Sheridan said, "the enemy could have been destroyed before he quit the state." But Sheridan enjoyed his first taste of military glory. Some newspapers wrote of his achievement, calling him the "Paladin of Perryville."

After Perryville, General Don Carlos Buell was replaced by General William Rosecrans, who on Christmas Day advanced the army to confront Bragg along Stone's River, near the town of Murfreesboro, Tennessee. Rosecrans intended to attack the Confederate right, but before he could, Bragg attacked him. Outnumbered and outgunned, Sheridan was forced to retreat. Enraged by the situation, Sheridan was swearing fervently as he led his men to the rear. Even in the midst of disaster, Rosecrans could not resist an admonition: "Watch your language. Remember the first bullet may send you to eternity."

During the battle at Stone's River, Sheridan's division had been engaged in savage fighting, and they had weathered the storm with flying colors. He had confirmed a truth that soldiers are not disheartened by death, only by pointless death.

Eight months later at the Battle of Chickamauga, Sheridan did not fare quite as well. Bragg had been reinforced by two divisions from Lee's Army of Northern Virginia under the leadership of James Longstreet. Sheridan was overwhelmed and driven from the field. On that day, it was Major General George Thomas who held against impossible odds and saved the army. For his achievement, Thomas would earn his title the "Rock of Chickamauga." The Army of the Cumberland had been beaten in the bloodiest battle of the war in the Western Theater.

Rosecrans's army dragged itself back to Chattanooga, where it was bottled up by Bragg. Grant joined the besieged army, replaced Rosecrans with General Thomas, and summoned Sherman's reinforcements and his own Army of the Tennessee. With the aid of Sheridan's division, the Federals were able to crack the Confederate center and send Bragg's army in a quick retreat.

The Union victory at Chattanooga convinced Lincoln that Grant was a winning general. On March 12, 1864, Grant was named general in chief of the Union armies. Sheridan was ordered to Washington. He arranged to leave the next day, without making the usual formal farewell to his troops. "I could not do it," he wrote. "The bond existing between them and me had grown to such depth of attachment . . . from our mutual devotion . . . and by general consent within and without the command were called 'Sheridan's division'." But his troops found out that he was leaving. As Sheridan boarded the train, he was surprised to see the hillsides around the station lined with his men, there to say farewell and demonstrate their affection.

In Chattanooga, Sheridan learned he had been named the chief of cavalry for the Army of the Potomac. He was "staggered," he wrote, by the thought of the "great responsibilities," but this was not his greatest concern. He was bothered even more by the political infighting for which the Army of the Potomac was famous. The problem lay with General George Meade, who had little use for cavalry. Sheridan's predecessor, Major General Alfred Pleasonton, had been replaced because of his difference of opinion on the use of cavalry. Like Pleasonton, Sheridan wanted his cavalry to be permitted to act independently of the main army. He too encountered resistance from Meade, who deemed cavalry fit for little more than guard and picket duty.

Their disagreement came to a head on May 6, when Grant ordered Meade to "make all preparations during the day for a night march to take position at Spotsylvania Court House." It was important that the Union forces reach Spotsylvania, which was north of Richmond, before Lee's army. The night was foggy and rainy, and the bulk of the army did not leave until the evening. Only one road was wide enough for large numbers of troops, which slowed their movement. For Lee to reach Spotsylvania, he had to cross the Po River. Meade should have sent Sheridan immediately to block or destroy the bridge crossing the river. Instead, he sent one cavalry division to Spotsylvania while another guarded the army's right flank. Lee was left to use the bridge as he pleased. Sheridan assigned James Wilson's 3rd Cavalry Division to head south, but they soon became entangled with the infantry, slowing their movement and causing confusion. In the meantime, the Confederates reached Spotsylvania before the Union troops and were able to beat off Wilson's cavalry.

Meade blamed Sheridan and gave him a severe tongue-lashing. Sheridan, whose aggressive streak was just as great, if not more so, struck back. It mattered nothing that Meade outranked him. He was not going to take the blame for what he saw as Meade's fault for hampering his cavalry's advance. Sheridan concluded angrily, "I could whip Jeb Stuart"—Lee's renowned cavalry commander—"if you would only let me. But since you insist on giving cavalry directions without even consulting or notifying me, you can command the cavalry corps yourself. I will not give it another order." He was quitting and he stormed out.

Meade went to see Grant, expecting him to get Sheridan under control by reprimanding him for his blatant insubordination. When Grant did not react the way he had expected, Meade repeated Sheridan's boast about defeating Stuart if given the opportunity. "Did he really say that?" Grant asked. "Well, he usually knows what he's talking about. Let him go ahead and do it."

By nightfall, Sheridan was leading ten thousand of his men to the outer suburbs of Richmond, where he encountered Stuart at Yellow Tavern, six miles north of the city. Outnumbering Stuart's cavalry by three to one, Sheridan ordered a charge. All along the line, Union troops drove forward, while Stuart tried personally to rally his troops. Earlier he had resisted pleas to remove himself from the center of the fight, shrugging, "I don't reckon there is any danger." This time, being a frontline commander betrayed him, and his luck ran out. He was shot by a dismounted Michigan cavalryman. Sheridan not only made good his boast, but Stuart was killed in the action. However, nothing that Sheridan accomplished helped Grant as he tried to capture the crucial crossroads at Spotsylvania. By separating Meade and Sheridan, Grant was able to maintain the peace; he did not want to lose the services of either.

Sheridan retained all of Pleasonton's appointments, most notably George Custer, Wesley Merritt, and James Wilson. All three men were in their twenties and became known as the boy generals. All three served Sheridan well, but it was Custer with whom he developed the closest bond, even friendship. Sheridan admired Custer's dash and flair, respecting the fact that Custer was as tenacious and persevering as he.

With his victory over Stuart, Phil Sheridan had made a dramatic point about the proper use of cavalry and helped to shatter the myth of the innate superiority of Southern horsemen. It was time for Sheridan to have an independent command. In July 1864, Jubal Early had put a scare into the politicians and bureaucrats of Washington when his raid threatened the capital. At the same time, both Grant's offensive at Petersburg and Sherman's movement through Georgia had stalled. With the presidential election coming up in the fall, Lincoln could ill afford another setback. While in Washington, Sheridan received a quick lesson in election-year politics. His main task, he was given to understand, was to avoid being beaten; a defeat of his army could well cost Lincoln the election.

Grant did not share the administration's concern. He was well aware of

Sheridan's capabilities and knew he could count on him. Sheridan was given the task of clearing the Shenandoah Valley of all Confederate forces. The Shenandoah Valley had twice before been used as a corridor for Confederate invasion of the North. It was known as the breadbasket of the Confederacy because of the food and forage it supplied the Southern forces. Grant hoped to close the valley down once and for all, giving Sheridan special instructions on the type of warfare to conduct there. "In pushing . . . it is desirable that nothing should be left to invite the enemy to return," Grant instructed. "Take all provisions, forage and stock wanted for use of your command. Such as cannot be consumed, destroy. . . . The people should be informed that so long as an army can subsist among them, recurrences of these raids must be expected."

Sheridan moved cautiously into the valley with 40,000 men, probing and skirmishing with Jubal Early's 12,000 Confederates. Gradually he made progress, mostly by attrition. The campaign came to be known as the Burning. Sheridan issued orders for his troops to destroy all the wheat and hay and to seize all mules, horses, and cattle that might be useful to the army. Sheridan, like Sherman, believed in total war; the population must be made to feel the sting. If the inhabitants were impoverished, then they would force the government to seek peace. To Sheridan, the torch was as important a weapon as the sword. When he left the Shenandoah Valley in late 1864, no crops were left in the fields for the fall harvest.

The South, with its tradition of chivalry and romantic self-image, had been much more considerate of noncombatants' property than had the North. Lee's strict orders to his troops during the invasion of the North were held up as examples of gentlemanly restraint in the enemy's country. Most Federal commanders had been careful to prohibit the mistreatment of civilians, but the Union Army of the Shenandoah seemed to take the destruction of the valley as a personal mission.

The middle of October found Sheridan's army encamped near Cedar Creek, twenty miles south of Winchester. Jubal Early was not far away, but he had been beaten twice and it was unlikely that he had any intention of attacking. Sheridan took this opportunity to leave the army and visit Washington. Early learned that Sheridan had ordered some of his troops back to Petersburg and that he, himself, was absent from the field. On the nineteenth, Early launched a surprise attack on the reduced Union army. The opening stages of engagement belonged to the Confederates; Early's men had the Federals reeling and in a near rout after just a few hours of fighting. Sheridan was on his way back from Washington and just fifteen miles away at Winchester when the fighting began. While riding back to join his army, Sheridan's attitude was casual and unhurried—until he met the first wave of retreating Union soldiers. When General William H. Emory rode over to him to report that a division of his corps was ready to cover the retreat to Winchester, Sheridan flared, "Retreat, hell! We'll be back in our camps tonight." Then he plunged into the work of re-forming the army.

Once his preparations were complete, Sheridan rode along his entire two-mile front, cap in hand, showing himself to every soldier in the line. "I'll get a twist on those people yet," he yelled. "We'll raise them out of their boots before the day is over!" Cheers from his men came from everywhere, and caps were thrown into the air. Sheridan then led a counterattack that drove the enemy back. Early's army was so badly damaged that they were no longer a menace. The battle cost the South one of its brightest stars, young Major General Stephen D. Ramseur, who was mortally wounded while rallying his men. It was clear to all that the Confederacy would never threaten the North by way of the Shenandoah Valley.

The Battle of Cedar Creek ended the major action in the valley, and both commanders began returning troops to Petersburg. After a final engagement at Waynesboro, Sheridan joined Grant for the final weeks of the war. Sheridan's army acted as Grant's shock troops, helping to force Lee's Army of Northern Virginia from Petersburg. On April 1, the battle at Five Forks ended the siege at Petersburg. Lee was forced to abandon his position there and retreat toward Richmond.

With the fall of Petersburg, the fall of Richmond quickly followed. On April 3, Union troops marched into Richmond unopposed and occupied the town. During the last week before Appomattox, as the Confederates retreated, they were repeatedly harassed by Federal cavalry. When Lee learned that Union cavalry had captured his supply trains, he made one last effort to break away from Grant's army. Custer and his riders moved in quickly to cut off Lee's retreat. Sheridan's cavalry held the Confederates at bay long enough for the Union infantry to advance. Lee had no choice but to surrender.

Sheridan, Ord, and other generals of Grant's waited outside the McLean house at Appomattox while Grant and Lee met inside to discuss the terms of surrender. Grant was magnanimous in his terms and forbade the firing of victory salutes and cheering in the Union lines, for there was sadness as well as joy in watching an honorable foe go down in defeat.

Unfortunately, there were many incidents in future years when the South would forget its dignity and the North, its example of magnanimity. Some of these incidents would involve General Sheridan, who could not easily forget the bloodshed and destruction he had witnessed during the war.

After Lee and Grant left, Sheridan and his fellow officers went on a frenzied souvenir hunt. Despite the protests of homeowner McLean, Union officers carried away tables, chairs, candlesticks, even chunks of upholstery. Sheridan paid twenty dollars for the pine table on which Grant had signed the surrender document. The next day he gave the table to Custer as a gift for his wife, Libbie, along with a note praising her "very gallant husband" for his part in bringing about the surrender.

Sheridan's contributions to the Union victory did not go unnoticed. Lincoln had said of him after Cedar Creek, "Phil Sheridan is all right." General Grant was more generous in his praise of Sheridan: "I believe General Sheridan has no superior as a general, either living or dead, and perhaps not an equal." Sherman described his Ohioan neighbor as "a persevering terrier dog, honest, modest, plucky and smart enough."

Although the war was over, the nation still needed Sheridan's service. The army was now turning its attention to the Indians on the western frontier and to a problem developing in Mexico. Sheridan was quickly given a new assignment. Grant was concerned about the presence in Mexico of 40,000 troops of French Emperor Napoleon III, who was supporting the puppet regime of Austrian Archduke Maximilian. Worse yet in the eyes of the federal government was the aid and comfort the French had given to the Confederacy during the war. The United States supported the restoration of President Benito Juarez. Without actually sending his troops across the Rio Grande, Sheridan did everything in his power to let the French know that armed intervention was possible if Benito Juarez was not returned to the presidency. In April 1866, Napoleon III grudgingly announced that he would begin to pull French troops out of Mexico. Sheridan believed his elaborate display of force at the border had been decisive in forcing the French to leave. But it is more likely that French domestic pressure and the diplomatic efforts of Secretary of State Seward had more impact on Napoleon's decision than did Sheridan's military theatrics.

In March of 1867, Congress passed the first and most sweeping of three Military Reconstruction acts, dividing ten of the eleven former Confederate states into five military districts. Nine days after the passage of the act, President Johnson gave Sheridan command of the 5th Military District, composed of Texas and Louisiana. Sheridan supported the Reconstruction Act and was able to quote it verbatim in his memoirs twenty years later. Sheridan was determined to see that the law was carried out in his district. Within eight days of being appointed, Sheridan removed New Orleans Mayor John Monroe, Louisiana Attorney General Andrew Herron, and District Judge Edmund Abell, all of whom he held responsible for an earlier riot. Grant supported Sheridan's moves, but President Johnson did not. He ordered that no more removals be made until the United States attorney general could rule on the legality of such actions. Grant passed along the president's order to Sheridan, but added a secret message warning him that "there is decided hostility to the whole Congressional plan of reconstruction at the White House, and a disposition to remove you from the command you now have. Both the Secretary of War and myself will oppose any such move, as will the mass of the people." He assured Sheridan that Congress wanted the individual districts to be "their own judges of the meaning of its provisions." He added, "Go on giving your own interpretation of the law."

In light of these and other instructions to Sheridan, it is easy to conclude that Johnson's later assessment that "Grant was untrue" was accurate. Grant saw the Radical handwriting on the wall and took advantage of it for his own political gain. Sheridan was now heeding Grant's advice, keeping his eyes on several other Southerners whom he eventually wanted to remove from office.

For the next few months, Sheridan busied himself with voter registration. The Second Reconstruction Act had authorized military commanders to register voters and hold elections. The language of the act was vague, and Sheridan and the other district commanders asked the U.S. attorney general to clarify the wording. The important question concerned who was ineligible to register to vote. Under the guidelines of the so-called Ironclad Oath, all those registering were required to swear that, before the war, they had never been an executive or judicial officer of a state that seceded from the Union. Defining what constituted an executive or judicial position was the key factor in determining who was permitted to be registered. While the attorney general continued to ponder the question, Sheridan and the other commanders had to interpret the registration requirements in their own way. Sheridan chose to give the law the widest possible interpretation, disenfranchising every official from governor to harbor pilot, auctioneer, and cemetery sexton. Sheridan, who told Grant that "his desire [was] to faithfully carry out the law as a military order," wanted to complete the process before a ruling could be made by the attorney general.

Troops were sent to towns throughout the state to protect the registration teams, and blacks were particularly encouraged to register. Whites were routinely turned away on the grounds they had served in the Confederate army, whether they had taken the oath of alliance or not. Sheridan's efforts had the desired effect: By the time registration ended on August 1, over sixty-five percent of those registered were black.

When Sheridan learned that an aide to the New Orleans police chief had intimidated prospective black voters, he dismissed the man from office and reorganized the entire department. He ordered the newly appointed mayor to make certain that at least half of the city's police force were Union veterans.

Sheridan continued to be drawn into controversy. When a political battle erupted between the Louisiana legislature and the governor over the appointment of two sets of commissioners, Sheridan removed both boards and appointed his own. When racial trouble escalated over segregated streetcars in New Orleans, officials of the transport company asked Sheridan to help enforce the segregated order. He refused, warning instead that he would ban streetcars altogether if the discriminatory practice continued. Soon the races were riding together, but not without mutual bitterness and suspicion.

Finally on May 24, U.S. Attorney General Henry Stanbery issued his opinion on the question of voter qualifications in the South. His ruling was more liberal than Sheridan's; but unlike other military commanders in the South, Sheridan did not issue new guidelines. Stringent loyalty tests continued to be applied to prospective white voters, while black voters in Texas were allowed to register even after listing their place of birth as Africa. This should have disqualified them from voting because of the way citizenship was defined in the Fourteenth Amendment. In his open defiance of presidential orders, Sheridan was supported, if not encouraged, by Grant. More and more, Grant was separating himself from Johnson's control and encouraging his subordinates to do the same. In mid-July 1867, Congress passed the Third Reconstruction Act rebutting the attorney general's ruling, redefining "executive and judicial offices." The new act gave military commanders the power to remove from office any official considered a detriment to the reconstruction process.

Alarmed by Sheridan's actions in New Orleans, President Johnson sent Brigadier General Lovell Rousseau to New Orleans to keep an eye on him. The pressure of Rousseau's presence had just the opposite effect. When faced with a direct challenge to his authority, Sheridan always lashed out quickly and instinctively. On July 30, Sheridan removed Governor James Throckmorton of Texas, replacing him with Republican Elisha Pease, the man Throckmorton had defeated in an election a year earlier. Sheridan told Grant that the removal was necessary to get rid of "an impediment to the reconstruction of the State." Two days later, Sheridan removed twenty-two New Orleans city councilmen. Still later, he removed the mayors of Lake Charles and Shreveport and three district judges in Texas.

Meanwhile, in Washington, Andrew Johnson fired Secretary of War Stanton, an act that would ultimately lead to his impeachment and trial by Congress. A reluctant Grant was appointed interim secretary of war. After a few days of cabinet-level discussion, Johnson finally relieved Sheridan of command on August 17. He was transferred to the Department of the Missouri, with headquarters at Fort Leavenworth. Perhaps because he saw it coming, Sheridan received the news calmly.

Sheridan's closest admirers could not claim that he had made a success of his position as military commander. "I was only following orders," he said. In fact, there is validity in his claim, because he did essentially what Grant wanted him to do. A more worldly commander would not have interpreted the Reconstruction acts as literally as he did. It was to Grant that he looked for orders and advice. There is no doubt that he had little compassion for the conquered South, especially for its aristocracy. In a letter to a former aide, he said, "I cannot and will not cater to rebel sentiment. . . . I did not care whether the Southern States were readmitted. . . . The more I see of these people, the less I see to admire."

After nearly two and a half years of controversial service in the Deep South, Sheridan left for his new assignment as commander of the Department of the Missouri, exchanging commands with General Winfield Scott Hancock. For many years the Plains Indians had been gradually pushed across the Mississippi and had then been settled permanently on a vast range of reservations west of the Arkansas, Missouri, and Iowa borders. There, they were promised they could live forever. Mormons, ranchers, farmers, miners, and railroad construction gangs invaded the land the Indians had been promised. The Indians began to resist these recurring invasions with all the fury they could bring to bear.

In 1867, public opinion demanded that the government try to make a peaceful settlement with the Indians. Congress appointed a peace commission to negotiate a more favorable settlement. Federal representatives agreed that whites would not make their homes in lands between the Arkansas and Platte Rivers, with the understanding that the Indians would not interfere with the building of railroads through those lands. The Indians also agreed to live on the land set aside for them. Unfortunately, the treaties looked much better on paper than they were in reality.

The Department of the Missouri was quiet when Sheridan took over the command, but it was a decidedly uneasy quiet. Rumors of renewed bloodshed by the Indians swept through the post. Sheridan quickly organized a personal inspection of the district. What he found was troubling. Among the Cheyenne, Kiowa, and Arapaho, he found a mood of surly discontent. "The young men were chafing and turbulent," he later wrote. Neither they nor their elders seemed to understand the terms of the new treaty. When a delegation of chiefs attempted to meet with Sheridan to air their grievances, he refused to see them, reasoning that "Congress had delegated to the Peace Commission the whole matter of treating with them, and a council might lead only to additional complications."

Sheridan found that he had only a small force on hand in the District of Upper Arkansas, where trouble was most likely to break out. His command was less than half the combined might of the Indians, and even that force was scattered among eight forts. Sheridan, who at the war's end had commanded well-trained, battle-worn troops, now had in their place a stripped-down regular army of recruits.

Not all western soldiers were poor soldiers, but the combination of poor living conditions, harsh discipline, bad food, tainted water, and brutal weather contributed to the lack of cohesion and esprit de corps. These conditions led to the staggering annual turnover rate of between twenty-five and forty percent. Those who stayed on were in constant danger of diseases such as cholera, malaria, pneumonia, and dysentery. The western soldier was five times more likely to contract a disease than he was to suffer a battle wound.

The Indian warriors they faced, by contrast, were the products of an age-old culture that glorified combat and the skills it required: courage, endurance, strength, cunning horsemanship, and use of weapons. The Plains Indians were more than a match for Sheridan's troops. Thus it was Sheridan's task to use his smaller force in such a way that he could take advantage of its firepower, discipline, organization, and leadership to balance the power.

In July 1868, the first sign of trouble came. The Cheyenne broke camp near Fort Dodge and moved off to the north of the Arkansas River instead of heading for the reservations south of it. Hostilities flared up when these bands raided a village of friendly Kaw near Council Grove, Kansas, near a white settlement. A little later, the Comanche and Kiowa tribes joined the Cheyenne in killing, raping, and robbing whites. That autumn the whole border was aflame.

The Indian tribes could put 6,000 warriors in the field, while Sheridan's command totaled only about 2,600. Nevertheless, he laid down the principle: "Punishment must follow crime." To punish the Indians who preferred raiding to farming, Sheridan could not fight them on their terms. Generals such as Hancock had been made to look foolish by the "best light cavalry in the World," the Plains Indians. But Sheridan reasoned that his soldiers were much better fed and clothed than the Indians, and he could gain an advantage if he conducted short, successful campaigns.

As always, Sheridan made careful plans. The Indians would be like hibernating bears, lying in their winter camp, he reasoned, so he would attack them then. He established his forward headquarters at Fort Hays, Kansas, gathering information and preparing his men for a winter campaign. He selected George Armstrong Custer, now a lieutenant colonel, and his 7th Cavalry to head the leading column. Custer was one officer who Sheridan felt he could rely on for quick and aggressive action. Custer, however, had little regard for those he slaughtered. He could ride into an Indian village populated with women and children as well as braves and kill, burn, and destroy with little feeling or regret. "Punishment must follow crime," and Custer followed the marauder, his wife, and children, exterminating all in his path.

By November 15, 1868, Sheridan and his men left Fort Hays. Sheridan's instruction to Custer had been brutally simple: "Proceed south. . . ; destroy their villages and ponies; kill or hang all warriors and bring back all women and children." At dawn Custer led the attack across the Washita River. He made no effort to ascertain whether the Cheyennes in the camp participated in the raiding parties. Carbines rattled in the stillness of the winter dawn. Chief Black

Kettle was shot to death at the door of his lodge. Braves, squaws, and children were shot as they attempted to flee. By the time the slaughter ended, 103 warriors and an unreported number of women and children were killed, while 53 were captured.

Despite the surprise attack, hundreds of Indians managed to escape. A young major named Joel Elliott, leading a few troops, spurred after them. Custer and the rest of his command withdrew, leaving Elliott and his men on their own, at the mercy of the Cheyennes. Never again did Custer have the respect of the 7th Cavalry. But Custer's victory on the Washita, whatever its moral and tactical deficiencies, had been an enormous psychological blow to the Indians, comparable in effect to the demoralization of the citizens in the Shenandoah Valley four years earlier. It also raised Custer's reputation back east to the status of the nation's preeminent Indian fighter. That opinion was not shared by his troops—and it would have unimaginable consequences for both Custer and his opponents a few years later.

The aftermath of Sheridan's rigorous winter campaign brought more controversy for him. The destruction of Black Kettle's village drew an outcry of protest in the East. Sheridan assured General Sherman that future fears of massacres were groundless. He also made clear his belief that the Indians who complied with the treaty's terms and lived on reservations should be adequately clothed and fed. Those who spent their summers in war parties, Sheridan said, should be quickly and sternly punished.

In November 1868, Ulysses S. Grant was elected president of the United States. Grant appointed Sherman as commander of the U.S. Army and Sheridan as commander of the frontier. This change in assignment meant that Sheridan would be farther from the action, tied to a desk in Chicago. He would never again come so close to an Indian fight as he had during the campaign against Black Kettle. Lieutenant generals do not lead cavalry charges.

In the fall of 1869, complaints flooded into Sheridan's headquarters concerning the actions of a small band of the Blackfeet tribe, the Piegans in northern Montana, who were stealing horses and other goods and selling them in Canada. Sheridan dispatched Major E. M. Baker to take care of the Piegans. "I want them struck hard," he instructed Baker.

Baker's attack on January 23, 1870, was an absolute debacle—and not just for the Indians who suffered his fury. Against the advice of his scouts, Baker ordered an attack on a Piegan village along the Marias River. This band had been given a safe-conduct pass by the Indian Bureau and had not participated in any hostile activities that fall. Despite being shown the safe-conduct pass, Baker attacked anyway. For more than an hour, his men blazed away, killing 173 Piegans, at least 53 of whom were women and children.

The Marias massacre provoked an immediate firestorm of protest back east.

Sheridan lashed out quickly and instinctively at his critics. He claimed that since 1862 at least eight hundred men, women, and children had been murdered within the limits of his command, some in the most fiendish manner; the men usually scalped and mutilated, women raped, then killed and scalped. The assaults in question had been committed by Cheyennes, not Piegans; but Sheridan conveniently omitted that point. Thereafter, Sheridan and his subordinates would face an increasingly skeptical and sometimes hostile public and Congress.

During the controversy, Sheridan was quoted as having made the statement, "a dead Indian is the only good Indian." Although he immediately disavowed the statement, it has continued to be attributed to him. This statement has been used by friends and enemies ever since to characterize and castigate his Indian-fighting career.

Sheridan's frontier remained quiet for the next few years. Taking advantage of the quiet during the fall of 1870, Sheridan traveled to Europe as an observer to the Prussian war with France. Sheridan corresponded frequently with Grant and Sherman about his observations, admiring the German leadership but feeling the French had allowed themselves to be outfought and outgeneraled.

Sheridan returned to Chicago in time for the Great Chicago Fire of 1871. At ten o'clock on the night of October 7, a fire broke out and continued to burn for five days. The heat of the flames was so intense that it could be felt as far as a hundred miles away. By the time the fire was brought under control, 250 people were dead and property loss reached $200 million. The quick assistance of the army as ordered by Sheridan aroused a political controversy. While the fire raged, Sheridan was engrossed in directing his soldiers and civilians in fighting the fire; he did not always remember to be tactful. Upon learning that a hotel owner, whose establishment had not been damaged by the fire, had raised his daily rates from $2.50 to $6.00, Sheridan dismissed the proprietor, installed one of his orderlies as manager, and dropped the rates to their original level.

His troops patrolled the city with bayonets, routing gangs of hoodlums, breaking up organized lootings, and restoring order as quickly as possible. Sheridan had his men supply blankets, set up tents for the homeless, and distribute food rations. For his efforts, his thanks came from Governor John Palmer—who was offended by Sheridan's intervention. Alleging that the mayor should have called out the militia, Palmer charged Sheridan with unconstitutional acts.

Palmer took the matter to the state supreme court. But Chicago's citizens, who were grateful to Sheridan for his assistance, rallied to his support. He received thousands of letters of thanks and support from Secretary of War William Belknap, but the Illinois Supreme Court upheld Palmer. Some believe that Palmer's ungrateful actions were the result of personal grievances that carried over from the Civil War.

Sheridan made frequent trips east. He began to eat, drink, dance, and keep company with the ladies. He made hunting trips to the western territories, on one occasion with visiting European royalty, on another with members of New York society. Sheridan approved the mass slaughter of buffalo taking place on the Great Plains, viewing their extermination as a way of eliminating the Indians. Every buffalo hunter should be given a medal, Sheridan told the Texas legislature in 1875, engraved on one side with a dead buffalo and on the other with a "discouraged-looking Indian."

When gold was discovered in the Black Hills of the Dakotas, many prospectors began moving into the hills. This land had been set aside for Indians, and whites were forbidden from entering. When Sheridan learned of the intrusion, he issued standing orders to burn wagon trains, destroy equipment, and arrest ringleaders of any expeditions into the hills. The treaty of 1868, he pointed out, "virtually deeds this portion of the Black Hills to the Sioux." He suggested instead that miners and homesteaders try their luck farther west in the unceded lands of Wyoming and Montana.

In the midst of the explosive situation out west, Sheridan was ordered back to New Orleans to monitor political problems developing there. Sheridan warned Washington that a "spirit of defiance to all lawful authority" had spread across the state. He urged that the government declare all opponents of Governor William Kellogg's regime "banditti" and arrest and try them as criminals. After suggesting to one congressman that "what you want to do is suspend the what-do-you-call-it," by which he meant the writ of habeas corpus, Sheridan sent troops with fixed bayonets into two legislative chambers. He was imposing the will of the electorate, not his own, but he managed to do it in a way that offended the North as well as the South. He was soon back in Chicago dealing with Indians—who had no constituency.

As the Indians waged war on the encroaching whites, Sheridan continued his forceful policies. For some years, Indians living in Mexico regularly crossed the Rio Grande and raided Texan herds, driving thousands of stolen horses and cattle back across the border. In 1873, Sheridan and Secretary of War Belknap traveled to Fort Clark, Texas, to confer with Colonel Ranald MacKenzie. Mackenzie was directed to pursue the hostile Indians into Mexico, regardless of the international repercussions. A few days later, the young colonel executed a raid into Mexico, destroying three villages of those Indian bands thought to be hostile. He then dashed back across the border ahead of the Mexican troops. Mexican officials protested vehemently, but to little effect.

Once back in Chicago, Sheridan turned his attentions to a young lady who had been a member of his mission to Louisiana. She was Irene Rucker, the youngest daughter of General Daniel Rucker, quartermaster general of the Division of the Missouri. Irene was described as "young, beautiful, bright, and accomplished, blond and vivacious." She was only twenty-two, half Sheridan's age. They were married on June 3, 1875, at the home of her father. Their marriage was close, stable, and blessed by a daughter, then twin girls, and finally a son.

For the next eight years, Sheridan continued to wear down the Plains Indians as civilization spread to the West. The Sioux had been outraged by the invasion of gold-seekers in their old hunting grounds in the Black Hills. Another cause of their growing desperation was the tragic slaughter of buffalo herds by white hunters. Sheridan was aware that white settlers, prospectors, gun runners, and corrupt bureaucrats were preying on the Indians and inviting a violent reaction. Sheridan recommended the enactment of laws to punish marauding whites who encroached on Indian lands and to punish Indians for their criminal acts. Congress, however, did little to solve these problems.

In June of 1876, Sheridan sent Generals Terry, Crook, and Custer to crush all resistance from the Sioux. Custer detached himself from Terry's command and, with his 7th Cavalry, followed the trail of a Sioux band up the Rosebud River and over to the Little Bighorn River. He had been ordered not to bring on a general engagement until Terry could bring up the rest of his command. Instead, when he sighted the Sioux encampment on the banks of the Little Bighorn, he decided to attack. As he had at Washita eight years earlier, he divided his command. Greatly outnumbered, the 225 men of his command all died in what has become known as "Custer's Last Stand." George Armstrong Custer, who had pursued glory all his life, instead found notoriety and death.

News of the massacre reached Sheridan in Philadelphia. The nation was not ready for such a disaster. Throughout the land, there was an outcry for vengeance. Even unreconstructed Southerners were eager to join in the hunt for Sitting Bull, Crazy Horse, and their followers. Sheridan, unavoidably feeling some responsibility for Custer's demise, had no time for the luxury of grief. The public demanded to know how the massacre could have happened, particularly with Custer in charge. Sheridan investigated the tragedy of Little Bighorn and concluded it had been caused by Custer's bravado, his faulty tactics, and his failure to ascertain the Sioux's strength before attacking.

In July 1877, thirteen months after Custer's death at Little Bighorn, Sheridan visited the battlefield. Saddle-high grass now grew over the battleground, and the smell of wildflowers had replaced the stench of dead bodies. More than ever, Sheridan was convinced that Custer could have survived his initial error, his hasty and "usual hurrahs," if only he had not divided his command. Sheridan consoled himself with the knowledge that now, after buffalo and Indians had freely roamed the countryside, there were "no signs of either . . . but in their places we found prospectors, emigrants, and tramps."

The last three years of the decade saw the final subjugation of the northern Plains Indians. The last resisting bands of Sioux and Cheyenne surrendered to the army, quietly bringing to a close the costliest and, from a military standpoint, most embarrassing campaign in frontier history.

Sheridan found himself constantly defending his policy toward the Indians. On one matter, at least, Sheridan did find himself in agreement with both the agency Indians and his junior officers—the near-criminal ineptitude of the Indian Bureau. Officers investigating Indian unrest reported that the Cheyenne were not receiving, either in quantity or quality, enough food to support themselves. "I am expected to see that the Indians behave properly whom the government is starving," Sheridan complained. There were times when Sheridan was willing to support an Indian cause if he felt they were not being treated fairly.

In 1882, during an expedition through Yellowstone National Park, Sheridan discovered the park in shambles. Poachers were indiscrimately slaughtering the wildlife. Sheridan also learned that a company run by the Northern Pacific Railroad was being granted monopoly rights to develop the park at a ridiculously low rent. Launching a national campaign to protect the wildlife and keep the park under federal control, Sheridan brought President Chester A. Arthur to Yellowstone the next year. In 1886, the army took over the supervision for the next thirty-two years. Due to Sheridan's concern, they were able to bring poaching under control, and with the help of breeding stock, the buffalo herds were saved from extinction.

At least three times in his later years, Sheridan's name was proposed as a candidate for president, but he turned down all such offers. He told an Associated Press reporter, "I don't want that or any other civil office." In the autumn of 1883, General Sherman reached retirement age. It was time to give younger officers a chance, he said. Sheridan, at the young age of fifty-two, was appointed to the highest military office in the army, replacing Sherman. Sheridan was not as popular as his predecessor; he was more fond of staying at home with his family than making appearances at social events.

Sheridan's subordinates found he was an understanding superior, one who was always willing to stretch regulations to help them, especially if they had served on the frontier. For an officer seeking a leave because his wife was ill, he would support the appeal. When the Rio Grande flooded and the soldiers at Fort Brown were menaced by a fever epidemic, he ordered a boat to evacuate the whole post, moving its personnel to a safer place until the fever season was over. Old comrades seeking appointment to West Point for their sons found him quick to endorse their applications. Sheridan strongly supported improved living conditions for soldiers in the field, particularly those serving on the frontier.

In the spring of 1888, Sheridan was ravaged by a series of heart attacks. He was fifty-seven and his luck was running out. In June, a bedridden Sheridan was promoted to full general. He spent the remaining days of his life sitting on the porch of his summer cottage at Nonquit, Massachusetts; on August 5, while he watched the waves roll in, death came to visit.

Sheridan was eulogized by Sherman, who said, "He was a great soldier and a noble man and deserved all the honors bestowed on him." Grant, who had died in 1885, had pronounced Sheridan "the embodiment of heroism, dash and impulse." But the most memorable tribute came from his wife. Asked by a friend why she did not remarry, Irene Sheridan responded, "I would rather be the widow of Phil Sheridan than the wife of any man alive." After a statue of their husband and father was erected in Washington, the Sheridans moved to a house on Massachusetts Avenue so they could be near it. For years thereafter, the morning ritual of the Sheridan girls included going to the window and calling to the image of Phil Sheridan, "Good morning, Papa."

12 Wizard of the Saddle

NATHAN BEDFORD FORREST

NATHAN BEDFORD FORREST was a fierce and controversial Civil War officer, an unschooled but brilliant cavalryman. In the course of rising from private to lieutenant general in the Confederate army, he revolutionized the way armies fought. He was a superb tactician, a ferocious fighter, and a courageous soldier. Untutored in war, on the battle-field, Forrest relied solely on intuition. His self-taught tactics made him the most feared man in the Confederate army. He was known as the Wizard of the Saddle and was reputed to have killed more than thirty Union soldiers in hand-to-hand combat and to have had twenty-nine horses shot out from under him. He was wounded on four separate occasions.

Forrest was a hero to the poor Southern white man and a symbol of what the Confederacy was willing to do to win. He consistently outmaneuvered his adversaries, exploiting every opportunity to confuse and deceive his opponents.

He struck fast and hard. It is said that in a battle "he was always first with the most." He routinely defeated forces twice his size, using tactical designs that combined shrewd simplicity with the most savage aggressiveness. General William T. Sherman ruefully dubbed him "that devil Forrest." While Sherman had defined war as hell, Forrest was more specific, saying, "War means fighting, and fighting means killing."

Nathan Bedford Forrest was a large man with a colorful personality, and he was a violent man with a fierce temper, struggling with it for most of his life. He thought nothing of killing other men and in fact was proud of it. He knifed to death a fellow Confederate who made the mistake of assaulting him. On another occasion, a courier interrupted Forrest as he paced about, mentally trying to solve a difficult military problem. Annoyed by the interruption, he knocked the man unconscious with a single blow and resumed his pacing.

Possessing only six months of schooling, Forrest displayed a knack for emphatic sentence construction and had an instinctive grasp of mathematics. Despite his lack of formal education, contact with businessmen and constant reading of newspapers gave him an excellent sense of the use of words and the construction of phrases. During the war, after dictating a dispatch, he would read it over for corrections. If he detected a grammatical error or an awkwardly constructed phrase, he would say, "That won't do it; it hasn't the right pitch." He would then change the wording and always seemed able to shape it into a forcible expression. He keenly felt the need for education and regretted not having spent more time in school. He once remarked: "No one knows the embarrassment I labor under when thrown in the company of educated persons."

Far from being perfect, Forrest felt the only personal vices that he was ashamed of were his fondness for gambling and his use of profanity. He neither drank nor smoked. He showed respect for women and clergymen, and he delighted in children. He loved horses and horse racing and had a pointed sense of humor. At a dinner during the war, when someone inquired why his hair had turned gray while his beard remained dark, he replied that it was probably because he tended to work his brains more than his jaws.

Stories of Forrest's episodes have been told and retold, until many of them take on mythologic qualities. Southerners are widely considered America's best storytellers and are known to outdo themselves venerating their heroes. None of the lore is more dramatic than the story of the horseman who, one late-summer day in 1845, came to the aid of two women and their black driver, stranded at a creek ford. The driver was struggling to free the carriage from a mudhole, while two young acquaintances of the women sat on horseback beside the stream, letting the slave try to free the vehicle's wheels alone. It was the Sabbath and the women did not want to soil their Sunday finery. The third horseman, when he arrived, showed no hesitation in getting his clothing wet.

After hitching his horse to a fence, he waded out to the carriage. Asking the women's permission, he carried them one by one to dry ground. Then he re-entered the water, set his shoulder to the carriage wheel, and helped the driver free the vehicle. Before helping the women back to their seats, he turned to the onlookers and soundly castigated them for their uselessness, threatening physical harm if they didn't leave at once.

The women turned out to be the widow Elizabeth Montgomery and her eighteen-year-old daughter, Mary Ann. Mother and daughter thanked the man for his help and were about to drive off when he introduced himself. He was Bedford Forrest, a twenty-four-year-old mercantile dealer. He asked for permission to call on Mary Ann at home. Driving away, Mary Ann was greatly impressed by young Forrest's aggressive manner. Although she had never seen him before, she had almost certainly heard of him. His reputation had been well established. Recently, he had received publicity from being involved in a shootout in which he was wounded and his opponents left in a "doubtful state." Bedford didn't waste time. Within days after their meeting, he called on the Montgomerys. When he arrived, he found two other prospective callers; the same two onlookers from the ford. With threats of bodily harm, Forrest ordered them away. Mary Ann invited him inside, where he proceeded to propose. She hesitated—after all, it was only the second time in her life she had spoken to him. He and his business, he told her, could support her comfortably and securely. He was determined to marry her and said he would bring a marriage license on his next visit. On the third visit, Mary Ann accepted Forrest's proposal, and in September, they were married.

Procuring the minister, the Reverend Samuel Montgomery Cowan—who was the bride-to-be's uncle and guardian—proved difficult. Rev. Cowan initially said no when Forrest asked for his niece's hand. "Why, Bedford, I couldn't consent." he replied. "You cuss and gamble, and Mary Ann is a Christian girl." Forrest's response was simple but difficult to argue. "I know it," he said, "and that's why I want her." The whirlwind courtship fits the pattern of Forrest's behavior in situations of challenge. This type of reaction was to follow him throughout the Civil War.

Nathan Bedford Forrest was born on July 13, 1821. Nathan was his paternal grandfather's name; Bedford was the Tennessee county in which he was born. His father, William Forrest, eked out a tenuous living in the backwoods of south Tennessee. During the course of his marriage, his wife Mariam Beck Forrest would give birth to eleven children, Bedford being the oldest. None of the five daughters lived to adulthood, but six of the eight boys did—and all became soldiers. The family moved to Tippah County, Mississippi, in 1834, hoping to improve their lot. Three years later, William died, leaving Forrest the head of the household.

Like many children of the southern frontier, Forrest had almost no formal education. Although he was functionally literate, Forrest's knowledge of spelling remained incomplete throughout his life. At times during the war, his semi-literacy presented problems for those who had to decipher his directives. Forrest, aware of his shortcomings, whenever possible dictated his letters to his adjutants. Major Charles Anderson, one of his adjutants, later recalled a moment when the general looked down at the pen in his hand and said, "I never see a pen but what I think of a snake."

When he was twenty-four, Bedford left his family and moved to Hernando, Mississippi, to seek his fortune. By this age, he had killed his first man, avenging the murder of his uncle. On the frontier, this was not unusual. There was little regard for the law, and a person often had to take care of wrongs done against him. Violence was believed to be the most basic solution to these problems. Forrest took a commonsense approach to a problem by killing the person who had wronged him; but it was murder, plain and simple.

This was not the only major event in his life that year. He also met and married Mary Ann Montgomery. In 1846, she gave birth to a son, William, and in 1847, to a daughter, Frances, who died six years later. Forrest remembered his childhood days of poverty and wanted a better life for his family. So in 1851, he decided to move them to Memphis to seek his fortune as a planter.

Memphis was a boom town on its way to becoming the inland slave-trading capital of the Southwest. By 1845, slaves were fast becoming the single most valuable commodity in the South. The value of slaves became greater than the value of the plantation itself and of all the livestock and crops associated with it. Extremely high prices were paid for slaves in the markets of Louisiana and Memphis. Slaves were bought and sold at the auction block. For the buyers, slaves were displayed and inspected in the same manner that livestock was sold. Frequently when slaves were sold, no allowance was made to keep families together. Forrest claimed that he tried to maintain his slaves' family structures and would not sell to some people because of their reputations as cruel masters.

Forrest quickly saw that the basis for becoming a successful planter was having a good labor force, which led him into trading slaves. By 1860, Forrest owned three thousand acres of land with a value of $190,000 and had forty-two slaves. His personal estate was valued at $90,000. At the age of thirty-nine, he had become one of the wealthiest men in the South.

Although slave trading had made him wealthy, he was not known to mistreat slaves. Forrest felt that slaves were property to be protected, and whipping or mistreating them would only make them less attractive to prospective buyers. The wealth he had acquired through slave trading was his ticket to social esteem. In 1855 Forrest was elected city alderman in Memphis. With his lack of education, uncouth way of expressing himself, and inability to read and write well, he could have been viewed as what Southerners called white trash. But Forrest was able to transcend these shortcomings to become a powerful member of the community. His determination and grit enabled him to achieve significant goals throughout his life and brought him victory after victory on the battlefield.

When Tennessee seceded from the Union in June 1861, Forrest enlisted as a private in a company of mounted rifles. He was not in the unit long when Governor Isham Harris ordered him to Memphis and authorized him to raise a cavalry regiment. With the assignment, Forrest received a commission as a lieutenant colonel. This method of raising troops was common during the war. Lacking any adequate structure for raising troops, state governments turned to prominent local citizens who could attract men willing to serve under them. Most were able to enroll a single company (50–100 men); Forrest enrolled ten companies.

Forrest's cavalry was mostly self-equipped and self-mounted. Even so, some needed guns; Forrest made a secret visit to Kentucky and purchased Colt's navy pistols, saddles, and other equipment for horses. Using his own money, he was able to equip a cavalry regiment of about 600 men. He also collected a detachment of new recruits. The *Memphis Avalanche* of June 24, 1861, observed: "No better man could have been selected for such a duty of known courage and indomitable perseverance. He is a man for the times."

The first significant military action for Forrest took place in Kentucky in late December 1861. A Union force of 500 troops was moving toward the village of Sacramento; their mission was to destroy a ragged band of Confederate raiders. Forrest received information of their approach, and he immediately ordered his 200 men to follow him at all possible speed. When he intercepted the Union troops, he split his unit into three sections. While dismounted skirmishers moved forward through the brush, one force on horseback was to move around the left flank, and another mounted section would circle the right end. With a loud rebel yell, Forrest led the charge as the Confederates attacked from all three sides, causing mass confusion among the Union ranks. Panic seized the demoralized Yankee line, and those who could reach their horses rode away. Forrest gathered his cavalrymen and pursued the fleeing enemy. Finally, the retreating Union forces were able to form a line and block the road. Forrest charged into their midst and killed or wounded three Yankees in the hand-to-hand struggle that raged until all the Union troops had been killed or captured.

During the skirmish at Sacramento, Forrest employed the guerrilla tactics that would contribute to his legend. In his battles, he fought side by side with his men, applying his standing rule of combat: "Forward men, and mix with them." In his report of the Sacramento engagement, General Albert Sidney

Johnston said: "For the skill, energy and courage displayed by Colonel Forrest, he is entitled to the highest praise, and I take great pleasure in calling the attention of the general commanding and of government to his service."

During the war, Forrest often found himself beyond the safety of his men, isolated and in danger. It happened first in the battle at Sacramento, when an aide of his was shot dead. He suddenly found himself fighting off three Union soldiers—a private and two captains. Forrest shot the private and dodged the officers' saber slashes, mortally wounding one officer and dislocating the other's shoulder.

Although Forrest was unorthodox in his approach to leadership, he was no madman. In some ways, he was a model commander; he never asked his men to do anything he was not willing to do himself. He was always considerate of the welfare of his troops, trying to hold the shedding of their blood to a minimum. Whenever possible, he used skill or trickery to win a victory. But when all else failed and a fight to the death was necessary, he did not hesitate. As in the battle at Sacramento, Forrest lacked in troop strength but gained by shock effect, surprise, aggressiveness, and valor.

Shortly after the Battle of Sacramento, Colonel Forrest was ordered to take his cavalrymen to Fort Donelson, a Confederate stronghold on the Cumberland River in northern Tennessee. Just prior to his attack on Fort Donelson, General Grant had captured Fort Henry, ten miles west. Grant then turned eastward to Fort Donelson to complete his campaign.

Fort Donelson was commanded by General John Floyd and garrisoned by 15,000 troops under Generals Gideon Pillow and Simon Bolivar Buckner. General Johnston, commanding general of the Department of the Tennessee, ordered the fort held if possible, but evacuated if necessary. If Fort Donelson fell, it would mean the loss of Nashville and probably all of western and middle Tennessee as well.

On February 14, in below-freezing weather, Union gunboats joined the Union forces and began shelling the fort. General Floyd, deciding his position was untenable, tried to break through the Federal lines. Early the next morning, he attacked and slowly pushed the Union forces back. Despite heavy sleet and snow, Forrest's cavalry cleared the Union soldiers from three roads leading from the fort to Nashville and provided an opportunity for the Confederates in the fort to escape. By the end of the day, Forrest had lost his horse, and his overcoat bore fifteen bullet holes. For some unknown reason, General Pillow ordered his men to withdraw to their original position. Grant quickly regained the ground lost earlier.

That night, General Floyd met with his officers and decided to surrender the fort. The lone dissenting voice was Forrest's. "I did not come here for the purpose of surrendering my command," he said, storming out of the meeting. Forrest had no intention of surrendering his command and had even offered to conduct a rearguard action so that the garrison might attempt to escape. His offer was rejected. Disgusted by the intentions of his superiors, Forrest returned to his men. "Boys," he said, "these people are talking about surrendering, and I am going out of this place before they do or bust hell wide open." By 4 A.M., he had his cavalry mounted and ready to leave. Finding an unguarded breach in the Union line, Forrest and his men splashed through the backwaters of the Cumberland River and made it to safety.

Behind them, at Fort Donelson, 12,000 Confederate troops surrendered. In his report of the battle, Forrest insisted that two-thirds of the army could have made it safely out of Fort Donelson by the route he followed. Later he tempered his feelings about the decision to surrender at the fort: "The weather was intensely cold; a great many of the men were already frost-bitten; and it was the opinion of the generals that the infantry could not have passed through the water and have survived it."

Forrest's determination at Fort Donelson earned him recognition, but his actions after the Battle of Shiloh cemented his reputation. In the process of screening the Confederate retreat, Forrest battled with the pursuing Union column led by General William Sherman at a place called Fallen Timbers. With a small number of men, Forrest attacked Sherman, forcing him to deploy his troops and allowing the Confederate army enough time to escape. As Forrest rode out in advance of his men, he was quickly surrounded by Union soldiers. "Kill him! Kill him and his horse!" they shouted. Forrest fought back, swinging wildly with his saber and firing his revolver. As he turned away, a soldier shot him at point-blank range, but he still managed to remain in the saddle. The ball penetrated Forrest's side and lodged against his spine. Forrest reached down, grabbed his assailant by the collar, and pulled him up on his horse. Using him as a shield, he galloped back to his own troops.

Forrest's wound required two operations, and he was unable to return to action for several weeks. While convalescing, he was able to recruit additional men; his ad in the *Memphis Appeal* read, "Come on, boys, if you want a heap of fun and to kill some Yankees."

After July 1862, Forrest was back in action, forcing the Union garrison at Murfreesboro to surrender after threatening to have all of the defenders "put to the sword." To his old pattern of shock and surprise, Forrest had added a new tactic—bluff. He had ordered his men to shoot anything they saw in blue and to "do all you can to keep up the scare." He was to use this technique time and time again, and his subordinates would too. In several instances, they forced the surrender of superior Union forces simply by demanding it in Forrest's name, even though he was miles away.

There was, however, one ominous element in the events at Murfreesboro. Forrest had made a fortune through slave trading and considered black Southerners to be mere commodities. During an interview by a reporter from the

New York Times later in the war, Union General D. S. Stanley claimed that Forrest had been involved in the cold-blooded killing of a mulatto man, who was a servant to one of the officers captured at Murfreesboro. Allegedly, Forrest asked him what he was doing with a Union officer. The mulatto man answered that he was a freedman and was acting as his servant. Hearing that, Forrest drew his pistol and blew the man's brains out. There is no doubt that Forrest was angered by the participation of blacks in the Union army and often resorted to violence to express his anger, but there is no conclusive evidence to support this claim.

There was another incident involving Forrest at Murfreesboro. Captain William Richardson, who had been a prisoner at the Murfreesboro jail, later recalled what had happened: "After the fighting had ceased and the Federal prisoners were all brought together, General Forrest came to me and said: 'They tell me these men treated you inhumanely while in jail. Point them out to me.'" Richardson replied there was one man he could identify—the man who had set fire to the jail in hopes of killing the prisoners before they could be rescued. Forrest asked for the man to be pointed out. Sometime later at the next roll call, the man's name was called and no one answered. Forrest said, "Pass on, it's all right."

Deception continued to work for Forrest. It was the key to his success in the spring of 1863 against Colonel Abel Streight. Forrest had pursued the colonel through the mountains of northern Alabama for several weeks. When he finally caught up with him, Forrest had only 600 men and two guns; Streight had 1,500 men. Stretching his men out in a line that appeared to overlap the Federals, Forrest had his men make as much noise as possible to give the impression that he had a larger force. Streight's men were exhausted from the chase, so exhausted that they could barely stay awake long enough to eat. At that point, Forrest sent in a flag of truce requesting Streight's surrender, "to avoid useless effusion of blood."

The two men met under a flag of truce. Forrest made sure that Streight could see his troops and his two artillery pieces moving around a nearby hill. Streight inquired about the size of his command. Forrest responded, "I've got enough to whip you out of your boots." When Streight did not surrender, Forrest gave the command "Sound to mount!" to his men as though ordering 5,000 men to attack. Forrest was so convincing that Streight surrendered. When his deception was exposed after the surrender, Forrest was alleged to have said, "Ah, Colonel, all's fair in love and war, you know."

Forrest intimidated and bluffed not only his enemies but also his Confederate comrades. His own troops and even his commanding officers feared his explosive temper; he was often perceived as an overbearing bully with a homicidal rage, capable of anything.

Following the Battle of Chickamauga in September 1863, General Bragg failed to follow up his victory and allowed the Union forces to regroup at Chattanooga. Infuriated by Bragg's action, Forrest went to the general's headquarters and verbally attacked him, listing a series of grievances and telling him: "You have played the part of a damn scoundrel, and are a coward, and if you were any part of a man I would slap your jaw . . . I say to you that if you ever again try to interfere with me or cross my path it will be at the peril of your life." He demanded a transfer, which Bragg passed on to Richmond. Forrest never again served under Bragg, nor was he ever charged with insubordination. Bragg knew that Forrest would have no compunction about killing him, so he let the matter drop. Two weeks later, Forrest met with Jefferson Davis and was transferred to the West.

Forrest continued to conduct raids into Union-controlled territory. These raids had important strategic value, as Union defenders felt the constant threat from Forrest and were forced to commit extra troops to establish strong points at positions where he might attack. During the winter of 1863–1864, Sherman sent numerically superior cavalry forces after Forrest, only to have them return from their botched attempts. The first failure came in February 1864 at Okolona, Mississippi, where Forrest defeated General Sooy Smith's cavalry—7,000 strong—in a running battle. Again Forrest led a frontal assault on the enemy's rear guard. "His presence seemed to inspire everyone," a subordinate remembered. The Union troops withdrew to Memphis, disheartened and panic-stricken, but the victory had been costly for Forrest. A Yankee bullet claimed the life of his 26-year-old brother, Jeffrey, whom he had raised as a son and who was serving as a colonel in his cavalry corps. Within an hour after his brother's death, Forrest avenged it, killing three enemy soldiers with his sword. In the process, he had two horses shot from under him.

Forrest's victory over Smith gained him greater respect from General Grant. Grant later wrote, "Smith's command was nearly double that of Forrest, but not equal man to man." Perhaps Napoleon said it best: "In war, men are nothing, a man is everything." Nathan Bedford Forrest was such a man in war.

Forrest's most controversial exploit was the capture of Fort Pillow on April 12, 1864. The garrison at Fort Pillow consisted of about 600 men, half of them black, mostly escaped slaves. After Forrest's men had surrounded the fort, he issued his usual demand for surrender. Forrest promised his prisoners good treatment if they laid down their arms at once; otherwise, "I cannot be responsible for the fate of your command."

The fort commander refused. A Confederate colonel later recalled that the Federals "openly defied us from the breastworks to come and take the fort." Come to take the fort, they did! The outcome was never in doubt. Within minutes, the fort was breached, and the hand-to-hand combat quickly favored the Confederates. Once they had gained control, the killing didn't stop. Forrest's men continued to shoot and bayonet many of the helpless Union soldiers, particularly the black ones. One Confederate sergeant recalled: "The poor deluded Negroes would run up to our men, fall upon their knees and with uplifted hands scream for mercy, but they were ordered to their feet and then shot down. The white men fared little better." When a Confederate soldier tried to stop the slaughter, Forrest came up and said, "No! No! Shoot them like dogs." The slaughter at Fort Pillow, and Forrest's failure to control or even discourage the actions of his men, constitutes the blackest mark on his service record.

Whether Forrest ordered the massacre is still debated, but he certainly watched the slaughter proceed. The least damning thing that can be said of his action is that he lost control of his men. By the time the slaughter was over, there were 230 Union dead and 100 more seriously wounded. Confederate losses were only 14.

Many Northerners believed that Forrest ordered the massacre. A congressional committee that investigated the incident reached the same conclusion. In Forrest's report, he admitted that a great many blacks had been killed, but he claimed they had been killed in battle or while trying to escape. Today, most historians doubt that Forrest planned the massacre at Fort Pillow; they believe, however, he did little to stop it once it started. If Forrest was upset at what happened, it was probably because he lost control of his men; it is unlikely that he had any remorse about the results.

The massacre galvanized the North, leading to redoubled demands that Forrest be stopped. To answer this cry, General Sherman sent General Samuel Sturgis to hunt him down. Sherman said the infernal Forrest had to be stopped and killed, "if it cost 10,000 lives and bankrupts the Federal Treasury."

On May 2, 1864, Sturgis went after Forrest as he was withdrawing back into Mississippi, but failed to catch him. In June, a mixed column of 5,000 infantry, 3,000 cavalry, and 22 artillery pieces caught up with Forrest. By ordinary standards, Forrest could not have defeated such a force—he had no more than 4,800 men. When Forrest learned of Sturgis's advance, he made plans to meet him head-on. Forrest realized that Sturgis's men had been on the march for a week in heavy, humid weather and through roads consisting of deep, boggy mud. Forrest was hoping to use the natural elements against his enemies. As he predicted, the long march had exhausted the Union soldiers. By midday, the two sides were locked in fierce combat. Forrest's men fought dismounted, each man armed with two Colt navy revolvers rather than a saber, which proved to be more effective in hand-to-hand combat. Applying the same strategy as he had in other battles, Forrest divided his outnumbered troops into two groups and attacked from both flanks, using the classic envelopment movement. The Union line collapsed and the battle turned into a rout. By the end of the day, Sturgis had lost half his command, and his demoralized force was in complete retreat. Order gave way to confusion and confusion to panic. Forrest continued to chase the retreating Federals far into the night. The Battle of Brice's Cross Roads proved to be one of Forrest's greatest victories.

With Forrest still creating havoc in Mississippi, Sherman diverted two divisions to the region, making a promise that neither he nor his subordinates would be able to keep. "I will order them to make up a force and go out to follow Forrest to the death," Sherman said. "There will be no peace in Tennessee until Forrest is dead!"

Forrest continued to wreak havoc on Union forces, but the situation for the Confederacy had become critical and no daring cavalry raids could prevent the inevitable. By the beginning of 1865, it was clear to Forrest that the war was lost. He had his last encounter with Union troops in April at Selma, Alabama. Union General James Wilson intercepted Forrest's cavalry and was prepared to attack its remnants when news of Lee's surrender at Appomattox arrived.

On May 4, Forrest's department commander, General Richard Taylor, surrendered. Although technically Taylor's action was binding on every soldier under his command, there was nothing to prevent Forrest from continuing to fight. Forrest, however, had had enough of war. His response was blunt: "Any man who is in favor of a further prosecution of this war is a fit subject for a lunatic asylum, and ought to be sent there immediately."

On May 9, Forrest issued his farewell address to his men: "That we are beaten is a self-evident fact, and any further resistance on our part would be justly regarded as the height of folly and rashness." Instead, he urged his men to accept the verdict of the war, submit to federal authority, and be good citizens. He concluded, "Obey the laws, preserve your honor and the government to which you have surrendered." In many respects, Forrest's farewell address was similar to that of Robert E. Lee.

After the war, Forrest returned to what was left of his plantations. His former slaves refused to leave him, and with their help, he soon restored his land. He was prosperous enough to support his family and a number of Confederate veterans who had lost everything during the war.

As a businessman, Forrest wanted to see the South restored to its rightful place in the Union. He said: "I did all in my power to break up the government but I found it a useless undertaking and I now resolve to stand by the government as earnestly and honestly as I fought it. I'm also aware that I am at this moment regarded in large communities of the North with abhorrence as a detestable monster, ruthless and swift to take life."

Forrest worked diligently to clear himself of charges stemming from the alleged Fort Pillow massacre. He was anxious for a presidential pardon. Because he had been a high-ranking Confederate officer and before the war owned property valued at above $20,000, he had to apply directly to the president for his pardon. Although the Fort Pillow massacre continued to be an obstacle to this effort,

Forrest found influential friends to intercede for him with Andrew Johnson. Johnson's lame-duck administration had nothing to lose by granting the pardon.

Like Lee, Forrest became a symbol of the Southern cause. Lee was careful to appear as reconciled to the new political order as possible and became the symbol for those in the South who desired a true reunion. Forrest, on the other hand, became deeply involved in the divisive politics of Reconstruction and became the symbol of white supremacy. Forrest could accept the death of slavery, but he never believed in political equality for African Americans. Their proper role in society, Forrest believed, was laboring under the domination of benevolent white employers.

Bedford Forrest, for the moment, followed the guidelines for Reconstruction. Knowing that he faced the threat of arrest at any time may have had something to do with his behavior. Friends advised him to go to Europe until he could return safely. Forrest declined, saying, "This is my country. I am hard at work upon my plantation, and carefully observing the obligations of my parole."

Then in the spring of 1866, two disturbing events befell Forrest. The first was connected with his indictment for treason. He was required to post a $10,000 bond until his trial in September. Although he had to renew the bond in September, the trial for treason never took place.

At the same time, Forrest was involved in another more serious trial—the murder of Thomas Edwards, a freedman on his plantation. A fight between the two men had led to Edwards's death. Edwards was a disgruntled worker who frequently abused animals and his wife. According to a laborer on the plantation, on one occasion Edwards "whipped his wife so unmercifully that a physician was called to attend her." Edwards, saying that his treatment of his wife was his business, threatened to shoot anyone who interfered. Fiercely defensive over what he saw as a personal choice, Edwards told a carpenter on Forrest's plantation, "I will whip my wife when I damn please." When the man warned him that his behavior was against Forrest's orders forbidding a man from whipping his wife, Edwards dismissed the warning: "I do not care a God damn for General Forrest or any other God damn man. If General Forrest or any other man attempts to interfere with me in the privilege I enjoy as regards whipping her or beating her, I'll cut his God damn guts out."

Finally, on March 31, matters came to a head between Edwards and Forrest. When Forrest asked Edwards for help, the man ignored the general's call and went into his cabin where, according to Forrest, he "commenced cursing and abusing his wife." Forrest followed Edwards into the cabin, ordering him to stop abusing his wife or he would whip him. With that, Edwards "stepped back" and holding a knife in his hand, remarked, "Damn you, I ask you no odds." There are several versions of what happened next, but whatever the exact sequence of events, Forrest killed Edwards. Again Forrest had taken out his rage on a black man and resorted to violence to solve a problem.

Word of the altercation spread throughout the plantation and the surrounding area. Within a short time, Deputy Wirt Shaw arrived to arrest Forrest. In the morning, they left for Friar's Point by steamboat. When Forrest noticed that the boat was filled with Federal soldiers, he asked Shaw not to let the men know who he was for fear of harassment or even worse. Shaw agreed, but Forrest was soon recognized; the results were quite unexpected. As Shaw remembered: "Instead of being insulted by them, he was very much honored and lionized. Nothing on the boat was too good for him. They were dined and champagned." When the Federals learned why Forrest was on the boat, they offered to toss the deputy overboard and take Forrest to Memphis. Forrest rejected their offer, saying that he wanted to get the affair over and assuring his would-be benefactors that he anticipated no trouble.

In April, Forrest was indicted for the murder of Thomas Edwards. Bail was set at $10,000 and the trial scheduled for the next term of the circuit court. Throughout the summer months, the court subpoenaed witnesses and summoned prospective jurors. On October 8, 1866, the trial began. Three days later, the jury found Forrest not guilty.

In 1867, the Republican majority in Congress began a political war with President Johnson for control of Reconstruction, a war it quickly won. The lenient terms of Johnson's policies were revoked, and a new policy that disenfranchised former Confederates was instituted. At the same time, African Americans were enfranchised. The purpose of the Reconstruction by the Radical Republicans, as seen by many Southerners, was to create a federal government controlled by die-hard Unionists and supported by the votes of recently freed slaves.

With white supremacy being threatened, reactionary organizations began to form in the South. The largest of these was the Ku Klux Klan, a secret, quasi-fraternal order. The Klan's purpose was to intimidate Republican voters and leaders and to control the black population that had been granted political rights in the South. The Klan became a night-riding organization that would abduct individual Republican leaders—black and white—beat them, and sometimes even kill them.

Forrest was initiated into the Klan by John Morton, his former artillery chief, a Grand Cyclops of the Nashville branch. He soon became very active and powerful within the organization. Despite his later claims of having no connection with the Klan, his denials are unconvincing. Most scholars have concluded that he was. Nathan Bedford Forrest fought to return rule of the South to the "proper hands." An intimidating person, he was willing to go to great lengths, employing violence when necessary. He publicly counseled peace and submission to federal authority, while privately he waged war against the new order in the South. Forrest could neither understand nor appreciate the concerns of former slaves, and he did not try to do so. He believed that their interests were best reflected in his own interests. It is easy to believe that Forrest was a member of the Ku Klux Klan. Although he may not have been the Grand Wizard, as is often claimed, he certainly wielded enormous influence in the Klan.

During the summer of 1868, Forrest traveled extensively throughout the South on what he claimed was business. It is interesting to note that shortly after his visits, the first Klan notices appeared in local newspapers. On one occasion, Forrest claimed that there were 40,000 Klansmen in Tennessee and more than half a million in the South. Forrest explained that the Klan had been formed as a "protective political military organization" designed to fight the influence of Republican organizations in the South. The Klan soon became a major force of counterrevolution in Tennessee and the rest of the South.

Many white Southerners, including Forrest, hoped to persuade black Southerners to return to the status quo antebellum, working much as they had when they were slaves. When persuasion failed, the Klan turned to more violent means of controlling the new voters. Forrest was walking a tightrope; he wanted to return the former prewar leadership to power and keep blacks in their "proper place." But he also wanted to avoid overt activities that might bring even greater wrath on the South from the federal government. The Klan's violent acts were certain to do just that.

Forrest's tenure with the Klan lasted only about a year, because he began to feel that the organization was getting out of control. In 1869, he issued "General Order Number One," calling upon Klansmen everywhere to curtail their activities; but it did not call for the organization to be disbanded. The order apparently formed the basis of his later claim that he had "suppressed" the Klan.

In 1871–1872, General Forrest was summoned before a committee of Congress appointed to look into the affairs of the Ku Klux Klan. The committee believed that he and General John B. Gordon could give them valuable information about the Klan. Forrest testified that while he did not take an active part in the Klan, he knew it was an association of citizens in his state organized for their own self-protection. Forrest stated that he had advised against their engaging in violence and urged them to disband.

Forrest's business ventures floundered after the war. In 1867, he became president of the Planter's Insurance Company; a year later, he filed for bankruptcy. In 1868, his request to have his U.S. citizenship rights restored was approved, and he received a pardon from President Johnson. For six years following his pardon, Forrest served as president of the Selma, Marion, and Memphis Railroad. He devoted himself to the railroad, displaying a strong business sense. He conducted his railroad business as he had his slave trading and his military career—in his own headstrong, independent way. In 1874, Forrest resigned from the debt-ridden railroad.

In Forrest's last years, he seemed to mellow with age. He became more respectful of his wife and with her encouragement, gave up his lifelong gambling habit. It was also through her influence that Forrest was baptized, and in 1875, he joined the Presbyterian Church. As his health began to decline, Forrest relied more and more on his wife for help, even though she insisted that he adhere to a bland, unappetizing diet. "I know Mary is the best friend I have on earth," he said.

Forrest's health was rapidly deteriorating. At one time, he admitted that he had "not been in good health since the war." On September 21, 1876, he attended a reunion of the 7th Tennessee Cavalry. In a moving address to his old comrades in arms, he concluded by saying, "Soldiers, I was afraid that I could not be with you today, but I could not bear the thought of not meeting with you." Forrest had always kept his promise to his men, but he was unable to keep the promise he made that day to continue meeting with them. His failing health would not permit it.

During the spring of 1877, Forrest's health failed even more rapidly. In an effort to improve it, he traveled to Hurricane Springs to "take the waters." By the end of August, reports of Forrest's health were extremely negative. He had for months been afflicted with chronic diarrhea and a malarial impregnation that had brought on a combination of diseases.

As he approached death, Forrest sought to settle his affairs in hopes of leaving his son free of the legal problems that had plagued him since the war, and particularly since the railroad failed. Near the end, Forrest reflected on his life: "My life has been a battle from the start. It was a fight to achieve a livelihood for those dependent upon me in my younger days, and independence for myself when I grew up to manhood, as well as the terrible turmoil of the Civil War."

The man who had a reputation for having a terrible temper and being a ferocious fighter would admit: "I have seen too much of violence and I want to close my days at peace with all the world, and I am now at peace with my Maker." For many of his war comrades, this statement must have come as a surprise; for Forrest it was the acceptance of religion in his life.

One of the last men to call on Forrest was Jefferson Davis, but the ailing cavalryman hardly recognized the former president of the Confederacy. On the evening of October 29, 1877, Forrest uttered his last words. Unlike Stonewall Jackson, Robert E. Lee, and other former Confederates, he did not refer to a scene of a distant battle. His last words were characteristically a command: "Call my wife!"

Forrest's funeral procession stretched for the three miles from Jesse Forrest's home to the Elmwood Cemetery. Twenty thousand people lined the streets or followed the casket. Former comrades, subordinates, and superiors came to pay homage to the fallen warrior. Jefferson Davis served as one of the pallbearers. At his request, Forrest was buried in his Confederate uniform.

He was eulogized throughout the country by both friend and foe. Sherman called him "the most remarkable man" the war produced, with a "genius for strategy which was original and . . . to me incomprehensible. . . . He seemed to always know what I was doing or intended to do, while I . . . could never . . . form any satisfactory idea of what he was trying to accomplish." Joseph Johnston, when asked the name of the greatest soldier of the war, replied without hesitation, "Forrest."

At the grave in Elmwood Cemetery, the many floral arrangements included a clutch of wildflowers brought by Colonel John Donovan. He had been handed them, Donovan said, when his train stopped at a station in rural Alabama. "Take these to Memphis and place them on General Forrest's grave," said a thirteen-year-old girl. "They are sent because General Joseph Wheeler's daughter loved him."

But everyone did not love him. The *New York Times* published an obituary that was understandably less positive. It noted that while Lee had been an example of the "gallant soldiers and dignified gentlemen" of refined Virginia, Forrest typified the "reckless ruffianism and cutthroat daring" of the Southwest. It reported that he was "notoriously blood-thirsty and revengeful." The *Times* chose not to mention Forrest's surrender address at Gainesville. It did, however, describe the "cold-blooded massacre" at Fort Pillow as an event with which his name would ever be associated. Since the war, the paper continued, Forrest's principal occupation seems to have been trying to explain away the Fort Pillow affair.

In 1905, the city of Memphis unveiled an equestrian statue of Forrest in a park named in his honor. Both Forrest and his wife, who died fifteen years after her husband, were reinterred at its base. Recently, several African American groups have insisted that the monument be dismantled and removed from the park. For them, Forrest remains the slave trader, the butcher of Fort Pillow, the Grand Wizard of the Ku Klux Klan, and a racist.

Some white Southerners and Civil War enthusiasts prefer to think of Forrest as the untutored military genius, the Wizard of the Saddle, the incredible soldier who rose from private to lieutenant general in four years of war. They recall the Forrest who killed thirty Yankees, as well as some of his own men, in personal combat during the war. They are amazed at the feats of the man who survived four wounds that would have killed most men. And they remember the brilliant raider, the matchless tactician, and the ruthless fighter.

In the final analysis, Nathan Bedford Forrest was a man out of control who solved his problems through violence. Above all else, he was a racist. It is difficult to see him as a man to admire.

13   General with the "Slows"

GEORGE B. MCCLELLAN

FEW Civil War figures have inspired as much passion and controversy during their own lifetimes as George B. McClellan. When the Civil War began in 1861, the North was confident that it could bring a speedy, victorious end to the war. After McClellan's early victory in western Virginia, it was believed he would be the man to lead the army to victory. At the age of thirty-four, he was named commander of the Army of the Potomac and general in chief of the entire Union army. By the fall of 1862, the hope for a quick victory had vanished, and McClellan had been relieved of his duties. To some, McClellan had been a failure; to others, a scapegoat. The war would continue three years longer, many believed, than it should have. Few American commanders had ever promised so much and delivered so little as General George McClellan.

McClellan's early life and military career gave no indication of the troubles that would plague him later. George McClellan was born on December 3, 1826, to Dr. George and Elizabeth McClellan.

George's father traveled in the upper ranks of Philadelphia society and numbered among his acquaintances many notables; his mother was also from one of Philadelphia's leading families. Together, the couple produced five children. Elizabeth was a woman of culture and refinement, ensuring that her children had the best education Philadelphia could offer. Young George attended an infant school at the age of five and then four years of private school. In 1838, he enrolled at a preparatory academy of the University of Pennsylvania. Two years later, at the age of thirteen, he entered the university.

Little is recorded of George McClellan's youth beyond his schooling. His sister Frederica remembered him as "the brightest, merriest, most unselfish of boys . . . , fond of books and study . . . and always the soul of honor." George enjoyed academic success early; he was gifted, bordering on genius. In 1842, at the age of fifteen, he entered the U.S. Military Academy at West Point.

George was legally too young to enter West Point, but the academic board waived the age requirements in his case. Despite his youth, he had already passed two years at the University of Pennsylvania, where he had developed an impressive command of language, the classics, and modern literature. He was even more accomplished in mathematics. From the age of ten, George had dreamed of going to West Point and becoming a soldier. Before final admission, entering students had to pass a mental and physical examination. Of the 122 entering cadets, the class lost thirty members after the examination. McClellan, whom the cut never came near, was elated at having passed the first hurdle. In a letter to his sister, Frederica, he wrote, "I feel in high spirits. . . . I know I can do as well as anyone in both my studies and my military duties. If this state of mind continues, I will be able to stay here for four years."

The general perception today of West Point before the Civil War is that it produced great military men. In reality, the program of study was designed to produce great engineers and did little to teach its graduates how to run an army. As one of the best and brightest in his class, McClellan became an engineer. When directing his military campaigns, McClellan utilized his engineering skills in almost everything he did.

McClellan, like others in his class, was greatly influenced by the military legacy of Napoleon. He soon came to regard himself as a young Napoleon. He did not call himself that, but did not discourage others when they made that comparison.

As a cadet, McClellan sometimes worked only as hard as was necessary. Many years later, Charles Stewart, recalling their academic rivalry, would say, "He was well educated, and, when he chose to be, brilliant." The competition between the two was intense. McClellan felt he deserved first place in the class of 1846 but had to settle for second behind Stewart. He did not accept the verdict gracefully. "I must confess that I have malice enough to want to show them that if I did not graduate head of my class, I can nevertheless do something," he wrote his family. In later years, he would look back with satisfaction. Forty-four of the fifty-eight classmates would fight in the Civil War. Of these, six would serve under him as generals in the Army of the Potomac—and four others against him in the Army of Northern Virginia. Two of these Confederates were Thomas Jackson, seventeenth in class rank, destined for military greatness as Stonewall Jackson; and George Pickett, who finished last, remembered for his famous charge at Gettysburg.

There was no doubt in the opinion of the class who their real star had been. It had not been Stewart, despite the final ranking. William Gardner, one of McClellan's classmates, spoke for them when he said that McClellan was thought to be "the ablest man in the class. . . . We expected him to make a great record in the army, and if opportunity presented, we predicted real military fame for him."

The Mexican War broke out in 1846, the year George McClellan graduated from West Point. When he heard the news, he was exultant; graduation had come with a gratifying bonus. "Hip! Hip! Hurrah!" he wrote home. "War at last, sure enough! Ain't it glorious!" McClellan had hoped this would happen. He had his heart set on going directly to Mexico after graduating. Now the government in Washington had answered his prayers by declaring war on Mexico.

McClellan and his classmates were delighted with the government's plans to double the size of the army to meet the needs of the war. This meant they were more likely to be quickly promoted from their lowly status as brevet second lieutenant. In peacetime, they could expect to remain at that rank until the second lieutenants above them were promoted, resigned, or died. In wartime, promotions came rapidly: Armies expanded and fought, and soldiers died. The war seemed promising and was very popular at West Point.

McClellan didn't go to Mexico immediately after graduation, as he had hoped. He was ordered instead to a newly formed engineer outfit, where he was to assist in their training. It took about four months to prepare the company for combat. In September, McClellan and Company A sailed from New York City for Mexico, arriving at Brazos de Santiago fourteen days later.

In Mexico, McClellan quickly made use of his training in engineering and mapmaking. Although his combat responsibilities were minimal, McClellan did see some action. The battle at Contreras was memorable to him because of his narrow escapes. In the course of battle, he lost two horses and was knocked to the ground by enemy artillery fire. His commander, Brigadier General Persifor Smith, noted that "nothing seemed to [McClellan] too bold to be undertaken or too difficult to be executed." McClellan was commended and promoted to brevet first lieutenant "for gallant and meritorious conduct."

From Mexico City, McClellan wrote to his brother John: "I feel so glad and proud that I have got safely through the battles of this war. . . . Thank God! our name has not suffered, so far, at my hands." He had reason to be proud. He had demonstrated his courage at Veracruz, Cerro Gordo, Mexico City, and Chapultepec and would earn a second brevet promotion to captain.

Following the war, McClellan was involved in surveying and exploring what was then the Wild West. It was during his western tour of duty that McClellan met Mary Ellen Marcy, the eighteen-year-old daughter of Captain Randolph B. Marcy, his commanding officer. Captain Marcy proved to be one of the few superiors under whom McClellan ever served without friction. Soon George was courting his daughter. Ellen Marcy was an attractive, vivacious young woman who was the apple of her father's eye and the subject of his anxious matchmaking. Captain Marcy was happy to see George show interest in his daughter, pointing out that he was "one of the most brilliant men of his rank" and came from a good family. McClellan was a catch, he said, "that any young lady might justly be proud of."

Ellen had a different idea about whom she wanted to marry. One morning in June 1854, George declared his love for her and proposed marriage. To his dismay, she rejected him. He was furious with himself for being foolish by "pushing too far and too quickly." He would bide his time and pray for a change of heart.

Perhaps the reason Ellen Marcy continued to put off McClellan's desire to marry her was the sheer number of suitors paying her court. Before she was twenty-five, Ellen had received at least nine proposals of marriage. But McClellan did not give up; he continued to write to her and hope.

McClellan quickly earned a reputation as one of the army's brightest military minds. As a result, he was chosen as a member of a team of army officers to observe and collect information about the war in the Crimea, in which both France and England were involved. That McClellan, not yet thirty, would be sent to Europe with a group of senior officers is some indication of his standing in the army. Owing to the ideas he would bring back from his European travels, McClellan was marked as a leading man in the military. His star was on the rise.

McClellan put to use some of the things he had learned in Europe. He proposed the McClellan saddle, which he adapted from those he had seen in Europe. He introduced the shelter tent, which later became known as the pup tent. The bayonet manual and drill that the army adopted were the result of translations and modifications McClellan had made from a French text.

Despite McClellan's success in the army, he realized that promotion was a slow process during peacetime, so in 1857 he left the military. He quickly went to work as chief engineer for the Illinois Central Railroad. McClellan welcomed the freedom and authority of his new position. He said he enjoyed the luxury of making decisions on his own without first referring to the adjutant general or the secretary of war. "I feel already as if a heavy load was removed from my shoulders," he said. His salary was $3,000 a year—more than twice his army pay—with a promise of advancement to vice president at $5,000 if he proved himself.

McClellan kept in touch with Ellen after leaving the army. In his letters, he tried to enlist her sympathy for his bachelor's existence. He described his lonely games of chess, which he was forced to play against himself. He "dread[ed] to think of the future," he said. "It seems so blank—no goal to reach, no objective to strive for!" Ellen continued to keep company with other men.

One suitor who began courting her was McClellan's friend from West Point, Ambrose Powell Hill. Hill quickly fell in love with Ellen and proposed; she accepted. Hill had already given her an engagement ring before the Marcys were aware of the situation. Both parents reacted with anything but joy. They urged their daughter to wait at least six months before marrying. Ellen's father painted a harsh picture of life on the frontier as an army officer's wife; moreover, he said, Hill's means were limited. To marry him, he warned Ellen, was to resign herself to "a life of exile, deprivation, and poverty." He also pointed out the differences in their backgrounds. The Marcys were Northerners; Hill was a Southerner, brought up in a "detested" slave environment. He wanted better for her, he said, and forbade her to see Hill again. Ellen's mother favored McClellan. After he returned from Europe, she wrote to Ellen: "How very kind he is . . . such a treasure you have lost forever . . . the time is coming sooner or later . . . when you will regret if ever a woman did—mark my words."

Quickly, Mrs. Marcy took action—with a vengeance. She began to circulate stories about Hill's medical problems, the most embarrassing of which was sex related. When McClellan learned what was happening, he immediately wrote to Mrs. Marcy defending his friend's honor: "You have been unjust to him, and you have said unpleasant and bitter things . . . about one of my oldest and dearest friends."

By then, the damage had been done, and in July Ellen told her parents the affair was over. She returned the engagement ring to Hill. Hill wrote to McClellan expressing his concern that people would have a false impression of his affair with Ellen. At the expense of his own vanity, he admitted to McClellan that it was she, not he, who had broken the engagement. The two continued to be good friends despite their love for the same woman.

Ellen's suitors came and went, but McClellan was always there biding his time. Finally she accepted, and they were married on May 22, 1860. Hill was a groomsman in the wedding. His best wishes were sincere and strong.

During the war, McClellan's army would be assaulted repeatedly by Hill's division. McClellan's troops formulated a theory that Hill's fierce attacks were an attempt to get revenge on his rival. After one of these attacks, a Union veteran exclaimed disgustedly, "My God Nelly (Ellen), why didn't you marry him (Hill)!" Later when this anecdote was told to McClellan at an 1885 reunion, he smiled and said: "Fiction no doubt, but surely no one could have married a more gallant soldier than A. P. Hill."

George and Ellen would have twenty-five years together. They were utterly devoted to each other. "My whole existence is wrapped up in you," he told her. During their engagement, he began his lifelong habit of writing to her at least once every day during their separation. He also underwent an evangelical religious regeneration, which would affect his outlook on life. Taking on the religious beliefs of the Presbyterian faith that he embraced, he believed that his union had been predestined, an example of God's will acting on those He elected. Later, when war began and McClellan was called to the world's stage, he accepted that, too, as God's will.

A month after his wedding, McClellan was offered the post of superintendent, and later president, of the Ohio and Mississippi Railroad. His salary was $10,000, double his Illinois Central salary. But his life was due for a drastic change in just a short time.

In 1860, with the clouds of war hanging over Washington, there was no doubt that George McClellan would play a major role in the federal army. The variety of his assignments, particularly his year of observing Europe's armies, had ranked him as one of the military intellectuals of the prewar army. In addition, his four years as railroad executive gave him valuable experience in the vital area of military logistics. It came as no surprise that after the firing on Fort Sumter, McClellan became the most sought-after former officer in the North. At age thirty-four, he reentered the army at the rank of major general, outranked only by the general-in-chief himself, Winfield Scott.

McClellan quickly took over the Ohio volunteers. Acting in concert with other forces in the East, he began his first successful Union campaign of the war. In an attempt to clear western Virginia of Confederate influence, McClellan, with a force of men, marched on Grafton. The Confederates retreated southward to the village of Philippi, allowing McClellan to occupy Grafton without a single shot being fired. On June 3, the small Confederate force at Philippi was routed, freeing the western part of the state of Confederate troops. Eight days later, delegates from Virginia's western counties met in convention, setting up their own provisional state government and naming Francis H. Pierpont governor. For McClellan, it was an excellent way to begin a campaign. He became the first Yankee hero of the war. The *New York Times* spoke highly of him: "We feel proud of our wise and brave young major general. There is a future behind him."

On July 21, 1861, in the first major engagement of the war, the Union experienced a disastrous defeat at Bull Run. The sight of leaderless soldiers running in panic through the streets had a tremendously demoralizing effect on the people of Washington and the government itself. Washington was threatened; danger was near, and someone was needed to bring order out of chaos. To do this, the Union turned to the heroic general of the war thus far—George B. McClellan. On July 22, Lincoln informed McClellan that he was to take command of the Army of the Potomac. To his wife, Ellen, McClellan wrote, "I find myself in a new and strange position here—President, cabinet, General [Winfield] Scott . . . all deferring to me. By some strange operation of magic, I seem to have become the power of the land."

McClellan might have been a better man had he encountered some humbling reverses in his early years. He might have been a better general when he took over the eastern command had he been tested in his first battle in western Virginia. He triumphed too easily and was convinced that he was a great soldier. The public was eager for a hero and went wild over him. He looked and acted the way a soldier and hero should act. He was handsome and had a magnetic personality. He had an aura that drew men to him. Admirers said he was the only general who, by simply riding up to them, could induce men to stop what they were doing and follow him. He stood only five feet, eight inches tall, but possessed tremendous shoulders and chest. In manner, he was courteous and sometimes boyish; and like a proper American hero of the time, he smoked and chewed tobacco. They said he looked like Napoleon, and photographers asked him to pose in a typical Napoleonic manner. The press referred to him as the young Napoleon. Wherever he went, crowds gathered to stare at him. He began to feel that people looked at him as their savior, the one who could protect them from danger. Later, when he was about to become general in chief, he wrote his wife: "I was called to do it; my previous life seems to have been unwittingly directed to this great end."

In the Western Virginia Campaign, McClellan revealed the military and personal characteristics he would later manifest in his operations and commands. He was an excellent organizer and trainer of troops. His men, sensing that he identified himself with them, idolized him. In preparing for battle, he was confident and energetic; but when it came time for battle, he was slow and timid. He exaggerated every obstacle; in particular, the size of the opposing army increased in his mind the closer he got to it. In battle, he hesitated to throw his entire force at the enemy at the critical time, and he withdrew when bolder men would have attacked.

Few generals were more popular with their soldiers than George McClellan. They were attracted by his sunny personality and confident smile. They affectionately called him "Little Mac." On an inspection trip, Lincoln was impressed with the enthusiasm of the soldiers for McClellan, especially when they cheered for him.

At first, Lincoln felt confident with his choice to lead the Army of the

Potomac, not realizing there were some serious flaws in McClellan's character, among which was his reaction to superiors and fellow officers. Though haughty and officious with them, McClellan was humble in front of his soldiers. At the beginning of the war, few realized the extent of McClellan's egotism. His unbridled ego quickly found him at odds with General Scott. Lincoln, soon realizing that General Scott had come to the end of his usefulness as a military leader, retired him with honors and tributes. The president then was ready to place the responsibility of the army in McClellan's hands. On November 1, 1861, at the age of 34, George McClellan assumed the nation's highest military position.

McClellan immediately faced the difficult task of restoring confidence in his army after their brutal defeat at Manassas. He issued his grandiose edicts and proclamations. He demanded and received the best for his troops. McClellan made every man under his command, down to the lowest private, believe that he cared about them—and indeed he did. In the end, it might be that he cared about his soldiers too much.

McClellan set up schools of instruction to train his men; camps encircled the entire city of Washington. He drilled the men constantly. As a result of his efforts, the Army of the Potomac gained confidence and began to see themselves as part of a coordinated military machine. Their sense of accomplishment and pride had much to do with the feelings the army had for McClellan. He wrote to Ellen of his success: "I have restored order very completely . . . you have no idea how the men brighten up now when I go among them. I can see every eye glisten. Yesterday they nearly pulled me to pieces in one regiment. You never heard such yelling."

McClellan felt that he was the leader of this army and that this army was his army. He referred to it that way almost to the day he died. McClellan was skilled in creating and training an army, but his motherly instinct hampered his ability to send them into battle. He wanted the army to be the best that ever took the field, but at the same time, he wanted no harm to come to it. To instill pride in the army, he staged grand reviews, not realizing the image the army had created would lead the people and politicians to press him to act. Throughout the summer and fall of 1861, McClellan did nothing. Pressure was increasing on him to take action. As the year advanced, McClellan had the perfect excuse for not moving his army—winter. Throughout the winter, he did nothing but stay in camp and build his army.

The pressure to move his army mounted, but McClellan held his ground. His response was: "So soon as I feel that my army is well organized and well disciplined and strong enough, I will advance and force the Rebels to a battle on a field of my own selection. A long time must elapse before I can do that."

McClellan had other problems, philosophical ones that would strain his relations with the president. He was far more conservative in his war aims than

Lincoln. McClellan was a Democrat who believed strongly in preserving the Union but opposed freeing the slaves. He did not get along with Lincoln and his administration and showed little respect for them. "The President is an idiot! I only wish to save my country and find the incapables around me will not permit it," he said.

McClellan's contempt for Lincoln grew to insubordination. One evening, Lincoln went to McClellan's house and asked a servant to tell him he wanted to see him. McClellan sent word back, "Tell him I have gone to bed." When Lincoln's friends asked why he put up with such rude treatment, he said humbly, "I would hold McClellan's horse if it would help win the war."

As the new year rolled around, McClellan had still not moved his army. After the spring of 1862, more and more often Lincoln spoke of McClellan as the general "with the slows." Finally Lincoln wrote to McClellan, ordering him to either attack Richmond or step down from commander of the Army of the Potomac. Faced with the need to act, McClellan proposed to attack Richmond by moving his army to the Virginia Peninsula and advancing on the Confederate capital from the Chesapeake Bay.

The Peninsula Campaign was launched in March. Transports carrying more than 120,000 of McClellan's men landed on the Virginia Peninsula. It was the largest water-borne military operation in American history. McClellan moved his troops up the peninsula to Yorktown, where they laid siege to the Confederate line. Commanding the army on the other side was General Joseph Johnston, a man similar to McClellan in leadership style. Both were brave men, but fearful of the ultimate responsibility for leading an army and risking defeat. Though McClellan's army was moving steadily up the peninsula with very little resistance from Johnston, McClellan still pressured the Lincoln administration for more troops.

In the Battle of Seven Pines in late May, Johnston was wounded. He was replaced by Robert E. Lee, and that changed everything. When McClellan learned that Johnston was being replaced by Lee, he was well pleased. General Lee, he assured President Lincoln, "is too cautious and weak under grave responsibility—personally brave and energetic to a fault, he yet is wanting in moral firmness when pressed by heavy responsibility and is likely to be timid and irresolute in action." McClellan was confident of victory. When finally they met in the Seven Days' Battles outside Richmond two months later, McClellan's assessment of Lee proved wrong. Ironically, he had precisely predicted not Lee's response to the pressure of command but his own. Each general had entered the contest as the commander of his nation's principal army; each was seen as a great leader. Lee eventually became one of the best generals America ever produced. McClellan is now dismissed as "merely an attractive, but vain and unstable man, with considerable military knowledge, who set on a horse well and wanted to be President."

McClellan, unable to defeat Lee's army, blamed it on having been outnumbered and needing reinforcements. On June 25, he reported: "The Rebel force is stated at 200,000. I shall have to contend against vastly superior odds if these reports be true. I regret my inferiority in numbers, but I feel that I am in no way responsible for it." Confederate strength was actually 80,000.

When his request for more troops was denied, McClellan anticipated defeat. He was less concerned with gaining victory in the coming battles and more on salvaging what he could from defeat. In July, McClellan was ordered to withdraw from his position on the peninsula.

General McClellan knew where to lay blame for his failure during the Peninsula Campaign. The authors of his defeat, he said, were the "heartless villains" in Washington who "have done their best to sacrifice as noble an army as ever marched to battle." From the very beginning, he said, "Stanton and his cohorts had wanted him defeated and overthrown, so that disunion would prevail and they could be free to rule unhampered in the North." McClellan believed that Stanton had recognized him as his enemy who must be destroyed. "They are aware that I have seen through their villainous schemes and that if I succeed my foot will be on their necks."

McClellan continued to rationalize his defeat, standing firm in his belief that everything that had happened to him on the peninsula was God's will. Consequently, nothing was his fault and everything was for the best. The hand of God had dictated the outcome of the Seven Days' Campaign, and he believed his defeat was actually a blessing in disguise. "I think I begin to see His wise purpose in all this." McClellan told his wife. "If I had succeeded in taking Richmond now, the fanatics of the North might have been too powerful and reunion impossible."

After McClellan's failure on the peninsula, Lincoln placed his army under the command of General John Pope to assist in the Second Battle of Manassas. Only two of his corps arrived in·time to fight, and the Union army suffered another crushing defeat. Pope's army and the rest of McClellan's army now crowded together in Washington. McClellan found himself a general without an army, but that did not last long. Despite Lincoln's frustrations with McClellan's cautiousness, he had no one else to whom he could turn.

On September 1, Lincoln restored McClellan to his former position at the head of the Army of the Potomac. For Lincoln, this was the most difficult   military-command decision he had to make during the war. It was counter to the wishes of most of his cabinet, which was about to present him with a petition calling for McClellan's dismissal. According to Attorney General Edward Bates's account, Lincoln "was in deep distress . . . seemed wrung by the bitterest anguish." Lincoln was faced with little choice despite his earlier statement that "McClellan can be trusted to act on the defensive, but having the 'slows' he is good for nothing for an onward movement." When the cabinet learned of Lincoln's decision, the two radical members, Stanton and Chase, angrily protested. Lincoln insisted that McClellan "had beyond any officer the confidence of the army. Though deficient in the positive qualities which are necessary for an energetic commander, his organizing powers could be made temporarily available till the troops were rallied." The infuriated Chase later wrote: "I could not but feel that giving the command to him [McClellan] was equivalent to giving Washington to the Rebels." Stanton was equally angry at Lincoln's renewed confidence in McClellan and felt so disgusted that for a while he considered resigning as secretary of war. But Lincoln stood strong in his defense of McClellan: "There is no man in the army who can lick these troops of ours into shape half as well as he. . . . McClellan has the army with him," he said.

When the Union army learned that Little Mac was returning, the men broke into cheers. Despite the failure of the Peninsula Campaign, they retained their faith in him. In a short time, McClellan had the army organized and ready to fight. Meanwhile Lee moved into western Maryland, hoping to draw McClellan out of the impregnable fortification of Washington and into the open.

Lee's strategy worked—McClellan's army began moving toward Frederick, Maryland, to intercept Lee. Then on September 13, McClellan had one of the most extraordinary pieces of luck; two soldiers accidentally found a copy of a Confederate dispatch indicating that Lee had divided his army. Lee's army was already smaller than McClellan's. To divide it, particularly in enemy territory, was a very dangerous action. One part of Lee's army under Stonewall Jackson was sent to Harpers Ferry, while the remaining part was deployed around Hagerstown to the north. "Here is a paper," McClellan said, "with which if I cannot whip Bobbie Lee I will be willing to go home."

With this important information in hand, McClellan set his troops in motion, but with his customary timidity on engaging the enemy. Not until the evening of September 16 did he bring his 70,000-man army in position to attack the Confederates. By then, Jackson had captured Harpers Ferry, and Lee had regrouped all his forces except A. P. Hill's division, which was still at Harpers Ferry. Lee took up a position behind Antietam Creek. He had fewer than 40,000 men when the battle began, but Hill arrived in time to save the day for Lee.

The Antietam campaign, McClellan believed, had secured his military reputation. Perhaps one day, he wrote, "history will, I trust, do me justice in deciding that it was not my fault that the campaign of the Peninsula was not successful. . . . I have shown that I can fight battles and win them!" His claim of victory was based on the tradition that the army holding the battlefield gains the victory. In that day's struggle, the Confederate line had been pressed back, but never broke. When Lee left the field, it was not a rout. Antietam was the only battle George McClellan ever directed from start to finish, and on it rests in large measure his reputation as a battlefield commander and tactician. Antietam was the bloodiest single day of the Civil War. One out of every four men who marched into the battle was killed, wounded, or missing—about 23,000 total. The Confederate deaths were 10,300; the Union deaths, 12,400. The campaign as a whole cost the Federals 27,000 men, including those captured at Harpers Ferry. In McClellan's official report, he more than doubled the Confederate losses to 30,000. But the fact that Maryland and Pennsylvania were now safe from invasion was a more realistic claim to victory.

Antietam was one of the greatest what-if battles of all time. Again, McClellan was tentative in his approach to battle, fighting less to win than to prevent his own defeat. McClellan almost surely would have defeated Lee—and probably ended the war—had he advanced his entire army simultaneously in assault on the Confederates and prevented Hill's division from joining Lee. He also held in reserve an additional 24,000 fresh troops, which he never used. Moreover, McClellan allowed two excellent opportunities to win a decisive victory to slip away: by not renewing the battle on September 18, and by not attempting to pursue the Confederates as they retreated across the Potomac on the 19th.

President Lincoln used what he labeled a victory at Antietam to issue the preliminary Emancipation Proclamation. Two days later, he suspended habeas corpus, a legal protection for those who might oppose governmental policies. McClellan, a Democrat, was bitter in his condemnation of those in Washington who were trying to create a social revolution. Thinking his troops would be opposed to Lincoln's position on slavery, McClellan called on them to repudiate the Emancipation Proclamation. As the days passed and there was little reaction from his troops, it became obvious that he was out of step with both his army and his political superiors in Washington.

McClellan was enough of a realist to know that the issue of slavery had to be faced when the war was over. "When the day of adjustment comes," he told his wife, "I will . . . throw my sword into the scale to force an improvement in the condition of those poor blacks." Although he would never join the fight for abolition, McClellan supported any gradual emancipation that would guarantee equally the rights of master and slave.

Lincoln was very disappointed that Lee's army had not been destroyed, as it should have been. He urged McClellan to advance promptly into Virginia. But Little Mac, asserting that he had won a great victory against great odds at Antietam, refused to move his troops until he felt they were ready. He needed, he declared, more men and equipment.

Ten days after the battle, McClellan still had not moved his army. He wrote to the president: "This army is not in condition to undertake another campaign nor to bring on another battle." Lincoln decided to visit McClellan in the field to press him into action. He arrived on October 1 and remained for four days.

He reviewed troops, visited hospitals, and toured the battlefield. The two spoke at length about advancing the army into Virginia, but McClellan continued to insist that his army was not ready to move. Later, while looking at the army from a nearby hill, Lincoln asked a friend what he saw. The man responded that it was the Army of the Potomac. "So it is called, but that is a mistake." Lincoln said. "It is only McClellan's bodyguard."

Not until late in October did McClellan move his army into Virginia. His plan was to move rapidly down the east side of the Blue Ridge and capture Richmond before Lee's army in the Shenandoah Valley could intercept him. McClellan's march was anything but rapid, advancing at a rate of six or seven miles a day. As a result, Lee had ample time to block McClellan's front and have Jackson attack his rear.

Lincoln had seen enough. On November 7, he relieved McClellan of his command. Twice McClellan had rescued the North from defeat, but Lincoln did not think he was the man to lead the Union to victory. Other than McClellan's not being aggressive enough, Lincoln had political reasons for relieving him. The general had become the most prominent opponent of the administration and its policies. He publicly accused Secretary Stanton of leading a traitorous conspiracy to destroy McClellan and his army on the peninsula. McClellan did nothing to restrain his supporters when they attacked Lincoln and his administration; in some cases, he even encouraged them. There was fear in Washington that McClellan might use his army to take over the government, especially a government in the midst of a civil war. Lincoln could not tolerate McClellan's inaction in the field, nor his insubordination, and so he fired him. McClellan was thirty-five when his military career ended.

For all his days, George McClellan regarded Antietam as a great victory. On September 17, he told his wife: "Those in whose judgment I rely tell me that I fought the battle splendidly and that it was a masterpiece of art." However, history does not support McClellan's analysis of the battle.

The tragedy of McClellan's failure is that he did not take advantage of his greatest asset—his army's love for him. They would have done anything for him, but he did not give them the opportunity. By being deliberate and slow to involve the full strength of his army, he jeopardized the lives of those engaged. He did not want to see his beloved army suffer. Generals expecting to win battles must be willing to sacrifice the lives of some men for the good of the others. McClellan was not willing.

On November 9, General McClellan began the painful process of bidding farewell to his army. That evening in his tent he received the officers on his staff. Expressing his dismay at being removed, McClellan said it was unexpected: "We have only to obey orders." Then he offered a toast: "To the Army of the Potomac, and bless the day when I shall return to it."

The next morning, McClellan's troops assembled for a review in his honor and to hear his parting words: "In parting from you I can not express the love and gratitude I bear to you. As an army you have grown up under my care. . . . The battles you have fought under my command will proudly live in our Nation's history . . . unite us still by an indissoluble tie. Farewell!" McClellan was deeply moved by the final display of affection from his men. "I did not know before how much they loved me nor how dear they were to me," he wrote Ellen. "The scenes of today repay me for all that I have endured." His army, as he always called it, saw McClellan no more.

Once the Union's best-known critic had been relieved of duty, the Lincoln administration faced the problem of what to do with him. There was no available administrative post for an officer of McClellan's rank in Washington. In any event, the capital was the last place the government wanted him. Secretary Stanton ordered him to Trenton, New Jersey—apparently for no better reason than its nearness to the Marcy's home, where Ellen was staying.

McClellan was given a hero's welcome in Trenton. He responded with a brief speech, urging his listeners to be sure the war was prosecuted "for the preservation of the Union and the Constitution, for your nationality and rights as citizens." This scene would be repeated wherever he went in the next few months.

After a brief stay in Trenton, McClellan moved to New York. The city was the largest Democrat stronghold in the North, and his greeting there was tumultuous. When McClellan attended the opera one evening, the orchestra struck up "National Airs" as the audience cheered.

The six weeks following the Union defeat at Fredericksburg, Virginia, were a time of crisis for the Army of the Potomac; it was remembered ever after as the Valley Forge of the Army's existence. This was largely due to McClellan's replacement, General Burnside, and his many failings—particularly, his neglect of his men. Every day, soldiers died senselessly in wretched hospitals and filthy camps. The food was so bad that they even died from scurvy. After McClellan's departure, the army's morale suffered. McClellan had been popular with his men because he was always careful to look after their welfare. It was a characteristic that came to be weighted equally with his military ability.

Even more noticeable in the wake of Fredericksburg was McClellan's mark on the officers who had served under him. His critics called it "McClellanism," describing its symptoms as bad blood and general paralysis. Burnside found himself being undercut by the generals friendly to McClellan. It appeared that the whole army had lost confidence in Burnside. Lincoln had no choice but to replace Burnside, appointing Joe Hooker and reassigning some of McClellan's strongest supporters. The Army of the Potomac's officer corps was put on notice that loyalty to the commander in chief was a higher duty than loyalty to McClellan.

Lacking any official duties, McClellan devoted most of his time during the early months of 1863 to reporting on his fifteen months as commander of the Army of the Potomac. In his report, McClellan was careful to rationalize his "reasons for delays" and the "enemy's positions and numbers," including important intelligence estimates of troops' size on which he had relied. After Joseph Hooker's defeat at Chancellorsville in May 1863, pressure began to mount on Lincoln to return McClellan to his command of the Army of the Potomac. The *Pennsylvania Herald* was the most prominent of the newspapers demanding the dismissal of Stanton and Halleck and the reinstatement of McClellan.

When the time came, it was General George Meade who replaced Hooker, not McClellan. After Meade's victory at Gettysburg, McClellan was to write, "most of the army thought at Gettysburg that they were fighting under my command. . . . I have been told by many officers that 'McClellan's ghost' won the battle because the men would not have fought as they did, had they not supposed that I was in command."

While he conspicuously courted Lincoln's political opposition, McClellan realized he had no chance for a command while the president was still in office. He resigned his commission and returned to private life. Although McClellan left the army, it would not be long before he was in the spotlight again. This time he was making political news; his name was being mentioned as a possible Democratic candidate for president in the 1864 election. Because of his military career, in the eyes of the Democrats, he would be a viable candidate to oppose President Lincoln. If he had failed during the Peninsula Campaign to capture Richmond, it was because the administration had failed to reinforce him and in some cases, actually withheld troops essential to his strategy. These actions, as McClellan had claimed, were taken with the deliberate, treasonous intent to destroy him and further the Radical Republicans' cause.

In the spring of 1864, McClellan backers believed that he would accept the Democratic nomination at the party's national convention that summer. While disclaiming ambition for the presidency, McClellan said he believed it was in God's hands. Earlier, he had told his mother that he wasn't interested in running for the presidency, but in March he wrote her: "I know that all things will prove in the end to have been arranged for the best and am quite willing to accept what I cannot avoid."

When it became known that McClellan might be the Democratic candidate, his political enemies brought charges against him. The most sensational of these was that McClellan had met with General Lee at Antietam, where the two agreed that the Confederate army would withdraw across the Potomac without interference, clearing the way for a compromise peace settlement that would preserve slavery. In New York, the *Tribune* and *Times* ran the story for several days—until the Joint Committee on the Conduct of the War, which had investigated the allegations, found them to be false.

In one of his few public appearances during the election year, McClellan delivered a speech at West Point dedicating the site of a monument to honor the Civil War dead. In his address, McClellan described what he saw as the appropriate goal of the war. The war was being fought, he said, for a cause "just and righteous, so long as its purpose is to crush rebellion and save our nation from the infinite evils of dismemberment. The Civil War should be a war for Union and Constitution and no other object."

As McClellan's prominence increased, Secretary Stanton's animosity grew. Former members of McClellan's staff had difficulty obtaining commissions in other commands. A movement by members of the Army of the Potomac to raise money for a presentation sword to honor McClellan was halted by Stanton's order. After McClellan's West Point address, Stanton dismissed or transferred the three members of the speaker's committee, including the superintendent.

In July 1864, General Grant met with Lincoln to discuss the command responsibilities for the Eastern Theater. McClellan's name came up. Lincoln and Grant agreed that if McClellan dropped out of the running for president, he would be invited to return to the army. McClellan refused to discuss the issue. He said it was his greatest wish to command the Army of the Potomac in one more great campaign, but that he was not willing to trade a presidential nomination for the possibility. By the end of the year, he had discreetly made known his availability for the presidency.

McClellan's views on the war had not changed since 1862. He still opposed emancipation but favored restoration of the Union by military victory. The peace wing of the Democratic party objected to this position, favoring an armistice followed by negotiations. Peace Democrats launched a last-minute effort to nominate Governor Horatio Seymour of New York, but when the fall came, they had no choice but to accept McClellan.

The convention bridged the gap between the party's two wings and nominated McClellan on the first ballot. They adopted a "peace" platform denouncing "arbitrary military arrest, suppression of freedom of speech and of the press, and the disregard of state rights." The key plank declared that after "four years of failure to restore the Union by the experiment of war . . . [we] demand immediate cessation of hostilities, to the end that at the earliest possible moment, peace may be restored on the basis of the Federal Union of the States."

McClellan's candidacy appeared to be a contradiction—a retired West Pointer who had fought the Confederates as Lincoln's commanding field general, McClellan was now running against Lincoln on what looked like a peace-at-any-price platform. McClellan was embarrassed by the antiwar plank and repudiated it in his letter accepting the Democratic presidential nomination. He tried to counteract the peace platform by stating: "I could not look into the face of my gallant comrades of the army and navy who have survived so many bloody battles and tell them that their labors . . . were in vain; that we have abandoned the Union for which we have so often paroled our lives."

The letter satisfied most War Democrats and upset some of those who were pushing for peace at any price. In their campaign, the Peace Democrats emphasized the platform, while the War Democrats stressed McClellan's letter. This split gave Republicans the opportunity they were looking for. "The truth is," said a Republican orator, "neither you nor I, nor the Democrats themselves, can tell whether they have a peace platform or a war platform."

In the main issues of the day, Lincoln and McClellan were not completely opposite in their position about the conduct of the war. They both agreed that secession was iniquitous and the war righteous. They agreed essentially to Reconstruction. The differences between them were more a matter of shading than of glaring contrasts. The great body of Democrats were loyal citizens who favored the vigorous prosecution of the war; but McClellan also had the backing of a small, though noisy, antiwar faction. Lincoln feared that if McClellan was elected, he might be controlled by the antiwar arm of the Democratic party.

By the end of the summer, it seemed that Lincoln would lose the election unless something very dramatic happened. On September 2, Atlanta fell. Sherman telegraphed the good news to Washington: "Atlanta is ours, and fairly won." The North was elated by the news. At Petersburg, the Army of the Potomac fired a hundred-gun salute. This was the news Lincoln had hoped for, and it came just before the election.

In November, the Republicans won the election. Lincoln defeated McClellan by a ten-to-one margin in the electoral race. McClellan had counted on the army's vote, but after three years of fighting, they knew the road to peace lay with Lincoln. The meaning of this was simple enough—the Union would see it through. McClellan told a friend that he was relieved not to have won the burden of the presidency: "For my country's sake I deplore the result—but the people have decided with their eyes wide open and I feel that a great weight is removed from my mind."

Addressing his supporters afterward, McClellan took comfort from his conclusion that he was not responsible for the outcome of the election. "As I look back upon it," he said, "it seems to me a subject replete with dignity. . . . I think we have well played our parts. The mistakes made were not of our making . . . . I trust that we will see that these apparent mistakes were a part of the grand plan of the Almighty."

Soon after the election, McClellan decided to leave the United States, traveling extensively in Europe in a kind of self-imposed exile. He did not return to the United States until after the 1868 election. Initially, there was interest among Democrats in running McClellan for the presidency again in 1868, but his support dwindled after the Republicans nominated General Grant. A newspaper wrote that the party would ensure a Republican victory "by running the man who didn't take Richmond against the man who did."

After returning to America, the general dabbled with some business dealings, but in 1873, he returned to Europe. He spent two years there and began to write his memoirs. He returned to the political arena in 1876, campaigning tirelessly for Samuel J. Tilden against Rutherford B. Hayes. McClellan's position on blacks remained the same as it had in 1861. He was forced to acknowledge that slavery was dead and that, legally at least, blacks were citizens and could vote. "Sectional harmony was paramount," he said, "and states' rights must prevail in all social and racial questions."

In 1878, McClellan was elected governor of New Jersey, serving three years and declining to run for a second term. In the election of 1884, he campaigned vigorously for Grover Cleveland. McClellan regarded the Democrats' victory in November as the beginning of a new era for the nation. He expected to be rewarded for his part in the victory by being invited to join Cleveland's cabinet as secretary of war, but was disappointed when it didn't happen.

McClellan loved speaking to veterans organizations and visiting the battlefields made famous by his army. He sensed that the bond he had had with Union soldiers was still strong, and indeed it was.

Early in October 1885, at the age of fifty-eight, McClellan suffered a severe attack of angina pectoris. Under his doctor's care and with rest, he seemed to make a complete recovery. On the evening of October 28, however, as McClellan was working on his Antietam article for *The Century* magazine, the chest pains returned. McClellan's condition deteriorated rapidly. At three o'clock the next morning, he murmured, "I feel easy now. Thank you . . . " and then died.

Messages of condolence arrived by the hundreds, from the president, from generals who had fought with and against him, and from men who had served in the ranks of the Army of the Potomac. "His death," Fitz John Porter said, "is crushing to me." General Beauregard described the great esteem he felt for McClellan as a man and soldier, and Joseph Johnston mourned "a dear friend whom I have so long loved and admired."

Obituaries appeared in newspapers throughout the country, each recounting and evaluating the events in McClellan's life. The *New York Evening Post* wrote: "Probably no soldier who did so little fighting has his qualities as a commander so minutely, and we may add, so fiercely discussed." The *New York World* was partisan to the end: "No general who fought in the war from its outbreak to its close was ever actuated by nobler sentiments and purer and more patriotic motives. Yet no soldier was ever more unjustly dealt with or more harshly, cruelly and unfairly criticized."

Funeral services were held on November 2 at the Madison Square Presbyterian Church in New York. The honorary pallbearers included old business and political friends as well as comrades from the army years. Burial was in the McClellan and Marcy family plot at Riverview Cemetery in Trenton.

No other Union general presents more of a paradox than George B. McClellan. In many ways, McClellan was the most brilliant strategist to defend the Union. Even General Lee admitted that McClellan was his brightest adversary. And yet history has not been kind to him. Today he is seen as overly cautious, vindictive, vain, and generally a detriment to his cause.

There is no doubt that McClellan was a complex man. He brought forth a love and admiration from his troops that has remained almost unparalleled in American history. In turn, he respected and loved his troops and experienced real sadness when his men were killed in battle. Ultimately, he is best understood as a military genius crippled by his own insecurity, a master of planning who could not boldly execute his own plans. McClellan's true character may best be described as Lincoln put it, "the general with the slows."

14   *Gallant Texan*

JOHN BELL HOOD

AT midnight in the northwestern hills of Georgia, about 135 years ago, an unusual ceremony took place. There, in a candlelit tent, a man was baptized. It was unusual for a number of reasons, not the least of them being that, at the moment, in the hills and valleys around them, more than 150,000 armed men slept—awaiting the dawn and one of the most highly contested campaigns of the Civil War. The man performing the baptism was Leonidas Polk, an Episcopal bishop from Louisiana who also served as an infantry corps commander in the Army of Tennessee. The candidate for baptism into the church was also a lieutenant general, thirty-three-year-old John Bell Hood, a tall young Kentuckian. Using a horse bucket and a tin washbasin, Bishop-General Polk administered the solemn rites to his fellow general. When it proved difficult for Hood to kneel because of the horrible mutilations he had received at Gettysburg and Chickamauga, Polk suggested that he remain in the chair. But Hood struggled for his crutches and declared that if he could not kneel, he could at least stand. He got to his feet and was received into the church.

Historians do not know why Hood chose to get religion at that time. Perhaps he had been caught up in the wave of revivalism that had recently swept the Confederacy. It may have been his love affair with a young socialite from South Carolina and the embarrassment he had experienced when he was not able to take communion with her in her church. Whatever the reason, within two months, General Polk would be dead, and Hood would be poised to march the Army of Tennessee into the battles of Atlanta and Nashville—and into oblivion.

Late in the evening of July 17, 1864, a fateful telegram from Richmond arrived at the headquarters of General Joseph E. Johnston, commander of the Confederate Army of Tennessee near Atlanta, Georgia. An orderly hurried the message to the general. "Lieutenant General J. B. Hood," Johnston read, "has been commissioned to the temporary Rank of General . . . you are hereby relieved from the command of the army . . . which you will immediately turn over to General Hood." And so the army's fate was sealed, for better or worse, as it now had its leader, a "fighting general," to contend with Sherman.

The decision to replace Johnston with Hood was not greeted with enthusiasm by the Army of Tennessee. In fact, it was viewed in most quarters with shock, and in some cases, with bitter disappointment and even tears. President Davis had decided to remove Johnston because he would not attack Sherman, as Davis requested. Everyone knew Hood's reputation as a fighter; serving under both Lee and Jackson, Hood had subscribed to the "get 'em on open ground and hit 'em with all you've got" school of military thought. Although not a man of genius or a great general in Davis's eyes, Hood was a bold fighter, and that's what Davis felt was needed.

The news that Hood was replacing Johnston was not welcomed by the officers' corps, either. When passed over for the promotion, Lieutenant General William Hardee, who had graduated from West Point fifteen years before Hood and was a year his senior in rank, asked to be relieved. One division commander remarked that Hood had "gone up like a rocket. It is to be hoped that he will not come down like the stick." Another general told Hood that he regretted Johnston's removal, but promised his cooperation. Others felt the same way—it was not an encouraging start for the new commander of the Army of Tennessee.

Hood recognized the immediate danger he faced. He did not know the position of his troops or have the confidence of all his subordinate officers. He went to see Johnston to request that he withhold the order, retaining command of the army until the impending battle had been fought. Johnston would hear none of it. Hood and the corps commanders appealed to Davis, asking that the command change be suspended until after the battle of Atlanta. Davis declined. Hood went to see Johnston one more time, urging him to remain "for the good of the country" and asking for the benefit of his counsel until Hood became oriented to the army. Johnston promised that he would. That evening, without a word to Hood, Johnston left for Macon, Georgia.

John Bell Hood, elevated to the Confederacy's highest military grade and most important field command, remains a fascinating individual. Hood was only thirty-three and crippled from wounds when he was given command of the Army of Tennessee. Having lost a leg at Chickamauga and the use of an arm at Gettysburg, he had already played a crucial role in the Civil War. Now, with his country struggling against long odds for its survival, he was the Confederacy's last hope.

Five months later at Nashville, Hood watched the remnants of his army fleeing through rain and mud in a desperate attempt to escape Union troops. His army had been destroyed and routed, the worst such experience any Confederate army had suffered during the war. Both Hood's promotion to army command and his ultimate defeat were predictable.

John Bell Hood was born in Owingsville, Kentucky, on June 29, 1831, to John and Theodosia Hood. His parents were considered part of the Kentucky aristocracy, and as John grew up, he acquired their values and customs. His father was a physician who owned more than 600 acres of farmland and several dozen slaves. Young Hood never knew poverty. He developed a taste for good living that stayed with him all his life. Even on the battlefield, he carried a silver cup given to him by the ladies of Richmond. When his tent was pitched, he used his own fine china and silver, which were laid out on the camp table.

As an adolescent, young John loved the pursuit of women; he would continue this endeavor until his marriage after the war. Charming women were as necessary to him as food and drink—and they, in turn, found him fascinating. Women were attracted to him because of his admirable physique—six feet two inches tall, broad shoulders, narrow hips, and blondish, auburn hair. They liked his shy, deferential manner and his great sad eyes. Most of all, women were attracted to him because they sensed his admiration of them and his enjoyment of their companionship.

Hood's father, who wished him to follow in his footsteps to study medicine, offered him the inducement of studying in Europe. But young John had other ideas; he wanted to be a soldier and seek adventure. In 1849, Hood's uncle, a congressman, was able to secure an appointment for him to West Point. His father signed the acceptance, giving his son permission to attend the academy.

Hood's first year at West Point was a sobering experience. During a plebe's first two months, he underwent basic training and was subjected to hazing at the hands of other cadets. Hood was a target of ridicule; his provincial accent, slow thinking, and large frame accentuated his awkwardness. It was not what young Hood had expected. He had come to the military academy dreaming of becoming an army officer, a knightly profession in which he could experience adventure, earn honors and titles, and gain entree into better society.

Hood, awed by his new surroundings, soon became aware of his relatively poor academic preparation. During his plebe year, he had to work hard to make up for his academic deficiencies. Despite his efforts, by the end of four years, his academic standing had not improved. To add to his problems at the academy, his conduct record became worse. It was presumed that boys who were conditioned by discipline and punishment would mature into cadets and then into officers who would conform to the army's standard of behavior. Obstreperous cadets often schemed to beat the system by smuggling women and liquor onto the post or sneaking off post, making a mockery of the school's regulation.

In September of his senior year, Hood was made a lieutenant in the Corps of Cadets. In December, after being found absent from his quarters without authority, he was reduced to the rank of a cadet private and given enough demerits to raise his year's total to 196, just four short of the number needed for expulsion. The experience demoralized Hood to the point that he considered leaving the academy and going home to farm. Instead, Hood buckled down for the rest of the year, managing to pass his January examination and keeping his number of demerits from reaching 200. He graduated in July 1853, forty-fourth among the fifty-two survivors of his class. He ranked last in his class in ethics.

The greatest influence on Hood while at West Point was his association with Colonel Robert E. Lee, who had become superintendent of the academy in 1852. Lee's brilliant service in the Mexican War had won wide acclaim. His self-control, personality, soldierly manner, and reputation won the enthusiastic admiration of the young cadets. One cadet wrote that Lee was "the personification of dignity, justice, and kindness and was respected and admired as the ideal of a commanding officer." Hood later wrote that he had "become very much attached" to Lee while he was at West Point.

But Hood's relationship with Lee at West Point was a painful one. It was Lee, as superintendent, who determined Hood's punishment for his absence from quarters in December. When reprimanding Hood for dereliction of duty, Lee was careful to handle the matter so tactfully that there were no lasting ill feelings. Lee never held the transgression against Hood. Although the relationship between Hood and Lee was strained during 1852 and 1853, it marked the beginning of an association that would profoundly influence the younger man.

The cadet corps included many men with and against whom Hood would serve. His class was headed by James McPherson, who had helped him with his studies; McPherson, unfortunately, would die in combat against Hood's army at Atlanta. J. E. B. Stuart and William Pender were in the class of 1854 and would emerge, along with Hood, as outstanding young officers of the Army of Northern Virginia.

Cadets who graduated high in their class were usually assigned to the engineering corps. There was never any doubt that Hood's record would not entitle him to an assignment in the engineering corps. To avoid being assigned to the infantry, Hood asked his uncle to use his influence to get him assigned to the cavalry. The congressman's letter either arrived too late, or he had lost his influence, because Hood was appointed a brevet second lieutenant in the infantry.

Hood's initial assignment was to the 4th Infantry Regiment, located in California. Two uneventful years later, he was transferred to the elite 2nd Cavalry Regiment at Fort Mason, Texas—a new unit Secretary of War Jefferson Davis had staffed with the most talented Southern officers. Hood reported to his new commander, Colonel Albert Sidney Johnston, later to be the first commanding general of the Army of Tennessee. The deputy commander was Colonel Robert E. Lee, and one of the majors was George H. Thomas. The staff also included William Hardee, Charles Field, and twelve others who would later become generals during the Civil War. Hood was fortunate to have the opportunity to learn his trade under such capable soldiers. Duty in Texas was tough. The country was barren and dull. Despite continued trouble from the Comanches, Hood loved Texas, its mood, and the temper of its people. Even after his tour there, Hood would consider himself a Texan.

In 1857, during a brush with a Comanche band, Hood had his hand pinned to his saddle by an arrow. It was an ugly wound that incapacitated him for almost two years. When he returned to duty, he was appointed instructor of cavalry for the regiment.

For his brief but savage action during the Comanche encounter, Hood received a commendation for gallantry from the department commander. A short time later, he was promoted to first lieutenant, a rank he retained until the end of his service in the United States Army. Aside from his combat experience in battling the Comanches, another interesting incident occurred during Hood's service in Texas. One day while riding in the country with his colonel, Robert E. Lee, Hood received some fatherly advice when their conversation turned to matrimony. Thinking that his young protégé might form an attachment to some of the young Texan ladies, Lee advised Hood: "Never marry unless you can do so into a family which will enable your children to be proud of both sides of the house." This pronouncement made such a deep impression on the dashing lieutenant from Kentucky that he repeated it in his memoirs many years later.

In the spring of 1861, when the United States was breaking apart, Hood went back to Kentucky to meet with Governor John Breckinridge, hoping to offer his services to his native state. After learning that Kentucky would not secede, Hood boarded a train for Montgomery, Alabama, the Confederate capital at the time. He was appointed first lieutenant in the Confederate army and sent to Richmond to report to his old mentor, Robert E. Lee. He was immediately dispatched to Yorktown, Virginia, to join Colonel John Bankhead Magruder, who was expecting an attack from Federal troops.

To the beleaguered Magruder, Hood was a godsend, a bona fide professional with a towering physique and a military bearing that indicated he was in command. Magruder put Hood in charge of all cavalry companies, promoting him to captain and then to major. This unusual rate of promotion was brought about to provide young Hood seniority over the other company commanders.

Hood was in his element, leading patrols into enemy lines in much the same way he had stalked Indians with the 2nd Cavalry in Texas. The war was providing opportunities undreamed of in times of peace. Quickly, almost effortlessly, Hood had become a major. He returned to Richmond to see the right people about another assignment. There he learned that Texas was sending troops to Virginia. The companies were organized into the 4th Texas Infantry Regiment, and Hood was promoted to colonel and placed in command. During the winter of 1861, Hood drilled and instructed his troops. In the spring of 1862, he was promoted once more, to brigadier general, and given command of a Texas brigade.

In eleven months, young Hood had advanced from first lieutenant to brigadier general. He had been an obscure soldier, undistinguished except for his brief encounter with Comanches in Texas, until he arrived in Virginia. Now he commanded a brigade of 2,000 officers and men—and his brigade grew daily in strength. It would be known simply as the Texas Brigade and would become a premier fighting force in the Army of Northern Virginia.

Hood had little difficulty establishing rapport with his men. "As a number of officers and men had known him on the frontier of Texas as a good Indian fighter, he was accepted without much opposition," one man wrote. Hood made no effort to curb the footloose behavior of his Texans. He was demanding in battle but turned his back on whatever else they did in camp. As one private put it: "West Pointer that Hood was, he not only knew Texas and Arkansas tastes and temperaments," but occasionally let his men indulge. On one such occasion, the Texans decided to go absent without leave—virtually en masse—while passing through Richmond. When one of his officers tried to prevent the disintegration of the command, Hood called to him: "Let 'em go. Let 'em go. They deserve a little indulgence and you'll get them back in time for the next battle."

On May 7, the Union army under General George McClellan advanced up the Yorktown Peninsula toward Richmond. Hood was ordered to drive them back. In their first serious action, Hood's Texans routed the Federals near Eltham's Landing in what Hood called "a happy introduction to the enemy."

Hood's daring action at Eltham's Landing was somewhat disturbing to Johnston, who had not wished to provoke a major engagement at that time. After listening to Hood's explanation of his actions, Johnston said: "General Hood, have you given an illustration of the Texan idea of feeling an enemy gently and falling back? What would your Texans have done, sir, if I had ordered them to charge and drive back the enemy?" "I suppose, General," Hood replied, "they would have driven them into the river, and tried to swim out and capture their gunboats." Johnston smilingly ended the conversation by saying, "Teach your Texans that the first duty of a soldier is literally to obey orders."

The Texans responded to the way Hood treated them by gaining a reputation for spirited fighting. The action at Gaines' Mill provided widespread attention for the performance during the Seven Days' Battles. The Texans pierced the center of the Union line with a wild, howling charge. Hood's men quickly noticed that he always went into the thick of the fighting with them, personally leading the Texas Brigade in a bayonet charge. Hood exulted in the excitement of combat. Those who saw him noticed how his eyes glowed, how the battle visibly changed him into a terrifying warrior whose fighting spirit enraptured his entire brigade. The Texans' action at Gaines' Mill helped to gain an important victory for Lee, and Hood's name was soon being spoken of with favor in Richmond.

Hood began to be noticed in Richmond. At first he was seen mainly in the poker parlors where he gained a reputation for playing recklessly and for high stakes. "I saw Hood bet $2,000 with nary a pair in his hand," one soldier said. Then Hood began infiltrating the more genteel society in the capital, making contact with high society as well as with the president himself. Hood was said to have "very winning manners" and to have used these "advantages actively for his own advancement." Mrs. Mary Boykin Chesnut, a diarist and close friend of Hood's, wrote extensively of his actions throughout the war. She thought his social behavior was not very subtle: "General Hood's an awful flatterer—I mean an awkward flatterer" and once I warned him "if you stay here in Richmond much longer you will grow to be a courtier. And you came a rough Texan." But Hood was very ambitious and beyond taking anyone's advice. Even a private in the ranks would note, "Hood was ambitious as he was brave and daring."

Hood emerged from the Seven Days' Battles with a shining reputation as a bold and able combat officer, for which he was rewarded by a promotion to division commander. Hood and his Texans were then detached to the command of General James Longstreet and would be involved in the Second Battle of Manassas. There, Stonewall Jackson's corps swiftly maneuvered around the army of General John Pope, while Longstreet, with Hood's division in a prominent position, destroyed the Yankees' left flank. Pope was thoroughly defeated and his army went reeling back to Washington. Hood called it "the most beautiful battle scene I have ever beheld." Again Hood had acquitted himself well; he had also become one of the Confederate's rising stars.

After his victory at Manassas, Lee did not wait long to go on the offensive, this time moving his army into Maryland. Hood's Texans were with Lee, but Hood was not at the head of his column; he had been put under arrest. On the final day at Manassas, Hood's men had captured several Union ambulances, putting them into action for the Texas Brigade. General N. G. Evans, who was senior to Hood, ordered him to turn the ambulances over. When Hood refused, Evans placed him under arrest for insubordination; Longstreet ordered him to remain in Virginia. Hood explained his action: "I would cheerfully have obeyed directions to deliver them to General Lee's Quartermaster for use of the army, [but] I did not consider it just that I should be required to yield them to another brigade of the division, which was in no manner entitled to them." Because the power of arrest was sacrosanct to Lee, he would neither intercede nor overrule Evans—thus allowing a petty feud to remove one of his best fighting generals. Hoping that Hood and Evans would reconcile, Lee compromised, ordering Hood to bring up the rear of his division and accompany them into Maryland.

When Lee came into contact with the Texans, they began to shout, "Give us Hood!" Lee sent for Hood and told him: "General, here I am just upon the eve of entering into battle with one of my best officers under arrest." Lee told Hood that if he would apologize about the ambulances, he would release him. Hood still refused, citing the justness of his position. Lee, shaking his head, told Hood his arrest was suspended until after the impending battle.

After their conference, Lee courteously raised his hand to the men and said, "You shall have him, gentlemen." Amid wild cheering, Hood moved to the front of his division.

Hood's star soared again as a result of the Maryland Campaign at Antietam, in which he commanded a small division. Hood's men fought in the cornfield sector near the Dunker Church, holding their ground under relentless pressure from Union troops. Hood's division suffered more than 2,000 casualties while holding his section of the line. As his ranks thinned, he could be seen pacing and crying aloud: "For God's sake, more troops!"

Hood's division was badly shattered and he would forever be bitter. The high command, he believed, had betrayed his men. Lee had placed his division in a dangerous position without giving them the means to defend themselves. When Hood asked for help from both Lee and Longstreet, they passed him along to Jackson, whom he found asleep. As a result, his division had suffered. His pleas for reinforcements had gone unanswered. When the ammunition was depleted, Hood withdrew his troops. Despite overwhelming odds and heavy losses, it had been his finest hour.

When the fighting subsided, Hood rode off to report to Lee on the conditions in his area. He was visibly and uncharacteristically shaken by the ordeal. Lee asked him how his men were. Hood's emotional reply was, "They're all dead on the field where you sent them."

The action on the Confederate left had saved the day for Lee and the Army of Northern Virginia. Fighting against nearly five-to-one odds, Generals Hood, McLaws, and Lawton had repulsed 30,000 Union troops. On September 27, 1862, General Jackson recommended that Hood be promoted to the rank of major general. Jackson said that at Antietam, Hood had fought with "such ability and zeal as to command my admiration. I regard him as one of the most promising officers of the army."

Hood also gained a measure of personal satisfaction after the battle. He expected to be placed back under arrest for the controversy over the ambulances, but Lee released him from the charges. Instead of arrest, Hood was recommended for permanent division commander and promoted. At the age of thirty-one, he had become the youngest of nine major generals of infantry. "In lieu of being summoned to a court-martial," Hood said, "I was shortly afterwards promoted to the rank of major general."

After Antietam, McClellan was replaced as Union commander of the Army of the Potomac, this time by General Ambrose Burnside, who promptly began to march his army toward Fredericksburg. Although greatly outnumbered, Lee decided to take the Union's assault on the heights of Fredericksburg. Longstreet's corps, with Hood's division at its center, was on the left; Jackson's corps defended the right flank. Burnside's troops were slaughtered in a series of charges up and down the Confederate line. It was there that Lee uttered his famous remark to Longstreet: "It is well that war is so terrible. We should grow too fond of it."

During the winter of 1862–1863, Hood was in great demand in Richmond society, becoming a welcome figure at dances and charades. During this time, Hood fell in love with Sally "Buck" Preston, an eighteen-year-old daughter of an aristocratic South Carolina family. Buck was staying in Richmond that winter at the home of family friends, Colonel and Mrs. John C. Chesnut. Chesnut was an aide to Jefferson Davis; his wife, Mary Boykin Chesnut, was a fashionable hostess in Richmond. Hood clearly impressed Mrs. Chesnut, who wrote in her diary: "When he came, with his sad Quixote face, the face of an old crusader who believed in his cause, his cross, his crown. . . . Tall-thin-shy, blue eyes and light hair, tawny beard and a vast amount of it covering the lower part of his face—an appearance of awkward strength. Someone said that great reserve of manner he carried only into ladies' society."

All through the spring, Hood pursued Buck Preston whenever he could get down to Richmond. She was a true beauty, smart and a born flirt. Caught up in the midst of war, Buck had many suitors. Added to that list was perhaps the handsomest and most famous and eligible bachelor of them all, thirty-two-year-old Major General John Bell Hood. The trouble was that Buck couldn't make up her mind.

The war, however, would interfere with Hood's pursuit of Buck. The next important battle in the East called Hood away from the Army of Northern Virginia. Lee had sent Longstreet's corps to scrounge up food and forage when yet another Union commander, "Fighting Joe" Hooker, was selected to replace Burnside. Hooker quickly tried to engage Lee at Chancellorsville, but was routed when Jackson attacked him from the flank. At Chancellorsville, the Confederates lost their ablest field commander, Stonewall Jackson. Hood, who had tried to model himself in Jackson's style, was deeply distressed at the news of his death.

Hood expressed his grief at the loss of Jackson to Lee and then introduced the issue of the reorganization of the Army of Northern Virginia. The corps were too large, said Hood. Four divisions were too much for one general to control in the rugged countryside of Virginia. Lee agreed with him. As much as he would miss Jackson, the loss gave Lee the opportunity of reorganizing his army into smaller corps. Realizing that Hood was angling for a corps command, Lee informed Hood that although he was good, he was not yet ready for corps command. "I rely much upon you," wrote Lee. "You must so inspire and lead your brave division as it may accomplish the work of a corps."

Gettysburg was to be Hood's last battle under Lee's command. On the second day of the battle, shortly after putting his troops into action, he was wounded. He had protested bitterly against a frontal attack on the enemy at Little Round Top. Hood's scouts reported that the way was clear to circle around the south end of Round Top and attack the enemy from the rear. Three times, Hood sent staff officers to Longsxztreet recommending that he be allowed to bypass Round Top. Three times, the request was denied by Longstreet, who continued to order a frontal attack. Under protest—"the first and only one I ever made in my military career," he later wrote—Hood ordered his four brigades to advance. Longstreet rode up and Hood pleaded again. "We must obey the orders of General Lee," was Longstreet's only reply.

Hood rode off toward his division into enemy fire. Within minutes after he entered the Peach Orchard, a bullet tore into his arm. Almost unconscious, Hood was taken to the rear and his troops proceeded without him. They struggled up the boulder-strewn hills and almost seized Little Round Top. Joshua Chamberlain's troops repulsed their attack. The Confederate survivors withdrew; half of Hood's division had been lost in the senseless frontal attack.

Amputation was not necessary, as first feared, but Hood lost practically all feeling in his arm, which remained useless for the rest of his life. His wound was tended at Staunton and then at Charlottesville, and finally he was moved to Richmond.

While Hood recovered from his wound, Longstreet's corps was moved out West to counter the threat posed to General Braxton Bragg's Army of Tennessee by General William Rosecrans's army, massing near Chattanooga for a thrust on Atlanta. Although Hood had only partially recovered from his wound, when he learned of his division's transfer, he placed his horse on the train and joined his troops in Georgia. Arriving on the battlefield at Chickamauga, he mounted his horse in the boxcar, leaped from the train, and joined his division already in action. Bragg gave Hood command of the Confederate forces in the center, nearly a full corps. It was Hood's command that led the breakthrough in the Union center. At the height of the action, Hood was struck high in the leg by a minié ball. He dropped his reins and slid out of his saddle. Lying on the ground, Hood gave his last orders to the Texans. "Go ahead," he shouted, "and keep ahead of everything." Then he was carried from the field on a stretcher.

Hood's wound proved more serious than originally thought; he had been shot through the right thigh, a few inches below the hip. His leg was amputated by Dr. T. G. Richardson, chief medical officer of the Army of Tennessee.

On September 20, the joy in Richmond at the news of the victory at Chickamauga was dampened by the report that Hood had been killed. When Lee heard of Hood's death, he commented, "I am gradually losing my best men, Jackson, Pender . . . Hood." Soon the news was corrected. Hood was still alive and "in fine spirits," despite the loss of his leg. The Texas brigade passed a hat, collecting nearly $5,000 to buy Hood an artificial limb. General Longstreet recommended Hood for promotion to the rank of lieutenant general for distinguished conduct and ability in the battle.

With nourishing food, skilled nursing, and much encouragement, Hood was soon sitting up and asking when he could return to duty. When offered a civil post, he declined: "No bombproof place for me. I propose to see this fought out in the field."

Hood returned to Richmond, where he had the opportunity to see Buck Preston again; but he made little impression on her. In fact, his attitude may even have hurt his chances of capturing her heart. On one occasion, after Hood turned on his black servant in a fit of temper, Buck became very annoyed. "I hate a man who speaks roughly to those who dare not resent it," she said. Later, on another occasion, she confided to Mrs. Chesnut that she wouldn't marry him "if he had a thousand legs, instead of having just one." Hood's hopes of marrying Buck were diminishing rapidly. "I was routed," he said. "She told me there was no hope."

Still Hood persisted. In love, as in war, he knew only one method of combat—full-scale attack. Despite being turned down at least twice by Buck when he proposed marriage, Hood kept after her. In Richmond, Hood's romance with Buck was the source of both merriment and sympathy. Colonel Charles Venable, related by marriage to the Preston family, observed: "Buck can't help it. She must flirt. . . . She does not care for the man. It is sympathy with the wounded soldier. Helpless Hood."

Hood was not as helpless as Venable thought. By pure persistence, he managed to win from Buck a somewhat contingent acceptance of marriage. "I am so proud, so grateful. The sun never shone on a happier man," he told Mrs. Chesnut. The worldly Mrs. Chesnut was still not convinced. "So the tragedy has been played out," she wrote in her diary, "for I do not think even now that she is in earnest."

Hood spent the winter of 1863–1864 in Richmond actively involved in the social life of the city. His wounds precluded any role other than spectator at balls and parties, but his presence was visible proof that he had given more than his share for the Confederacy. "Richmond," Mrs. Chesnut observed, "was a hero-worshipping community," and the wounded Hood was lionized by idolatrous citizens.

Although Hood's love affair slowly dissolved, his military reputation prospered. His public association with President Davis provided the most visible recognition of his favored status. Davis's carriage was at Hood's disposal, and Hood shared the president's pew at church. It was in their mutual interest to be seen together. Davis, who had battled politically with his senior officers, for once was arm in arm with a popular hero. Hood, in return, was ambitious for promotion, which Davis could make that happen.

Undoubtedly, Hood and Davis often discussed the course of the war and the options open to them. Davis considered himself a military expert, and Hood praised his abilities, going so far as to suggest that Davis might personally take command of the army. "I would follow you to the death!" Hood told the president. The two agreed that the South must take the initiative and attack the Union armies before they could consolidate their strength. These talks helped to increase Davis's opinion of Hood's military ability. This relationship raised the question of whether Hood was praising Davis to flatter him and thus win promotion or whether he really was sincere.

Common sentiment among the army, government, and public favored

Hood's promotion to lieutenant general. Some, however, questioned his ability for such a high command. Lieutenant generals commanded corps. The only corps position available at the time was one in the Army of Tennessee. To free up a corps position for Hood, Davis withdrew an earlier nomination of D. H. Hill. Hill had commanded a corps at Chickamauga but had lost favor with Davis. On February 2, 1864, Hood was promoted to lieutenant general with the date of rank from September 20, 1863, the day that he had fallen at Chickamauga.

At the end of February, Hood reported at Dalton, Georgia, to Joseph Johnston, who had replaced Braxton Bragg. The Army of Tennessee was attempting to recover from its humiliating defeat at Missionary Ridge in the fall. Hood energetically organized his corps for battle. To build their self-esteem, he had them marching in review and maneuvering in mock battles, improving both readiness and morale.

The pain in Hood's shattered left arm and the stump of his right leg was steady and throbbing, sometimes dulled by laudanum, but still always there. It was something he had learned to live with, much as he had adjusted to the artificial cork leg. The leg was a badge of honor; the pain was the price of honor. Some days the pain left him testy and morose, but his staff had learned to live with these moods.

Before Hood left Richmond, he agreed to send Davis confidential reports on the condition of the Army of Tennessee. As a corps commander in Johnston's army, the ambitious Hood seized the opportunity to further his career. He sent secret letters to Richmond, overstating the army's perilous condition, downplaying Johnston's frequent requests for cavalry, and openly expressing his belief that Johnston should have taken the initiative and advanced into Tennessee and Kentucky—exactly what Davis and the Confederate high command had repeatedly urged Johnston to do. Later, Hood would justify his actions by arguing that he wanted to encourage Davis to send reinforcements to Johnston. Unprofessional as it was for Hood to send these letters, it was equally unprofessional for Davis and his staff to accept them without informing Johnston that Hood was sending them.

Patience with Johnston wore increasingly thin among members of the Confederate high command, who concluded that only Johnston's reluctance prevented the recovery of Tennessee. Hood's frustration increased; he had come to Georgia expecting to advance against the enemy. Hood sensed that his opportunity was at hand. On July 14, he told General Braxton Bragg, a close friend and adviser to Jefferson Davis, "We should not, under any circumstances, allow the enemy to gain possession of Atlanta." Georgia Senator Benjamin Hill believed that Atlanta was in extreme danger of falling into Union hands. After visiting the beleaguered general, the senator returned to Richmond to brief

Davis on the situation in Georgia. Loss of Atlanta's railroads, hospitals, and industries would be a staggering blow to the Confederacy. Just as important would be the impact on the morale on both sides. Davis decided it was time to change the command of the Army of Tennessee.

Some of President Davis's advisers suggested that longtime corps commander Lieutenant General William Hardee would be a good choice. Davis cared little for Hardee either personally or politically. In the end, Davis preferred his young friend and protégé, John Bell Hood.

Davis, knowing that his choice was a risky one, turned to Lee for advice. He telegraphed Lee: "Johnston has failed, and there are strong indications that he will abandon Atlanta. . . . It seems necessary to relieve him at once." Davis wanted to know if Hood was capable of succeeding Johnston. Lee could only offer lukewarm commendation: "Hood is a bold fighter. I am doubtful as to other qualities necessary." In a tactful way, Lee let Davis know that Hood was gallant, zealous, and earnest but had never been tested with so much responsibility. Lee suggested Hardee; but to their peril, Davis and Bragg ignored Lee's advice. On July 17, Johnston was removed from command of the Army of Tennessee.

When learning Johnston had been replaced, Hood panicked. He immediately telegraphed Davis, requesting him to postpone the change: "The enemy being now in our common front and making as we suppose a general advance, we deem it dangerous to change commanders." Davis declined to suspend the order. Hood must command.

The news of Johnston's removal and replacement by Hood was received by the Army of Tennessee with stunned disbelief. Johnston's cautious style of fighting, beating a slow, strategic retreat in face of overwhelming Union odds, had kept morale high among his troops. According to one Tennessee private, Johnston was "loved, respected, admired: yea, almost worshipped by his troops."

If anyone was pleased about Hood's leading the Army of Tennessee, it had to be Grant and Sherman. In his postwar memoirs, Grant recalled: "Sherman and I rejoiced. Hood was unquestionably a brave, gallant soldier and not destitute of ability. But unfortunately his policy was to fight the enemy wherever he saw him without thinking much of the consequences of defeat."

Sherman's army and corps commanders rejoiced in the change too. They believed Hood would "hit like hell, now before you know it." For Sherman, this would mean an increase in Union casualties, but it was still a welcome change. Hood would take the Confederates into the open, where Sherman hoped to destroy his army. With an advantage of better than two to one in troop strength, Sherman had every reason to believe he had all the aces in the deck. Just a few years earlier, they had been calling Cump Sherman crazy. In fact, in the fall of 1861, the War Department had relieved him of his duties as head of the military department of the Cumberland and sent him home on sick leave. Less than four years later, Sherman was at the threshold of Atlanta; he was the right man in the right place at the right time, the commander of the Union Army of the Tennessee. No one was calling Sherman crazy now.

Hood, the new Confederate commander, realized his promotion was due to his reputation for aggressiveness. He was a disciple of the Lee and Jackson school of fighting, which had favored large open-field attacks. Now Lee had given up mass assaults in favor of fighting behind breastworks. Times had changed, but Hood had not.

On July 20, just two days after taking command, Hood hurled two-thirds of his army at the enemy at Peach Tree Creek. The attack failed; Hood had gained nothing at a cost of 5,000 men. This was the first of four attacks, none of them successful. In his frustration, Hood began to blame his subordinates, particularly Hardee, for the failure of his plans.

Hood fought Sherman in the only way he knew. The losses were large, gaining nothing for the Confederacy. Around Atlanta and again at Franklin, Hood flung his army in hopeless assaults against strong positions, always deluding himself by thinking his demoralized army was made up of spirited, confident troops like his old Texas Brigade. On September 2, Sherman's army entered Atlanta. Hood's army fled into Tennessee, clearing the way for Sherman to destroy Atlanta and then cut a blazing path to the Georgia seacoast.

Sherman did not pursue Hood into Tennessee, allowing him the opportunity to rest and reorganize his army. By mid-October, Hood was ready to act with breathtaking boldness. His object was to retake Tennessee and Kentucky. As Hood came north, General George Thomas shifted his forces to meet him. At Franklin, despite Confederate General Patrick Cleburne's strong argument for a flanking movement, Hood again reverted to a suicidal head-on assault. Again he failed, losing 6,300 men—nearly a quarter of the attacking force. Among those who paid with their life for Hood's reckless assault was General Cleburne. The Army of Tennessee was shattered; for all practical purposes, it was destroyed as an effective fighting force.

The subsequent defeat at Nashville two weeks later ended Hood's military career. Despite a magnificent fight, the Confederate army suffered its most crushing defeat of the war, followed by a vigorous Union pursuit.

The pursuit of Hood's army was a brutal nightmare, conducted in the foulest weather imaginable. Between Nashville and the Tennessee River, the remnants of a defeated army lay strewn along the line of retreat: busted caissons, overturned wagons, bloated horses, and human corpses, frozen in the grotesque poses of the dead. John Bell Hood was no Napoleon, but Nashville had been his Moscow.

A bandaged Tennessee private who had seen Hood prior to Nashville described him as "feeble and decrepit, with an arm in a sling and a crutch in the other hand, trying to guide and control his horse," and felt sorry for him. After the battle, when the private went to secure "a wounded furlough," he felt even more sorry for Hood. The general was alone in his tent, "much agitated and affected" by the events of the past six hours "and crying like his heart would break." The private received his furlough paper, then went back into the darkness, leaving Hood to his pain. "I pitied him, poor fellow," the soldier wrote later, remembering the event. "I always loved and honored him, and will ever revere and cherish his memory. . . . As a soldier, he was brave, good, noble and gallant, and fought with the ferociousness of a wounded tiger; but as a general, he was a failure in every particular."

Hood did the only thing left for him to do. He asked to be relieved. General Lee, now Confederate general-in-chief, reinstated General Joseph Johnston, whose campaign against Sherman was being viewed with less disapproval in light of Hood's failure. Johnston was assigned the task of stopping Sherman's advance through the Carolinas.

Hood returned to Richmond but found the city that had once hailed him as a hero now barred its doors to him. Senator Wigfall later commented on Hood's career: "That young man had a fine career before him until Davis undertook to make him what the good Lord had not done—to make a great general of him. He had thus ruined Hood and destroyed the last hope of the Southern Confederacy."

Mrs. Chesnut continued to welcome Hood into her home, but she hardly recognized him when he first reappeared, deep in combat fatigue. "His face speaks of wakeful nights and nerves strung to their utmost tension by anxiety," Chesnut wrote in her diary. He spoke plainly of his defeat and said he had nobody to blame but himself.

On February 7, the *Constitutionalist* published an apologia that equated Hood's actions to those of Robert E. Lee. In doing so, the newspaper placed the blame for the destruction of the Army of Tennessee on General William Hardee for his failure to coordinate with General Benjamin Cheatham at Nashville during Hood's assaults in July 1864. Hood did nothing to correct that supposition. When Hardee learned of the article, he immediately wrote to Hood saying he believed it had been written and published with Hood's knowledge and approbation and asking if that impression was correct. Hood's reply was that if he wanted to know who had written the article and the rationale for its content, he should contact the paper that had published it. A series of letters passed between the two generals, with no final conclusion reached. Both believed they had had the last word.

Trouble with another Confederate general soon confronted Hood. On April 1, Johnston notified President Davis's office that he had read Hood's report on the Atlanta Campaign and was going to prefer charges against him as soon as he could find time. In his report to Davis, Hood had set forth an argument that Johnston's conduct of the first half of the campaign had been both a disaster in itself and responsible for the catastrophes that befell the army when Hood took over. Johnston's actions, Hood said, had demoralized the army to such an extent that it had never completely regained its old esprit and prowess.

When Hood went to Richmond, he stopped in South Carolina to see Buck Preston. Although depressed by his defeat in Tennessee, he still hoped to marry her. Buck's family objected to the match. When Hood sought to marry her, he encountered a wall of opposition. He who had been in the thick of battle and fought gallantly at Gaines' Mill and Antietam was driven away by Buck's family.

On May 31, accompanied by two members of his staff, Hood surrendered to federal officials in Natchez and was paroled. For him, at last, the war was over. He was almost thirty-four. The cause he loved was lost, and he was overwhelmed with humiliation at the failure of his leadership.

In June, a depressed Hood returned to Texas. Once Hood reached Texas, however, his outlook brightened. He was welcomed by the people who had known him before the war and by those who knew him as the commander of the Texas Brigade. His arrival was hailed by a San Antonio paper that stated "It does our heart good to welcome him back . . . this truly great, good and gallant officer, soldier and gentleman." Old friends helped ease Hood's pain of failure and defeat.

The attacks on his military record continued to irritate him. As a result of these attacks, Hood headed to Washington. He was hoping to talk with Jefferson Davis, who was being held prisoner there. Davis, he felt, would clear his record and support his position. But his request to visit with Davis was denied by President Johnson. Hood continued to be interviewed by the press, but he limited his remarks to one subject—defending himself and his conduct of the Atlanta and Tennessee campaigns. It was virtually a repetition of his statement in his final report. It was the account he was to give repeatedly in the next few years, and one that finally became the substance of his book, *Advance and Retreat.*

In the winter of 1865–1866, Hood decided to move to New Orleans. He borrowed $250 from each of forty friends in Kentucky, planning to go into business in the Crescent City. Hood lived in New Orleans for the rest of his life but left frequently, traveling for either business or pleasure. Hood became a cotton factor and commission merchant, buying and selling cotton and other goods for a profit. After an unsuccessful venture as a commission merchant, Hood went into the insurance business, selling policies and managing the Louisiana investments of the Life Association of America.

On April 13, 1868, Hood married Anna Marie Hennen, the only surviving child of a prominent Louisiana Catholic family. Hood had been baptized as a Protestant in 1864. Because of the difference in their religious faiths, a special dispensation was required for the marriage. An eyewitness to the wedding noted that "it was a touching sight to see the tall slender form of the maimed soldier move slowly up, by help of crutches, to the altar rail, where he knelt, with the poorest and humblest to partake of the most solemn rite of his faith, the Communion."

Very little is known about the life and personality of Anna Marie, the woman Hood married, except that she had been educated in Europe. Her father, who died just before her marriage, had been a successful member of the New Orleans bar. Although the family's wealth had suffered some during the war, they were still able to live in comfortable circumstances. They owned a plantation near Hammond, Louisiana, and an apartment in the exclusive part of New Orleans. Some time after their marriage, Hood and his wife, along with his mother-in-law, moved to a larger house that would be their home until 1879. In the eleven years of their marriage, the Hoods had many children, including eight girls, three boys, and three sets of twins. Their last child, Anna Gertrude, was born just a few weeks before the deaths of Hood and his wife. When the family traveled, tradition has it that they were known as "Hood's Brigade" and sometimes had to telegraph ahead for milk.

Hood's business provided an adequate living, enabling him to spend time trying to clear his military career. Increasingly, as the years went by, he corresponded with ex-Confederates to obtain information about the war. His friend Stephen D. Lee advised him not to rush into print with a defense of his career because "prejudice was there too hight [sic] for him to have an impartial hearing." Hood's response was somewhat contradictory: "I agree with you. . . . The injustice done me by my countrymen has ceased to trouble me. How beautiful it is to have a God to look to in all our afflictions. . . . I trust to be able to forgive all who have wronged me. To conquer self is the greatest battle of life." Nevertheless, Hood continued to collect material about his military career.

Hood was also active in veterans organizations. He served as president of the Southern Hospital Association of New Orleans, an organization established to care for "diseased and maimed soldiers," and was vice president of the Louisiana branch of the Southern Historical Society. He was also active in both the Association of the Army of Northern Virginia and the Louisiana Division of the Army of Tennessee. From time to time, he was invited to speak to various veterans groups.

In 1874, Johnston's book, *Narrative of Military Operations Directed During the Late War Between the States*, prodded Hood into an effort to defend himself. Johnston's book depicted Hood as an incompetent officer whose errors were largely responsible for the loss of northern Georgia. Johnston stated that Hood had often proposed impractical plans, took unnecessary chances in battle, had lied, and generally had been a handicap in the effort to stop Sherman. Hood's own battle record as an army commander was further proof of his ineptness as a military leader. As Hood read these comments, he was determined to write a "Reply to General Johnston" to present his side of the dispute.

In 1875, Hood's ego received another jolt when William Sherman published his memoirs. Although not as harsh as Johnston's book, it did not paint a favorable impression of Hood's actions at Atlanta. Sherman said that Hood was "rash" and had "played into our hands perfectly" by marching into Tennessee and leaving the main Union force free to march across Georgia.

Sherman's memoirs encouraged Hood to increase the scope of his own work. He decided to write an account of the siege of Atlanta and his battles in Tennessee to add to the "Reply to General Johnston." The major theme of the second part of his memoirs was an effort to shift the blame for failure in the campaign onto others—Johnston, Hardee, and Cheatham.

By 1879, Hood had nearly completed his writing, but his economic situation was beginning to change. To offset his business losses, Hood tried to sell the federal government the letters and other historic papers that he had collected while working on his memoirs. For the documents, he was hoping to receive $12,500; the sale, however, had to wait for the appropriation of funds by Congress. Unfortunately, Hood never lived to receive the money.

Hood returned to New Orleans. Yellow fever attacked the city that summer. Hood's wife died first, the eldest child next, and then Hood himself. His death left his children destitute. The maimed hero of the Confederacy, who had survived the shot and shell of war, had at last succumbed to an innocuous mosquito. It was not a particularly valorous end for a gallant warrior; almost certainly, he would have preferred death on the battlefield as the proper end to his life.

Hood's friends decided on a quick, quiet funeral. Only a few former comrades in arms followed his casket from Trinity Episcopal Church to Lafayette Cemetery on the afternoon after his death. A detachment from a local company added a military touch to his last rites.

Hood's memory would live on, thanks largely to his friend General P. G. T. Beauregard. Seeing the plight of Hood's children, Beauregard organized the Hood Orphan Memorial Publication Fund; taking subscriptions for the publication of Hood's memoirs, with profits going to the children's support. Titled *Advance and Retreat*, it was an angry, bitter book that made no friends of former enemies.

Hood's faults and virtues were those of the mid-nineteenth century South.

After the war, Hood took no part in politics, nor did he make any public state-ments about Reconstruction. He was too involved trying to save his military reputation and earning a living.

Hood proved to be a fine combat leader in situations where his bravery and example would inspire his men. Unlike other Southerners of his generation, however, Hood rose to a position where courage and combat leadership were not enough. As an army commander, he was unable or unwilling to thorough-ly plan his operations. A writer for the *Clark County* (Kentucky) *Democrat* summed it up best: Hood was a man "born and bred to be a soldier" who "had no apti-tude for any other pursuit." It was Hood's tragedy that he was such "an excel-lent soldier but such a poor general."

15 Gentle Hero

JOSHUA LAWRENCE CHAMBERLAIN

HE seemed an unlikely candidate to become a military hero. He was soft-spoken, philosophical, deeply religious, and a professor at Bowdoin College in Maine when the Civil War began. On July 2, 1863, on a rocky slope overlooking the Gettysburg battlefield, this quiet academic proved that a man of the pen could be just as mighty with the sword. His name was Joshua Lawrence Chamberlain, and for his efforts he would be awarded the Medal of Honor and a permanent place among the heroes in American history, much to the surprise of those who thought him little more than an ivory-tower intellectual.

Most believed that a college professor would be the least likely person to be able to lead men in battle. Chamberlain seemed soft, effete, and too lost in intellectual pursuits to be a man of action, but in fact he was just the opposite.

He became the ideal example of the citizen answering his country's call. Though not a man of war, when a crisis arose, he went forward in battle and excelled at it.

The lofty dreams and high ideals that were to guide Chamberlain throughout his life had their roots in Down East Maine, a region that acquired its values from the early Puritan immigrants. This heritage bred people with a firm dedication to principle, to duty, and to a sense of fulfilling God's will in their lives by doing the best they could with the talents God had given them.

Joshua, called Lawrence by his parents, was born on September 8, 1828, in Brewer, Maine. Lawrence's father, also named Joshua, was a farmer who took an active part in civil and military affairs. At one time, he held the office of county commissioner and served as lieutenant colonel commanding the local militia regiment. Lawrence's grandfather, the first Joshua, and Ebenezer, his great-grandfather, had both served in the army during times of need. From Ebenezer to Colonel Chamberlain to Lawrence's father, there was a tradition of military service—and it was particularly strong in the later generations.

Lawrence's mother was Sarah Dupee Brastow. When she and Joshua married, it seemed to be a case of "opposites attract." Joshua was quiet, independent, indulgent toward his family, and tolerant on the political and social issues of the day. He showed little of the aggressiveness or business judgment that had made his father a financial success. One of his childhood heroes was Captain James Lawrence, the American naval captain of the frigate *Chesapeake*. It was Captain Lawrence who fought a losing battle with H.M.S. *Shannon* in 1813 and, after being mortally wounded, cried out, "Don't give up the ship!" Young Lawrence's father admired the South and believed in states' rights, but when the war started, he was loyal to the Union. Although he liked military activities and had three sons who served, he deplored the conflict and considered it unnecessary.

Lawrence's mother was altogether different from his father. While her husband was quiet and serious in appearance, she was outgoing and full of fun. Where he was indulgent, she was firm. She was energetic and industrious, helping her children with their studies. Though she loved all of her five children, her eyes glowed most brightly when she spoke of her oldest son, Lawrence. She had hopes that he would devote himself to the Lord's work; his father was equally determined that he pursue a military career. Sarah's husband and children adored her for her winning ways and power of persuasion.

Joshua and Sarah wanted to make certain that their children would continue the family tradition of hard work as the only sure path to heavenly reward. Religion played an important part in the Chamberlain home, and the family regularly attended the Brewer Congregational Church. Their religious beliefs were simple: Church attendance was required; family quarreling was forbidden;

profanity was not allowed; discipline was strict; modesty and moderation were displayed in all things; and public expression of any kind of emotion was viewed as undignified. Lawrence rebelled only slightly against these rules and, in his earlier years, tended to follow the path dictated by his mother, who had a gentle and studious personality.

Young Chamberlain was full of life as a boy. He worked on the family's hundred-acre farm plowing, planting, weeding, and harvesting. Lawrence learned that few things are so difficult that they cannot be resolved or mastered. Once when he told his father that he and his brothers could not clear away a large rock from a field, his father looked down at him and said, "Move it." He asked how and his father replied, "Move it, that's how. Do it." That became the solution for all his problems and an order of action for life.

But life was not all work. Bangor was a great lumber port and among the largest builders of ships. Lawrence loved boats and enjoyed being around the water. He learned to swim, became a skillful player of the old game of "round ball," and learned to shoot, although he preferred observing wildlife to shooting at it. He took great pleasure in the music he heard at church and school. He learned to sing and loved choral music, but of all the instruments the bass viol was his favorite.

Joshua sent Lawrence to Major Whiting's military academy in Ellsworth, Maine. Lawrence did well and enjoyed school, excelling at military drill, Latin, and French. For financial reasons, he even tried his hand at "keeping school," as teaching was often called. His early introduction to teaching was the beginning of his love for this avocation. Still, teaching was not without its problems. Lawrence had to thrash the usual school bully, a boy as large as himself, in order to establish control of the classroom. Thereafter, he had no trouble.

By the end of his teens, Lawrence had to make a decision about a career. His father hoped he would consider West Point and a military career; his mother hoped he would become a minister. Sarah Chamberlain won—at least up to a point. Having joined the Congregational Church in Brewer, Lawrence agreed to become a minister of the gospel. He would be a missionary to some country, he hoped, where he could teach and preach. Bowdoin College in Brunswick, Maine, produced many aspirants to the Congregational ministry. For entrance, a knowledge of Latin, French, and Greek was required. Though Lawrence was well prepared in Latin and French, he knew nothing about Greek. He threw himself into learning it with the same determination for which he later became celebrated. For the next six months, he spent most of his time studying Greek. It is said he memorized Kuhner's entire grammar in the unabridged Greek. His effort proved fruitful and he was admitted to Bowdoin in 1848.

Lawrence's academic record at Bowdoin was outstanding; he received honors in both languages and mathematics. His election to the honor society Phi Beta Kappa set the seal on a fine beginning as a scholar. He became a member of the Peucinian Society and composed poems for it. He joined the Alpha Delta Phi fraternity and continued his interest in religion by teaching Sunday school and directing the church choir.

It was at the First Parish Church that Lawrence met a trim, lively girl, Fannie Adams. She was the pastor's daughter and church organist. Lawrence began taking Fannie to prayer meetings and various college social events. Soon he found himself deeply in love with her. Lawrence and Fannie decided they would marry as soon as he finished his education. Finishing his education meant graduating from Bowdoin and then completing his study for the ministry at Bangor Theological Seminary. Fannie's father, Dr. George Adams, was less encouraging about Lawrence's plan to marry his daughter. He thought it unwise for Fannie to marry a man two years her junior, with three more years of study facing him.

With his marriage deferred until he completed his ministerial studies, Lawrence entered Bangor Theological Seminary in the fall of 1852. He studied theology in Latin and church history in German. He also began the study of Arabic, Hebrew, and Syriac, a task he would complete six years later. To help finance his schooling, Lawrence taught German to classes of girls and supervised the schools in his hometown of Brewer. When he finally completed his studies at the seminary, he received calls from three churches.

Having decided that he preferred teaching to the ministry, Lawrence turned down all three calls. Rather, he accepted an invitation to deliver an oration at Bowdoin in hopes of earning a master's degree and a teaching job. His presentation was well received, and he was offered a faculty position at Bowdoin for the academic year 1855–1856. Lawrence promptly accepted and celebrated by marrying Fannie Adams in December.

Chamberlain remained at Bowdoin from the fall of 1855 to midsummer 1862. After teaching logic and natural theology his first year, he was promoted to the professorship of rhetoric and oratory. Chamberlain was a gifted teacher as well as a patient, understanding man. He often spent extra time with students needing individual attention. But by 1858, he had become dissatisfied with the educational tradition of the college. He told his colleagues that Bowdoin needed to change, that it was preparing its students to work and not to think. The college was providing training, he argued, instead of educating its students. He later instituted a number of teaching innovations that provided for greater student participation, more science offerings, and less reliance on the classics. All this he did without gaining permission from either Bowdoin's president or the board of trustees.

During his Bowdoin years, Chamberlain was greatly influenced by Harriet Beecher Stowe, the wife of a professor at the college. She was in the process of writing her novel *Uncle Tom's Cabin* and would host reading groups with Bowdoin students, reading them passages from her book. This was Chamberlain's indoctrination into the issue of slavery, and he developed strong feelings on the question. "Slavery and freedom cannot live together," he said emphatically.

In 1861, Chamberlain had a secure position as a professor at Bowdoin College, had married and fathered two children, and bought a home in Brunswick. Life seemed predictable and settled, but the outbreak of the war changed all that.

Lawrence watched the war from afar. Throughout 1861, the students and faculty at Bowdoin talked of the war, although few at the college believed the conflict would last much past the summer of the next year. Chamberlain thought otherwise. He was convinced that the war would last for many years and be more bloody than his colleagues believed. As the national crisis deepened with Union defeats, Chamberlain grew uneasy. He strongly disapproved of slavery on religious and moral grounds. What angered Chamberlain most about the South was not their "slave-holding spirit" but secession, which he viewed as political heresy and an erosion of the law. Although slavery was an important issue for Chamberlain, he was not a committed abolitionist. When the Confederates fired on Fort Sumter, his anger was inflamed. "The flag of the nation had been insulted," he later wrote. "The honor and authority of the United States had been defied. The integrity and existence of the People of the United States had been assailed in open and bitter war." Although he came to greatly admire the Confederate soldiers, he denounced, as long as he lived, the South's withdrawal from the Union.

Chamberlain had every reason and every excuse to avoid going to war; but he was determined to go because for him, it was the right thing to do. He had a respect for all life as a manifestation of God; he hated killing, even of animals. But neither concern for family nor life hindered his belief that he should commit himself wholeheartedly to the war.

The Bowdoin people tried to persuade him to remain, saying that his duty lay in educating young men for the future. Chamberlain secretly wrote to the governor, asking what he could do for the war effort. When the college learned of Chamberlain's interest in going to war, they were not happy with the prospect of losing him. They offered him the chairmanship of the department of modern language and a two-year European sabbatical in hopes of enticing him to stay. Chamberlain accepted the sabbatical; but rather than going to Europe, he went to war.

Governor Israel Washburn offered Chamberlain a colonelcy and command of a new volunteer regiment, the 20th Maine, but he declined in favor of the number-two position, lieutenant colonel. Although he aspired to command, Chamberlain realized he had a great deal to learn about the military. Thus began the active career of one of the most remarkable officers—and hardest fighters—to serve in any American war.

Despite Chamberlain's patriotism, there were detractors among his colleagues at Bowdoin who did not want to see him leave the college. In part,
some of the faculty and administration felt betrayed by Chamberlain's action,
especially because he had kept his request to the governor a secret. They even
went so far as to contact several Maine politicians, telling them that not only
was Chamberlain needed at Bowdoin, but that he was too much an intellectual to make a good soldier. Such politicking had little influence on the governor and even less on Chamberlain.

The colonelcy of the 20th Maine went to a West Point graduate and veteran of the Battle of First Bull Run, Adelbert Ames. The volunteers making up
the 20th Maine were rugged men with no military experience and badly in
need of discipline. Nonetheless, Ames succeeded in making these ragtag civilians into a fighting outfit. Under Ames's tutelage, Chamberlain too began to
learn the art of soldiering. He read military manuals diligently and formed a
study group with other officers new to the military. He wrote home: "I study,
I tell you, every military work I can find and it is no small labor to master the
evolutions of a battalion and brigade. I am bound to understand everything."

In September 1862, the 20th Maine was assigned to the 5th Corps of the
Army of the Potomac and ordered north to head off the Army of Northern
Virginia's invasion of Maryland. Although the 20th Maine was held in reserve
during the Battle of Antietam, Chamberlain had an opportunity to see the results
of the battle. The sight of the dead was unsettling for him. In describing a dead
Confederate soldier, he wrote: "He wore the gray. He was my enemy, this boy.
He was dead—the boy, my enemy—but I shall see him forever."

The 20th Maine spent the rest of the fall honing its military skills and
preparing for the Union army to make its move on Fredericksburg. For any new
regiment, there could not have been a worse battle for its first action. The battle was poorly planned and its execution was even worse. The Federals began
their offensive on December 11, 1862, using pontoon bridges to cross the Rappahannock River. After fighting through the town of Fredericksburg, the Union
army assaulted Marye's Heights two days later. Lee's Confederate forces held
a strong position at the top of the heights. Wave after wave of Federal troops
advanced on the nearly impregnable position, and rank after rank was mowed
down. Federal troops did all they could that day to take the heights but were
never able to cross the wall. From across the river, Chamberlain watched the
initial attacks literally in tears, witnessing what appeared to be the sacrificial
deaths of so many men.

At around three o'clock, the 20th Maine was moved to the foot of Marye's
Heights and ordered to advance up the hill. The men kept in line despite having to step over the dead and the dying on the field. Years later, Chamberlain
would remember the bitterly cold day and the shouts of those who lay on the

ground: "No one lives who goes there." Chamberlain and Ames could see the flashes of rebel muzzles as the 20th Maine went across the field. "God help us now," Ames said softly. Turning to the men he yelled, "Forward the 20th."

The 20th moved forward. The air was thick with flying, bursting shells. "On we pushed up slopes slippery with blood," Chamberlain recalled. The Rebels were unmoved, and Chamberlain ordered his men to lie down where they were and return fire as best they could. When darkness came, they were still there below the wall, the forward line of the Army of the Potomac, building breastworks with the bodies of dead men, now frozen in grotesque poses.

Chamberlain and his men had to spend the night on the field in freezing temperatures. It was a gruesome experience for all concerned. "The living and the dead were alike to me," Chamberlain remembered. "I slept though my ears were filled with cries and groans of the wounded, and the ghastly faces of the dead almost made a wall around me. We lay there hearing the dismal thud of bullets into the dead flesh of our lifesaving bulwarks."

The 20th Maine stayed on the field the next day, trading fire with the Rebels, while the commanding general, Ambrose Burnside, attempted to find a way out of the dilemma. As evening approached, the 20th moved back into Fredericksburg. "We had to pick our way over a field strewn with incongruous ruin," Chamberlain wrote, "men torn and broken and cut to pieces in every describable way, cannon dismounted, gun carriages smashed. . . . It was not good for the nerves, that ghastly march, in the lowering night." Chamberlain thought the battle was a waste of lives; the Union army had lost—12,000 dead, wounded, and missing—at Fredericksburg.

The battle at Fredericksburg had been the 20th Maine's baptism by fire, and the men had proven themselves up to the challenge of battle. In the spring of 1863, Ames was promoted to general and Chamberlain became colonel of the 20th Maine. His chance to prove himself in his new position would come on a hot July day at Gettysburg.

By the spring of 1863, Chamberlain the professor had completed the transition to Chamberlain the soldier. "No danger and no hardship ever made me wish to get back to the college life again," he wrote. In the camps of the army, he found excitement and a new camaraderie that he had not known before. He knew it would be difficult to return to his old way of life.

On July 1, 1863, the V Corps, of which 20th Maine was a part, was ordered to proceed with all haste to Gettysburg. When Chamberlain arrived at Gettysburg, his regiment was ordered to occupy Little Round Top, a strategic location on the battlefield. Colonel Strong Vincent, Chamberlain's brigade commander, positioned his regiment on the far left flank of the entire Union army, a position that would receive a great deal of attention from the Confederates. Vincent's last words to the 389 men of the 20th Maine were: "This is the end of the Union line. You understand? You are to hold this ground at all costs!"

Advancing against them was the 15th Alabama Regiment and seven companies of the 47th Alabama—a contingent of 644 men, all under the command of Colonel William Oates. The Alabama troops struck at 6 P.M. and the fighting became intense. When the first attack was repulsed, Oates ordered another advance. Five times the Confederates attacked and were driven back.

Chamberlain had sustained heavy casualties, and his men were running out of ammunition after the repeated assaults by the Confederates. "At times I saw around me more of the enemy than my men," Chamberlain remembered. "Gaps, openings, swellings, closing again with convulsive energy. In the midst of this struggle our ammunition utterly failed. Half my left wing already on the field." It was time, Chamberlain realized, for desperate measures. In that intense moment, he chose to charge in a great right wheel. "The words 'Fix bayonets!' flew from man to man," Chamberlain recalled. "The click of the steel seemed to give new zeal to all. The men dashed forward with a shout."

The sight of two hundred screaming men advancing downhill with fixed bayonets was enough to terrorize the most courageous men, and the 15th Alabama was no exception. Chamberlain described the charge as having the effect of "a reaper cutting down the disconcerted foe." Stunned, the Confederate troops in the front ranks dropped their rifles and surrendered. The rest broke and retreated toward a stone wall in the rear. Oates described the retreat simply, saying, "We ran like a herd of cattle."

By the time the Confederates could regroup, Union reinforcements had poured into position. This discouraged further Confederate attempts to take Little Round Top. The golden opportunity to turn the Union left was gone, and the Confederates would pay dearly for it the next day. Chamberlain's courageous defenders had saved the left end of the Union line, the Battle of Gettysburg, and perhaps the entire Union.

Chamberlain viewed the war as a personal test. He knew he was rising to the challenge. But the most difficult part of the test was yet to come when, in the spring of 1864, the V Corps was ordered south as part of Grant's push toward Richmond. During the spring and summer, Grant's army lost 50,000 men. Most of his men expected to die; it was just a question of when. By June, Grant's army reached Petersburg. Now commander of the 3rd Brigade, replacing Colonel Vincent who had been killed at Gettysburg, Chamberlain prepared to do his part in the assault of Petersburg.

Taking over a brigade of Pennsylvanians, Chamberlain led them on June 18 in a series of attacks against heavily fortified Confederate works at Petersburg. He had received orders directing him to move forward. Incredulous at the request because of the Confederate's strong position, he responded by pointing out how exposed his brigade was. There was little coordination in the Union attacks, and the orders came back repeating that he was to attack. Chamberlain did, knowing that it was a terrible sacrifice, but as a man of conscience, he was at the head of his men. He said, "I felt it was my duty to lead the charge in person and on foot."

Defensive fire from the Confederates was intense. When his brigade's color-bearer was shot dead at his side during the assault, Chamberlain picked up the V Corps flag and raced forward. His troops forced a Rebel battery and supporting infantry to retreat. Later that day, Chamberlain and his men assailed another Confederate fortification, but this time they were met with stiff resistance. As Chamberlain turned to signal his Pennsylvanians to move up, a bullet slammed into his right hip joint and passed out his left hip. Supporting himself by leaning on his saber, he urged his men forward before loss of blood caused him to collapse.

The attack failed just short of the Rebel intrenchment. Chamberlain was carried from the field, and it was thought that his wounds were fatal. Chamberlain, thinking he was mortally wounded, told the doctors to attend the less seriously wounded. They ignored his orders and transported him to a field hospital behind the lines. Chamberlain wrote his wife: "I am lying mortally wounded. . . , but my mind and my heart are at peace. . . . You have been a precious wife to me. . . . Cherish the darlings. . . . Do not grieve too much for me. We shall all soon meet."

After lingering near death for weeks, Chamberlain recovered. General Grant, affected deeply by Chamberlain's heroism, immediately promoted him to brigadier general. It was one of the few field promotions Grant made during the war.

Chamberlain's survival was amazing, but the damage done internally would cause him terrible suffering and numerous operations the rest of his life. He spent five months convalescing at home in Brunswick. By August 1864, Chamberlain had recuperated so remarkably that he spoke about returning to duty. In November, he rejoined the V Corps despite being unable to walk without excruciating pain. Although he didn't like it, he often had to be helped up on his horse.

By March, Chamberlain was ready to lead his men again and was given the honor of attacking Lee's retreating army. At daylight on the 29th, his brigade hit Lee's divisions near Petersburg. After initial success, the Federals were stopped in front of a Confederate breastwork of logs and earth. Regrouping his men, Chamberlain led a new charge. As the volume of fire increased, Chamberlain's horse dashed far ahead of the charging column. When he tried to slow the horse down, it reared. At that moment, a bullet ripped through his horse's neck, hitting Chamberlain just below the heart and passing through the back seam of his coat. The bullet was partially deflected in its movement by a leather case and brass mirror in his breast pocket, thus sparing his life. To Brigadier General Charles Griffin, who rode up quickly to aid him, Chamberlain looked like a dying man. "My dear general, you are gone," he said, putting a steadying hand around Chamberlain's waist.

As Chamberlain slowly regained full consciousness, he saw that the Confederates had broken the right of his line. "Yes, General, I am gone," he gasped, and rode off from the astonished Griffin. It was a strange and ghastly sight, and it inspired his men. With tattered clothing and covered with blood, Chamberlain galloped to rally his line as officers and men stared in amazement. To many he was unquestionably a dying man on his last mission. Someone sent a wire to a New York paper reporting his death. Chamberlain dashed among the retreating men, exhorting and threatening them to rally. So inspired were they by the force of his personality and courage, troops of both sides cheered him.

Chamberlain had had quite an afternoon. Until reinforcements arrived, he had battled for two hours with four brigades of Lieutenant General Richard Anderson's corps, numbering more than 6,000 men. His own brigade amounted to only 1,700—of whom he had lost 400 killed and wounded in action. His wound, although bloody, had not been serious. He was able to return to duty within a few days. All told, his action had been a remarkable example of inspired leadership. After the battle, General Gouverneur Warren met him and said, "General, you have done splendid work. I am telegraphing the President. You will hear from it."

Chamberlain had little time to think about rewards. He was more concerned with the welfare of his men than with any reward he might receive. As it began to grow dark, a cold rain fell. On foot, weak and barely able to walk from the pain of his old wound and the new one, Chamberlain's thoughts were of his men. When he looked in on the wounded, he discovered General Horatio Sickel, who had been wounded in the battle. He sat down beside Sickel to cheer him as best he could. But Sickel, who could smile despite his pain, thought Chamberlain needed comforting himself. "General," he whispered, "you have the soul of the lion and the heart of a woman." "Take the benediction to yourself," Chamberlain replied, "You could not have thought that, if you had not been it."

On March 31, Chamberlain led a new attack on Lee's retreating army. Once again confronting a heavily defended position held by Southern infantry, he spaced his troops in a loose-order pattern to keep casualties low, and they swarmed over the defenders. Chamberlain's leadership in these last two actions resulted in his promotion to brevet major general "for conspicuous gallantry and meritorious service."

Chamberlain continued to perform superbly, including his role in the April Battle of Five Forks, called the Waterloo of the Confederacy because Lee lost such a large part of his army there. Chamberlain would remember the victory with great sadness because of the death of one of his men, Major Edwin Glenn. He had ordered Glenn to break a small line of Confederates, saying, "If you will break that line you shall have a colonel's commission." Glenn's unit achieved their objective, but in the process, Glenn was mortally wounded. When Chamberlain learned of Glenn's condition, he went immediately to see him. Glenn could only whisper, "General, I have carried out your wishes." Chamberlain, anguished by this, said, "Oh, my orders. My orders were never worth your life." This instant would haunt him all his life. After the battle, Chamberlain forwarded a recommendation for Glenn's brevet promotion.

After Lee's surrender on April 9, Chamberlain learned that he had been given the honor of accepting the formal capitulation of the Confederate arms and colors at Appomattox Court House. Grant had been instructed by Lincoln earlier to "let 'em up easy." Grant sensed in Chamberlain his quiet character and knew he would be willing to conduct a dignified surrender.

The morning of April 12 dawned cold and gray. Chamberlain lined his troops on both sides of the road leading through Appomattox. As the gray ranks marched forward to stack their arms and flags, there were no bands, no drums, just the shuffling sound of tramping feet. "On they come," Chamberlain wrote, "with the old swinging route step and swaying battle flags." General John Gordon led the column; the first unit behind him was the Stonewall Brigade, now reduced to 200 men. All the Confederate units were greatly reduced in size. The crimson battle flags were "crowded so thick, by thinning out of men," said Chamberlain, "that the column seemed crowned with red."

Chamberlain ordered his men to "shift arms," in an unmistakable marching salute of the Southern army. Major General John Gordon raised his sword and brought its tip down to his toe in a sweeping response to the Union tribute. Gordon shouted a command and the Confederates returned the salute. "It was," said Chamberlain, "honor answering honor." "Many of the grizzled veterans wept like women," said Major Henry Kyd Douglas. "On our part," Chamberlain wrote, "not a sound of trumpet more, nor roll of drum; not a cheer, nor word . . . but an awed stillness rather, and breath-holding as if it were the passing of the dead."

After the exchange of salutes, the Confederates fixed their bayonets and stacked their muskets. Then, Chamberlain wrote, "lastly, and reluctantly, with agony of expression, they folded their flags, battle-worn and torn, blood-stained, heart-holding colors, and lay them down." This was the most painful part of the ordeal; said one North Carolinian: "We did not even look into each other's faces." One soldier, Jonathan Archibald of the 48th Alabama, hid the regimental colors under his shirt, brought them home with him, and was buried with them when he died.

On the morning of May 23, 1865, Chamberlain led his division for the last time in the Grand Review of the Army of the Potomac. After riding past the reviewing stand, at the invitation of the president, Chamberlain dismounted and joined the dignitaries there. When he saw the remnants of the regiments that had charged with him on the day he had been wounded at Petersburg, he broke the protocol by returning their salute.

When the war was over, not only the nation had to heal but also Chamberlain himself—not just physically, but emotionally and spiritually. He returned home to Brunswick in July, but the town seemed unnaturally quiet after the excitement of the battlefield on which he had earned his fame. Nothing throughout the rest of his life could come close to what he had experienced during the war.

Chamberlain enjoyed his notoriety when he returned to Brunswick, but was soon plagued by periods of depression. He enjoyed the security from his teaching position but at the same time, loathed the boredom of Bowdoin's predictability. The physical disabilities caused by his crippling wound added to his dilemma because he realized that the life he had led as an army officer was no longer possible. He longed for the excitement of his army days.

During the year following his return home, Chamberlain made a number of speeches on Reconstruction before citizens' groups in Portland and Augusta, and his position on certain issues became widely known. Like many Northerners, Chamberlain believed the South should be punished, but not if that meant enfranchising the newly freed slaves. Lincoln had fought to preserve the Union first and then to abolish slavery. Lincoln had not wanted the war to spark a social revolution, but by late 1862, he believed he had little choice. Lincoln's goal, Chamberlain believed, was to reunite the nation. Chamberlain followed his example. The war was fought to save the Union and end slavery, and that was all. After that, the freedmen were on their own.

Chamberlain and his wife celebrated their ten-year wedding anniversary in December. He gave his wife an expensive gold-and-diamond bracelet that he designed himself, inscribed with the names of the twenty-four battles in which he fought. The band also depicted the shoulder boards of a major general, inset with two diamonds. The gift was opulent by any measure and was intended to show his wife his love. Though Fannie treasured the gift, it could not mend the rift that had grown between them during the four-year war. She knew her husband was considering running for governor and had been talking to Republican party leaders about his prospects. Fannie strongly disapproved, hoping her husband would overcome his restlessness, stay at home, and continue to teach.

Chamberlain went on without his wife's approval, welcoming the chance for the new adventure that political office promised. When he met with Republican leaders, he was pleased with the outcome. The party leaders selected Chamberlain to head their ticket, hoping his wartime record would give him the edge in the election. He agreed to stand as the Republican party's nominee and returned to Brunswick to announce his candidacy to his wife. She was not pleased with his decision to run for public office.

Chamberlain's opponent in the September election was Eben F. Pillsbury, an anti-Lincoln Democrat. Chamberlain's war record was enough for him to gain popular support. When all the votes were counted, the results showed that Chamberlain had gained the largest majority of any candidate for a state office in Maine's history—nearly seventy percent of all votes cast.

Fannie was not happy with the results of the election. She had tried to meet her husband's needs and had coped with his fame as best she could. When Chamberlain went off to war, she supported his decision. She stood by him when he was near death and helped nurse him back to health. For her, it was no surprise when he accepted the nomination for governor, nor that he was elected. And apparently it came as no surprise to him that Fannie now refused any further participation in his public life. Fannie Chamberlain, who had faithfully supported her husband during the war, now felt she had been discarded by him.

Chamberlain enjoyed being governor and wished his wife could have enjoyed it with him. Instead, Fannie stayed in Brunswick while he lived at a boarding house in Augusta. He visited his home as often as he could, but this did not satisfy his wife. Their marriage continued to deteriorate, and by 1868, Fannie was considering divorce. She took no action but elected to live a reclusive life, painting and tending to her children and in time, her grandchildren. Eventually, after Chamberlain came home as a private citizen again and returned to teaching, they reconciled their differences; their marriage would survive for nearly fifty years. As she grew older, Fannie began to lose her sight: Chamberlain would spend hours reading to her.

As a Republican governor of Maine, Chamberlain took the party's position on Reconstruction and supported ratification of the Fourteenth Amendment. Declaring that Congress was the rightful authority in the politics of Reconstruction, Chamberlain believed the terms proposed for the South were neither "hard nor humiliating." Although Maine had been one of only six states to allow free black men to vote, Chamberlain was more conservative when it came to allowing recently freed slaves that same right. He opposed such an early and sweeping reform.

In 1869, Chamberlain traveled to New York City to attend the founding convention of the Society of the Army of the Potomac. As governor of Maine and a national war hero, Chamberlain was much in demand as a speaker. Despite knowing that the army's top generals, including Phil Sheridan and Ulysses Grant, were members, Chamberlain was not intimidated. He decided to use time during his speech to remind Society members that they should honor not only those who gave their lives for the Union but even those who had run afoul of Grant, Sherman, and Sheridan. Chamberlain was championing the cause of what he considered the unfair and unwarranted treatment of General Gouverneur K. Warren by General Sheridan. At the Battle of Five Forks in April 1865, Sheridan had charged Warren with being overly cautious in his actions in the battle. As a result, Sheridan had relieved him of command. "Nor do they forget tonight those officers, once the favorites of fortune, whom misunderstanding, impatience, or jealousy has stricken from our rolls," Chamberlain said in even tones. The crowd knew he could only be referring to Warren. He continued: "Pardon me comrades if I venture here to express the hope, knowing all the pains and penalties of so doing, that tardy justice may be done to officers whose character and service in behalf of the Republic deserve something better than its hasty and lasting rebuke." It was a biting statement aimed squarely at those who now stood at the peak of political power. In defending Warren, Chamberlain was reaffirming his long-held suspicions of federal power and also jeopardizing his own political career.

Despite Chamberlain's rebuke of Sheridan—and by implication Grant—the president continued to support him. Chamberlain would go on to serve four one-year terms as governor of Maine. Although there was never any doubt that Chamberlain could have won a fifth term, the Republican leaders let him know that another term was out of the question. Chamberlain was not disappointed. He had tired of the job, and he realized new blood was needed to revitalize the party. Democratic party leaders approached him about standing for election as governor at the head of their party. He quietly refused, although inwardly he was pleased.

After his four years as governor, Chamberlain was unanimously elected to the presidency at Bowdoin College in 1871, serving in that capacity until 1883. He reformed curriculum by replacing Greek and Latin for most students with French and German and adding courses in science and engineering to the program. He changed the reading of the classics to translations from their original language. He revised many harsh disciplinary practices that he recalled as unnecessary from his years as a student. Chamberlain introduced military drill into the program, believing it would provide a means for students to acquire military knowledge, cultivate their bodies, and develop character. To carry out this enlargement of the curriculum, Chamberlain had to increase the faculty from sixteen to twenty-six. Such an increase, even with a growth in the student body, cost a great deal of money. During Chamberlain's administration, he was able to raise a sum of $200,000—an enormous amount for that time.

Because of the innovations introduced by Chamberlain, some members of the board of trustees, faculty, alumni, and student body were highly critical. Chamberlain offered to resign, but the board of trustees refused to accept his resignation, calling on all friends of the college to support his more liberal program.

The next academic year brought new difficulties that tested Chamberlain's good sense and resolve. The difficulty rose as a result of student opposition to his military program. The idea of soldiering had no glamour for the Bowdoin students, particularly when they were required to purchase uniforms. The students bypassed Chamberlain and the faculty and took their complaints directly to the board. The board of trustees met with a student committee, but no action was taken. Rebuffed, the students brooded over their future course of action.

When spring came, Chamberlain was faced with a major college revolt, an incredible and shocking situation to conservative sensibilities in 1874. Chamberlain met with the faculty and, as a result of an investigation, six of the revolt's ringleaders were dismissed from school. Far from intimidated, most of the student body voted never to drill again. Again Chamberlain met with the faculty, and a committee was formed to meet with students in an effort to divert them from "the folly and wrong of their intended course of action." All weekend the professors met with students, but the problem was not resolved. On Tuesday, students signed a pledge never to drill at Bowdoin College. When a group of juniors failed to report for drill, they were immediately sent home. Soon, practically all members of the sophomore and freshman class were likewise suspended when they failed to report for drill. Letters were sent to the homes of all students who were suspended, advising that they must agree within ten days to comply with the rules of the school—including the requirement for drill—or be expelled. If, after their return, they continued to object to the drill, they would receive an honorable dismissal at the end of the term.

When Chamberlain learned that Dartmouth College might open its doors to the recalcitrant students, he immediately wrote to Asa Smith, Dartmouth's president. Smith informed Chamberlain that he had no plans to admit the rebellious students. Chamberlain ordered letters reproduced and distributed to the student body informing them of Dartmouth's decision. To Chamberlain's great relief, all the students returned to school.

The revolt at Bowdoin excited interest throughout the country. Even papers critical of military training insisted that college authority must be maintained and respected. Chamberlain received both support and criticism. The Drill Revolt, however, doomed his military program. The board voted in June to make the program optional, although they continued to support it in principle and practice. Chamberlain still defended its worth: "Our educated young men," he said, "should be instructed as to be able to assume command of men, and to direct the defense of society against its foes." In 1879, the faculty expressed itself in favor of abolishing the drill. Three years later, the board discontinued the entire military program. A former student of the class of 1875 later spoke of the revolt: "Of course, we were wrong, and we all went back and submitted to the rules of the College, but the backbone of the drill was broken, and it died a speedy and unregretted death." The only person who was sorry to see the program go was Chamberlain himself.

In 1876, Democrat Rutherford Hayes was elected president. He withdrew the Federal troops from the South. Chamberlain defended the president's policies, saying Hayes was correct in "declining to maintain the surveillance of the United States army over local affairs." Individual wrongs done to freedmen should not be redressed by the federal government but only by state and local laws. Chamberlain made it clear that he supported this limitation of federal power. His defense of the status quo illustrates how some of his attitudes had changed since the war.

At Bowdoin, Chamberlain was continuing to have difficulty with students and the academic program. The criticism now shifted to the science program. Chamberlain was also assailed by those who opposed his de-emphasis of religion—and by those who thought he had not gone far enough. One wealthy alumnus threatened to discontinue his financial support, claiming that the school was too sectarian. Chamberlain's predicament was painful: He had not elected to carry out Bowdoin's already established traditions, but rather had tried to adjust to changing times. As a reformer, he found himself in constant trouble. In 1880 and 1881, the board discontinued the scientific and engineering programs.

Chamberlain was indeed ahead of his time. His successor, President William De Witt Hyde, observed that Chamberlain had "advocated the very reforms, using often the very phrases, that are now commonplace in progressive educational discussions." Throughout Chamberlain's career at Bowdoin, ill health caused by his wounds continued to dog him. His strenuous schedule did little to ease the pain. Finally, on March 12, 1883, after a winter of acute pain, Chamberlain was forced to take a leave of absence for the rest of the term. During the leave of absence, his doctor advised him to have an operation and to change his surroundings, recommending Florida. Chamberlain submitted to the operation, coming very close to dying, but his strong constitution and will to live pulled him through again.

Although Chamberlain recovered quickly from surgery, he remained physically weak for months and resigned his presidency. The reforms he regarded as most significant had failed; he had made enemies whose opposition to him threatened Bowdoin's growth as long as he was president; and his physical condition continued to weaken. It was time for him to step down, he thought. Chamberlain was truly a "Renaissance man," displaying versatility and a remarkable record of service to Bowdoin. At one time or another between 1855 and 1885, he taught every subject in the college curriculum except mathematics and physical science. Chamberlain never ceased to love Bowdoin.

While president of Bowdoin, Chamberlain made several important contributions in addition to his college duties. In 1880, a political situation threatened the state with riots. As major general of Maine's militia, Chamberlain was ordered by Governor Alonzo Garcelon to take command of the 1st Division and move to Augusta to protect life and property. The situation grew increasingly tense and bitter over the next two weeks. Chamberlain received death threats and was forced to sleep at different residences each night for fear of being killed or kidnapped. Augusta's mayor assigned a bodyguard to escort Chamberlain through the city. One night a gang of men formed outside the statehouse, and it was reported that they were waiting to kill him. Chamberlain decided to face the danger head-on. He went out through the dark and cold to meet the gang, calmly buttoning up his coat as he approached, saying: "Men, you wish to kill me, I hear. Killing me is no new thing to me. I have offered myself to be killed many times, when I no more deserved it than I do now. Some of you, I think, have been with me on those days. . . . I am here to preserve the peace and honor of this State. . . . But it is for me to see that the laws of this State are put into effect. . . . I am here for that, and I shall do it. If anybody wants to kill me for it, here I am. Let him kill!"

Chamberlain then threw open his coat as an old veteran who knew him stepped from the crowd: "By God, General, the first man that dares to lay a hand on you, I'll kill him on the spot." And with that, the gang moved away. Within a few days, the problem was settled by the State Supreme Court. The gangs that had patrolled the streets dispersed, and the state returned to normal. Chamberlain's nonpartisan stance in the issue pleased neither side, and newspapers of both parties were critical of him. Democratic papers called him a "traitor"; Republicans, a "Republican renegade." Chamberlain's role in keeping the peace had hurt his future political aspirations, and he would never win his party's nomination for a Senate candidacy.

In 1885, Ulysses Grant died. When Winfield Scott Hancock organized the funeral, he made sure to give Chamberlain's carriage a place in the front ranks of the mourners. Chamberlain was surprised by the honor bestowed upon him by Hancock. "I would not have chosen that position," Chamberlain wrote his wife, "because it was too much." Hancock did not think so and directed Chamberlain to stand near the door of Grant's tomb during the final ceremony.

Chamberlain had good reason to be surprised by his treatment at Grant's funeral. Grant and he had been friends, but on one issue they had not seen eye to eye—the questionable actions of Gouverneur K. Warren. In 1880, after years of attempting to clear his name, Warren had been granted a hearing before a special court of inquiry to review charges made by General Phil Sheridan about Warren's conduct at the Battle of Five Forks. Sheridan's action had left Warren a broken man. Chamberlain had always supported Warren, even though he knew Grant disapproved. By 1880, Chamberlain was known as a strong Warren supporter and Sheridan critic. Chamberlain testified on Warren's behalf before a court of inquiry in Washington. In preparing for his testimony, Chamberlain made notes on some of the actions in which he had been involved. He thus began his work on a manuscript on the Battle of Gettysburg. Chamberlain had always wanted to write a book about the war, but his busy schedule had never allowed him the time.

Before his court testimony, Chamberlain met with Sheridan and Hancock; Sheridan's greeting was cool and distant, which didn't bother Chamberlain. During his testimony, he denied that Warren had ever purposely circumvented or ignored an order. He was able to convince the court that in the turmoil of battle, the orders Warren had received were confusing and ambiguous. On November 1882, the court exonerated Warren from wrongdoing in his actions. The court also stated that Grant and Sheridan were wrong in their disciplining of him. Warren had not jeopardized the Union victory, the court held. There was no solace for Warren, however; he had died three months before the findings were released.

After Grant's funeral, Chamberlain bought land in Ocala, Florida, and organized a land-developing company. He was careful not to stake his future entirely on his development company, however, and accepted offers from other firms to lend his name to their investments. By 1885, he was serving on the boards of several investment and financial firms and became so busy managing his own business network that he moved to New York and opened a Wall Street office.

In 1888 and 1889, Chamberlain traveled to Gettysburg to make speeches and to attend reunions. He was elected president of the Society of the Army of the Potomac. By 1890, he continued to be in demand as a speaker. He was not as successful with his business ventures, and his land-developing project was nearly bankrupt. The 1890s were a time of economic impoverishment for many people, but Chamberlain was by no means near that level. In 1893, Congress voted to present him the Medal of Honor for "distinguished gallantry" for his action at Gettysburg.

In the latter part of the 1890s, Chamberlain's life was marked with bouts of illness. Gradually, he withdrew from all formal business and educational duties, returning to Brunswick for good. The new year, 1898, found him once again a full-time resident of his home next to the Bowdoin campus. But if people thought, as some did, that the general would settle down and just fade away, they were profoundly wrong. Within a few weeks after the explosion of the battleship *Maine* in Havana harbor, Chamberlain was ready to return to the army, perhaps even service in the field.

In March, Chamberlain began writing a series of articles on the crisis of the *Maine*, which were published in the *Bangor News*. He wanted the government to prepare for war, but he hoped it could be avoided. Writing about the crisis, however, was not all he did. He offered his service to the governor and later said he would like to organize a division of New England troops. Unfortunately, he was denied a role in the war. The secretary of war politely acknowledged Chamberlain's request, but turned to younger men.

In March 1900, President McKinley appointed Chamberlain as surveyor of the port of Portland. Chamberlain, who had hoped for a position of greater visibility and importance, was scornful. "It is essentially an obscure office," he said, "tending to keep me out of notice, as well as out of responsibility." Nevertheless, he was thankful to have a well-paid job that was not too strenuous for his failing body. The position allowed him to maintain his residence in Brunswick; he was still able to serve Bowdoin College and pursue his speaking and writing. Rarely did his daily routine vary; he always wore a dark suit, a blue shirt with a starched collar, and a black tie. People still sought him out and he was always willing to talk with them.

During the summer of 1905 Fannie, now blind, fell and broke her hip. "Your husband and children 'rise up and call you blessed'—as the old Scripture represented the crowning grace of woman," Chamberlain wrote to Fannie on her eightieth birthday. Shortly after, on October 18, she died. Her death broke his heart. "We pass now quickly from each other's sight," Chamberlain wrote, "but I know full well that where beyond these passing scenes you will be, there will be heaven." Whatever differences may have existed between Chamberlain and Fannie early in their marriage, the two had been very close for many years. For a time after her death, Chamberlain was overcome by melancholy.

Now alone, Chamberlain spent more and more of his time writing and completing his account of the last days with the Army of the Potomac. His work was later released as *The Passing of the Armies*. Chamberlain did not attempt to tell the story of the war through its battles; rather, his account is a defense of his view that God somehow intervened and blessed the Union.

During Chamberlain's last days, he was surrounded by the men of Bowdoin, who often came to visit him. He visited Gettysburg one last time in May 1913 before falling ill early in 1914. He never rose from his bed and died on February 24, at the age of eighty-five.

President Hyde of Bowdoin delivered the eulogy from the place where Chamberlain himself had so often stood as president of Bowdoin. It was a superb analysis and appraisal of his character and career. Chamberlain had stood in advance of his time in many ways, Hyde said, particularly as a reform-minded president of a college that did not have the money to afford his reforms. As a statesman, Chamberlain had courageously opposed the leaders of his party when convinced that to comply with their wishes was to misuse the power that the people had given. At Appomattox, saluting the defeated Confederate troops whom he looked upon no longer as enemies, but as friends and fellow Americans, was a deed "in which military glory and Christian magnanimity were fused." Hyde concluded, "All he said and did was bright and burning with an ardor of idealism which in the home was devotion; in the college was loyalty; in State and Nation was patriotism; toward humanity and God was religion."

Chamberlain was buried in Pine Grove Cemetery, next to the Bowdoin campus where he had spent so much of his life.

16

Principled Lawyer

JOHN SINGLETON MOSBY

N
O single battalion was feared more during the Civil War than the 43rd Battalion of the Virginia Cavalry. Known as Mosby's Rangers, they were an elite guerrilla unit that operated with stunning success in northern Virginia and Maryland from 1863 to the end of the war. John Singleton Mosby was not yet twenty-eight when the war began and he joined the Confederate cavalry. His daring and ingenuity brought him to the attention of J. E. B. Stuart. Through Stuart's influence, Mosby was authorized to raise a company of his own, which evolved into the 43rd Battalion. With seldom more than a few dozen men on an operation, Mosby's Rangers struck supply wagons and railroads, harassing and pinning down Union troops that sometimes greatly outnumbered them. They obtained valuable intelligence for General Lee and the Confederacy. General Grant was so frustrated by Mosby's operations that he ordered the immediate execution without trial of any Ranger

who was captured. By some, he was called "Gray Ghost;" to others, he was the devil incarnate. To his own men, he was more than just a hero.

John Singleton Mosby was born at Edgemont in Powhatan County, Virginia, on December 6, 1833. His parents were Alfred and Virginia McLaurine Mosby. When John was young, his family moved to a farm outside Charlottesville in Albemarle County, where his father prospered. Alfred owned slaves and earned enough to ensure the education of his eight children. John's early schooling took place in a one-room schoolhouse, but at the age of ten, he transferred to a school in Charlottesville. He was an avid learner, and even though he had to walk four miles to school, he rarely missed a day. Unlike most boys of his age, John disliked physical activities and preferred to read. "I always had a literary taste," he later wrote.

On October 3, 1850, John enrolled as a student at the University of Virginia in Charlottesville. He excelled in Latin, Greek, and English, but did poorly in mathematics. Chronic illness plagued him during his stay at the university. From 1852 through 1853, Mosby entered the social life of Charlottesville. It was then that he revealed the traits that were to make him a leader of men during the war.

In the course of events, Mosby had the chance to meet the town bully, George Turpin. In conversation with some of Mosby's friends, Turpin insulted Mosby. When Mosby learned of Turpin's statements, he sent him a note asking him to explain himself. Such a note from a frail-looking nineteen-year-old enraged Turpin, who went to Mosby's boardinghouse to confront him. As Turpin approached, Mosby leveled his pistol and squeezed the trigger. Turpin collapsed, a bullet having entered his mouth and lodged in his neck.

Mosby was arrested and charged with the "malicious and unlawful shooting" of Turpin. While few townsfolk liked Turpin and knew he had a record of prior assaults, Mosby had nearly killed an unarmed man. A jury found Mosby not guilty of "malicious shooting," but guilty of "unlawful shooting." He was sentenced to one year in the local jail and required to pay a fine of $500.

Mosby served nearly seven months of his one-year sentence, but Governor Joseph Johnson, after reviewing the evidence, pardoned him, and the state legislature rescinded the fine. During his incarceration, Mosby had begun the study of law, borrowing law books from his prosecutor, William Robertson. Upon his release from jail, he continued studying law and trained in Robertson's law office. He was admitted to the bar several months later and opened his practice in Howardsville in Albemarle County.

In 1857, John met and married Pauline Clarke, daughter of Beverly Clarke, a former United States congressman. The newlyweds moved to Bristol, Virginia, where Mosby opened a law office. He did well with his practice and they began a family.

When Abraham Lincoln was elected president in 1860, talk of secession was prevalent in Virginia. Mosby opposed secession, but when his native state left the Union, he reluctantly joined a militia company, the Washington Rifles. He answered his states' call, explaining: "Virginia is my mother, God bless her! I can't fight against my mother, can I?" Always a romantic—he carried volumes by Shakespeare, Plutarch, Byron, and others in his saddlebag—he naturally enlisted in the cavalry.

Frail and weighing a mere 125 pounds, Mosby was an unlikely candidate for the cavalry. Moreover, he was not an experienced horseman. Mosby soon found that war was a great equalizer. "I was glad to see," he said later, "that little men were a match for big men through being armed."

Mosby's first six months of service were under Colonel William "Grumble" Jones. Those serving with Mosby at the time described him as an ambivalent soldier. A member of J. E. B. Stuart's staff recalled: "He was rather a slouchy rider, and did not seem to take an interest in military duties. . . . [W]e all thought he was rather an indifferent soldier."

Mosby did not care for routine camp life; he preferred assignment to the outposts. From the summer of 1861 to the spring of 1862, he served along the picket line and also scouted. Jones was impressed with Mosby and soon installed him as a staff adjutant. His scouting abilities were then noticed by General Stuart, and Mosby was promoted from private to lieutenant.

When Colonel Fitzhugh Lee assumed command of the 1st Virginia Cavalry, Mosby resigned his commission and volunteered his services as a scout to General Stuart. In this capacity, he distinguished himself. In June 1862, during Stuart's famous ride around General McClellan's army in the Peninsula Campaign, Mosby's exploits were cited by Stuart as "a shining record of daring and usefulness." Mosby brought Stuart a report that changed the course of the war. He scouted and found the entire Union army, telling Stuart that he believed that all 100,000 troops could be circled in a matter of days. With Lee's approval, Stuart made the spectacular raid, with Mosby leading the way. Mosby's enthusiasm for the military was greatly increased after this episode. To his wife he wrote: "My dearest Pauline, I returned yesterday with General Stuart from the grandest scout of the war. . . . Everyone said it was the grandest feat of the war. I never enjoyed myself so much in my life."

Mosby had a keen intellect. John Cooke, from Stuart's staff, asserted that Mosby had "one of the most active, daring and penetrating minds." He was a deep thinker and when in thought, had the habit of picking his teeth with a toothpick or a small twig. As a partisan commander, Mosby left nothing to chance. He constantly sifted, planned, and calculated for each raid, seldom talking while on the raid as he plotted in his mind details of the attack.

Mosby possessed untiring energy. He could spend hours in the saddle scouting Union lines, gathering information from civilians; then he would study the information and prepare his men to attack. His tireless efforts, his daring, and his intellect made Mosby a formidable opponent. He worked at waging war.

Sometime during the winter of 1862, Mosby suggested to Stuart that he and a small, independent force be allowed to operate behind enemy lines. Stuart gave him nine men and left them in Loudoun County while he and his cavalry went to winter quarters near Fredericksburg. At the time, Mosby had no plans to organize a partisan command, but the nine-man detail proved to be very effective. As a result, the command grew until it reached battalion size. It was the beginning of two years of raids, ambushes, and attacks against any Union forces that entered a small area—the Virginia counties of Fauquier, Loudoun, Fairfax, and Prince William—which became known as "Mosby's Confederacy."

Mosby's Rangers were authorized by the Confederate government. Because they responded to their authority and wore Confederate uniforms, the laws of war accorded them full belligerent rights. Other guerrillas who fought covertly, masquerading as noncombatants, were simple outlaws for whom the war was an excuse to indulge in mayhem. If caught, these guerrillas were treated as criminals. It was difficult to distinguish among these types of guerrillas, and it was not uncommon for individuals to gravitate from one group to another.

Unlike the true guerrilla, who cloaked himself in the innocence of a noncombatant's clothing, Mosby rode in a fine Confederate uniform brightened with gold braid. His cap was lined with scarlet, while his broad-brimmed felt hat, like that of his hero J. E. B. Stuart, was decorated with an ostrich plume. His men did not often carry sabers or carbines, instead relying on at least two and sometimes as many as six Colt revolvers. Each man had at least two mounts, and many had more. They maintained their supply of mounts from local farmers in Mosby's Confederacy, an area known for the quality of its horses, and from those captured from Union troops. Mosby and his men employed deception and speed as well as audacity and surprise. Well acquainted with the section of Virginia where they operated, Mosby's Rangers could count on its inhabitants to give them food and shelter and to protect their identities and whereabouts. By operating in the dark or at dusk, they were able to penetrate the Federal lines at will. After each surprise attack, they would scatter and vanish into the countryside.

Mosby's chance at independent command had come and he made the most of it. Within a few days of taking command, Union officers in the area began reporting a series of nighttime raids against their outposts. By the middle of January, Mosby had taken twenty-two prisoners. He and his men enjoyed the hospitality of many families throughout the region. One resident noted in her diary: "The arrival of Mosby's men is like bright sunshine after dark cloud."

Men flocked to join Mosby's Rangers. During the course of war, more than a thousand men at one time or another served with him. By and large, they were young, obedient, and skilled horsemen. They rode as if born to the saddle. They were daredevils, but they had to be discreet, guarding what they said. Above all else, they had to follow orders; Mosby was an iron disciplinarian.

Mosby's first notable achievement came in March 1863. After a series of raids around Washington, he had drawn the anger of a British soldier of fortune, Colonel Sir Percy Wyndham. Wyndham charged Mosby with being a horse thief. Mosby, resenting the allegation, decided to capture the Englishman. On the night of March 8, Mosby raided Fairfax Court House, Colonel Wyndham's headquarters. Once there, he discovered that Wyndham was in Washington, but Brigadier General Edwin Stoughton was in town.

The riders—twenty-nine in all—split into several groups, one of which headed for Stoughton's residence. Mosby tricked Stoughton's aide into opening the door, saying he had a dispatch for the general. He quickly convinced the aide to reveal Stoughton's sleeping quarters. Seconds later, Mosby entered the general's room. He pulled down Stoughton's covers, pulled up his nightshirt, and slapped him on the rear end with his sword.

"Get up, general, and come with me," Mosby said. Stoughton angrily asked the stranger what he wanted. "Did you ever hear of Mosby?" Mosby asked. "Yes, have you caught him?" Stoughton asked. "No," replied Mosby, "but he has caught you." Less than an hour after their arrival in town, Mosby and his men left with General Stoughton, two captains, the aide-lieutenant, 30 privates, and 58 horses. From then on, Mosby was one of the most famous soldiers in America.

Mosby's exploit raised a cheer from Robert E. Lee, who wrote with rare exuberance: "Hurrah for Mosby!" Mosby was rewarded in June 1863 with a promotion to the rank of major and was authorized to recruit an entire battalion: the 43rd Battalion of Virginia Cavalry, Partisan Rangers. When President Lincoln was told that Mosby had captured a brigadier general and 58 horses, he murmured reflectively: "Well, I'm sorry for that. I can make new brigadier generals, but I can't make horses."

The terrain in Mosby's Confederacy was conducive to guerrilla warfare. It contained hundreds of square miles of forested mountains, woodlots, and hills, interspersed with fertile farmlands. A single sentry on horseback, stationed on a knoll, could scan miles of territory for enemy troops. Obscure trails provided a network for easy movement without detection. Small towns and homes of planters and farmers offered places of refuge and a network of informants. It was a region of beauty.

The effectiveness of Mosby's Rangers at disrupting Union operations was expressed by Lieutenant Colonel Henry Gansevoort, commander of the 13th

New York, when he wrote: "In fact, the whole country, in our rear, front and flanks is full of guerrillas. The chaps murder, steal and disperse. . . . They fight with desperation when attacked, but principally confine themselves to dashes here and there, and long pursuits of small bodies of our forces. The night does not know what morning may disclose."

No matter how the Union cavalry responded, the Rangers frustrated their efforts. The Yankees were engaged in warfare with shadows; the darkness of the night brought the unknown. Though they killed, wounded, and captured their nemeses, arrested civilians, and burned buildings, the Rangers always returned. Mounted Union patrols rode forth daily, companies guarded supply trains, and large picket details guarded the camp at night. Their grinding efforts yielded few rewards—only a handful of partisans were captured.

News of the Rangers' escapades reached the office of Major General Henry Halleck, the general in chief. "Most of the difficulties are caused," Halleck wrote in an analysis of Mosby's success, "by the conduct of the pretended non-combatant inhabitants of the country. They pretend to act the part of neutrals, but do not. They give aid, shelter, and concealment to guerrilla and robber bands like that of Mosby. . . . If these men carried on a legitimate warfare no complaint would be made." To Halleck, those who supported the Rangers "forfeited their lives by their actions when captured within Union lines." Halleck said he understood why Yankee troopers "shoot them down when they can." These feelings toward Mosby's civilian supporters pervaded the Union chain of command, from the top to the trooper in the saddle. The Northerners correctly understood that Mosby's Rangers could not continue to exist without the assistance of the residents of Mosby's Confederacy.

Despite the danger to their lives and property, the people "believed implicitly" in Mosby. Underlying the trust and support the Rangers enjoyed were the personal stakes of many people in the success and safety of Mosby's Rangers. One young woman wrote, "We all had brothers, cousins, and lovers with Mosby, and each one thought of her loved one" when fighting was heard nearby. The bond between inhabitants and Rangers was close. The partisans, for the most part, opened their doors for Mosby's men. Even the poorest resident would not refuse shelter and food to Mosby's troopers. Each Ranger boarded with civilian families or stayed at his own home as frequently as prudence and safety permitted. "Safe houses," as the Rangers called them, dotted the area.

Each safe house had a hiding place for the Rangers. Mosby's men called them secret closets, and they varied from house to house. Some contained underground passageways leading to the outside; others had rooms with a false wall panel behind which Rangers could hide. When the cry "Yankees coming" was heard, Rangers scrambled to one of the secret closets. Local folks were always on the alert, serving as a vast warning and intelligence network for the

Rangers. Nearly every house in the region held either a spy or a messenger for the guerrilla network. All this assistance carried a risk for the civilian population; people knew that the consequences were incarceration or worse.

Mosby expected his Rangers to be models of decorum. He accepted no breach of proper conduct; if he learned of a violation, he either reprimanded the offender or returned him to the regular army. The certainty and swiftness of his justice helped to keep his troopers' conduct under control.

Mosby's authority extended beyond the 43rd Battalion. For two years, he enforced the civil laws after the war had destroyed the governments and court systems in the area. Mosby, with his legal background, stepped in to fill the void. He regarded his powers a "trust" with the Rangers performing the "duties of police as well as soldiers." Mosby acted as both judge and jury, ordinarily holding hearings or a trial at a convenient place with his men present to act as witnesses. He settled disputes between neighbors, ruled on complaints made against his command, and punished perpetrators for various crimes. He meted out swift justice, allowing no appeal. Mosby's word was law. His exercise of military and civil power received the approval of the vast majority of area residents. He operated fairly, and the Rangers protected the civilians from many of the scourges that plagued Southerners in other parts of the country.

Many Union units that engaged Mosby's men thought the devil himself had hit them. When a swarm of screaming men suddenly appeared in their midst, firing pistols and riding through them, the Union soldiers often broke in panic. As quickly as the Rangers struck, they would disappear. The Union cavalry were constantly searching for Mosby, hoping to catch him off guard.

In June of 1863, Mosby's wife was visiting him at the home of James and Elizabeth Hathaway when they had unexpected Yankee visitors. Union cavalrymen entered the house and began to search for Mosby, going from room to room, but they were unable to find him. When the Union soldiers entered the house, Mosby had exited through a window and climbed onto a limb of a nearby tree. He clung there while the Federals searched his room and questioned his wife. When the Yankees left, satisfied that he wasn't there, Mosby crawled back into the house and went back to bed.

After his narrow escape, Mosby stayed under cover. With Lee moving through the Shenandoah Valley toward Pennsylvania, the Union Army was shadowing his march. That placed too many Union troops in Mosby's Confederacy for him to act. Once again, Stuart called on Mosby to scout for him. It was Mosby's information that helped convince Stuart to get permission from Lee to ride around the federal army during the Gettysburg Campaign. In Mosby's scouting report, he advised Stuart of a break in the Union column at Thoroughfare Gap, which Mosby thought was the best route to Pennsylvania. Unfortunately, Mosby's intelligence was out of date, forcing Stuart to detour around the Union flank. This caused Stuart to arrive at Gettysburg late. Though many criticized Stuart for his late arrival, Mosby believed he was partially at fault. Mosby would defend Stuart for the rest of his life, even to his grave.

For Mosby, Union wagon trains were regular targets. In July, Mosby reported to Stuart that he had captured 29 sutler's wagons, along with 100 prisoners and 140 horses. The wagons were loaded with food, tobacco, alcohol, newspapers, and books. Instead of destroying the wagons, Mosby decided to deliver them to Middleburg. In the meantime, the Union cavalry pursued the Rangers, overtaking the slow-moving convoy. The outnumbered Rangers were forced to abandon the wagons and flee. One of the Rangers groaned that with the wagons, they could have opened the first department store in Mosby's Confederacy.

In August 1863, Mosby was wounded, shot in the thigh and groin. He was disabled for nearly a month. During that time, he turned the command over to his subordinates, and there is evidence that discipline suffered while he was away. It was Mosby's personality that held the command together.

By the beginning of 1864, Mosby was back in the saddle again. In January, he suffered his worst defeat at Loudoun Heights, the mountains above Harpers Ferry, Virginia. In the action, Mosby lost eight men: Four were killed and four mortally wounded. Most critical was the loss of two of the most efficient officers in his battalion. The debacle of Loudoun Heights devastated Mosby and his men. It ended all romantic notions of war and was a preview of the long, bloody, and bitter events to follow in that year.

In May, there was more bad news for Mosby—the death of Stuart at Yellow Tavern. Lee had lost the eyes of his army, and Mosby had lost his good friend. Following Stuart's death, Mosby would report directly to Lee, the only commander of a unit below corps level to do so.

The year 1864 had not exactly turned out the way Ulysses Grant had hoped either. The Army of the Potomac had fought three bloody battles at the Wilderness, Spotsylvania, and Cold Harbor, but had little to show for it. Moreover, Confederate General Jubal Early was active in the Shenandoah Valley and threatening the capital. To ensure Washington's continued safety, Grant dispatched Sheridan to manage affairs in the valley.

In August, Sheridan arrived in the valley with a mandate to clear it of all Southern forces and to eliminate it as a food source for the Confederacy. Mosby threw all his men and resources into an effort to harass and frustrate the Federals.

Shortly after arriving in the valley, Sheridan realized he had an additional problem to face—John Singleton Mosby. Sheridan's initial response to Mosby and his Rangers was the joking comment that they were "substantially a benefit to me as they prevented straggling and kept my trains well closed up."

When Sheridan found that Mosby's raids were becoming a serious problem for him, he decided to form an elite unit of independent scouts to combat it. The scouts were to be led by Captain Richard Blazer. Blazer's first encounter with a portion of Mosby's Rangers occurred in September when he caught them by surprise. The Confederates were routed; thirteen were killed, six wounded, and five captured. When Mosby learned of their defeat, his derision of those who escaped was harsh and relentless. "You let those Yankees whip you," he thundered. "Why, I ought to get hoop skirts for you! I'll send you all into the first Yankee regiment we come across!"

By November 1864, Blazer's scouts had begun to take their toll on Mosby's operations. Mosby had paid little attention to them, concentrating still on harassing Sheridan's army and disrupting the Manassas Gap Railroad. But a defeat of one of his squadrons at Vineyard had exhausted his patience. He immediately ordered Dolly Richards to take the 1st Squadron and "wipe Blazer out! Go through him!"

A key factor in the success of Blazer and his scouts, besides their tactical methods, was their treatment of Shenandoah Valley citizens. Blazer was not only a brave fighter, but a humane and kind man. This was a striking contrast to the behavior of other Union officers who had come through the valley. Because of Blazer's fair treatment of the valley people, he was able to gain their cooperation and, in some cases, even their support. But Blazer's days were numbered. Within a few weeks, Blazer was captured and his threat to Mosby's Rangers ended.

Mosby continued to be a thorn in the Union's side. By that time, he had been elevated to the rank of lieutenant colonel and finally to colonel. In October, Mosby and his Rangers derailed a Baltimore and Ohio train outside of Harpers Ferry, capturing $173,000. The Rangers divided the loot, each receiving $2,100, though Mosby took none. Again he had embarrassed Sheridan, but on that same day, one of Mosby's men was hanged. The Union had now declared the Rangers outlaws because they had seized private property along with Union spoils. At the express orders of Grant, several Rangers were hanged without a trial.

When Mosby learned that George Custer was responsible for the executions, he instructed his men that whenever a member of Custer's command was captured, he should be held back and not sent to Richmond. In October, Mosby informed Lee what he had decided to do: "It is my purpose to hang an equal number of Custer's men whenever I capture them." Lee and Secretary of War James Seddon both gave their approval.

Mosby rode to Rectortown, where twenty-seven Yankee prisoners were being held. Twenty-seven slips were placed in a hat, and the prisoners were instructed to draw one slip each. Seven of the slips had been marked, and the men who drew the marked slips were those chosen to be executed.

Not all the men belonged to Custer's command, but no one protested. Some of the men prayed aloud. Mosby ordered that four of the condemned men be shot and the other three hanged. Two of the men to be shot were able to escape; the other two later recovered from their wounds. The Rangers placed a note on the body of one of the three men who had been hung: "These men have been hung in retaliation for an equal number of Colonel Mosby's men hung by order of General Custer at Front Royal. Measure for measure."

The escape of two of the prisoners did not bother Mosby. As he explained later, "If my motive had been revenge, I would have ordered others to be executed in their place and I did not. I was really glad they got away as they carried the story to Sheridan's army." His objective, he said "was to prevent the war from degenerating into a massacre. . . . It was really an act of mercy." Mosby also wrote a note to Sheridan explaining that he would hereafter treat any prisoner falling into his hands with kindness "unless new acts of barbarity shall compel me to adopt a course of policy repulsive to humanity."

Later, Mosby offered justification for his actions: "I determined to demand and enforce every belligerent right to which the soldiers of a great military power were entitled by the laws of war. . . . It was not an act of revenge, but a judicial sentence to save not only the lives of our men, but the lives of the enemy. It had that effect. I regret that fate thrust such a duty upon me; I do not regret that I faced and performed it."

Mosby had many close calls during the war, but perhaps the narrowest escape from death came in December 1864 at the home of Ludwell Lake. Mosby had stopped there for the night and was having dinner when he heard a noise in the yard. He peeped out the door to see Union cavalrymen approaching. Quickly he extinguished the lamp and started for the bedroom, hoping to escape through a rear window. As the Union troops entered the house, several shots were fired. In the dark and confusion, Mosby was shot in the abdomen, blood gushing from the wound. Mosby lay on the floor, bloody saliva running from his mouth. When confronted by the Union soldiers, Mosby gurgled between what sounded like death gasps that he was Lieutenant Johnson of the 6th Virginia Cavalry. The Federals searched the house but failed to find Mosby's uniform coat with his colonel's insignia. Just before being shot, he had stuffed it under a bureau. The Federals never realized that Mosby was in their grasp, and not wishing to bother with a dying guerrilla, they left. Mosby was not dying, however. Just before the Union soldiers entered his room, he had the presence of mind to take blood from his wound and place it around his mouth. Later Mosby was moved to his father's house in Lynchburg, where he recovered. At the end of January, he appeared—pale and thin—in Richmond, where he was given a hero's welcome. By the end of February, he was back with his command.

Mosby and his Rangers had one last fight left in them. Just before the end of the war, they defeated Federal guerrillas known as the Loudoun Rangers; but their efforts were wasted. On April 9, 1865, the Army of Northern Virginia surrendered at Appomattox Court House.

Mosby, however, never surrendered his command formally. Instead, on April 21, he summoned his men to the crossroads hamlet of Salem. There, in a field, each company formed in ranks, and Mosby officially disbanded the 43rd Battalion of the Virginia Cavalry. He said: "Soldiers! I have summoned you together for the last time. The vision we have cherished of a free and independent country has vanished, and the country is now in the spoil of a conqueror. I disband your organization in preference to surrendering it to our enemies. I am now no longer your commander. After association of more than two eventful years, I part from you with a just pride, in the fame of your achievements, and grateful recollections of your generous kindness to myself. And now at this moment of bidding you a final adieu, accept the assurance of my unchanging confidence and regard. Farewell!"

After disbanding the battalion, Mosby went south in hopes of joining up with Joseph Johnston's army. Upon learning that Johnston had surrendered to Sherman, Mosby abandoned any thought of continuing to fight. With a $5,000 reward for his capture, Mosby went into hiding in the area around Lynchburg until being paroled two months later by Grant.

On June 29, the Washington press announced that Mosby had been paroled on the same conditions as other officers of Lee's army and had returned to Culpeper to open a law office. Mosby was staying at Culpeper only temporarily, and it was not his plan to enter the practice of law there. When Mosby entered Alexandria, word spread. Wherever he moved, crowds surrounded him to shake his hand and to cheer him. Later his presence brought trouble when a large group of blacks tried to insult him. A commotion followed as whites came to defend him. To disperse the crowd, Mosby was removed and arrested. He spent two days behind bars until the provost marshal received instructions from headquarters to release him. Mosby was glad to leave Alexandria but confessed that he was pleased to have been such a thorn in the side of his enemies that they were reluctant to bury the hatchet.

By early September, Mosby was back in Fauquier with his shingle hanging from the California Building. He was soon joined by his wife and children, and with his home once more organized, he turned to making a serious living. Unfortunately, his trouble with the government wasn't finished. While on business in Leesburg, Mosby was arrested again. These surprise infringements on her husband's freedom disturbed Mrs. Mosby. After failing to obtain help from President Johnson, she turned to General Grant. General Grant graciously received her, treating her as if she was the wife of a Union officer. Her story found a patient and sympathetic ear. When they had finished their talk, General Grant wrote a letter that exempted Mosby from arrest unless he violated his parole or by instructions from the president, secretary of war, or from Grant's headquarters. With this letter, Mosby was once again free.

Mosby took up civilian life with the same fervor he had displayed in the military. He managed to stay clear of the political field and added successful cases to his practice, enhancing his legal reputation.

While in Richmond during March 1870, Mosby met General Lee and his daughter, Agnes, at the Ballard hotel. As they talked, Mosby made a conscious effort not to discuss the war. After meeting with General Lee, Mosby met George Pickett and casually mentioned that he had been to see Lee. Pickett asked Mosby to return to the hotel with him, explaining that he would like to pay his respects but did not want to be alone with his former commander. Mosby agreed to go with him, but later regretted it, finding himself in a meeting that was extremely embarrassing. When they left, Pickett spoke bitterly of Lee, referring to him as "that old man" and adding that he "had my division massacred at Gettysburg." Mosby, very supportive of Lee, replied, "Well, it made you immortal."

Mosby was a devoted family man. By 1870, at thirty-six, he was the father of five children—ranging in age from eleven to infancy. He was a doting father who liked to have his children with him, even on business trips. He encouraged his children to read and rewarded them for every book they completed. He sent his children to private schools and did all he could to encourage their education.

Mosby had few vices; he did not drink hard liquor or smoke, but he consumed coffee in much the same way that Grant smoked cigars. He welcomed an occasional lager or glass of claret. He liked music, but played no musical instruments and had trouble carrying a tune. He disliked games, considering cards a waste of time. He kept a few fast horses and enjoyed watching them race.

Politics during the opening months of the election year 1872 were lethargic and dull. A spark of interest was created, however, by the gradual easing of the shackles of military control on the Southern states to a stage of some political independence. During his first term as president, Grant had shown marked leniency and consideration toward the South. The president's behavior captured the hearts of some Southerners, yet failed to impress the diehards in Dixie. Defeat had removed the social order from the South, but not its party loyalties.

It was during this time that Mosby went to see President Grant. Grant's reception of the former raider was informal and friendly. Their conversation began with recollections of Grant's escape from capture at the hands of his visitor while returning to the Army of the Potomac during the spring of '64. "If I had captured you," Mosby remarked, "things might have changed—I might have been in the White House and you might be calling on me." "Yes," agreed Grant.

As the conversation continued, Mosby became convinced that Grant wanted to help the Southern people. After their meeting, Mosby was determined to support Grant, believing it was the best way to aid the crippled South. It proved to be a milepost in Mosby's life: deciding to back Grant, the man who had commanded the forces that had conquered the South.

The South refused to follow or sympathize with the example set by Mosby in his sudden change of faith. Quick to idolize him as a soldier during the war, they were just as quick to turn against him as a politician. In time, the switching of political parties would be accepted with complacency; but in 1872, with the country still bitter and feeling the effects of the war, it was political and social suicide. Mosby was denounced by the press and public alike, by people who had been close to him and those who knew him only by reputation, and even by some of his old command. Mosby accepted this condemnation with the same indifference he had displayed in accepting the hatred of the North.

When Grant's second nomination came at Philadelphia, Mosby began campaigning in the incumbent's behalf. Mosby's disdain for Grant's opponent, Horace Greeley, made him overbearing to all those who did not share his viewpoint. Even the press, sympathetic to Greeley, admitted that Mosby's opposition to their candidate had an effect on the election in Virginia. As early as August, Mosby promised Grant that he could count on Virginia's votes. When the final ballots were counted in November, Mosby wired Grant: "Virginia casts her vote for Grant, peace, and reconciliation." It was the first time that a Republican had carried the state of Virginia.

Grant wanted to reward Mosby with a political appointment, but Mosby refused, explaining that he could be more influential by taking nothing for himself. He refused to share in the election spoils just as he had refused to take part in the rich loot from the Union army raid during the war.

During the election of 1874, Mosby was a candidate for Congress, running as an independent. In July, the death of his seventh child diverted his attention temporarily from politics. When August arrived and the time drew near for political action, Mosby realized it would be useless to continue in the race.

In 1876, Mosby announced that he would support Hayes, Grant's choice for president. His political views continued to be controversial, sometimes placing him in danger. One night, as Mosby stepped off the train at Warrenton, Virginia, someone took a shot at him. Grant, hearing of this, was concerned for Mosby's safety. He appealed to his successor, newly elected President Hayes, to help Mosby. In time, it was announced that John Singleton Mosby, lawyer of Warrenton, would be the next consul to Hong Kong.

For the next seven years, 1878 to 1885, Mosby made his home in the British crown colony, his consulship ending with the inauguration of Grover Cleveland. Hearing he would not be reappointed, he wrote to Grant asking him for help in locating employment. Mosby could see little promise in returning to Warrenton; his law practice there had dwindled. July came, and Mosby prepared to return to the United States; but he still had not heard from Grant. The day before Mosby set sail for America, a message arrived for him—Grant was dead.

Even in the pain of his last days, Grant had not forgotten the man who had bucked the South to bring him political support. One of the last pieces of correspondence that Grant wrote was a note to railroad executive Leland Stanford. When Mosby stepped off the boat on American soil, he was notified by Stanford that an attorneyship with the Southern Pacific railroad awaited him.

Once back in the United States, Mosby found his popularity picking up. A lecture bureau in Massachusetts offered him a contract to tell the inside story of his Civil War activities. He accepted, travelling for weeks throughout New England on a strenuous speaking schedule. His success on the lecture tour soon led to an offer to write. Soon Mosby was preparing his talks for publication in the *Boston Herald*. By 1887, the newspaper series had been compiled into book form and called *Mosby's Reminiscences*. Other books followed. Mosby gave a defense of his war idol in *Stuart's Cavalry Campaigns*, later taking his side again in *Stuart's Cavalry in the Gettysburg Campaign*, a dissertation that caused other military leaders to sharply challenge him. Other efforts included *The Dawn of the Real South* and finally, his *Memoirs*.

Throughout the waning years of the nineteenth century, there would be many Ranger reunions, but Mosby attended only one. In January 1895, he went to the 43rd Battalion's reunion at Alexandria. More than 150 Rangers were present, some coming up and gripping his hand. At age sixty-two, with gray hair, and heavier than he had been during the war, Mosby was still their hero. This was the first time some had seen him since their final meeting at Salem. The reunion reached its climax at a banquet, an affair that left few dry eyes. An address by Mosby started the tears: "Your presence here this evening recalls our last parting. I see the last line drawn up to hear read the last order I ever gave you. I see moisten eyes and quivering lips. I hear the command to break ranks. I feel the grasp of hands and see the tears on the cheeks of men who had dared death so long it had lost its terror. And I know now as I knew then, that each heart suffered with mine the agony of the Titan in his resignation to fate." He continued, saying: "Life cannot afford a more bitter cup than the one I drained when we parted at Salem, nor any higher reward of ambition than that I received as commander of the 43rd Virginia Battalion of Cavalry."

On a lovely summer day in 1896, Mosby would have one more narrow escape with death. While driving a friend, he leaned over the dashboard of the buggy to lift the horse's tail from the reins. The animal became frightened and kicked out with one of its hoofs, striking Mosby a hard blow in the face. He was rushed to the University of Virginia hospital, where he lay unconscious for days. Diagnosis revealed that his skull was fractured and his left eye would be of no use again. One of the war's best-known surgeons, Dr. Hunter McGuire, Stonewall Jackson's army physician, was called to consult on treatment.

With skilled care, the period of danger passed, and Mosby began to fight his way back to health. But never again would he look the same: His physical appearance was marred by an eye that no longer functioned. Moreover, his energy had dissipated and he became dependent on naps, insisting on having one every afternoon.

In January 1897, his mother died. While helping to settle her affairs, Mosby took advantage of the time to see newly elected President William McKinley. He was hoping McKinley would find him a political position. Mosby felt that the Republican party owed him a favor for all his past support. There was only one problem: The new President had served in the Shenandoah Valley, and Mosby wasn't sure whether he would still be harboring some hidden resentment against him for his guerrilla actions there. If any apologies for his past misdeeds were expected, Mosby knew he would not be able to offer them. When calling upon the president, Mosby found him "very cordial" as he told a friend. He said that "I used to make him miserable in the Shenandoah Valley." But there was no talk of an appointment.

In February 1898, the battleship *Maine* was sunk in Havana harbor, killing 260 American sailors. Although there was no real evidence of sabotage or involvement by the Spanish government in the catastrophe, America went to war. The words "Remember the Maine" were headlines in many newspapers. Mosby, although cynical about the war, offered his services to the government.

Mosby, now sixty-four, telegraphed his friend Nelson Miles, an ex-Union soldier who was currently major general commanding the army, and asked for a military appointment. Miles responded by saying that Mosby would need some senatorial influence if he wanted to carry this one off. Mosby fired back, "I have no influence except my military record." When Mosby was pressed by the *New York World*, he said: "I was surprised to hear that congressional influence was required to secure the privilege of fighting the battles of the country. . . . I cannot imagine what any congressman could say that would add anything to the endorsement I have received from General Grant and General Robert E. Lee."

In a letter a few days later to the *Richmond Times*, Mosby explained that he was "indifferent about rank" and would be satisfied to go in as a lieutenant. But no offer came from the army. By late June, Mosby had formed his own unit, calling them the Hussars. The newspaper noted that the old Confederate was drilling his light cavalry troops, "instilling the same vim that he showed when at the head of his raiders."

By early August, the war was nearly over, and Mosby's Hussars disbanded without having drawn a drop of blood. Mosby, against this war as much as he was against Virginia's secession from the Union, was relieved. "After all," he said, "although I was rejected, I think I got the best of it."

In 1901, in an unexpected move, Southern Pacific was reorganized—and Mosby's worst fears were realized. The sixty-seven-year-old attorney was without a job, facing the world without Grant. But again his political friends came to his rescue. In July, President McKinley appointed him special agent to the General Land Office. His headquarters were in Sterling, Colorado, and he spent much of his time on the trail of cattle barons who were fencing land illegally. Then in 1904, President Theodore Roosevelt, listening to the pleas of some of Mosby's friends, named him an assistant attorney in the Department of Justice.

As Mosby aged, his disposition seemed to change. He talked fast, expecting his orders to be obeyed just as promptly as if he were still heading a battalion. At times, he was an irascible, intolerant, rude old man. In 1863 and 1864, he had been an important part of the excitement of the war. Now seated in a swivel chair, in a job more fitted to his age, he was surrounded by men and women who knew of his war reputation only by hearsay. It was a hard pill for him to swallow.

Despite all his peculiarities and his social misbehaviors, Mosby had one trait that was typical of years as a leader. Until his dying day, he maintained a personal and paternal interest in his men. When he learned that one of them was in financial difficulty, he took it upon himself to find the man's son a responsible job, reminding the young man that he must send a part of his salary to his father. He frequently shared with others, even though he himself needed more.

As the years passed and the ranks of his veterans thinned, he felt more separated from his battalion. "I am beginning to feel very lonely in the world now," he once remembered. "Nearly all my friends are gone and I have made no new ones."

In June 1910, Mosby was fired. With Roosevelt gone and a new man in the attorney general's office, Mosby's influence with the government was lost. He was told that he was too old to hold a job. His friend James Keith, president of Virginia's Supreme Court of Appeals, protested at once, assuring Attorney General George Wickershaw of Mosby's competence. "I've met no man with a more acute and veracious mind than Colonel Mosby," said Keith. If Mosby hadn't thrown success away for conscience sake, he would have stood "in the front ranks of the bar of his day," he said. Others spoke up to both the attorney general and President Taft, but to no avail. He was seventy-six, and his working life was over.

Occasionally, in his moments of reminiscence, Mosby remarked: "I pitched my politics in too high a key when I voted for Grant. I ought to have accepted office under him. My family would now be comfortably supplied with money." But those who knew him best knew he did not mean it. He was a man of honor, they said, and these words did not come from the heart.

In 1915, a delegation from the University of Virginia, the school that expelled him in 1853, visited Mosby. They brought a token of appreciation, a bronze medal and an embossed statement expressing the affection and esteem of his friends and admirers at the university. "Endowed with the gift of friendship, which won for you the confidence of both Lee and Grant," it stated, "you have proven yourself a man of war, a man of letters, and a man of affairs worthy the best tradition of your University and your State, to both of which you have been a loyal son." He accepted the award joyfully and said, "My chief regret is that I could not do for my prison what Tasso did for his dungeon at Ferrara—confer immortality."

By the close of 1915, Mosby was confined to his home because of deteriorating health. Three months later, he was at Garfield Hospital; six months after that, he was dead. He died at 9 o'clock on the morning of May 30, 1916. He was eighty-two years old. Mosby was conscious almost to the last. As the end drew near, one of his daughters poured the water of baptism over her dying father's head. Other members of the family were there to witness the ceremony, but few believed the baptism would stick.

Two days later his body, escorted by a uniformed guard, was taken by train to Warrenton to lie in state briefly in the county courthouse. The governor sent a wreath, and three thousand people attended the funeral. He was buried in Warrenton, surrounded by the graves of his wife, Pauline, and their infant children. Fittingly, he rests on the brow of a hill.

It was a bloody business in which the Rangers engaged. But one important fact emerges—John Mosby and the 43rd Battalion had no equal as guerrilla fighters during the war. Primary credit for that belongs to the commander. Possessing a keen intellect, uncompromising discipline, and a complete grasp of the potential of guerrilla warfare, Mosby built the Rangers into a matchless partisan command that played havoc with Union forces in the valley. The casualties the Rangers inflicted, and the supplies and armament they captured, far outweighed their losses.

In the end, Mosby and his Rangers prevailed in their "war of wits" against Union cavalrymen, earning a place among some of the finest guerrilla warriors in history. Ulysses S. Grant, in his memoirs, wrote of Mosby: "There were probably but few men in the South who could have commanded successfully a separate detachment in the rear of an opposing army, and so near the border of hostilities, as long as he did without losing his entire command."

Mosby's military record brought him fame and notoriety, which was to condition his life for the half century he lived after the war. His postwar career was varied, but, regardless of the situation, he lowered his shoulders into the prevailing wind and moved forward. He practiced law, watched his family grow, and reconciled himself to the outcome of the war. He became friends with Ulysses S. Grant, switching to the Republican party. He stood among a mere handful of Southerners who called for healing, who announced that the war was over and the South had lost, and who spoke of cooperation with the North and the oblivion of the past. His message was one of reconciliation. He spoke out for union. He preached that the uncooperative South had no worse enemy than itself. For this, he was treated as a leper by some who had earlier cheered him. To Southerners, he was a "political turncoat," but Mosby ignored the firestorm of condemnation that followed. He was his own man. He endured much bitterness and loneliness during the latter part of his life. For Mosby, his actions were a matter of principle—and he was a principled man.

17   Boy General

GEORGE ARMSTRONG CUSTER

A T daylight on April 9, 1865, Robert E. Lee's hard-pressed infantry
advanced against the Union 3rd Cavalry Division near Appomattox
Court House, Virginia. Once invincible, its ranks now thinned by
death and desertion, the proud Army of Northern Virginia made one
last attempt to break out of the Union trap. But they were no match for the
superior Union forces. Federal infantry had reached the front during the night
opened fire, while Union cavalry repulsed a Confederate sortie and prepared
to charge. The Union cavalry commander watched from a nearby ridge as his
men wheeled into formation. His name was George Armstrong Custer.

Custer was without question one of the most controversial and intriguing
American military figures of the nineteenth century. Rambunctious as a young
man, he possessed unwavering courage and gallantry. At the tender age of twenty-four, he became a major general. During the Civil War, he captured more

prisoners and armaments than any other commander, North or South, an achievement respected by his peers and acknowledged by his enemies. During the Indian Wars, he became both a resolute martyr and hated butcher while capturing the imagination of the entire country. Whether his actions are viewed as brave or foolhardy, his conquests cannot be ignored.

Custer was rash and egotistical. His unique military uniform reflected his flamboyant nature. It consisted of a black velvet suit, trimmed with gold lace, and a navy-blue shirt turned down over the collar of his jacket. His suit was set off by a brilliant crimson necktie. Accounts of his life tell of his wanderlust and temerity. It may be said that there was hardly a more colorful character in American history.

George Armstrong Custer was born in the peaceful small village of New Rumley, Ohio, on December 5, 1839. His father, Emanuel Custer, was the village blacksmith. Emanuel's father fought in the Revolution, and his grandmother, Sara Martha Ball, was a cousin of George Washington's mother. Emanuel's first wife, Matilda Viers, gave birth to three children, only two of which survived. Matilda died in 1835, leaving Emanuel a widower with two young sons.

Emanuel did not wait long to find a new wife, marrying Maria Kirkpatrick in 1836. Like Emanuel, she had lost her spouse just a year earlier, and she had a son and a daughter. Emanuel and Maria were a year apart in age, both with young children. Five months after their marriage, Emanuel's three-year-old son died. In December 1839, she gave birth to George Armstrong Custer.

Soon George would have three younger brothers and a sister in addition to the half-brothers and a half-sister from his parents' first marriages. The most famous of these siblings was Thomas Custer, who would have the unique distinction of being awarded two Medals of Honor during the Civil War and would die with his older brother George at Little Bighorn.

As a boy, George—or Autie, as his father called him—was always full of fun. He enjoyed a practical joke, even if it was on himself, had a gentle disposition, and displayed an even temper. Even though he was very strong for his age and excelled in wrestling, he was never known to use his strength in bullying others.

Autie's father was a member of the militia. Whenever Emanuel drilled, Autie accompanied him, wearing a small militia uniform. After the drill, his father often would have young Autie drill through the Scott's manual of arms with his toy musket. Autie's father later recalled hearing him repeat the line that his older brother was committing to memory for school: "My voice is for war."

Although Custer's interest in military affairs began when he was young, he also developed a fondness for horses at the same time. Emanuel divided his time between farming and blacksmithing, so Autie was regularly around horses. The tasks he performed while growing up provided opportunities for him to develop his love of animals.

The Custer household was filled with life and love. There was no difference between the Custer brood and the children from the previous marriages; all in the family got along with each other. To the Custers, family meant inclusiveness, devotion, and loyalty, a lesson Autie never forgot.

At the age of six, young George began attending the one-room log school in town. The school gave him fertile ground for his mischievousness and new victims for his pranks. "He was rather a bad boy in school," claimed a classmate. Bright and impulsive, Autie was "irrepressible as a boy," according to one of his teachers. He hated homework and seldom was prepared for class, relying on last-minute skimming just before it was time for his recitation. Once he learned to read well, he smuggled novels into class, placing them inside a textbook during reading periods.

When Autie was ten, his half-sister, Lydia, married David Reed of Monroe, Michigan. Separated from her family, Lydia was lonely, so it was decided to send young Custer to live with the Reeds. Autie was excited about the move; he adored his sister. Young George spent three years with the Reeds in Monroe, where he attended the New Dublin School and later the Stebbins Academy for Boys.

At the age of sixteen, Autie returned to Harrison County, Ohio, to teach at the Beech Point School and later at the Locust Grove School. Between terms, he attended the McNeely Normal School to enhance his teaching skills. Autie's students remembered him as "socially inclined," jovial and full of life. Another recalled him as pleasant and well liked. Referring to his long blond hair, one female student said of him: "What a pretty girl he would make." Custer's students observed the traditional practice of locking out the teacher until he brought them Christmas treats. When the boys of the class barred the door, Custer refused to play the game. Instead, he went off to protest to the district school directors. This pattern of demanding respect and maintaining good discipline would be a mainstay of his military career.

Twenty-six dollars a month and room and board was his pay for teaching. To him, that was a small fortune, yet he took it all home and gave it to his mother. In later life, he spoke of this as one of the happiest times of his life. He knew his parents had made sacrifices to allow him to get a fine education, and it was with a sense of deep gratitude, love, and devotion that he made this token payment.

In the summer of 1856, Autie fell passionately in love with Mary Jane Holland. The couple spent as much time together as possible, talking of marriage and a future together. When Mary Jane's father found they were doing more than kissing, he forbid his daughter to see Custer, but she continued to meet with him anyway.

About the same time, Autie decided to try for an appointment to the United States Military Academy at West Point. His motivation rested more on pragmatic grounds than on any burning ambition to be a soldier. West Point would earn him twenty-eight dollars a month for five years, and he would receive an education. Obtaining the appointment, however, would prove difficult for him. Autie wrote to his congressman but did not receive an encouraging response. When Alexander Holland, Mary Jane's father, learned of Custer's aspiration, he went to his congressman and requested that his daughter's suitor be given the appointment. Holland knew that a cadet could not be married, and with Autie at West Point for five years, he hoped that his daughter's and Custer's passions would subside. The intervention worked, and in January 1857, Custer received an appointment to West Point.

Later, when the one-time candidate had become a famous general, Congressman John A. Bingham said that Custer's letter of application had immediately impressed him. Read today, the letter seems merely an unvarnished request for information. The letter was hardly original as Bingham had claimed it was, thus stressing the importance of Mr. Holland's intervention.

Custer achieved considerable distinction at West Point, although it was nothing to be proud of. He accumulated demerits at an alarming rate, usually for trivial rule violations such as dress code and lateness. One hundred "skins" in six months earned dismissal; repeatedly, Custer came to within less than ten of the limit. His four-year total stood at 726. Custer did not flourish in academics either. He still had difficulty applying himself to subjects that did not interest him. The books he checked from the library featured dashing cavaliers, flashing swords, and beautiful women.

Custer did well, however, in the strenuous outdoor instruction. He excelled at horsemanship, riding bareback effortlessly, and he was expert in using a saber. Whenever low marks threatened to cause his expulsion, he dug into his books and staved off disaster. Whenever his demerits neared the maximum, he went for months at a time without a single infraction.

On at least one occasion, Custer resorted to extreme measures to avoid being dismissed. In January 1861, the academic board found him and thirty-two other cadets deficient. This meant reexamination and failing that, dismissal. Custer broke into the instructor's room in an attempt to make a copy of the test. Upon hearing steps in the hall he panicked, tore the pages from the book, and fled. The instructor discovered the evidence of the tampering and altered the questions. Paradoxically, of the thirty-three cadets taking the new examination, only Custer passed and remained at West Point.

This episode revealed not only the lengths to which Custer would go to win but also the incredible good luck that had blessed him from childhood. Time and time again, fortune smiled, either to extricate him from a scrape or to see him through a difficult situation. "Custer's Luck" became his hallmark. He began to believe himself fated to win, regardless of the risks. His over-confidence would cost him his life in the end.

Custer was very popular with his classmates, earning nicknames such as Fanny, Cinnamon, and Curley because of his reddish-blond, wavy hair. He was viewed by his fellow cadets as a free spirit and an indifferent soldier, a "roys-tering, reckless cadet, always in trouble, always playing some mischievous pranks and liked by everyone." Custer's roommate, Tully McCrea, asserted that he "never studied any more than he can possibly help," adding that he "admired and partly envied Custer's free and careless way, and the perfect indifference he had for everything. It was all right for him whether he knew his lesson or not; he did not allow it to trouble him."

Cadet Custer was friendly with many of his Southern classmates and was anti-Black Republican. But when Fort Sumter was fired upon, there was no doubt where his allegiance was—with the Union. Custer knew what war would mean; he would be fighting many of his friends from the South. One day, he told his friend from Georgia, Cadet Pierce Young, "We're going to have war. It's no use talking. I see it coming . . . and who knows but we may move against each other during the war?" Custer proved prophetic; he was to meet Young in bat-tle near Huntertown, Pennsylvania, on July 2, 1863.

After the surrender of Fort Sumter, graduation at West Point was acceler-ated so that the fifth year of study was dropped. The class of 1862, Custer's class, graduated on June 24, 1861. Custer stood last; his four-year total of 726 demerits led the class.

Looking back on his career at West Point, Custer candidly wrote that future cadets would not benefit from a study of his career "unless as an example to be carefully avoided." Despite his record, Custer was always devoted to West Point, expressing a wish to be buried there. After graduation, Custer went direct-ly to the battlefield, where he consistently distinguished himself.

Second Lieutenant George Custer reported to Washington, and was instruct-ed to join General McDowell's army at Manassas. He arrived just in time to join the 2nd United States Cavalry as they retreated. Only four days after leav-ing West Point, Custer had his first taste of combat. "I remember well," Custer wrote in his memoirs, "the strange hissing and exceedingly vicious sound of the first cannon shot I heard as it whirled through the air." He had heard cannon fire before at the academy, "but a man listens with changed interest when the direction of the balls is toward instead of away from him."

The Bull Run debacle resulted in the removal of McDowell and the appoint-ment of Major General George McClellan to command the Army of the

Potomac. Brigadier General Philip Kearny was given command of the Jersey Brigade, with Custer assigned as an aide-de-camp, later becoming his assistant adjutant general. The cavalry's idleness at Bull Run reflected the state of military thought at the beginning of the war. The Confederates quickly learned the usefulness of cavalry, but it took two years for the Union generals to see the benefits of employing cavalry as a separate arm. As a result, the horsemen were assigned to infantry generals, who could think of no better use for them other than as couriers, pickets, scouts, and personal escorts. When Custer was assigned to the cavalry, he could not look forward to much fighting. His regiment wound up in the defense of Washington—not exactly what he had hoped for. Again Custer got lucky. He was removed from the cavalry during its two years in oblivion. Officers who had been trained at West Point were in great demand for staff duty. Custer was delighted when he was promoted to captain of volunteers and appointed to the staff of General McClellan as an aide-de-camp. "Upon this," wrote McClellan, "he brightened up, assured me that he would regard such service as the most gratifying he could perform."

Custer had great admiration for McClellan, writing that he would "follow him to the end of the earth." Perhaps no other superior officer would have deep affection from Custer. In turn, McClellan described Custer as "simply a reckless, gallant boy undeterred by fatigue, unconscious of fear, but whose head was always clear in danger, and he always brought me clear and intelligible reports of what he saw when under the heaviest fire. I became attached to him."

Staff duty involved a variety of responsibilities. Custer conducted reconnaissance, delivered messages, relayed intelligence from subordinate commanders, acted as the commander's representative with units in action, and oversaw troop movements. The duties would mean hours in the saddle, infrequent meals, and exposure to enemy fire. It was training that would prove invaluable for Custer when he got his own command.

Two characteristics marked Custer's career as a staff officer. He knew what the generals needed to know, where to get it, and how to report it precisely and accurately. Second, Custer ranged over a wide area of operation, not always with the approval or even the knowledge of his chief. He usually could be found at the point of heaviest fighting, often in the midst of it himself, enabling him to obtain the best possible information on the strength and location of the enemy.

McClellan's command did not survive. When the "slows" that first surfaced during the Peninsula Campaign reappeared after Antietam, McClellan was replaced by Major General Burnside. Early in November 1862, when McClellan went home to New Jersey, Custer returned to Michigan. Custer spent the winter of 1862–1863 in Monroe, awaiting orders. During this time, he began his famed courtship of Miss Elizabeth "Libbie" Bacon. While attending a party at Boyd's Seminary, Custer was formerly presented to Libbie, and the romance began.

Libbie had a beautiful face, slim figure, and chestnut hair. She was full of zest for life. Many of Monroe's young men competed for her attention. Smitten, Custer tenaciously courted her. Libbie's response, however, was only tepid.

Libbie was Custer's match in charm, spirit, and ambition. The daughter of an Ohio judge, she was adoring and strong-minded. Her father took a dim view of soldiers in general and Custer in particular. Gradually, Custer began to win her over. They made a sparkling couple and she was often seen with him. Finally, he proposed. She refused to marry him until he swore that he would never drink, a promise he kept, and that he would never swear or gamble—pledges he largely ignored.

They were married on February 9, 1864. Custer and his bridegrooms in military blue and gold, and Libbie with her bridesmaids equally radiant in white, dazzled the crowd that filled the church. It was a storybook wedding that launched a lasting marriage. Throughout the war, Libbie stayed as close to Custer's side as possible. When he decided to remain in the army after the war and go west to command the 7th Cavalry, she went too.

Warfare seemed to suit Custer very well. In fact, he reveled in it. In his memoirs, Custer wrote of killing a Confederate officer, describing the act as "the most exciting sport I ever engaged in." In a letter to his cousin in October 1862, he spoke of his enjoyment of combat: "I, of course, must wish for peace, and will be glad when the war ends, but if I answer for myself alone, I must say that I shall regret to see the war end and I would be willing, yes glad, to see a battle every day during my life."

Custer returned to the Army of the Potomac late in April 1863. No longer McClellan's aide-de-camp, Captain Custer, U.S. Volunteers, reverted to First Lieutenant Custer, 5th Regular Cavalry. Detailed to Brigadier General Alfred Pleasonton's command, Custer soon demonstrated himself as a bold, aggressive officer. In cavalry actions of June 1863, which exposed Lee's northward move into Pennsylvania, Custer demonstrated his fearlessness and ability to lead and direct soldiers in battle. Pleasonton recognized that in addition to his talent for gathering and reporting important information, Custer was gifted in combat leadership. Pleasonton admired and encouraged it. When Pleasonton received his second star, Custer was promoted to brevet captain.

General Pleasonton was an active officer who expected the same of those serving under him. He constantly demanded knowledge of his front, and it was Custer who kept him supplied with information about enemy movements and positions. Custer took an active part in every cavalry fight, making it his responsibility to place every picket. He did much of the dangerous reconnoitering, often across enemy lines. The cavalry under General Pleasonton was rapidly becoming a force to be dealt with, and Custer was playing a significant role in establishing his reputation.

On June 16, Union Colonel Judson Kilpatrick's cavalry engaged the Confederate cavalry, under the famous J. E. B. Stuart, in battle. When it appeared that the Confederates would have the upper hand, Custer led a fierce charge against the enemy. When Colonels Kilpatrick and Calvin Douty saw this, they directed their men to follow Custer. Soon Kilpatrick and Douty were beside him, waving their sabers together, as the three led the charge. Custer looked back and beckoned with his sword. "Come on boys," he shouted. Kilpatrick's horse was shot from under him, and Douty was killed; but Custer continued on, swinging his saber every step of the way. At one time, he was completely surrounded by Rebels but was able to fight his way free by cutting down one who rushed him.

At the end of June 1863, Lee's Army of Northern Virginia crossed the Potomac and moved into Pennsylvania. The Army of the Potomac hurried to intercept the Confederates. The same day, an envelope reached Pleasonton's headquarters in Frederick, Maryland, that stunned Captain Custer. It was addressed to Brigadier General George A. Custer. It was hard for him to believe the document inside—orders jumping him four grades, from captain to brigadier general. At the age of twenty-three, he had become the youngest general in the Union army. Custer would now command the 2nd Brigade of the 3rd Division, which consisted of four Michigan regiments and became known as the Wolverines.

Pleasonton had not acted impulsively. He had not singled out Custer alone. Colonels Kilpatrick and Alfred Duffie had received promotions earlier in June, and Captains Wesley Merritt and Elon Farnsworth got their stars at the same time as Custer. Pleasonton wanted men who could lead his brigades.

Less than a week later, General Custer made his debut at Gettysburg. For two days, the Army of Northern Virginia fought fiercely to dislodge the Union army from its strong position. On the third day, in a desperate attempt to break Meade's line, Lee sent 12,500 infantrymen under George Pickett against the Union's center. As Pickett prepared for his epic charge, Confederate cavalry, led by J. E. B. Stuart, moved into position three miles to the rear of the Union center. These were the feared gray horsemen of the Confederacy.

Under General David Gregg, three Union brigades faced Stuart, two of his own and Custer's Wolverines. When one of Gregg's brigades was in danger of being overrun, he ordered Custer's 7th Michigan to charge. As the horsemen moved to the front, sabers drawn, Custer galloped to the head of the column to lead the charge, shouting, "Come on, you Wolverines!" With a wild cheer, the regiment charged and drove the Southerners back in confusion. The battle raged on until another Confederate force hit Custer's flank. Prudently, Custer led his regiment back to the cover of artillery.

Stuart launched another attack. Again Gregg called on Custer's brigade, and again Custer dashed to the head and led the charge, calling upon his Wolverines to follow him. With a loud cheer, Custer's Michigan Brigade responded. The gray cavalry briefly stood firm, but then collapsed under the momentum of the assault. For the first time, Federal cavalry had stopped Stuart. Stuart fell back, if not defeated at least prevented from going where he had intended. His repulse coincided with Pickett's repulse. What might have happened had Stuart been able to overrun Gregg and attack the Union rear just as Pickett reached his objective, is one of the Civil War's most intriguing questions.

Custer had reason to be proud of his first week in command. Within a few days, he had earned a reputation based not on his gaudy appearance but on leadership in combat. Neither Custer nor the Michigan Brigade had time to bask in their glory. General Meade ordered the cavalry to harass Lee as he retreated.

In September, Custer received a superficial leg wound while leading a cavalry charge near Brandy Station. Taking time off to recuperate, Custer was soon back to lead his Wolverines again at Brandy Station, in one of the storied charges of the war. When Custer found himself cut off by Stuart, he removed his hat so that his men could see his hair. Leading the charge, he shouted: "Boys of Michigan, there are some people between us and home. I'm going home; who else goes?" The Wolverines joined him in fighting his way "home." Not even those contemptuous of his flamboyance or jealous of his rapid rise could help admiring his battlefield courage and leadership. "No soldier who saw him that day at Brandy Station," recalled an officer, "ever questioned his right to wear a star, or all the gold lace he felt inclined to wear. He at once became a favorite in the Army of the Potomac."

The spring of 1864 brought change for Custer and the entire Union Cavalry Corps when the army's high command was changed. Sam Grant, as his friends called him, was forty-one years old when Lincoln appointed him general in chief of the army. Grant had fashioned an unrivaled string of victories in the West—Forts Henry and Donelson, Shiloh, Vicksburg and Chattanooga. President Lincoln rewarded Grant by bestowing authority that no other soldier had enjoyed since George Washington. Grant's accession to command meant changes in the Army of the Potomac. Major General Pleasonton was relieved as commander of the Cavalry Corps. The selection of Major General Philip Sheridan as his replacement brought uncertainty to, and speculation from, those he would command. Among the Michigan troops, the fear was that Custer might be transferred. "'Bad luck' to those who are instrumental in removing him," Major James Kidd told his father about the prospects of losing Custer. "We swear by him. His move is our battle cry. He can get twice the fight out of his brigade than other men can possibly do."

Custer was troubled by the removal of Pleasonton. The two men had become close friends. "I do not believe a father could love his son more than General Pleasonton loves me," Custer told Libbie. It was more than his affection for Pleasonton that motivated Custer in his reaction to his friend's transfer. Custer believed he deserved promotion to divisional command; with Pleasonton gone, he would be less likely to receive it.

Sheridan, meanwhile, prepared for the corps' spring operations with drills, inspections, and reviews. Custer welcomed the resumption of field operations. Despite his disappointment with command changes and in his opportunity for promotion, Custer accepted Sheridan, writing to his wife, "General Sheridan from what I learn and see is an able and good commander and I like him very much."

In early May, the Army of the Potomac marched toward south toward the Rapidan and Rappahannock Rivers. The collision of Grant and Lee came on the killing ground of the Wilderness, where General Joseph Hooker had suffered his defeat a year earlier. During the quiet before the battle, Custer prayed, "inwardly, devoutly," as he had written to Libbie earlier. "Never have I failed to command myself to God's keeping," he wrote, "asking Him to forgive my past sins, and to watch over me while in danger. . . . I feel that my destiny is in the hands of the Almighty. This belief, more than other fact or reason, makes me brave and fearless as I am."

Custer's fame continued to grow as he racked up one triumph after another with the Michigan Brigade. His performance quickly earned him Sheridan's approval and esteem. By midsummer 1864, Sheridan also had won over Custer, replacing McClellan and Pleasonton as his idol and gaining his lasting loyalty and devotion.

Just as Custer proved himself to Sheridan, Sheridan proved himself to Grant. With Grant's support, he established the cavalry's utility as an independent arm. As the Army of the Potomac moved around Lee and gradually worked its way southward, Sheridan led the Cavalry Corps in a successful raid to the very edge of Richmond. There, at the Battle of Yellow Tavern, one of Custer's Wolverines killed J. E. B. Stuart himself. The Southern cavalry would never again measure up to the Union horsemen.

In September, Sheridan attacked General Jubal Early in the valley around Winchester, Virginia. At Winchester, Custer again demonstrated his generalship and added new laurels to his fame. Custer's Wolverines rolled over an entire brigade of infantry, captured 700 prisoners, two artillery caissons, and seven battle flags, and forced Early's army to flee up the valley. Custer was rewarded for his efforts by being given command of the 3rd Division. The 3rd Division happily welcomed its new leader.

The news of Custer's promotion to division command hit the Michigan Brigade like a bombshell. Under his leadership, the brigade had become the

George Armstrong Custer during the Washita campaign, 1868

most renowned in the 1st Division and well known throughout the army. Serving under Custer meant hard fighting and casualties, but he never took them into battle unless he rode with them. The red neckties that they wore attested to their pride. The downcast Wolverines circulated petitions asking for the Michigan Brigade to be transferred under Custer's command. Custer tried to console the men by telling them that General Sheridan had promised to consider moving them to the 3rd Division after this campaign. They were never moved.

The men left behind grumbled that the 1st Division had accomplished nothing since Custer left. "Now, all you hear about is the 3rd Division. The 3rd Division captured so many battle flags, nothing but the 3rd Division, while the 1st Division is scarcely heard of. The fact is you have Custer now."

In October, Custer repeated his victory at Winchester by smashing into the Confederate left and forcing the entire line to disintegrate. The next day, Custer was off to Washington commanding a squad of thirteen troopers, each carrying a Confederate battle flag that he had captured. The troopers presented the flags to Secretary of War Stanton. Stanton's response was to announce Custer's promotion to major general. Shaking Custer's hand, Stanton concluded, "General, a gallant officer always makes gallant soldiers."

In the spring of 1865, the Confederates were finally driven from the Shenandoah Valley and, fittingly, Custer and his 3rd Division were in the forefront. Then Sheridan was free to join Grant in the siege of Petersburg. Petersburg had been Lee's last attempt to hold off Grant. If it fell, the fall of Richmond would follow quickly. The mission of Sheridan's cavalry, as Lee's army limped westward in a desperate effort to break free, was to slow the retreat until Grant's infantry and artillery could finish the job. Impoverished in weapons, ammunition, food, and clothing and a mere shadow of its once mighty strength, the Army of Northern Virginia was easy prey for Custer's cavalry. At Sayler's Creek on April 6, a fifth of the Confederate army—seven generals and 7,000 troops—surrendered, many of them to Custer's 3rd Division.

By April 8, Custer, bolstered by the 1st Division, lay squarely across Lee's line of escape. At daybreak on April 9, Lee found himself surrounded. As Custer's 3rd Division formed for yet another charge, a lone gray horseman approached, bearing a soiled white towel attached to a pole. He presented himself to General Custer and declared that General Lee wished to meet with General Grant. Their meeting would end the war.

After the meeting, Lee descended the front steps of the McLean house and mounted his horse. As he moved off, there was silence. Suddenly the silence was broken by the stirring notes of "Dixie," played by Custer's band. General Lee, moist-eyed, turned in his saddle as he looked at Custer, and then touched his hat. Custer responded by removing his hat and bowing. There was no need to exchange words, for both were West Pointers who knew the pledge of Duty-Honor-Country. "Dixie" expressed it all.

Fittingly, the symbol of the war's end, the flag of surrender, had come to Custer. By the age of twenty-five, he had achieved a record few others had accomplished in a lifetime. Sheridan recognized his achievement and after Lee's surrender in McLean's parlor at Appomattox, purchased a writing table from McLean. The next day, he wrote a note to Libbie Custer: "I respectfully present to you the small writing table on which the conditions of the surrender of the Army of Northern Virginia were written by Lieutenant General Grant—and permit me to say, madam, that there is scarcely an individual in our service who has contributed more to bring about this desirable result than your gallant husband."

Custer loved war; it nourished and energized him. It provided an environment in which he could gain the obedience and adulation of those under his command. He was able to lead and inspire men to fight and die for him. The return of peace found him an adult in achievement and renown, but still a boy in years. For the decade remaining to him, the boy and the man would struggle for dominance; this struggle would mark his behavior during his frontier years.

Custer's first test came scarcely a month after the Grand Review in Washington. His new assignment was to organize a cavalry unit located in New Orleans for duty in Texas. The task proved difficult. Many of the 4,000 men now under his command were volunteers who had never fired a gun during the war. They had enlisted for three years, or the duration of the war. Now that the war was over, they wanted to go home. Custer and his staff faced many weeks of hard work in organizing the division before the march to Texas.

Custer quickly realized that these men lacked the regimental pride often gained by the bond of battle. They received every order with grumbles and growls, but Custer was determined to whip his troops into a well-disciplined unit. Some men deserted and others were insubordinate. These men had not served under his command during the war, and Custer had not earned their respect. With his efforts came a smoldering resentment toward Custer and his staff. This was Custer's first major encounter with desertion and insubordination, and he was not willing to accept either lightly. As he enforced his discipline, Libbie feared for his life. "Threats began to make their way to our house," she said. Even his staff tried to persuade Custer to lock his doors and bolt the windows.

Things reached crisis level when an officer's tent was fired upon by one of the officer's men. He might have been killed had he not been lying flat on the ground. Another officer was so disliked that his men threatened him, then drew up and signed a petition demanding his resignation. Custer interpreted their action as mutinous. On his demand, all apologized and were restored to duty except for one. This lone sergeant refused to admit he was wrong and was immediately court-martialed and sentenced to be shot. Friends of the sergeant appealed to Custer to pardon him, but he refused. Now there were rumors of a plot to kill Custer.

Preparations were made for the execution of the sergeant and one of the captured deserters. Both were to be shot on the same day. Custer insisted that his men witness the executions. The two men were placed before recently dug graves and their eyes bandaged. A lone figure, under orders, approached the sergeant and moved him aside. In an instant, the command "Fire!" was given, and the deserter fell dead at the side of the waiting grave. The sergeant fainted and was revived from his shock. It was explained to him that General Custer, thinking he had been unduly influenced by others, had decided to pardon him. Custer said he could not permit his troops to coerce him. He continued to maintain a firm hand, but lawlessness among the troops continued.

The benefit of Custer's firmness was evident on the march to Texas. The

240-mile trek took nineteen days and was a tedious one of heat and discomfort. The country, one trooper thought, seemed "as if even God himself had abandoned it." There were daily desertions. The men, with inadequate rations and unable to forage without risk of punishment, were frequently hungry.

Many men resented the way they were treated, feeling Custer did not consider the safety and comfort of those under his command. On the trip to Texas, Custer had an ambulance especially fitted for Libbie so she could go with him. On other campaigns, Custer often indulged himself luxuriously, maintaining a large, well-appointed tent, attended in the field by a female cook.

Within twenty-four hours of the division's march to Texas, local citizens complained to Custer about the theft of property. He responded by issuing an order that forbade foraging unless authorized by his headquarters: "Every violation of this order will receive prompt and severe punishment . . . any enlisted man violating the above order . . . will have his head shaved, and in addition will receive twenty-five lashes upon his back, well laid on." If any officer failed to report a violation, he would be arrested and dishonorably discharged from the army.

Custer was determined to gain control of the discipline of his troops, but in the process, he had issued an arbitrary, inflammatory, and illegal order. The Articles of War required that any officer or enlisted man charged with violating specific orders be tried before a general court-martial or a civil magistrate before punishment could be administered. In addition, the punishment of flogging had been abolished by an act of Congress in 1861. With this action, Custer had exceeded his authority and ignited a test of wills between him and his troops. In Custer's defense, however, he had received instructions from Sheridan to be conciliatory in the treatment of civilians and to enforce "rigid discipline among the troops and to prevent outrages on private persons and property."

Custer's orders to desist from foraging were soon tested. His men were issued rations that were not fit to eat. As a result, some of the troops foraged, including the killing of a calf. When the owner protested to Custer, he investigated and made several arrests. He ordered the men to be flogged and their heads shaved. Two weeks later, a similar situation occurred, and the guilty men were each given twenty-five lashes. His men were enraged by this treatment. The lieutenant colonel of the 1st Iowa Regiment swore that Custer would not touch another of his men. The governor and legislature of Iowa officially condemned Custer for his cruelty.

Custer's troops never forgave him for his cruel actions, and their later writings indicated the depth of their hatred for him. They blamed him for "incompetence or criminal negligence" in not fighting for adequate supplies for them. They described his orders as "inconsistent and tyrannical." One of them offered a rationale for Custer's actions: "He was only twenty-five years of age and had the usual egotism and self-importance of a young man. . . . He had no sympathy in common with the private soldiers, but regarded them simply as machines created for the special purpose of obeying his imperial will." It was a damning indictment of Custer, in stark contrast to the view of his Civil War comrades from the members of the Michigan Brigade and the 3rd Cavalry Division.

Nothing in Custer's experience had prepared him for the situation he encountered in Texas. During the war, he had known only loyalty and devotion from the men under his command. The men he had encountered in Louisiana and Texas felt they had been betrayed by their government. This fostered poor discipline and strong resentment. Probably any general would have had difficulty with these men, but Custer's reacting to them with illegal punishment and unbending discipline made it even worse. Had Custer—supported by Sheridan—not imposed his discipline, the men could have become marauders throughout the countryside. For that, he deserved credit; but his methods, which violated the Articles of War, are difficult to justify.

Despite Custer's problems with his men, he liked Texas. He had been fascinated with the Southern way of life since his West Point days and had counted among his closest friends cadets from that region. Texas found a sympathetic, if not kindred, fellow in him. While Custer empathized with the planters' difficulty with the reality of freedmen labor, he saw slavery for what it was. While in Louisiana, he and Libbie had attended black prayer meetings. Although Custer was opposed to suffrage for freedmen, he stated that "I am in favor of elevating the Negro to the extent of his capacity and intelligence, and of doing everything in our power to advance the race morally and mentally as well as physically and socially."

Meanwhile, in Washington on December 28, 1865, the War Department mustered out over a score of generals, including Custer. For Custer, the order meant he reverted to the rank of captain in the 5th United States Cavalry. On January 31, 1866, Custer relinquished command and returned to Washington.

Custer, uncertain about his future in the army, wondered whether to seek employment elsewhere. Now reduced in rank, Custer found that both his ego and income suffered. His salary as a major general had been $8,000; his captain's pay now would be only $2,000 per year. Custer's war fame, however, assured him entry into the circles of the wealthy and led to offers of employment. He rejected positions with the railroad and in the mining industry. While in New York, Custer was contacted by the Mexican government, which was hoping to have him serve in its army at a yearly salary of $16,000. He was forced to turn down the offer when he couldn't obtain a leave of absence. Twice Custer refused an appointment as lieutenant colonel of the black 9th Cavalry, because he wished "to be attached to an organization of white troops." Later in the year, his professional status was settled when General Sheridan secured for him the lieutenant colonelcy of the newly formed 7th Cavalry.

Custer was ordered to report for duty at Fort Riley, Kansas, to take over his new command. The fort was one of several posts the army had established in Kansas to guard settlements and was a route west to Denver, Colorado. In the summer of 1866, Fort Riley had been officially established as the headquarters site for the 7th Cavalry.

Custer reported for duty on November 1 and assumed temporary command of the regiment. By December, Colonel Andrew J. Smith arrived at the fort to take command, but his association with the regiment was nominal. On February 27, 1867, Smith assumed command of the district of the Upper Arkansas, relinquishing direction of the regiment to Custer.

The 7th Cavalry fell far short of being a crack regiment. The desertion rate was symptomatic of the caliber of recruits and the harshness of military life in the postwar army. Those troops assigned to a frontier regiment soon encountered the reality of life on an isolated post in an unforgiving land. Privates earned $13 a month; they endured monotony, rigid rules, poor food and quarters, disease, and occasional danger. Each year during the postwar years, the army lost one-fourth of its personnel to desertion. Replacements arrived and the cycle renewed itself. Despite the hardships, some men served for years, constituting a nucleus of veterans amid the turnover of troops in the regiment.

From its inception, the United States offered its citizens the opportunity for betterment. America rewarded hard work and ambition. To Americans, progress characterized the human saga; in America, it meant the conquest of a wilderness. Conquest of the wilderness meant the subjugation of Native Americans. At the end of the Civil War, the Great Plains remained the largest final homeland for the Indians, and it was there that Americans sought further expansion and progress.

By government estimates, there were 270,000 Indians in 125 groups. Of these, 100,000 would oppose the army and white settlers. Most of them—the Sioux, Cheyenne, Arapaho, Kiowa, and Comanche—lived in nomadic tribes on the Great Plains. These Plains warriors were superb horsemen and excellent guerrilla fighters. Though tribal animosities weakened their resistance to whites, the Indians were still formidable opponents.

The army saw its role in dealing with the Indians in stark terms. Major General William T. Sherman, commander of the Military District of Missouri, took a firm stand on the treatment of the Indians: "We must act with vindictive earnestness against the Sioux, even to their extermination, men, women and children." Unfortunately for the army, neither Sherman nor the ranking officers had a strategy for conquering the tribes.

Sherman assigned the campaign against the southern tribes to Major General Winfield Scott Hancock. He gathered a force of 1,400 troops; Custer's 7th Cavalry was a part of it. Hancock assigned Custer the task of pursuing a band of Sioux. Custer pushed ahead, but soon discovered that the size of the track narrowed as bands of Indians dispersed from the main body. This was a common native tactic, making it very difficult for the army to bring them to battle.

While on this campaign, Custer's troops rode toward the Smoky Hill River. It was then that Custer decided to hunt buffalo. Accompanied only by his dogs, Custer left his men behind. He was deep in Indian territory but didn't seem concerned. Somehow, while aiming his revolver at a buffalo and pulling the trigger, he shot his own horse in the head. On foot, bruised, and lost, he was finally rescued by his own troops. The energy and foolhardiness of that hunting foray, endangering himself and his men, was typical of Custer's behavior.

Whenever he went into the field, Custer was a fierce driver, setting a pace that he enjoyed—and expected everyone else to maintain. He could ride a full day with no liquids except a cup of cold tea or coffee, and only a small amount of food, and still retain his energy. When tired, he stretched out on the ground in a deep sleep for an hour or two and then sprang up fully refreshed. He often pushed his men through the day and then, while they wearily made camp, would take a fresh horse and ride off to hunt or scout the trail. While everyone around him slept, Custer sat in his tent writing long letters to Libbie. Men who did not share his energy found his pace cruel, particularly when it was ordered on a whim. The fact that he never noticed their suffering, or didn't care, was a mark of his egocentricity.

Catching Indians was no easy task. The Lakota warriors attacked Custer's column, stole his horses, and were still able to make a clean getaway. After weeks of fruitless campaigning, forage and supplies failed to materialize. "The inaction to which I am subjected now," Custer wrote Libbie, "is almost unendurable." The rugged terrain and the endless periods of boredom took a heavy toll on Custer's men and horses. Soon the men began to desert, one at a time and in pairs. Once, when thirteen of his men left camp at the same time, Custer ordered them hunted down and shot. One of the men was killed and two more brought back wounded. For two days, Custer refused them medical treatment; one subsequently died.

Custer had no qualms about looking after his own comfort while his men suffered the hardships of the wilderness. His scouts helped supply him with fresh game even as his men ate moldy bacon and hardtack. Sometimes, he took along an iron stove for his tent and even a woman to do the cooking. The night before his attack on Chief Black Kettle, Custer remained comfortably in his tent while a blizzard raged outside and his men huddled together under shelter halves and wet blankets. Other officers routinely watched over their men; George Crook, the famous Indian fighter, would painstakingly check his men's equipment and supplies, making certain that they were well fed and equipped. Custer seemed interested only in his own welfare.

Custer had been duped by the Lakota, knew it, and allowed it to gnaw at him. In his first independent operation with the 7th Cavalry, he had lost the quarry—a Civil War hero outwitted by the Indians. The experience sobered and depressed him. As discipline infractions and desertions mounted, he reacted severely.

Custer had been on the march for nearly two months with little to show for his efforts. Frustrated and missing his wife, he inexplicably left his command in the field and with a small personal escort, left for Fort Riley, 275 miles away. As usual, Custer set a furious pace. When a favorite horse fell behind, he sent six men on worn-out mounts to find it. Indians attacked them; one of the troopers was killed, another wounded and left for dead. Custer refused to go back for their bodies and later blamed them for bringing about their own deaths. Later he would offer several contradictory excuses for the strange forced march, but the real reason seemed to be nothing more than a desire to see his wife.

Eventually, the remainder of the tired and demoralized 7th Cavalry arrived at Fort Wallace in western Kansas. The man who had ordered deserters shot had now deserted his command. When Colonel Smith learned of the situation, he ordered Custer to return to Fort Wallace immediately. Custer ignored the order and continued on his quest to meet with his wife. After three days with her, he returned to Fort Wallace. He was placed under arrest for leaving his command without permission. Department commander Winfield S. Hancock supported Smith, saying that "Custer's action was without warrant and highly injurious to the service, especially under the circumstances."

In August of 1867, Lieutenant General Ulysses Grant ordered a general court-martial of Custer to convene at Fort Leavenworth on September 17. Smith charged Custer with "absence without leave from his command" and "conduct to the prejudice of good order and military discipline." He was also charged with overmarching the horses, using the ambulances without authority, and neglecting his duty by not trying to "recover or bury" the bodies of troopers. Additionally, Captain Robert West filed a charge that Custer had ordered deserters to "be shot down" without a trial and had denied wounded men medical treatment.

Custer pleaded not guilty and with the assistance of his counsel, spent the weeks before the trial preparing a defense. The trial began on September 17 and lasted until October 11. The court found Custer guilty of all charges, but cleared him of criminality in regard to the ambulances and treatment of deserters. The members ruled that he should be "suspended from rank and command for one year and forfeit his pay for the same time." The court's punishment was mild enough, explaining that "General Custer's anxiety to see his family at Fort Riley overcame his appreciation of the paramount necessity to obey orders."

The Custers reacted with indignation at the verdict and sentence. Libbie dismissed the verdict as "nothing but a plan of persecution" of her husband, the act of envious officers trying to cover up the shortcomings of the Hancock Campaign. The couple moved back East, to Michigan, where Custer did his best to forget his disgrace by recalling earlier success on other battlefields. During that time, he began working on his Civil War memoirs.

Before Custer's suspension was up, Phil Sheridan overrode the court, calling him back to the 7th Cavalry for a winter campaign. Sheridan had assumed command of the Department of Missouri. "The proper strategy," he once said, "consists in the first place in inflicting as telling blows as possible upon the enemy's army and causing the inhabitants so much suffering that they must long for peace, and force their government to demand it. The people must be left nothing but their eyes to weep with over the war." During the Civil War, he had applied his grim theory to the Shenandoah Valley. Now he was ready to apply similar tactics in the West, wherever Native Americans continued to resist. Sheridan planned to attack the Cheyenne during the winter, when they were most vulnerable. Sheridan told Sherman, "I have to select the season when I can catch the fiends; and if a village is attacked and women and children killed, the responsibility is not with the soldiers, but with people whose crimes necessitated the attack." Sherman heartily agreed.

To head the winter campaign, Sheridan selected Custer. It was what Custer had hoped for—a chance to redeem himself and erase the bitter memory of the Hancock Campaign by winning a great victory. During the campaign, Custer's casual readiness to leave his troops behind had fatal results. In November 1868, he attacked Chief Black Kettle's village on the Washita River. Custer's plan was to surround the village and, at daybreak, make a concerted attack from all sides. To accomplish this, he divided his command into four units. Before the attack, despite freezing air, the already chilled men were ordered to remove their overcoats for greater freedom of movement. During the surprise attack, the 7th Cavalry captured the village and, by Custer's report, killed 103 Indians, including the chief and his wife. He also claimed to have captured 53 women and children and destroyed an enormous amount of Indian property. In his field report to Sheridan, he wrote that "the Indians were caught napping." Despite their surprise, the Indians fought vigorously and inflicted serious casualties, the extent of which Custer would not realize until later in the day.

In the course of the battle, Major Joel Elliott, with 18 men, pursued some fleeing Indians. By the evening, Elliott had not returned. Custer faced a dilemma: By the time the group's absence was noticed, they were probably beyond help; frontier army policy, however, was very clear—you did not leave your men to the Indians. The tightening noose of the enemy and the large number of captured and wounded compelled Custer to turn his attention to withdrawal. He made a brief attempt to search for Elliott, but soon realized it was a fruitless effort.

Despite Custer's victory at Washita, the matter of Major Elliott and the other missing men would remain a blot on his record. When Sheridan learned of Custer's victory, he fired off a communication to him generously commending the 7th Cavalry and expressing his "special congratulations to their distinguished commander."

The Battle of the Washita is the victory on which Custer's reputation as an Indian fighter largely rests. Even this acclaim is tarnished by controversy. Critics protested that Black Kettle was peaceful; Custer's defenders agree that he was but point to the presence of captives and trophies of raids on settlers found in the Indian village as evidence of Kettle's guilt. Critics spoke out against the massacre of women and children; defenders retorted that there were few, they could not be distinguished in dress from the men, and they fired back. Critics blamed Custer for abandoning the field without searching for Elliott and his men; defenders argue that a search for Elliott would have jeopardized the whole command. Despite the controversy over Washita and the absence of other important victories, Custer remained in the public eye as the most prominent frontier commander.

After a time, Custer was able to mold the 7th Cavalry into a crack regiment. Each man rode the same color horse, and Custer instituted a training program, an unusual practice among frontier units. The program featured daily target practice, and the best forty marksmen were formed into an elite unit of sharpshooters who were exempt from menial duties. Nonetheless, many of Custer's officers and men continued to resent his disregard for their safety and comfort.

In 1873, Custer led the 7th Cavalry during the Yellowstone Expedition, which comprised 1,500 officers and men, over 2,300 horses and mules, and 275 wagons and ambulances. The force was out for three months, traveling over 900 miles. Custer was assigned to protect Northern Pacific survey parties. While reconnoitering with his troops, Custer was attacked by Sioux warriors. Although outnumbered more than three to one, Custer coolly told his men to dismount and then conducted a determined defense for three hours. Selecting the right moment, he ordered his troops into the saddle and led a smashing charge that routed the superior force.

Just a week later, Custer set out in pursuit of a large band of warriors along the north bank of the Yellowstone River. When several hundred braves approached his column, Custer ordered the band to play "Garry Owen" and led a charge. The braves scattered, and the cavalry pressed a close pursuit before finally breaking off the chase. During the skirmish, Custer's first mount was shot from under him, but he soon got another horse and continued in the pursuit.

In 1874, Custer commanded the Black Hills Expedition, reconnoitering the sacred Sioux land in violation of recent treaties. With 1,000 men, Custer explored the region, verifying reports of gold deposits. As a result, he earned the title "Chief of Thieves" from the Sioux. The gold rush that followed to the Black Hills triggered unrest with the Sioux and a massive campaign in which Custer was to a play a prominent part.

On June 25, 1876, Custer and his 7th Cavalry went in search of a large Sioux-Cheyenne encampment reported by scouts to be on the Little Bighorn River. Custer left one company to guard the supply train while he prepared to engage the enemy. Despite warnings from his scouts that the enemy numbered as many as the "blades of grass" on the ground, Custer split the regiment into three battalions. Custer and Major Marcus Reno approached the encampment, while Captain Frederick Benteen was sent to reconnoiter the bluffs along the river.

The two commands, Custer's and Reno's, continued until they were within two miles of the river. Custer ordered Reno to "move forward at as rapid a gait as prudent and charge afterwards." At the same time, Custer and his force left the trail and moved to the right. Shortly after, Reno and his contingent were caught in a surprise attack by the Sioux. "The Death Angel," wrote Private William Taylor, "was very near." Without water for thirty-six hours, the battalion dug in until reinforcements from the 7th Cavalry arrived.

In the meantime, the Indians, led by Gall, made a frontal attack against Custer's column, while Crazy Horse and Two Moon struck the flank and rear. An eyewitness to the attack, Pte-San-Waste-Win, described it: "I could hear the music of the bugles and could see the column of soldiers turn to the left to march down to the river where the attack was to be made. . . . Soon I saw a number of Cheyennes ride into the river . . . until there were hundreds of warriors in the river and running up the ravine . . . many, hundreds in number, were hidden in the ravine behind the hill upon which Long Hair [Custer] was marching, and he would be attacked from both sides."

Custer took a position on a knoll about a half-mile above the Little Bighorn. Custer did not fear the Indians, even though his troops were outnumbered; he believed they would flee when attacked, as they had in the past. Indians usually fought mainly in guerrilla fashion, running, striking, and running again. It was not to be the case this time. Custer was to encounter more than a thousand warriors, while having only 200 men to face them. The Indians came across the ford and swarmed up the gullies all around. Kill Eagle, a Blackfoot Sioux chief, later said that the movement of Indians toward Custer's troops was "like a hurricane . . . like bees swarming out of a hive." Crazy Horse led his warriors in a furious attack against Custer. In less than an hour, Custer's men were overwhelmed; there were no survivors. The ground was suddenly quiet, and the Indians later said they were surprised "as men are when a tornado passes and leaves quiet behind its awful roar."

"The smoke of the shooting and the dust of horses shut out the hill," Pte-San-Waste-Win said, "and the soldiers fired many shots, but the Sioux shot straight and the soldiers fell dead. The women crossed the river after the men . . . when we came to the hill there were no soldiers living and Long Hair lay dead among the rest. . . . The blood of the people was hot and their hearts bad, and they took no prisoners that day."

The reports of what happened during the battle varied. Crow King said that all the soldiers dismounted when the Indians surrounded them. "They tried to hold on to their horses, but as we pressed closer, they let go of their horses. We crowded them toward their main camp and killed them all. They kept in order and fought like brave warriors as long as they had a man left."

Red Horse's report of the battle was different. Near the end of the fighting, according to him, Custer's soldiers "became foolish, many throwing away their guns and raising their hands saying, 'Sioux pity us; take us prisoners.' The Sioux did not take a single soldier prisoner, but killed all of them; none were alive for even a few minutes."

On the 27th, General Terry's troops found Custer and his men, 197 by count, dead on the hill. Custer was naked, but he had not been scalped or mutilated. He had two wounds, one in the heart and one in the temple. The Indians themselves did not know who killed Custer, nor how or when he was killed. It wasn't until later that they learned that Custer had even been there that day.

The battle of the Little Bighorn was the army's most decisive defeat during the Indian wars. It also sealed the final defeat of the Indians and destroyed whatever chance remained for a fair resolution of the differences that existed between Native Americans and whites. After the death of Custer and his men, the nation's mood hardened. There was an all-out effort to crush the Indian resistance once and for all.

Newspapers editorialized about the battle, placing blame on Custer, the army, and the president and demanded revenge against the Indians. Sheridan blamed the defeat on Custer, the officer whom he had said had never failed him. In Washington, President Grant stated publicly, "I regard Custer's massacre as a sacrifice of troops, brought on by Custer himself, that was wholly unnecessary—wholly unnecessary." In Monroe, Michigan, "a great silence came over" the city, with bells tolling every hour.

When Libbie learned of her husband's death, she said, "I wanted to die." But Custer had impressed upon her the responsibilities of a commander's wife, and so she composed herself and began to comfort others. Later she would say, "To lose him would be to close the windows of life that let in the sunshine."

To Libbie Custer, her husband was a demigod whose character and military record had no blemish. Their thirteen-year marriage is one of history's great love stories. Widowed at age thirty-four, she dedicated the rest of her life to extolling her husband's deeds and virtues and defending his reputation. Her books—*Boots and Saddles* (1885), *Following the Guidon* (1890), and *Tenting on the Plains* (1893)—reached a wide audience. Many who had no other standard of comparison saw Custer as she had described him. Others who would have attacked him kept quiet out of consideration for the personable Libbie. Not until 1933 did she join her husband in the post cemetery at West Point.

From Gettysburg to Appomattox, George Armstrong Custer distinguished himself. His generalship combined audacity, courage, leadership, composure, and an uncanny instinct for doing the right thing at the right time. Individually, he fought with a fury and tenacity that astonished all who witnessed his feats of daring. Custer and others attributed the fact that he emerged from the war with so few scars to "Custer's Luck." He seemed to live a charmed life. But Custer's luck ran out at Little Bighorn. The glitter was authentic, and at the close of the war, Custer was considered second only to Sheridan as a cavalry general.

Almost at once, Custer's experiences during the Civil War gave way to his service on the frontier. His command on the frontier tarnished his name and dimmed his outstanding record during the war. Had he died just prior to Appomattox, he would have been remembered as the great cavalry general that he was; unfortunately, his service on the frontier would not be viewed in the same light. Custer had been denied greatness, but not immortality.

Epilogue

IT was all but over, the four-year nightmare. Robert E. Lee's once seemingly invincible Army of Northern Virginia had surrendered on the grassy roadside at Appomattox. General Joseph E. Johnston was ready to surrender his Army of Tennessee to his antagonist William T. Sherman. The stars and stripes once more flew over the ruins of Fort Sumter, where the war began. The Confederate government was in flight after the fall of Richmond. There was nothing more to fight for.

But there was one more senseless act to be performed, and who better to do that than the actor, John Wilkes Booth. Booth chose a theater for his crime. On April 14, 1865, at Ford's Theater, during the evening performance of *Our American Cousin*, Booth shot and killed President Abraham Lincoln. A blow intended to avenge and aid the South had the opposite effect.

The North went into mourning, a grief more prolonged than any in its history. The public outpouring of sorrow from the pulpit and press was staggering. For as long as two weeks after the murder, the dark days of mourning continued. The hunt for Booth and his accomplices spread throughout the nation. Finally, on April 26, Booth was cornered in a barn near the Rappahannock River in Virginia. Refusing to surrender, he too fell to a bullet. He died shortly after on the same day that General Johnston surrendered at last to General Sherman. On May 10, Confederate President Jefferson Davis was captured without a struggle.

Retribution was inevitable, yet slow in coming. The feared consequences of the war did not materialize. There were no bloodbaths of vengeance. No Confederates were tried for treason. Jefferson Davis was imprisoned without trial for two years but then released to live a quiet life and write his memoirs. The lack of reprisals was unique in history after a civil war, especially those wars fought on a scale as large as this one.

Perhaps there was little time for retribution because the men of both armies, North and South, were too busy returning home to find what remained of the life they left behind. The Union armies were demobilized quickly. Within two months, 641,000 men had been mustered out. By November 1866, only 65,000 men remained in an army that only eighteen months earlier had numbered over a million. Most of the returning Union soldiers seemed to readjust quickly to civilian life, apparently without the psychological and social problems that plagued so many veterans of recent wars.

How different it was for the defeated Confederates—yet it could have been worse. Thanks to Grant's magnanimity at Appomattox, there was no punishment or recrimination when other Southern armies surrendered. Men and officers were simply ordered to take their paroles, surrender their arms, and go home. For weeks following the surrender, the roads of the South were filled with passing Confederates: Ragged men, often in tears, stopped to ask for food or water and told the news of their surrender.

The reception of the Union soldiers when returning home was as different from that for the men in gray as the flags for which they fought. Throughout the North, there was jubilation. As regiment after regiment came marching home, they were met by cheering crowds. The conflict lay behind them—so did much of the best of their youth. Nothing would ever be the same again for anyone else in the country. The war left an indelible imprint on the nation's consciousness. A three-time-wounded captain and future Supreme Court justice expressed his view: "The generation that carried on the war has been set apart by its experience," said Oliver Wendell Holmes in 1884. "Through our great good fortune, in our youth our hearts were touched with fire. It was given to us to learn at the outset that life is a profound and passionate thing."

There was joy in the South too, but of a different kind. They had lost the war and no one could be joyful about that, but at last it was over, and the men were coming home. But so many men did not. Hundreds of thousands lay buried in the soil of Tennessee, Virginia, and Pennsylvania. As soon as possible, families on both sides began the ordeal of trying to find the remains of their sons and husbands to bring them home and give them a proper burial.

Even before the end of the war, a movement began in the North for the creation of national military cemeteries to honor the fallen brave. Lincoln had spoken at the dedication of one in Gettysburg. Others were established at Alexandria, Vicksburg, and most notably Arlington, Virginia. There on the grounds that were once part of Robert E. Lee's estate, one of the most beautiful cemeteries was established. As the North memorialized its dead, it began to do the same for the living. Confederates, too, joined in the drive to preserve the memory of those who had served their cause, but understandably, in a land depressed by war, the immediate impetus was more economic.

The war's impact fell heavily on the South. Emancipation played a major role in the social order. Years later, older ex-slaves vividly recalled the day they had learned of their freedom. For many, it was the central event of their lives.

The South was not to pass from war to peace without paying some price. For nearly two years, there was surprisingly little interference in the South's affairs, as white Southerners once more elected men with their viewpoint to state legislatures and tried to send others to Congress. Worse for the freed slaves, Southern states passed "Black Codes," which restricted their freedom. At first, most Republicans supported President Johnson's Reconstruction plan, but soon many abolitionists and Radicals were at odds with him. In time, this difference would create a schism between the president and Congress. After the election of 1866, the Radical Republicans were successful in instituting a plan of reconstruction of their own. The schism would grow.

Coming first as destroyers, many Yankees remained in the South to help rebuild it. The day of the carpetbaggers had come, Yankee opportunists who went south to profit from cheap land and labor. There were others, however, such as entrepreneurs who brought with them an influx of capital and energy and played a strong part in reviving the Southern economy.

Republicans went south, where some Southerner scalawags joined them to run the Reconstruction state governments. Often it was good, honest government; but in some cases, it was corrupt and abusive. Fearful that the newly freed slaves would cause serious social threats to their former masters, groups such as the Ku Klux Klan arose to intimidate freed slaves and maintain their control over blacks.

There were some Southerners, perhaps as many as 10,000, who simply refused to take part in the rebuilding of the South. Beginning with the flight of cabinet members and generals in 1865 and followed later by thousands of others, they abandoned the country to go into exile, fearing indictments against them or unwilling to live under Yankee rule. Most of those who left went to Mexico; others went to Central or South America, Europe, and Canada.

In the United States, Southerners looked for ways to rebuild the South and their own personal fortunes. Because the South's transportation system had been completely destroyed, there was a need to rebuild and modernize the railroads. This was often financed by Northern entrepreneurs. Former Confederate military luminaries became active in or figureheads of the new lines. Joseph Johnston, Nathan B. Forrest, John Breckinridge, P. G. T. Beauregard, and others became railroad presidents and participated in the rebuilding. Scores of former Confederates entered the life insurance business; Jubal Early supervised a state lottery. Robert E. Lee turned down more lucrative positions to accept the presidency of Washington College (renamed Washington and Lee after his death).

Of course, the old Confederates could not stay out of politics. After taking a loyalty oath and applying for restoration of their citizenship rights, their voices were once more heard in state legislatures and the halls of Congress. Many Union veterans entered politics, too, relying on their military record to help get them elected. Every elected president until 1904, except for Grover Cleveland, had served in the Union army. But none of them, not even Grant, was a military president; all except Grant were civilians who had gone to war in the crisis of 1861 and returned to civilian life at the end of the war.

The compromise that settled the disputed presidential election of 1876 would lead to the end of Reconstruction and the removal of Federal troops from the South. Civil affairs were once more entirely in the hands of Southerners. The final vestiges of war and defeat were removed. Now it remained for emotional wounds to heal.

The states in the North continued to grow and prosper after the war, virtually forcing the rest of the world to take notice. Yankee trade expanded throughout the world, dominating both North and South America. America began to have a greater influence in the affairs of others. The years of fighting during the war had a profound impact upon the settlement of the uncharted West. Even before the war ended, the massive migration of white settlers began as a direct result of the conflict. In addition to the soldiers and civilians who went west, there were thousands of deserters from both armies. Few returned after the war, for fear of capture and certain disgrace. When the war ended, thousands more who were accustomed to the practice of raiding and near-lawless episodes made the trek west. The James and Younger brothers, who had been Confederate guerrillas, now became outlaws. "Wild Bill" Hickok, western lawman, had served the Union. For these and many more, their days in the West were little more than an extension of the adventure of war. The settlement of the West, with all the dangers and struggles involved, restored a fraternal bond that the war had broken. Were it not for the West, reconciliation might have taken longer than it did.

Time would be the greatest healer. As the years passed, the soldiers grew older and more compassionate. By the end of the century, nostalgia and fading memories had erased much of the bad feelings. Veterans on both sides had banded together in fraternal organizations. Homes for indigent and helpless veterans were established in both the North and South. The old generals and leaders met to talk of their comrades and of their past glories.

In time, they would all die. Of the great men, Lee was the first to depart. The war hastened his death as surely as a bullet could have struck him down. He lived to only 1870, a symbol of peaceful acceptance of the war's fate, a champion of reconciliation. Tolerant to the end, he threatened to fire one of his professors at Washington College if the man ever spoke disrespectfully of General Grant again in his presence. The mourning was universal at the passing of Lee. Lee's old adversary, Ulysses S. Grant, outlived him by fifteen years. As president, Grant had endured scandal, disgrace, and financial disaster; but to the end of his days, he was still admired for his role in the war. He struggled to complete his memoirs, beating by days the cancer that killed him. Grant's example of courage during his last days was admired even by his former enemies.

The president of the Confederacy would answer the final call in 1889. Jefferson Davis devoted the last years of his life to writing his history of the Confederacy, trying to win with the pen what he had lost by the sword. Davis never fully admitted defeat or error and never entirely forgave his old foes.

More and more, the vestiges of the old war reminded Americans of their common bonds and virtues rather than their one-time differences. The Civil War had marked a decisive turn in the nature of American nationality. The word *union* was replaced by *nation*. No longer was America a voluntary confederation of sovereign states. The war had strengthened the national government at the expense of the states. The United States had truly become one nation under God.

Organization of the Union and Confederate Armies

The Union and Confederate armies were both organized in much the same way. That is not surprising because the senior officers on both sides were graduates of West Point, often having served together in the Regular army. For both North and South, the regiment was the basic unit for infantry and cavalry. The battery was the basic unit for artillery. Companies were grouped into regiments, regiments into brigades, brigades into divisions, divisions into corps, and corps into armies.

Theoretically, a company's strength was 100; a regiment's, 1,000; a brigade's, 4,000; and a division's 12,000. Rarely did either army reach these numbers. Union and Confederate corps and armies' sizes varied greatly. For both sides, a company was considered any unit of 50–100 soldiers commanded by a captain. Each company in a regiment was required to have an official letter (or number); for example, Company A, 4th Virginia Regiment.

At the time of the Civil War, the regiment was considered the largest body of troops that could be directly commanded by a single leader. In modern times, the size of the unit that a single leader can direct has shrunk to a platoon, which is a part of a company containing 24–50 soldiers. The volunteer infantry regiment at full strength as prescribed by U.S. Army regulations consisted of ten companies, each composed of ninety-seven men and three officers. The regiment was commanded by a colonel. Most regiments were seldom, if ever, up to full strength. By 1863, the average Union regiment could muster only 425 effectives. When Union regiments dwindled to 150 to 200 men, they were often merged to form a new regiment.

In most instances, Southern regiments were kept together by mustering in recruits. As the war progressed and there were few new recruits, many of these regiments dropped below recommended strength. In some cases, they were skeletons of their original strength but were kept together to maintain the regimental esprit de corps.

Although some soldiers were part of renowned brigades and divisions, they identified most with their regiments. Composed of men usually from the same area and state, the regiment became their wartime home. Both Union and Confederate regiments were known by their number and state: the 10th New York or the 48th Mississippi.

Regiments were only as good as the officers who commanded them. Officers were responsible for the regiment's training and discipline. A regimental commander who took interest in his men's health and welfare and who stood fire well meant the difference between a regiment that held its position under fire and one that broke and ran. Bravery was a prime requisite for leadership; a regiment that had confident leaders was likely to have confident soldiers.

In early stages of the war, regimental commanders attempted to increase morale by using distinctive uniforms. There was a rash of enlistments in the Zouave regiments in both the North and South. With their colorful uniforms, baggy pants, fezzes, and vivandières, it was an easy matter to fill the ranks of the Zouave regiments.

Battle flags and regimental colors were also means of developing esprit de corps and were carried into action. The color guard for a regiment was considered a position of honor, despite the hazard associated with it. The flag drew fire like a magnet, and many brave men lost their lives carrying it. The colors acted as a rallying point and were used as markers on the battlefield. Men were willing to risk their lives to prevent the regimental flag from falling into enemy hands.

The common tactical infantry and cavalry unit of the Civil War was the brigade. The brigade generally consisted of four to six regiments. Near the end of the war, the size could have been as few as two. When Confederate regiments were forced to consolidate, some brigades contained remnants of as many as fifteen regiments.

By definition, a brigadier general commanded a brigade, but colonels were often used where brigades were too small to justify a brigadier. Regimental and company commanders played a major role in the brigade's effectiveness in battle. It was their job to instruct the men in complicated battle maneuvers and to coordinate these movements with other regiments in the brigade.

Some brigades became famous during the war, and men served in them with great pride. The Stonewall Brigade and Hood's Texas Brigade were two of Robert E. Lee's best units. On the Union side, the Iron Brigade earned fame in the Army of the Potomac.

In the South, the regiments that formed brigades were usually from the same state. There was the same feeling of pride and loyalty among Southerners toward their brigades as Union troops had toward their corps or regiments. Units often took the name of their original leader, especially in the Confederacy, and kept them after the command passed to another. The Stonewall Brigade, for example, proudly bore that name throughout the war.

The standard division consisted of three brigades. Confederate divisions were usually commanded by major generals; Union divisions, by either a brigadier or major general. Because Southern regiments tended to be somewhat stronger than Union regiments, Confederate divisions were also larger. Until late in the war, the average strength of Confederate corps and divisions was about double that of the Union's. This often led to considerable confusion. For instance, the four Confederate divisions involved in the first days of fighting at Gettysburg—those of Early, Heth, Pender, and Rodes—totaled 28,000 men. The six divisions of the I and XI Corps of the Union army that faced them totaled a little under 21,000. At one time, Confederate General Ambrose P. Hill's famous Light Division had seven brigades, giving it a strength of about 17,000 men.

Corps were established in the Union army in March 1862 by General George B. McClellan. Before the war ended, a total of forty-three corps had been formed in the Union army. Each corps was commanded by a major general, and each corps was designated by a number from I to XXV. Corps badges such as triangles, crescents, and arrows were adopted by most corps and worn by its officers and men.

In the Confederate army, corps were organized in November 1862 and were commanded by lieutenant generals. Confederate corps were also designated by numbers but were more likely to be referred to by their commander's name. Confederate corps were usually larger than those of the Union. At Gettysburg, the Army of the Potomac was made up of seven army corps, with fifty-one infantry brigades, grouped in nineteen divisions. Total Union troops involved numbered 93,000. The Army of Northern Virginia consisted of three army corps, divided into nine divisions, with thirty-seven brigades. The Confederate troops engaged totaled 70,000. In 1864, the Army of the Potomac was reorganized, and the five corps were consolidated into three, each corps averaging 26,000 men.

The largest organizational unit for both Union and Confederate troops was the army. Armies were usually named for the department in which they were found. Union armies were named for rivers; Confederate armies, for states or regions. For example, the main Confederate army in the East was the Army of Northern Virginia while the main Union army was the Army of the Potomac. There were sixteen Union and twenty-three Confederate armies.

Chronology of the Civil War and Reconstruction

1860

Dec 20   South Carolina is the first Southern state to secede from the Union.

1861

Feb 18   Confederate States of America is formed, with Jefferson Davis as president.

Apr 12–13   Confederates bombard and capture Fort Sumter in the harbor of Charleston, South Carolina.

Apr 15   Lincoln issues a call for 75,000 troops.

Apr 17   Virginia secedes.

May 21   Richmond, Virginia, is selected as the Confederate capital.

July 21   First major battle of the war (Bull Run) is fought at Manassas, Virginia. Confederate Generals P. G. T. Beauregard and Joseph E. Johnston defeat Union army under General Irvin McDowell.

1862

Feb 6–16   General Ulysses S. Grant captures Forts Henry and Donelson in Tennessee.

Apr 4   General George B. McClellan opens Union campaign on peninsula, east of Richmond.

Apr 6   Grant wins important battle at Shiloh, Tennessee and moves southward into Mississippi. Confederate General Albert S. Johnston is killed in the battle.

Apr 16	Confederates begin to conscript soldiers.
May 4	McClellan's troops occupy Yorktown, Virginia, and advance on Richmond.
May 23	Thomas "Stonewall" Jackson opens his campaign in the Shenandoah Valley of Virginia in an attempt to draw troops from McClellan's Peninsula Campaign.
May 31	Joseph E. Johnston is wounded in the Battle of Seven Pines just east of Richmond. He is replaced by Robert E. Lee.
June 6	Memphis, Tennessee, falls to Union troops.
June 25–July 1	General Robert E. Lee fights the Seven Days' Battle outside Richmond, driving Union forces from Richmond.
Aug 29–30	Lee and Jackson defeat the Union army under General John Pope at Manassas for a second time.
Sept 4	Lee mounts an offensive into Maryland.
Sept 17	After a bitter battle at Antietam (Sharpsburg, Maryland) a McClellan–led Union army forces Lee to withdraw into northern Virginia.
Sept 22	President Lincoln issues the preliminary Proclamation of Emancipation.
Oct 8	Union General Don Carlos Buell ends Confederate General Braxton Bragg's invasion of Kentucky at Perryville.
Nov 7	Lincoln replaces McClellan with General Ambrose E. Burnside.
Dec 13	General Lee's Army of Northern Virginia hands General Burnside a crushing defeat at the Battle of Fredericksburg.

1863

Jan 1	Lincoln issues the Emancipation Proclamation.
Jan 3	Union troops under General William S. Rosecrans force Confederate troops under Bragg to retreat after the Battle of Murfreesboro (Stone River), Tennessee.
Jan 25	Lincoln replaces General Burnside with General "Fighting Joe" Hooker as commander of the Army of the Potomac.
Mar 3	The North passes a conscription act for all able-bodied men between the ages of 20 and 45.
May 2	Lee and Jackson win a stunning victory at Chancellorsville, Virginia. Jackson is accidentally shot by his own men.
May 10	Stonewall Jackson dies.

June 23	General J. E. B. Stuart receives orders from Lee to harry the Union line of communication.
June 27	Hooker resigns as commander of the Army of the Potomac and is replaced by General George C. Meade.
July 1–3	Lee invades Pennsylvania but is defeated at Gettysburg; this marks the turning point of the war.
July 4	Vicksburg, Mississippi, falls to Grant.
Sept 20	Bragg's Army of Tennessee defeats Rosecrans at the Battle of Chickamauga, Tennessee.
Nov 19	Lincoln delivers his Gettysburg Address.
Nov 25	Generals Grant and George H. Thomas defeat Confederates at Chattanooga, Tennessee.
Dec 8	Lincoln proposes his Ten-Percent Plan for Reconstruction.
Dec 16	General Joseph E. Johnston replaces General Bragg as commander of the Army of Tennessee.

1864

Mar 2	Grant is promoted to lieutenant general and becomes commander in chief of all Union forces.
Apr 12	General Nathan Bedford Forrest storms Fort Pillow, Tennessee, massacring numerous black Union soldiers.
May 4	Grant launches drives by George Meade against Lee in Virginia and by William T. Sherman against Johnston in northwest Georgia.
May 5–6	Union and Confederate troops clash in the Battle of the Wilderness.
May 7	Despite heavy losses to the Army of the Potomac, Grant continues to advance toward Richmond.
May 11	J. E. B. Stuart is mortally wounded in a battle with General Phil Sheridan at Yellow Tavern, Virginia.
June 3	Lee inflicts heavy losses on Grant in the Battle of Cold Harbor, Virginia.
June 20	Grant lays siege to Petersburg, Virginia.
July 17	Jefferson Davis replaces Johnston with General John Bell Hood as commander of the Army of Tennessee.
Aug 10	General Sheridan begins his campaign to clear the Shenandoah Valley of General Jubal Early's troops.
Sept 1	Hood evacuates Atlanta and Sherman enters the city.
Oct 19	Sheridan defeats Early in the Battle of Cedar Creek and begins to burn crops in the Shenandoah Valley.

Oct 31	Hood invades Tennessee in hopes of drawing Sherman north.
Nov 8	Lincoln is reelected president, defeating McClellan.
Nov 15	Sherman begins his March to the Sea.
Nov 30	General John M. Schofield defeats Hood in the Battle of Franklin, Tennessee.
Dec 15–16	Hood's Army of Tennessee is defeated at Nashville, Tennessee.
Dec 22	Sherman captures Savannah, Georgia. General William Hardee's Confederate army escapes into South Carolina.

1865

Jan 19	Lee is appointed general in chief of all Confederate forces.
Jan 20	Sherman begins his march into South Carolina.
Feb 23	Joseph Johnston replaces Hood as commander of the Army of Tennessee.
March 3	Congress creates the Freedmen's Bureau.
March 19	Johnston's Confederates attack Union forces at Brentonville, North Carolina. Sheridan joins Grant at Petersburg.
Apr 2	Federal troops break the thin Confederate line at Petersburg. Richmond is abandoned. General A. P. Hill is killed.
Apr 9	Lee surrenders the Army of Northern Virginia to Grant at Appomattox.
Apr 14	President Lincoln is assassinated by John Wilkes Booth at Ford's Theater.
Apr 15	Andrew Johnson assumes the presidency.
Apr 26	Johnston surrenders the Army of Tennessee to Sherman.
May 4	President Lincoln is buried in Springfield, Illinois.
Dec 18	Thirteenth Amendment is ratified.

1866

Apr 9	Congress passes a Civil Rights Act over President Johnson's veto.
July 23	Grant is promoted to full general.
Oct	Radicals take over Congress after congressional election.

1867

| Mar 2 | Radicals override Johnson's veto of a Congressional Plan for Reconstruction, dividing the South into five military regions. They also pass the Tenure of Office Act. |

Aug 5   Johnson tests the Tenure of Office Act by firing Secretary of War Edwin Stanton.

1868
Mar 13–May 26 Impeachment trial of Andrew Johnson is held.
July 14   Fourteenth Amendment is ratified.
Nov 3   Grant is elected president.

1870
Mar 30   Fifteenth Amendment is ratified.
Oct 12   Robert E. Lee dies at Lexington, Virginia.

1871
Apr 20   Congress enacts the Ku Klux Klan Act.
Nov 5   Grant is elected president for the second time.

1875
July 31   Andrew Johnson dies at Carter Station, Tennessee.

1876
June 25   George A. Custer is killed in the Battle of Little Bighorn.

1877
Mar 3   Rutherford B. Hayes becomes president.
Apr   Last federal troops leave the South.
Oct 29   Nathan B. Forrest dies at Memphis, Tennessee.

1879
Aug 30   John B. Hood dies at New Orleans, Louisiana.

1885
July 23   Ulysses S. Grant dies at Mount McGregor, New York.
Oct 29   George B. McClellan dies at Orange, New Jersey.

1888
Aug 5   Phil Sheridan dies at Nosquitt, Massachusetts.

1889
Dec 9   Jefferson Davis dies at Beauvoir near Biloxi, Mississippi.

1891
Feb 14   William T. Sherman dies at New York, New York.
Mar 21   Joseph E. Johnston dies at Washington, D.C.

1904
Jan 2   James Longstreet dies at Gainesville, Georgia.

1914
Feb 24   Joshua L. Chamberlain dies at Portland, Maine.

1916
May 30   John S. Mosby dies at Warrenton, Virginia.

Endnotes

p. 1 "In 1865, spring came" B. Davis, *The
      Long Surrender*, New York: Random
      House, 1985, 5.

p. 1 "In May 1861" J. Cullen, "Richmond
      Falls!" *American History Illustrated* (Jan.
      1974): 11.

p. 2 "Richmond was destined" Cullen,
      12–13.

p. 2 "When the war began" Cullen, 13.

p. 2 "The inevitable outcome" Davis, 5.

p. 2 "Richmond was once active" Davis,
      6.

p. 3 "Reagan was on the way" Davis, 19.

p. 3 "The service was underway" R.
      Wheeler, *Witness to Appomattox*, New
      York: Harper & Row, 1989, 91.

p. 3 "The city had lost" Cullen, 14.

p. 3 "Fear swept the city" Davis, 23.

p. 4 "Davis left his executive" H. Strode,
      Jefferson Davis, Tragic Hero, New York:
      Harcourt, Brace & World, 1964,
      168.

p. 5 "When Davis reached" Davis, 26–29.

p. 6 "When the official" Cullen, 14.

p. 6 "Confusion, panic, and fear" Cullen,
      14.

p. 6 "In the evening" Cullen, 15.

p. 6 "Despite the chaos" Davis, 31–32.

p. 7 "In the meantime" R. Lee , *General

Lee's City*, McLean: EPM Publica-
      tions, 1987, 37.

p. 7 "In the early morning" Lee, 37–38.

p. 7 "Just before daylight" Lee, 38.

p. 7 "Richmond was now" Cullen, 16.

p. 7 "Late in the night" Davis, 36.

p. 8 "The next morning" Cullen, 16–17.

p. 9 "Early in the morning" Lee, 38.

p. 9 "Major Stevens accepted" Lee, 38–39.

p. 10 "I never knew" A. Hoehling and M.
      Hoehling, *The Day Richmond Died*,
      New York: A. S. Barnes & Compa-
      ny, IX.

p. 10 "In the defenseless city" Davis,
      39–40.

p. 10 "When Major General Weitzel" Lee,
      39.

p. 10 "The Federal infantry" Lee, 39.

p. 11 "Some citizens of Richmond" Davis,
      40–41.

p. 11 "The Federal soldiers" Davis, 41.

p. 11 "The stars shone" Cullen, 19.

p. 11 "Despite the ruins" N. Trudeau, *Out
      of the Storm*, Baton Rouge: Louisiana
      State University Press, 1994, 84.

p. 11 "The next day dawned" J. Korn,
      Pursuit to Appomattox: The Last Battle,
      Alexandria: Time-Life Books, 1987,
      108.

p. 12 "When news of Richmond's" Trudeau, 83.

p. 12 "In the meantime" Trudeau, 85.

p. 12 "About midmorning, Lincoln" Wheeler, 129–130.

p. 12 "The walk was long" Wheeler, 133–135.

p. 14 "The winter of 1864–65" A. Marrin, *Unconditional Surrender: U. S. Grant and the Civil War*, New York: Macmillan, 1994, 163.

p. 15 "Nakedness went along" B. Catton, *A Stillness at Appomattox*, Doubleday & Company, 1957, 329–330.

p. 15 "Lee's Army of Northern Virginia" Marrin, 163–164.

p. 15 "For Grant and the army" Marrin, 161.

p. 15 "On March 25" D. Freeman, *Lee of Virginia*, New York: Charles Scribner's Sons, 1958, 188.

p. 16 "Heading southward with" Editors of Time Life, *The Time-Life History of the Civil War*, New York: Barnes and Noble, 1990, 395397.

p. 16 "Lee soon ascertained" Freeman, 189–190.

p. 16 "That night Petersburg" Freeman, 190.

p. 17 "On April 3, General Grant" Korn, 108.

p. 17 "As Lee passed his soldiers" Freeman, 191–192.

p. 17 "During the night" Freeman, 192.

p. 18 "The absence of food" Korn, 113.

p. 18 "The Federal troops" Korn, 113.

p. 18 "Lee waited until darkness" Korn, 115–116.

p. 18 "An earlier attack" Korn, 116.

p. 19 "Before Lee moved on" Freeman, 196.

p. 19 "That night Sheridan" Korn, 128.

p. 19 "With those of his men" Freeman, 197.

p. 19 "Peace for them" Freeman, 197.

p. 19 "By the evening" Freeman, 198.

p. 20 "That evening General Grant" Korn, 133.

p. 20 "That evening Grant" C. Dowdey, *Lee*, New York: Bonanza Books, 1965, 567.

p. 20 "Saying nothing to Longstreet" Dowdey, 568.

p. 20 "Although weary and burdened" Korn, 134.

p. 21 "The hopelessness of their" E. Thomas, *Robert E. Lee*, New York: W. W. Norton, 1995, 360.

p. 21 "Before long, a courier" Korn, 134.

p. 21 "That evening Lee" Korn, 135–136.

p. 22 That evening, having still" W. McFeely, *Grant*, New York: W. W. Norton, 1981, 217.

p. 22 "It was Palm Sunday" Korn, 140.

p. 22 "For a moment" Freeman, 201.

p. 23 "Lee talked with Longstreet" P. Alexander, "With Lee at Appomattox," *American History Illustrated* (Sept. 1987): 51.

p. 23 "At the start" McFeely p. 218.

p. 23 "The two armies" Catton, 378.

p. 23 "Off toward the south" Catton, 378–379.

p. 24 "All up and down" Catton p. 379.

p. 24 "One of General Ord's" Catton, 379–380.

p. 25 "The men were" Korn, 145.

p. 25 "At Grant's request" R. Wilson, "Meeting at the McLean House," *American History Illustrated* (Sept. 1987): p. 48.

p. 25 "Grant was motivated" Korn, 148.

p. 25 "It was difficult" Dowdey, 578.

p. 25 "Grant's reply must" Dowdey, 578.

p. 25 "Lee suggested that" Dowdey, 579.

p. 26 "When Lee read" Korn, 149.

p. 26 "This will have" Dowdey, 580.

p. 26 "Meanwhile, the Federal" Korn, 151–152.

p. 26 "The early halt" Freeman, 205.

p. 27 "Lee's misery made" Freeman, 205–206.

p. 27 "Lee had another" B. Catton, *The American Heritage New History of the Civil War*, New York: Viking, 1996, 571.

p. 27 "That night, after" Dowdey, 583.

p. 28 "Grant too was" Catton, 570.

p. 28 "On the morning" Korn, 153.

p. 28 "As the column" Korn, 155.

p. 29 "After the exchange" Korn, 155.

p. 29 "It was nearly" Trudeau, 150.

p. 31 "Booth had plotted" J. McPherson, *Ordeal by Fire*, New York: Alfred A. Knopf, 1982, 483.

p. 31 "John Wilkes Booth's" H. Williams, et al., *The Union Restored*, New York: Time Incorporated, 1963, 109.

p. 31 "The death of Lincoln" Williams, et al., 109–110.

p. 32 "On April 15, 1865" D. Donald, *Lincoln*, New York: Simon & Schuster, 1995, 567–568.

p. 32 "Everyone in Washington" McPherson, 485–486.

p. 33 "For more than a week" N. Trudeau, "Last Days of the Civil War," *Civil War Times Illustrated* (July–Aug. 1990): p. 64.

p. 33 "It had been decided" Trudeau, "Last", 66.

p. 33 "At 9:00 A. M." Trudeau, "Last," p. 66–67.

p. 33 "After the Grand Review" I. Tarbell "How the Union Army Was Disbanded," *Civil War Times Illustrated* (Dec. 1967): p. 5.

p. 34 "A long series of orders" Tarbell, 6.

p. 34 "But there were some" N. Trudeau, *Out of the Storm: The End of the Civil War, April–June, 1865*, Baton Rouge: Louisiana State University Press, 1994, 378–379.

p. 34 "Others worried about" Trudeau, *Storm*, 379.

p. 35 "Finally the Yankee" Trudeau, *Storm*, 380.

p. 35 "Most of the returning" A. Nevins, *The War for the Union: The Organized War to Victory, 1864–1865*, New York: Charles Scribner's Sons, 1971, 373.

p. 35 "For many Northern" R. Murphy, et al., *The Nation Reunited*, Alexandria: Time Life Books, 1987, 25.

p. 35 "Some returning veterans" Nevins, 374.

p. 36 "The majority of enlisted" Nevins, 374.

p. 36 "For the most terrible" Williams, et al., 127.

p. 36 "The government that" I. Tarbell, "Disbanding the Confederate Army," *Civil War Times Illustrated* (Jan. 1968): p. 13.

p. 36 "Penniless as they were" Tarbell, 13.

p. 37 "As the Rebels made" Trudeau, *Storm*, 382.

p. 37 "The South suffered" S. Foote, *The Civil War—Red River to Appomattox*, New York: Random House, 1974, 1041–1042.

p. 37 "The war had laid" Trudeau, *Storm*, 381.

p. 38 "Many Southerners lost" Trudeau, *Storm*, 381–382.

p. 38 "Once back home" Williams, et al., 127–128.

p. 38 "Through the North" P. Batty and P. Parish, *The Divided Union*, Topsfield, Massachusetts: Salem House Publishers, 1987, 198–199.

p. 39 "The direct physical" Williams, et al., 128.

p. 39 "Even before the fall" W. Davis, "Confederate Exiles," *American History Illustrated* (June 1970): p. 31.

p. 39 "Some of the exiles" Davis, 31.

p. 39 "When the war ended" Davis, 33.

p. 40 "Further to the south" Davis, 37.

p. 40 "Never before had so" Davis, 43.
p. 40 "The experience of war" P. Smith, *Trial by Fire*, New York: McGraw-Hill, 1982, 590–591.
p. 40 "The idealism that" Murphy, 25.
p. 40 "The society to which" Murphy, 25–26.
p. 41 "In 1865, the South" E. Foner, *Reconstruction, America's Unfinished Revolution*, New York: Harper & Row, 1988, 125.
p. 41 "Material losses in" Murphy, 26.
p. 41 "The railroad system" Murphy, 26.
p. 41 "Loathing the North" Murphy, 28.
p. 42 "To help the newly" H. Graff, *America, the Glorious Republic*, Boston: Houghton Mifflin, 1988, 446–447.
p. 42 "The bureau's critics" Foner, 168–169.
p. 43 "Many white Southerners" Murphy, 28.
p. 43 "For African Americans" Murphy, 29.
p. 43 "A persistent rumor" Murphy, 29.
p. 43 "Few blacks had the" Murphy, 29.
p. 43 "Despite the grim" Foner, 128.
p. 44 "Southern planters emerged" Foner, 128–129.
p. 44 "For those planters" Foner, 130–131.
p. 44 "Kindness proved to" Foner, 131.
p. 44 "Even as the Freedmen's Bureau" Graff, 447–448.
p. 45 "Many white Southerners" Graff, 443.
p. 45 "The political fate" J. Randall and D. Donald, *The Civil War and Reconstruction*, Lexington: D. C. Heath, 1969, 552.
p. 45 "Abraham Lincoln had" Graff, 444.
p. 46 "The most ardent advocates" Williams, 112.
p. 47 "Johnson had executed" Williams, 113.
p. 47 "Johnson's attempt at" Murphy, 33.

p. 47 "The Thirteenth Amendment" Graff, 448–449.
p. 47 "In the election of 1866" Graff, 449–450.
p. 48 "In 1867, the Radicals" Williams, 116.
p. 48 "Despite the passage" Graff, 450–451.
p. 49 "The trial began on" Williams, 117.
p. 49 "From 1868 until Reconstruction" Murphy, 63.
p. 49 "The realities, however," Murphy, 63–64.
p. 49 "Scalawags often have" Williams, 133.
p. 50 "When the warning failed" Murphy, 36.
p. 50 "The rise of the Klan" Graff, 454.
p. 50 "Between 1868 and 1871" E. Foner and O. Mahoney, *America's Reconstruction*, Baton Rouge: Louisiana State University Press, 1995, 122.
p. 51 "Despite the Grant administration's" Foner and Mahoney, 125.
p. 51 "Other factors weakened" Foner and Mahoney, 128.
p. 51 "Long before the end" Randall and Donald, 678–679.
p. 51 "The Reconstruction period" Randall and Donald, 535.
p. 52 "To many white" Randall and Donald, 535–536.
p. 52 "The Civil War" Smith, 994.
p. 53 "On Saturday afternoon" A. Hoehling, *After the Guns Fell Silent*, New York: Madison Books, 1990, 3.
p. 53 "One of Lee's aides" Hoehling, 4.
p. 54 "When Lee reached" Hoehling, 5.
p. 54 "Lee was not allowed" Hoehling, 5.
p. 54 "Lee was born" W. Davis, et al., *Civil War Journal: The Leaders*, Nashville: Rutledge Hill Press, 1997, 134.
p. 54 "Henry Lee's early years" Freeman, 5.

p. 54 "In the absence" Davis, et al., 134–136.

p. 55 "Lee was a studious" M. Grimsley, "Robert E. Lee: The Life and Career of the Master General," *Civil War Times Illustrated* (Nov. 1985): p. 14.

p. 55 "Lee's excellent West Point" Grimsley, 14–15.

p. 55 "As he commenced" Davis, et al., 136–138.

p. 56 "In the Spring of 1846" B. Sell, *Leaders of the North and South*, New York: Michael Friedman Publishing Group, 1996, 78.

p. 56 "On the other" E. Bonekemper III, *How Robert E. Lee Lost the Civil War*, Fredericksburg: Sergeant Kirkland's Press, 1997, 19.

p. 56 "After the excitement" Grimsley, 16.

p. 57 "While at West Point" Freeman, 44.

p. 57 "In October 1857" Grimsley, 16–18.

p. 57 "Lee had listened" Thomas, 37.

p. 58 "After Lincoln's election" Grimsley, 19.

p. 58 "In April 1862" Grimsley, 19.

p. 58 "In September 1862" Dowdey, 330.

p. 59 "Climaxing Lee's six" Davis, et al., 145.

p. 59 "In the spring of 1863" Freeman, 117–119.

p. 59 "Following Chancellorsville and" Bonekemper III, 104.

p. 60 "When Lee encountered" Bonekemper III, 107.

p. 60 "On the second day" Bonekemper III, 15.

p. 60 "After two days" Thomas, 296.

p. 60 "At one o'clock" Freeman, 133–134.

p. 61 "Lee rode out" Freeman, 134.

p. 61 "Lee in the evening" Thomas, 301.

p. 61 "On July 4, Lee" Freeman, 135.

p. 62 "Lee's army fought" H. Commager, et al., *America's Robert E. Lee*, Boston: Houghton Mifflin, 1951, 98–99.

p. 62 "It was Grant's inability" Commager, et al., 100–103.

p. 63 "Even with the war" J. Stanchak, "Behind the Lines," *Civil War Times Illustrated* (Nov. 1985): p. 52.

p. 63 "With the war" Commager, 106–108.

p. 63 "Lee made one last" Commager, 109–110.

p. 63 "On the afternoon" Davis, et al., 133–134.

p. 64 "When Grant arrived" McFeely, 219–220.

p. 64 "Lee did not attend" C. Dubowski, *Robert E. Lee and the Rise of the South*, Englewood Cliffs: Silver Burdett, 1991, 120–121.

p. 64 "The next morning" Dubowski, 121.

p. 64 "Once Lee was home" Grimsley, 47.

p. 65 "Robert E. Lee had reason" Grimsley, 47.

p. 65 "Lee's personal example" M. Marshall, "A Soldier No Longer," *Military History* (Dec. 1990): p. 12.

p. 65 "Knowing the eyes of" S. Horn, *The Robert E. Lee Reader*, New York: Bobbs-Merrill, 1949, 462.

p. 65 "On another occasion" Marshall, 13–14.

p. 65 "In applying for" Grimsley, 47.

p. 66 "Nothing could be greater" M. Preston, "Robert E. Lee After the War," *Civil War Times Illustrated* (Jan. 1969): p. 5.

p. 66 "Wherever Lee went" Marshall, 14.

p. 66 "A short time after" Preston, 5.

p. 66 "Lee was eager" Horn, 468–469.

p. 66 "Lee had been" Horn, 469.

p. 67 "At the next board" Grimsley, 47–48.

p. 67 "Lee considered the college" Grimsley, 48.

p. 67 "Washington College was" Preston, 6.

p. 68 "Lee quickly established" Freeman, 218.

p. 68 "Lee immediately embarked" Thomas, 377.

p. 68 "At Lexington, Lee" M. Fishwick, *Lee After the War*, New York: Dodd, Mead, 1963, 88–89.

p. 68 "Lee was unsparing" Horn, 476–477.

p. 69 "Lee set a goal" Freeman, 219.

p. 69 "Lee had discovered" C. Flood, *Lee, the Last Years*, Boston: Houghton Mifflin, 1981, 156.

p. 69 "Although Lee believed" Fishwick, 89.

p. 69 "This was the spirit" Fishwick, 106–107.

p. 69 "Lee continued to hear" Grimsley, 48–49.

p. 70 "To the widow" Grimsley, 49.

p. 70 "By the end of the second" Freeman, 220–221.

p. 70 "In November 1867" Grimsley, 50.

p. 70 "As a result" Freeman, 223.

p. 70 "On the afternoon" Freeman, 224–227.

p. 71 "Lee was known" Marshall, 10.

p. 71 "Lee's postwar policy" Marshall, 14.

p. 71 "Quietly he did his duty" Freeman, 234–235.

p. 72 "Word of Lee's illness" P. Stern, *Robert E. Lee, The Man and the Soldier*, New York: McGraw-Hill, 1963, 243.

p. 72 "During that last" Stern, 244.

p. 72 "Mary spoke of her husband" Davis, et al., 158.

p. 72 "Word of Lee's death" Stern, 247.

p. 72 "Funeral services were" Stern, 247.

p. 73 "After the war" R. Gragg, *The Illustrated Confederate Reader*, New York: Harper & Row, 1989, 224.

p. 73 "Robert E. Lee's life" Davis, et al., 159.

p. 74 "He was 5 feet 8 inches" A. McFall,

"Grant's Early War Days," *America's Civil War* (Nov. 1994): p. 34.

p. 74 "One Grant's closest" Davis, et al., 183.p. 75 "Grant was a mystery" Davis, et al., 184.

p. 75 "Grant was not much" Davis, et al., 184.

p. 75 "Ulysses' father decided" M. Grimsley, "Ulysses S. Grant," *Civil War Times Illustrated* (Jan.–Feb. 1990): p. 21–22.

p. 76 "As a cadet, Grant" Editors of American Heritage, *The American Heritage Pictorial History of the Presidents*, Great Neck, New Jersey: American Heritage, 456.

p. 76 "Grant put in" Grimsley, "Grant," p. 22.

p. 76 "Before reporting to his" Grimsley, "Grant," p. 22–23.

p. 77 "In the 1880s" G. Perret, *Ulysses S. Grant, Soldier and President*, New York: Random House, 1997, 39–40.

p. 77 "In 1843, Grant" Perret, 40.

p. 77 "Julia was five feet" Perret, 40.

p. 77 "In April 1844" Perret, 41.

p. 77 "Four years later" Perret, 43.

p. 78 "Grant was opposed" Perret, 51.

p. 78 "In March 1847" Grimsley, "Grant," p. 24.

p. 78 "Like Lincoln, Grant" Editors of American Heritage, 457.

p. 78 "When the war ended" Editors of American Heritage, 458.

p. 78 "After leaving the army" Perret, 107–108.

p. 79 "The capture of Fort Donelson" Grimsley, "Grant," p. 31.

p. 79 "Rumors and whispers" Perret, 202–208.

p. 80 "Grant continued his" Sell, 26.

p. 80 "After assuming the" Sell, 26–28.

p. 80 "After crossing the Rapidan" Perret, 306.

p. 80 "When the battle" Perret, 312.

p. 81   "Again Grant suffered" Sell, 28.

p. 81   "The spring campaign" Davis, et al., 199.

p. 81   "After Cold Harbor" Davis, et al., 199–200.

p. 81   "Grant's strategy to keep" Davis, et al., 200–201.

p. 81   "On April 2, Lee's" Perret, 358.

p. 81   "On the evening of" Perret, 358.

p. 83   "At Appomattox, Grant" Korn, 108.

p. 83   "As they rode away" Perret, 360.

p. 83   "Back at headquarters" Perret, 360.

p. 83   "The surrender at Appomattox" McFeely, 216.

p. 84   "No one ever mistook" Grimsley, "Grant," p. 47.

p. 84   "Grant possessed his full" Grimsley, "Grant," p. 47–48.

p. 84   "In some respects" Grimsley, "Grant," p. 48.

p. 84   "Grant made little" W. Nye, "Grant—Genius or Fortune's Child," *Civil War Times Illustrated* (June 1965): 8.

p. 84   "Some believe Grant" Nye, 8.

p. 85   "Loyalty was an important" Nye, 8.

p. 85   "The stories about" Grimsley, "Grant," p. 48.

p. 85   "After Appomattox, the" Editors of American Heritage, 459.

p. 85   "With Lincoln's death" Perret, 368.

p. 86   "In a short time" Davis, et al., 202.

p. 86   "In the 1866 Congressional" Grimsley, "Grant," p. 61.

p. 86   "While serving as interim" Grimsley, "Grant," p. 61–62.

p. 86   "For the first time" Foner, et al., 86.

p. 87   "In early 1868" Perret, 377–378.

p. 87   "The bitterness between" Davis, et al., 203.

p. 87   "'The office,' said Grant" Perret, 381.

p. 87   "When Grant took office" Perret, 412.

p. 87   "On March 30, 1870" Perret, 412.

p. 88   "The new legislation" Perret, 412.

p. 88   "The last of the enforcement" Perret, 412–413.

p. 88   "Grant's presidency was" Grimsley, "Grant," p. 63.

p. 88   "One scandal broke" L. Frost, *U. S. Grant Album*, New York: Bonanza Books, 1966, 160.

p. 89   "When Grant first heard" Frost, 160.

p. 89   "Although Grant was" Williams, 154.

p. 90   "In August 1879" Editors of American Heritage, 466.

p. 90   "Throughout the autumn" L. Poggiali, "The Death of U. S. Grant, and the Cottage on Mount McGregor," *Blue and Gray* (Feb. 1993): p. 61.

p. 90   "The book when completed" Poggiali, 61.

p. 90   "Grant left New York" Perret, 473–474.

p. 91   "A few days after" Perret, 477.

p. 91   "On July 16, 1885" Davis, et al., 207.

p. 91   "Without the writing" Editors of American Heritage, 466.

p. 92   "Even at the very end" Gragg, 221.

p. 92   "President Davis and" Gragg, 221.

p. 93   "Faced with the reality" Gragg, 221.

p. 93   "Jefferson Davis was born" R. Potter, *Jefferson Davis, Confederate President*, Austin: Steck Vaughn, 1994, 9–12.

p. 93   "Jefferson Davis's early" M. Grimsley, "We Will Vindicate the Right: An Account of the Life of Jefferson Davis," *Civil War Times Illustrated* (July–Aug. 1991): 32.

p. 93   "Jefferson's older brother" Grimsley, "Davis," p. 33.

p. 94   "In 1824, when Davis" Grimsley, "Davis," p. 33.

p. 94   "In 1828, Davis graduated" C. Canfield, *The Iron Will of Jefferson Davis,*

New York: Harcourt Brace Jovanovich, 1978, 9.

p. 94 "Davis began his military" Grimsley, "Davis," p. 33.

p. 94 "The marriage was" Grimsley, "Davis," p. 34.

p. 94 "Davis devoted himself" Davis, et al., 53–54.

p. 95 "From 1835 through 1843" Grimsley, "Davis," p. 34–35.

p. 95 "Like Sarah, Varina was" Canfield, 27–28.

p. 96 "When the Mexican War" Sell, 72–73.

p. 96 "In 1851, Davis resigned" Davis, et al., 57.

p. 96 "The issue of slavery" B. Wiley, "Jefferson Davis, an Appraisal," *Civil War Times Illustrated* (Apr. 1967): 8.

p. 96 "In 1860, Davis introduced" Grimsley, "Davis," p. 39.

p. 97 "Davis's tactic worked well" Grimsley, "Davis," p. 39.

p. 97 "As it turned out" Grimsley, "Davis," p. 39.

p. 97 "For all his protests" Davis, et al., 59–60.

p. 97 "When Davis returned" Sell, 73.

p. 97 "Varina did not like" Grimsley, "Davis," p. 41.

p. 97 "Davis spent the first" Grimsley, "Davis," p. 41.

p. 98 "The confederacy's aim" Grimsley, "Davis," p. 46.

p. 98 "Leonidas Polk was given" Davis, et al., 61–62.

p. 98 "Braxton Bragg had" Davis, et al., 62.

p. 98 "Davis's problems were not" Davis, et al., 63.

p. 98 "Davis had successes too" Davis, et al., 64.

p. 99 "In assembling his cabinet" Davis, et al., 64.

p. 99 "Initially the Confederate" Davis, et al., 64.

p. 99 "Davis ran the war" Grimsley, "Davis," p. 60.

p. 99 "The conduct of military" Grimsley, "Davis," p. 60.

p. 99 "As president, Davis was" Sell, 73.

p. 100 "With the help" P. King, *Jefferson Davis*, New York: Chelsea House Publishers, 1990, 90.

p. 100 "The early victory" King, 90–91.

p. 100 "Despite the huge losses" Davis, et al., 66.

p. 100 "It was the president" King, 93.

p. 100 "Tragedy visited Davis" Davis, et al., 68–69.

p. 101 "On March 31" W. Davis, *Jefferson Davis, the Man and His Hour*, New York: Harper Collins, 1991, 601–602.

p. 101 "Davis had expected" Grimsley, "Davis," p. 70.

p. 102 "A wanted man now" Canfield, 123.

p. 102 "Davis was still convinced" Grimsley, "Davis," p. 70.

p. 102 "When Davis met" Grimsley, "Davis," p. 71.

p. 102 "Davis left the meeting" W. Davis, 616–617.

p. 102 "On April 19, Davis" Canfield, 122.

p. 103 "Davis became a familiar" W. Davis, 621.

p. 103 "Davis arrived in Abbeville" W. Davis, 628–630.

p. 103 "On the morning of" Murphy, 21.

p. 104 "The war might be over" W. Davis, 640.

p. 104 "Weary and ill" Grimsley, "Davis," p. 71.

p. 104 "Davis was imprisoned" H. Strode, *Jefferson Davis, Tragic Hero*, New York: Harcourt Brace & World, 1964, 238.

p. 104 "Other indignities befell" Davis, et al., 73.

p. 104 "Davis's suffering, however" Davis, et al., 74.

p. 105 "Gradually, the terms" Grimsley, "Davis," p. 71.

p. 105 "As the months dragged" Davis, et al., 74.

p. 105 "Varina, in the meantime" Hoehling, 241.

p. 105 "As Davis's carriage" Hoehling, 241.

p. 105 "At the order from" Hoehling, 242.

p. 106 "Immediately after being" Strode, 301.

p. 106 "Davis was free now" Canfield, 129.

p. 106 "After Davis was released" B. Davis, 241–242.

p. 106 "Davis spoke of his" B. Davis, 242.

p. 106 "Shortly after, Davis" Grimsley, "Davis," p. 72.

p. 107 "Davis was finally" Grimsley, "Davis," p. 72–73.

p. 107 "The last dozen years" Potter, 114–115.

p. 107 "Immediately after the" Grimsley, "Davis," p. 73–74.

p. 107 "In the spring of 1886" M. Ballard, "Cheers for Jefferson Davis," *American History Illustrated* (May 1981): 9.

p. 107 "At ceremonies honoring him" Ballard, 10.

p. 108 "The next day" Ballard, 11.

p. 108 "On the morning" Ballard, 11.

p. 108 "Davis continued to tour" Ballard, 11.

p. 108 "Davis lived well into" Grimsley, "Davis," p. 14.

p. 108 "On December 6, 1889" Grimsley, "Davis," p. 74–75.

p. 109 "Despite Davis's unpardonable" Wiley, 9.

p. 109 "For better or worse" W. Davis, 690.

p. 109 "The myth that the South" S. Woodworth, *Jefferson Davis and His Generals*, 314.

p. 110 "Jefferson Davis remained" Davis, et al., 77.

p. 111 "Andrew Johnson once said" Editors of World Book Encyclopedia, *World Book of America's Presidents*, Chicago: World Book Encyclopedia, Inc. 1982, 106.

p. 112 "He went to work" H. Trefousse, *Andrew Johnson*, New York: W. W. Norton & Company, 1989, 24–25.

p. 112 "Although Andrew and Eliza" Trefousse, 28.

p. 112 "Johnson's political career" Editors of American Heritage, 430.

p. 112 "A Jacksonian Democrat" McPherson, 496.

p. 112 "Andrew Johnson was" Editors of American Heritage, 430.

p. 113 "An admirer of Thomas Jefferson" Editors of American Heritage, 430–431.

p. 113 "As governor, Johnson" Editors of American Heritage, 431.

p. 113 "Although Tennessee was" Trefousse, 123–127.

p. 114 "Between Lincoln's election" C. Smith, *Presidents of a Nation Divided*, Brookfield: Millbrook Press, 1993, 64.

p. 114 "In 1862, Grant took" Editors of American Heritage, 432.

p. 114 "In the summer of 1864" Trefousse, 179.

p. 114 "Lincoln and Johnson" C. Smith, 66.

p. 115 "After the victorious" Editors of American Heritage, 432.

p. 115 "Just a little more" C. Smith, 66.

p. 116 "On the evening" R. Baily, et al., *The Time-Life History of the Civil War*,

New York: Barnes & Noble, 1990, 410–411.

p. 116 "No inheritor of" Editors of American Heritage, 432.

p. 116 "Andrew Johnson was" Williams, 112.

p. 116 "Andrew and Eliza" Editors of World Book Encyclopedia, 108109.

p. 116 "As president, Johnson" McPherson, 496.

p. 117 "At first Johnson " Baily, 411.

p. 117 "When the news reached" Baily, 411–412.

p. 117 "In April of 1865" McPherson, 504.

p. 117 "The White House" McPherson, 504.

p. 117 "As the postassassination" McPherson, 496.

p. 118 "It didn't take" Editors of American Heritage, 432–433.

p. 118 "Johnson's dealings with" Foner and Mahoney, 33–34.

p. 118 "Congress also passed" Foner and Mahoney, 34.

p. 118 "Johnson was opposed" McPherson, 498.

p. 119 "Although Johnson initially" McPherson, 498.

p. 119 "Radical Republicans criticized" Editors of World Book Encyclopedia, 109.

p. 119 "Johnson's plan quickly" Foner and Mahoney, 80.

p. 119 "Early in 1866" Foner and Mahoney, 78–79.

p. 119 "Enraged, the Radical" Editors of American Heritage, 434.

p. 119 "In April 1866" Foner and Mahoney, 80.

p. 120 "In the fall" Foner and Mahoney, 81.

p. 120 "The conflict between" Editors of American Heritage, 435.

p. 120 "A bill to impeach" Editors of American Heritage, 435–436.

p. 120 "But the Supreme Court" Editors of American Heritage, 436.

p. 121 "Under the Constitution" Editors of American Heritage, 436.

p. 121 "On May 16, the Senate" Hoehling, 251.

p. 121 "Johnson received word" C. Smith, 72.

p. 121 "By one vote" Hoehling, 252.

p. 122 "Johnson had hoped" C. Smith, 84.

p. 122 "With Grant safely" Editors of American Heritage, 438.

p. 122 "Johnson was still" P. Smith, 802.

p. 122 "When Secretary Wells" Editors of American Heritage, 438.

p. 122 "Johnson managed to fire" Trefousse, 351–352.

p. 122 "Johnson was now" Trefousse, 353–354.

p. 123 "When he reached Tennessee" Trefousse, 354.

p. 123 "When Johnson moved back" C. Smith, 75.

p. 123 "In March, Johnson" Editors of American Heritage, 438.

p. 123 "When Andrew Johnson came" Trefousse, 375–377.

p. 123 "News of the former" Trefousse, 377–378.

p. 124 "With Johnson's passing" P. Smith, 802–803.

p. 124 "Johnson's behavior was" P. Smith, 803.

p. 124 "It was only fitting" C. Smith, 75.

p. 125 "Confederate Lieutenant General" R. DiNardo and A. Nofi, editors, *James Longstreet*, Conshohocken, Pennsylvania: Combined Publishing, 1998, 77–78.

p. 126 "Few figures from" J. Wert, "Lee's Old War-Horse," *American History* (March 1998): 17.

p. 126 "James Longstreet was" J. Wert, *General James Longstreet*, New York: Simon & Schuster, 1993, 19–20.

p. 126 "Young James, called Pete" Wert, *Longstreet*, 22.

p. 126 "On October 7, 1830" Wert, *Longstreet*, 22.

p. 127 "The academic demands" Wert, *Longstreet*, 29–30.

p. 127 "Longstreet was popular" Wert, *Longstreet*, 31.

p. 127 "Longstreet's first assignment" Davis, et al., 212.

p. 128 "On April 23, 1846" Davis, et al., 212–213.

p. 128 "Longsteet's wound was" Wert, *Longstreet*, 45–46.

p. 128 "After Republican Abraham Lincoln" Wert, *Longstreet*, 51.

p. 128 "For Longstreet the choice" Wert, *Longstreet*, 51–52.

p. 128 "When Alabama seceded" Wert, "War-Horse," p. 18.

p. 129 "The first time Longstreet" Davis, et al., 213–214.

p. 129 "When Longstreet reached" Davis, et al., 214–217.

p. 129 "Longstreet was a prudent" C. Dowdey, *Death of a Nation*, New York: Alfred A. Knopf, 1958, 9.

p. 130 "On March of 1862" Wert, "War-Horse," p. 18.

p. 130 "As the battle" H. Eckenrode and B. Conrad, *James Longstreet, Lee's War Horse*, Chapel Hill: University of North Carolina Press, 1986, 49.

p. 130 "Longstreet won praise" W. Piston, *Lee's Tarnished Lieutenant*, Athens: University of Georgia Press, 1987, 21.

p. 130 "Following the successful" Davis, et al., 217.

p. 130 "Lee and Longstreet" Piston, 22–23.

p. 131 "The first full year" J. Wert, "General James Longstreet," *Civil War Times Illustrated* (Nov.–Dec. 1993): p. 106.

p. 131 "Shortly after Second" J. Murfin, The Gleam of Bayonets, New York: Bonanza Books, 1965, 115–116.

p. 131 "Lee split the army" Piston, 25.

p. 131 "The fighting at Antietam" Piston, 25.

p. 132 "Lee's stand at Antietam" Wert, *Longstreet*, 202.

p. 132 "At Antietam, Longstreet" Wert, "War-Horse," p. 19.

p. 132 "As time moved on" Piston, 30.

p. 132 "By December 1862" Piston, 31.

p. 133 "At Fredericksburg, Longstreet" B. Catton, *Never Call Retreat*, New York: Pocket Books, 1965, 23.

p. 133 "As the war progressed" Dowdey, 166.

p. 133 "Although Longstreet was" Piston, 38.

p. 134 "When Jackson died" Dowdey, 167.

p. 134 "The campaign that followed" Dowdey, 170.

p. 134 "The campaign was" Piston, 45.

p. 134 "Unfortunately for Lee" Wert, "War-Horse," p. 22.

p. 134 "When Longstreet reached" Dowdey, 167.

p. 135 "Lee was in no mood" Davis, et al., 221–222.

p. 135 "Lee also felt" Sell, 96.

p. 135 "On the second day" Davis, et al., 222.

p. 135 "The following day" Wert, "War-Horse," p. 23.

p. 135 "Longstreet told General Lee" Davis, et al., 224–225.

p. 135 "Two hours before the attack" Davis, et al., 225.

p. 136 "Just before the attack" Davis, et al., 225.

p. 136 "Pickett's three brigades" Sell, 99.

p. 136 "Following the withdrawal" Davis, et al., 220.

p. 136 "After Gettysburg and" J. Wert, "Generals at Odds," *Military History* (Aug. 1994): 52.

p. 136 "Colonel Edward Porter Alexander" Wert, "Generals," p. 52.

p. 136 "Seventy-five years" Wert, *Longstreet*, 297.

p. 137 "In September, at" Wert, "War-Horse," p. 23.

p. 137 "In April of 1864" Wert, *Longstreet*, 387–388.

p. 137 "From the battlefield" Davis, et al., 227–228.

p. 137 "Longstreet was with Lee" Davis, et al., 228.

p. 138 "At Appomattox, Longstreet" G. Faeder, "The Best of Friends and Enemies" *Civil War Times Illustrated* (Oct. 1987): 23.

p. 138 "Longstreet's feelings toward" Davis, et al., 228.

p. 138 "After the surrender" Piston, 92.

p. 138 "Longstreet rode away" Wert, "War-Horse," p. 24.

p. 138 "Two months after" Piston, 95.

p. 138 "Longstreet made a speedy" Piston, 95–96.

p. 138 "In late October 1865" Wert, *Longstreet*, 408–409.

p. 138 "As businessmen and citizens" Wert, *Longstreet*, 410.

p. 139 "Southerners reacted to" Wert, *Longstreet*, 410–411.

p. 139 "On June 8, the" Wert, *Longstreet*, 412.

p. 139 "His words were" Wert, *Longstreet*, 412.

p. 139 "Longstreet's political naivete" Wert, *Longstreet*, 413.

p. 140 "In 1871–1872, Longstreet" D. Sanger and T. Hay, *James Longstreet*, Gloucester: Peter Smith, 1968, 352–359.

p. 140 "Longstreet's image continued" Sanger and Hay, 370–371.

p. 140 "After Lee's death" Wert, "War-Horse," p. 24.

p. 140 "The first public criticism" Dowdey, 168–169.

p. 140 "Much of Longstreet's time" Piston, 129–130.

p. 140 "After the war" G. Tucker, "Longstreet: Culprit or Scapegoat?" *Civil War Times Illustrated* (April 1962): 6.

p. 140 "Longstreet had proved" Piston, 130.

p. 140 "In 1875, Longstreet's brother" Wert, *Longstreet*, 417–418.

p. 140 "Longstreet's participation in Republican" Wert, *Longstreet*, 419.

p. 142 "As the years passed" Davis, et al., 229.

p. 142 "Old men get lonely" Wert, *Longstreet*, 425.

p. 142 "Longstreet canvassed for" Wert, *Longstreet*, 426.

p. 142 "By 1903, Longstreet" Wert, *Longstreet*, 426.

p. 143 "When Longstreet died" Wert, "Generals at Odds," *Military History* (Aug. 1994): 52.

p. 143 "On January 6, Longstreet's" Wert, *Longstreet*, 426–427.

p. 144 "November 16, 1864" O. Dunphy, "March to the sea," *America's Civil War* (July 1990): 43.

p. 144 "The March to the Sea" Dunphy, 43–44.

p. 145 "Sherman's father, Charles" J. Marszalek, *Sherman, a Soldier's Passion for Order*, New York: Vintage Books, 1993, 2–4.

p. 145 "Although Charles was" Marszalek, 4–5.

p. 145 "Cump Sherman spent" Marszalek, 5.

p. 145 "In June 1829" Marszalek, 6.

p. 145 "His father's sudden" Marszalek, 6–9.

p. 146 "Father Dominic Young" Marszalek, 9–10.

p. 146 "Although Thomas Ewing" Marszalek, 15.

p. 146 "Young Sherman was" Marszalek, 17.

p. 146 "At the military academy" A. Castel, "The Life of a Rising Son, Part I: The Failure" *Civil War Times Illustrated* (July 1979): 4.

p. 146 "One of Sherman's" Marszalek, 22–23.

p. 146 "After Sherman graduated" Marszalek, 23.

p. 147 "In an early letter" M. Fellman, *Citizen Sherman*, New York: Random House, 1995, 9–10.

p. 147 "In 1850, Sherman" Castel (Part I), 4–6.

p. 147 "As unfortunate as" Castel (Part I), 7.

p. 148 "On December 20, 1860" L. Lewis, *Sherman, Fighting Prophet*, New York: Harcourt Brace & World, 1958, 1.

p. 148 "The South has put" Lewis, 1–2.

p. 148 "Sherman returned to" Castel (Part I), 7.

p. 148 "After the Confederates" Castel (Part I), 7, 42.

p. 148 "Sherman was assigned" Castel (Part I), 42.

p. 149 "Late in August" Castel (Part I), 42.

p. 149 "Fearing attack by" Castel (Part I), 43.

p. 149 "Secretary of War Simon" Castel (Part I), 44.

p. 149 "Upon General Buell's" Castel (Part I), 45.

p. 150 "The newspapers again" Castel (Part I), 45.

P. 150 "On December 23, Halleck" Fellman, 102.

p. 150 "Starting in 1862" Castel (Part I), 46.

p. 150 "Under Grant, Sherman" A. Castel, "The Life of a Rising Son, Part II: The Subordinate," *Civil War Times Illustrated* (Aug. 1979): p. 15.

p. 151 "In Grant's report" Castel (Part II), 15.

p. 151 "As a result of" Castel (Part II), 16.

p. 151 "Sherman continued to" Castel (Part II), 20.

p. 151 "During the Visksburg" Sell, 35.

p. 151 "At the end of August" Fellman, 199–200.

p. 151 "In October 1863" Castel (Part II), 21.

p. 152 "Grant's plan for ending" A. Castel, "The Life of a Rising Son, Part III: The Conqueror" *Civil War Times Illustrated* (Oct. 1979): p. 10.

p. 152 "In May 1864" Castel (Part III), 10.

p. 152 "On May 2, two" Castel (Part III), 13.

p. 152 "Hood marched his army" Davis, et al., 335.

p. 152 "On November 15" Davis, et al., 335.

p. 153 "Sherman's March to" Davis, et al., 352.

p. 153 "Before Sherman started" Davis, et al., 353.

p. 153 "The army marched" Davis, et al., 358–360.

p. 153 "Along with Sherman's army" E. Miers, *The General Who Marched to Hell*, New York: Collier Books, 1951, 266–267.

p. 153 "Lincoln replied with" Dunphy, 49.

p. 154 "The extent to which" M. Grimsley, *The Hard Hand of War*, New York: Cambridge University Press, 1995, 199.

p. 154 "Sherman did little" Marszalek, 312–313.

p. 154 "All in all, Sherman" Grimsley, *Hard Hand*, 200.

p. 154 "By the end of" C. Roland, *An American Iliad*, Lexington: University Press of Kentucky, 1991, 242.

p. 154 "Sherman's men devastated" Lewis, 493.

p. 155 "Later reflecting on his" Davis, et al., 362–363.

p. 155 "While the Southerners" Davis, et al., 363.

p. 155 "At the beginning of April" J. McDonough and J. Jones, *War So Terrible*, New York: W. W. Norton, 1987, 323–324.

p. 155 "Sherman ordered all soldiers" McDonough and Jones, 324.

p. 155 "The next day" Marszalek, 344–345.

p. 156 "Sherman, who had vowed" Castel (Part III), 19.

p. 156 "Calling in reporters" T. Fleming, "The Big Parade," *The Civil War Chronicles* (Summer 1991): 60.

p. 156 "On May 23, the eastern" Fleming, 62.

p. 157 "Precisely at 9:00 A.M." Fleming, 63–64.

p. 157 "After Sherman passed" Fleming, 64.

p. 157 "In retaliation for" Castel (Part III), 19.

p. 157 "As soon as the war" O. Eisenchiml, "Sherman: Hero or War Criminal?" *Civil War Times Illustrated* (Jan. 1964): 35.

p. 157 "The time had come" Marszalek, 358.

p. 157 "Sherman's tumultuous reception" Marszalek, 361.

p. 157 "But the nation" Marszalek, 361–362.

p. 158 "Even in the South" Marszalek, 362.

p. 158 "Sherman's fame extended" Marszalek, 362–363.

p. 158 "With the Civil War" Fellman, 259–260.

p. 158 "The removal of" Fellman, 261.

p. 158 "Sherman admitted he" Fellman, 263.

p. 159 "Sherman never used" Fellman, 271–276.

p. 159 "On one occasion" Marszalek, 416.

p. 159 "During the postwar" Marszalek, 417.

p. 160 "Sherman knew many" Marszalek, 418.

p. 160 "Sherman enjoyed an" Fellman, 356–358.

p. 160 "In the early 1880s" Fellman, 358–362.

p. 161 "Her visit did not" Marszalek, 420.

p. 161 "Sherman made little" Marszalek, 421.

p. 161 "Being commanding general" Marszalek, 422.

p. 161 "Sherman believed that Grant" Marszalek, 424–425.

p. 162 "Some of Sherman's" C. Royster, *The Destructive War*, New York: Alfred A. Knopf, 1991, 375–376.

p. 162 "Old soldiers and their" B. Davis, *Sherman's March*, New York: Random House, 1980, 299–300.

p. 162 "Sherman opposed the" B. Davis, *Sherman's March*, 300.

p. 163 "Retirement brought major" Marszalek, 479–483.

p. 163 "By the time Sherman" Marszalek, 484–488.

p. 163 "General William Tecumseh Sherman" McDonough and Jones, 331.

P. 163 "Sherman lived to be" McDonough and Jones, 331–332.

p. 164 "General Johnston was" McDonough and Jones, 332.

p. 164 "William Tecumseh Sherman" Marszalek, 499 and XVIII.

p. 165 "One afternoon in May" C. Anders, *Fighting Confederates*, New York: Dorset Press, 1968, 67.

p. 165 "Suddenly, a bullet" Anders, 67.

p. 165 "When Johnston opened" Anders, 67.

p. 166 "Within a few minutes" G. Govan and J. Livingood, *A Different Valor*, New York: Bobbs-Merrill, 1956, 156.

p. 166 "Although Johnston's wounds" Anders, 68.

p. 166 "Johnston was the most" C. Symonds, *Joseph Johnston*, New York: W. W. Norton, 1992, 3.

p. 166 "Johnston's military career" R. Welch, Review of *Joseph Johnston: A Civil War Biography*, *America's Civil War* (Nov. 1993): 58.

p. 167 "Young Joseph, like" Govan and Livingood, 13.

p. 167 "Joseph's father and mother" Govan and Livingood, 13.

p. 167 "Joseph's mother gave" Govan and Livingood, 13–14.

p. 167 "In June, the two" Govan and Livingood, 14.

p. 167 "Although Cadet Johnston" Symonds, 19.

p. 168 "West Point was" Symonds, 19.

p. 168 "In 1830, the Regular" Symonds, 23.

p. 168 "By the time Johnston" Symonds, 24.

p. 168 "Johnston found his" A. Mapp, *Frock Coats and Epaulets*, Lanham, MD: Hamilton Press, 1963, 369.

p. 168 "In May 1832" Symonds, 25–27.

p. 169 "Johnston participated in" Symonds, 25–27.

p. 169 "Trouble with the Seminoles" Anders, 70–71.

p. 169 "Although he had" Anders, 71.

p. 169 "The war in Florida" Symonds, 43.

p. 169 "When Johnston returned" Symonds, 45.

p. 170 "Surrogate parenthood was" Govan and Livingood, 17.

p. 170 "Lydia was not beautiful" Symonds, 52.

p. 170 "In 1864, when Johnston" Anders, 71.

p. 170 "The voltigeurs were" Anders, 71.

p. 171 "Johnston was badly hurt" Anders, 71–72.

p. 171 "During the war" Symonds, 71.

p. 171 "In 1848, Johnston" Anders, 72.

p. 171 "In 1858, Johnston" Anders, 72.

p. 171 "The crisis over secession" Symonds, 94.

p. 171 "Windfield Scott pleaded" Anders, 72–73.

p. 172 "Johnston, however, felt" Anders, 73.

p. 172 "The trip south" Symonds, 97.

p. 172 "When the Virginia" Symonds, 97.

p. 172 "Lydia Johnston left" Symonds, 97.

p. 172 "In May, Johnston" J. Glatthaar, *Partners in Command*, New York: The Free Press, 1994, 97.

p. 172 "In this moment" Glatthaar, 98.

p. 173 "This charisma extended" Glatthaar, 98.

p. 173 "But Johnston had problems" Anders, 74.

p. 173 "Finally, after an exchange" Anders, 74.

p. 173 "From the outset" Anders, 75–76.

p. 174 "Shortly after nightfall" Glatthaar, 103–104.

p. 174 "The controversy over rank" Glatthaar, 104.

p. 174 "In addition to his" D. Bailey, *Forward to Richmond*, Alexandria: Time-Life Books, 1983, 78.

p. 174 "Johnston was genial" Bailey, *Forward*, 78–79.

p. 174 "Johnston, of course, was" Bailey, *Forward*, 79.

p. 175 "Over the next few" Glatthaar, 112–113.

p. 175 "Johnston repeatedly and" Welch, 58.

p. 175 "During the Peninsula" Woodworth, 178.

p. 175 "As the retreating" Woodworth, 178.

p. 175 "Under the threat" Anders, 84.

p. 175 "Lee was appointed" Anders, 84–85.

p. 176 "While recovering from" Symonds, 178–179.

p. 176 "Davis's confidence in Johnston" Woodworth, 178.

p. 176 "On November 12, 1862" Anders, 86.

p. 176 "Johnston arrived in" N. Boothe, *Great Generals of the Civil War*, New York: Gallery Books, 1986, 147–148.

p. 177 "When Grant attacked" Welsh, 62.

p. 177 "The fall of Vicksburg" Woodworth, 221.

p. 177 "By the end" A. Julian, "From Dalton to Atlanta," *Civil War Times Illustrated* (July 1964): p. 4.

p. 177 "Pleased with the" Anders, 90.

p. 177 "Johnston spent the winter" Anders, 95.

p. 177 "Johnston was not" Anders, 95.p. 177 "Just as he did" Glatthaar, 129–130.

p. 178 "Removing Johnston from" Woodworth, 303.

p. 178 "That was it." Glatthaar, 130.

p. 178 "The reaction to" Govan and Livingood, 320.

p. 178 "Before Johnston left" Govan and Livingood, 320–321.

p. 179 "For five months" Welch, 63.

p. 179 "The meeting was held" Symonds, 354.

p. 179 "Then, in his" Symonds, 354–355.

p, 179 "Davis's head was still" Symonds, 355.

p. 180 "Johnston suggested that" Symonds, 355.

p. 180 "On April 17" Symonds, 356.

P. 180 "Sherman originally offered" Symonds, 356.

p. 180 "A few days later" Symonds, 356.

p. 180 "On May 2, 1865" Symonds, 357.

p. 181 "Johnston's critics have" J. Luvaas, "Joseph Johnston," *Civil War Times Illustrated*, (Jan. 1966): 29–30.

p. 181 "Although the war" Symonds, 358.

p. 181 "Before Johnston took" Symonds, 359–360.

p. 181 "Johnston found temporary" Symonds, 360.

p. 181 "Johnston wrote to" Symonds, 360.

p. 182 "It was pretty clear" Symonds, 361.

p. 182 "Johnston's lengthy volume" Symonds, 362–364.

p. 182 "Hood was quick to" Symonds, 365.

p. 183 "Hood finished his book" Symonds, 366.

p. 183 "Johnston continued to" Symonds, 370.

p. 183 "When comparing the behavior" Symonds, 371.

p. 183 "Like most professional" Govan and Livingood, 388–389.

p. 183 "The spirited race" Govan and Livingood, 389–390.

p. 184 "Johnston was elected" Govan and Livingood, 390–391.

p. 184 "Soon after he left" Govan and Livingood, 391–392.

p. 184 "The Democratic party finally" Symonds, 378.

p. 184 "By the beginning" Symonds, 379.

p. 184 "Johnston lost his" Symonds, 380.

p. 185 "The very next month" Symonds, 380.

p. 185 "Johnston's duty as" Anders, 68.

p. 185 "This attitude was typical" Anders, 68–69.

p. 185 "Johnston's funeral was held" Symonds, 381.

p. 186 "He was an unimpressive" R. Morris, *Sheridan*, New York: Vintage Books, 1992, 1.

p. 187 "Sheridan was born" Morris, 10–11.

p. 187 "The exact location" T. Lewis, *The Guns of Cedar Creek*, New York: Harper & Row, 1988, 35–36.

p. 187 "At the age of ten" T. Lewis, 36.

p. 187 "Phil's childhood was" T. Lewis, 36.

p. 187 "School was not" Morris, 13–14.

p. 188 "Little Phil was" Morris, 14–15.

p. 188 "Sheridan recognized his" Morris, 17.

p. 188 "Sheridan, who had" T. Lewis, 38.

p. 188 "Sheridan's low class" T. Lewis, 38–39.

p. 189 "In November 1854" T. Lewis, 39.

p. 189 "Young Sheridan had" T. Lewis, 39–40.

p. 189 "By the spring" Morris, 39–40.

p. 189 "News of the firing" P. Sheridan, *The Personal Memoirs of P. H. Sheridan*, New York: De Capo Press, 1992, 65–66.

p. 189 "After the Union defeat" R. O'Connor, *Sheridan, the Inevitable*, Indianapolis: Bobbs-Merrill, 1953, 56–60.

p. 189 "As late as April 1862" Sheridan, 75–77.

p. 190 "A few days later" Sheridan, 84.

p. 190 "His first important" R. Weigley, "Philip Sheridan, a Personal Profile," *Civil War Times Illustrated* (July 1968): 8.

p. 190 "It was not a large" T. Lewis, 43.

p. 190 "When Sheridan reported" T. Lewis, 44.

p. 191 "In October, during" J. Street, *The Struggle for Tennessee*, Alexandria: Time-Life Books, 1985, 58.

p. 191 "In writing about" Street, 80–81.

p. 191 "After Perryville, General" Street, 124.

p. 191 "Eight months later" T. Lewis, 46–47.

p. 192 "The Union victory" Morris, 152.

p. 192 "In Chattanooga, Sheridan" Davis, et al., 338.

p. 192 "Their disagreement came" Perret, 314–315.

p. 192 "Meade blamed Sheridan" Perret, 316.

p. 193 "Meade went to see" Perret, 316.

p. 193 "By nightfall, Sheridan" Perret, 316.

p. 193 "Sheridan retained all" Davis, et al., 340.

p. 193 "With his victory" Morris, 183.

p. 193 "Grant did not share" Davis, et al., 340.

p. 194 "Grant hoped to close" Morris, 184.

p. 194 "Sheridan moved cautiously" Davis, et al., 314–342.

p. 194 "The South, with" T. Lewis, 59.

p. 194 "The middle of October" T. Lewis, *The Shenandoah in Flames*, Alexandria: Time-Life Books, 1987, 153.

p. 195 "Once his preparation" T. Lewis, *Flames*, 153–154.

p. 195 "The battle cost" B. Catton, *American Heritage*, 499.

p. 195 "The Battle of Cedar Creek" Davis, et al., 342.

p. 195 "With the full" Davis, et al., 344.

p. 195 "Sheridan, Ord, and other" O'Connor, 270–271.

p. 195 "After Lee and Grant" Foote, 950.

p. 196 "Sheridan's contributions to" Morris, 258.

p. 196 "Although the war" Morris, 269.

p. 196 "In March of 1867" Morris, 285–287.

p. 197 "For the next few months" Morris, 287–288.

p. 197 "Troops were sent" Morris, 288.

p. 197 "When Sheridan learned" Sheridan, 434–435.

p. 197 "Sheridan continued to be" Morris, 289

p. 198 "Finally on May 24" Morris, 289–291.

p. 198 "Alarmed by Sheridan's" Morris, 292–293.

p. 198 "Meanwhile in Washington" Morris, 293–295.

p. 198 "Sheridan's closest admirers" Morris, 295–296.

p. 199 "After nearly two" O'Connor, 294–295.

p. 199 "In 1867, public opinion" O'Connor, 295–296.

p. 199 "The Department of" Morris, 300.

p. 199 "Sheridan found that" Morris, 300.

p. 199 "Not all western troops" Morris, 301.

p. 200 "The Indian warrior" Morris, 301.

p. 200 "In July 1868" O'Connor, 298.

p. 200 "The Indian tribes" O'Connor, 299.

p. 200 "As always, Sheridan" O'Connor, 301–302.

p. 200 "By November 15, 1868" O'Connor, 302–303.

p. 201 "Despite the surprise attack" Morris, 323.

p. 201 "In November 1868," O'Connor, 306–307.

p. 201 "In the fall of 1869" Morris, 326.

p. 201 "Baker's attack on" Morris, 326.

p. 201 "The Marias massacre" Morris, 327.

p. 202 "During the controversy" Morris, 328.

p. 202 "Sheridan's frontier remained" O'Connor, 310.

p. 202 "Sheridan returned to" O'Connor, 312–314.

p. 202 "His troops patrolled" O'Connor, 314.

p. 202 "Palmer took the matter" O'Connor, 314–315.

p. 203 "Sheridan made frequent" O'Connor, 325.

p. 203 "When gold was discovered" Morris, 348–349.

p. 203 "In the midst" O'Connor, 330.

p. 203 "As the Indians" J. Crutchfield, et al., *Legends of the Wild West*, Lincolnwood, : Publications International, 1995, 228.

p. 203 "Once back in Chicago" O'Connor, 333–334.

p. 204 "For the next" O'Connor, 337.

p. 204 "In June of 1876" O'Connor, 339–340.

p. 204 "News of the massacre" O'Connor, 341.

p. 204 "In July 1877" Morris, 367–368.

p. 205 "Sheridan found himself" Morris, 371.

p. 205 "In 1882, during" G. Ward, *The West, An Illustrated History*, Boston: Little Brown, 1996, 406.

p. 205 "At least three times" O'Connor, 349.

p. 205 "Sheridan's subordinates found" O'Connor, 350.

p. 205 "In the spring of 1888" T. Lewis, 305.

p. 206 "Sheridan was eulogized" O'Connor, 356–357.

p. 207 "Nathan Bedford Forrest" Davis, et al., 373.

p. 207 "Forrest was a hero" Davis, et al., 373.

p. 208 "Nathan Bedford Forrest" M. Grimsley, "Millionaire Rebel Raider," *Civil War Times Illustrated* (Sept.–Oct. 1993).

p. 208 "Processing only six" J. Wyeth, *That Devil Forrest*, Baton Rouge:

Louisiana State University, 1989, 554–555.

p. 208 "Far from being perfect" J. Hurst, *Nathan Bedford Forrest*, New York: Alfred A. Knopf, 1993, 9.

p. 208 "Stories of Forrest's" Hurst, 15–16.

p. 209 "The women turned" Hurst, 15–17.

p. 209 "Procuring the minister" Hurst, 17.

p. 209 "Forrest's response was" B. Wills, *A Battle From the Start: The Life of Nathan Bedford Forrest*, New York: Harper-Collins, 1992, 25.

p. 209 "Nathan Bedford Forrest" Grimsley, "Millionaire," p. 61.

p. 209 "Like many children" Davis, et al., 377.

p. 210 "When he was twenty-four" Davis, et al., 378.

p. 210 "Memphis was a boom town" Davis, et al., 375–376.

p. 210 "Forrest quickly saw" Davis, et al., 316.

p. 210 "Although slave trading" Davis, et al., 379–380.

p. 211 "When Tennessee seceded" Grimsley, "Millionaire," p. 63.

p. 211 "Forrest's cavalry was" Grimsley, "Millionaire," p. 63–64.

p. 211 "The *Memphis Avalanche*" Davis, et al., 380.

p. 211 "The first significant" J. Ward, "Forrest's First Fight," *America's Civil War*, (Mar. 1993): 51–56.

p. 211 "During the skirmish" Anders, 111.

p. 212 "During the war" Grimsley, "Millionaire," p. 65.

p. 212 "Although Forrest was" Anders, 112–113.

p. 212 "On February 14" Davis, et al., 380–381.

p. 212 "That night, General Floyd" Grimsley, "Millionaire," p. 68.

p. 213 "Behind them, at Fort" Grimsley, "Millionaire," p. 68.

p. 213 "Forrest's determination at" D.

Nevin, *The Road to Shiloh*, Alexandria: Time-Life Books, 1983, 152.

p. 213 "After July 1862" W. Brooksher and D. Snider, "Surrender or Die," *Military History* (Feb. 1985): 29–33.

p. 213 "There was, however" Wills, 77.

p. 214 "There was another" Wyeth, 77–78.

p. 214 "Deception continued to" R. Domer, "Rebel Rout of Streight's Raiders," *America's Civil War* (Sept. 1996): p. 36.

p. 214 "The two men met" M. Grimsley, "The Great Deceiver," *Civil War Times Illustrated* (Nov.–Dec. 1993): p. 73.

p. 214 "Forrest intimidated and" Davis, et al., 384.

p. 214 "Following the Battle" Davis, et al., 384–385.

p. 215 "Forrest continued to" R. Rogge, "Devil at the Crossroads," *America's Civil War* (Sept. 1990): 44.

p. 215 "Forrest's victory over" R. Domer, "Sooy Smith and 'That Devil Forrest,'" *America's Civil War* (May 1998): 40.

p. 215 "Forrest's most controversial" Grimsley, "Deceiver," p. 37.

p. 215 "The fort commander" Davis, et al., 384–386.

p. 216 "The massacre galvanized" G. Tucker, "Forrest—Untutored Genius of War," *Civil War Times Illustrated* (June 1964): 36.

p. 216 "On May 2, 1864" M. Grimsley, "Leader of the Klan," *Civil War Times Illustrated* (Jan.–Feb. 1994): 41, 63.

p. 217 "With Forrest still" Rogge, 49.

p. 217 "Forrest continued to" Davis, et al., 388–389.

p. 217 "On May 4, Forrest" Grimsley, "Leader," p. 66.

p. 217 "On may 9, Forrest" Grimsley, "Leader," p. 68.

p. 217 "As a businessman" Davis, et al., 389–390.

p. 217 "Forrest worked diligently" Davis, et al., 391.

p. 218 "Like Lee, Forrest" Grimsley, "Leader," p. 68.

p. 218 "Bedford Forrest, for" Wills, 323–324.

p. 218 "At the same time" Wills, 325–326.

p. 218 "Finally, on March 31" Wills, 327–328.

p. 219 "Word of the altercation" Wills, 329.

p. 219 "In April, Forrest" Wills, 330.

p. 219 "With white supremacy" Davis, et al., 390.

p. 219 "Forrest was initiated" Wills, 336.

p. 220 "During the summer" Grimsley, "Leader," p. 69.

p. 220 "Forrest's tenure with" Grimsley, "Leader," p. 69–70.

p. 220 "In 1871–1872, General" Wyeth, 551.

p. 220 "In Forrest's last years" Grimsley, "Leader," p. 72.

p. 221 "Forrest's health was" Wyeth, 551.

p. 221 "As he approached death" Wills, 377–378.

p. 221 "The man who had" Wills, 378.

p. 221 "One of the last men" Davis, et al., 391.

p. 221 "He was eulogized" Davis, et al., 392.

p. 222 "At the grave" Hurst, 380–381.

p. 222 "But everyone did not" Hurst, 381–382.

p. 222 "In 1905, the city" Wills, 380.

p. 223 "Few Civil War" Davis, et al., 108.

p. 224 "George's father traveled" S. Sears, *George B. McClellan, the Young Napoleon*, New York: Ticknor & Fields, 1988, 2–3.

p. 224 "Little is recorded" Sears, *Young Napoleon*, 4.

p. 224 "George was legally" J. Waugh, *The Class of 1846*, New York: Warner Books, 1994, 13–14.

p. 224 "The general perception" Davis, et al., 108–109.

p. 224 "As a cadet" Sears, *Young Napoleon*, 12.

p. 225 "There was no doubt" Waugh, 66.

P. 225 "The Mexican War" Waugh, 73.

p. 225 "McClellan and his classmates" Waugh, 74–75.

p. 225 "In Mexico, McClellan" Davis, et al., 109–110.

p. 225 "From Mexico City" Sears, *Young Napoleon*, 24.

p. 226 "Following the war" Sears, *Young Napoleon*, 42.

p. 226 "Ellen had a different" Sears, *Young Napoleon*, 42.

p. 226 "McClellan quickly earned" Sears, *Young Napoleon*, 43–44.

p. 226 "McClellan put to use" Davis, et al., 111.

p. 226 "Despite McClellan's success" Sears, *Young Napoleon*, 51.

p. 227 "McClellan kept in touch" Sears, *Young Napoleon*, 60–61.

p. 227 "One suitor who" J. Robertson, *General A. P. Hill, The Story of a Confederate Warrior*, New York: Random House, 1987, 27–28.

p. 227 "Quickly, Mrs. Marcy took" Robertson, 28–29.

p. 227 "During the war" W. Hassler, *A. P. Hill: Lee's Forgotten General*, Chapel Hill: The University of North Carolina Press, 1957, 22.

p. 228 "George and Ellen" Sears, *Young Napoleon*, 62–63.

p. 228 "A month after his" Sears, *Young Napoleon*, 64.

p. 228 "In 1860, with" Sears, *Young Napoleon*, 66–67.

p. 228 "McClellan quickly took" Davis, et al., 112.

p. 228 "On July 21, 1861" Davis, et al., 113.

p. 229 "McClellan might have" H. Williams, *Lincoln and His Generals*, New York: Alfred Knopf, 1952, 24–25.

p. 229 "In the Western Virginia" Williams, 25.

p. 229 "At first, Lincoln felt" R. Reeder, *The Northern Generals*, New York: Duell, Sloan & Pearce, 1964, 20.

p. 230 "McClellan immediately faced" Davis, et al., 113.

p. 230 "McClellan set up schools" B. Catton, *Mr. Lincoln's Army*, New York: Doubleday & Co. 1951, 68.

p. 230 "McClellan felt that" Davis, et al., 115–116.

p. 230 "The pressure to move" Davis, et al., 118.

p. 230 "McClellan had other" Davis, et al., 118.

p. 231 "McClellan's contempt for" Reeder, 21.

p. 231 "The Peninsula Campaign" Davis, et al., 121–122.

p. 231 "In the Battle" S. Sears, "McClellan vs. Lee: The Seven-Day Trial," *Military Quarterly* (Autumn 1988): 11–12.

p. 232 "McClellan, unable to" Davis, et al., 121–123.

p. 232 "General McClellan knew" S. Sears, *To the Gates of Richmond, The Peninsula Campaign*, New York: Ticknor & Fields, 1992, 347.

p. 232 "McClellan continued to" Sears, *Gates*, 347.

p. 232 "After McClellan's failure" Davis, et al., 124.

p. 232 "On September 1, Lincoln" S. Sears, "Lincoln and McClellan," *Lincoln's Generals*, Ed. G. Boritt, New York: Oxford University Press, 1994, 40.

p. 233 "But Lincoln stood" R. Luthin, *The Real Abraham Lincoln*, Englewood Cliffs: Prentice Hall, 1960, 329.

p. 233 "When the Union army" A. Castel, "George McClellan: 'Little Mac,'" *Civil War Times Illustrated* (May 1974): p. 9.

p. 233 "Lee's strategy worked" Castel, "Little Mac," p. 9–10.

p. 233 "With this important" Castel, "Little Mac," p. 10.

p. 233 "The Antietam campaign" Castel, "Little Mac," p. 10.

p. 234 "Antietam was one" Castel, "Little Mac," p. 10.

p. 234 "President Lincoln used" J. Stokesbury, *A Short History of the Civil War*, New York: William Morrow, 1995, 118.

p. 234 "McClellan was enough" Sears, "Lincoln and McClellan," p. 43.

p. 234 "Lincoln was very" Castel, "Little Mac," p. 11.

p. 234 "Ten days after" Davis, et al., 126.

p. 235 "Lincoln had seen" Sears, *Young Napoleon*, 339.

p. 235 "The tragedy of" Davis, et al., 125.

p. 235 "On November 9, General" Sears, *Young Napoleon*, 341.

p. 236 "The next morning" Sears, *Young Napoleon*, 341–343.

p. 236 "Once the Union's best" Sears, *Young Napoleon*, 344.

p. 236 "The six weeks" Sears, *Young Napoleon*, 348.

p. 236 "Even more noticeable" Sears, *Young Napoleon*, 349–350.

p. 237 "Lacking any official" Sears, *Young Napoleon*, 350–354.

p. 237 "When the time" Sears, *Young Napoleon*, 354.

p. 237 "In the spring" Sears, *Young Napoleon*, 361.

p. 237 "When it became" Sears, *Young Napoleon*, 361–362.

p. 238 "In one of his" Sears, *Young Napoleon*, 363.

p. 238 "As McClellan's prominence" Sears, *Young Napoleon*, 363–364.

p. 238 "In July 1864, General" Sears, *Young Napoleon*, 366–367.

p. 238 "McClellan's views on" McPherson, 441.

p. 238 "The convention bridged" McPherson, 441.

p. 238 "McClellan's candidacy appeared" Luthin, 553.

p. 239 "The letter satisfied" McPherson, 441.

p. 239 "In the main issue" Randall and Donald, 478–479.

p. 239 "By the end of" Stokesbury, 280.

p. 239 "In November the" Davis, et al., 130.

p. 239 "Addressing his supporters" Sears, *Young Napoleon*, 386.

p. 239 "Soon after the election" Sears, *Young Napoleon*, 391.

p. 240 "After returning to" Sears, *Young Napoleon*, 395.

p. 240 "Early in October 1885" Sears, *Young Napoleon*, 400–401.

p. 240 "Messages of condolence" Sears, *Young Napoleon*, 401.

p. 240 "Obituaries appeared in" Sears, *Young Napoleon*, 401.

p. 241 "No other Union general" Sell, 38.

p. 242 "At midnight in" W. Groom, *Shrouds of Glory*, Atlantic Monthly Press, 1995, 5–6.

p. 243 "Historians do not" Groom, 6.

p. 243 "Late in the" R. McMurry, *John Bell Hood and the War For Southern Independence*, Lincoln: University of Nebraska Press, 1982, 1.

p. 243 "The decision to" Groom, 22–24.

p. 243 "The news that Hood" Groom, 24.

p. 243 "Hood recognized the" Groom, 24–25.

p. 244 "John Bell Hood" McMurry, 1.

p. 244 "Five months later" McMurry, 1.

p. 244 "John Bell Hood was" J. Dyer, *The Gallant Hood*, New York: Smithmark Publishers, 1995, 21–22.

p. 244 "As an adolescent" Dyer, 23.p. 245 "Hood, awed by his" T. Buell, *The Warrior Generals, Combat Leadership in the Civil War*, New York: Crown Publishers, 1997, 9.

p. 245 "In September of" McMurry, 8–9.

p. 245 "The greatest influence" McMurry, 10.

p. 245 "But Hood's relationship" McMurry, 10.

p. 246 "The cadet corps" McMurry, 10–11.

p. 246 "Hood's initial assignment" G. Patterson, "John Bell Hood," *Civil War Times Illustrated* (Feb. 1971): p. 12.

p. 246 "In 1857, during" Patterson, 12.

p. 246 "For his brief" Groom, 28–29.

p. 247 "In the spring" Groom, 29.

p. 247 "Hood was in his" Buell, 53.

p. 247 "The companies were" Groom, 30.

p. 247 "Hood had little" Patterson, 14–15.

p. 248 "On May 7" Groom, 30.

p. 248 "Hood's daring action" Gilbert and Livingood, 127.

p. 248 "The Texans responded" Buell, 93.

p. 248 "Hood began to" Patterson, 15.

p. 249 "Hood emerged from" Groom, 30–31.

p. 249 "After the victory" Buell, 113.

p. 249 "When Lee came" Groom, 31.

p. 249 "After the conference" D. Davis, "Tumult in the Gaps," *America's Civil War* (Nov. 1988): 31.

p. 249 "Hood's star soared" Patterson, 16.

p. 250 "Hood's division was" Buell, 17.

p. 250 "When the fighting" Patterson, 10.

p. 250 "The action on the" McMurry, 60.

p. 250 "Hood also gained" Groom, 34.

p. 250 "After Antietam, McClellan" Wert, *Longstreet*, 223.p. 250 "During the winter" M. Chesnut, *Mary Chesnut's*

Civil War, New Haven: Yale University, 1981, 441.

p. 251 "All through the spring" Groom, 37.

p. 251 "Hood expressed his grief" Buell, 219.

p. 251 "Gettysburg was to be" Buell, 231.

p. 252 "Hood rode off" Buell, 231.

p. 252 "While Hood recovered" Patterson, 18.

p. 252 "On September 20, the joy" Patterson, 18.

p. 252 "Hood returned to Richmond" Patterson, 18–19.

p. 253 "Still Hood persisted" R. Morris, "John Bell Hood" *America's Civil War* (Sept. 1988): 6.

p. 253 "Hood was not" Morris, "Hood," p. 6.

p. 253 "Hood spent the winter" McMurry, 81.

p. 253 "Although Hood's love" Buell, 349.

p. 253 "Undoubtedly, Hood and Davis" McMurry, 87.

p. 253 "Common sentiment among" Buell, 349.

p. 254 "The pain in Hood's" J. Keenan, "The Gallant Hood of Texas," *America's Civil War* (Mar. 1994): 43–44.

p. 254 "Before Hood left" Symonds, 264.

p. 254 "Patience with Johnston" P. Nobbitt, "Confederate Breakout Attempt at Peachtree Creek," *America's Civil War* (Sept. 1998): 56–57.

p. 255 "Some of President" Nobbitt, 57.

p. 255 "Davis, knowing that" R. Neul, "Battle Most Desperate and Bloody," *America's Civil War* (Jan. 1995): 31.

p. 255 "When learning Johnston" Patterson, 20.

p. 255 "The news of Johnston's" Neul, 31.

p. 255 "If anyone was pleased" W. Davis, et al., *Civil War Journal: The Battles*, Nashville: Rutledge Press, 1998, 433–434.

p. 255 "Sherman's army and corps" Neul, 32.

p. 256 "Hood, the new" Nobbitt, 57.

p. 256 "Sherman did not" W. Sword, "The Other Stonewall," *Civil War Times Illustrated* (Feb. 1998): p. 38.

p. 256 "Again he failed" Buell, 395.

p. 256 "The pursuit of Hood's" J. Keenan, "Fighting with Forrest in Tennessee Winter," *America's Civil War* (Nov. 1995): 72.

p. 256 "A bandaged Tennessee" Foote, 706.

p. 257 "Hood did the only" Randall and Donald, 523.

p. 257 "Hood returned to Richmond" Patterson, 20.

p. 257 "Mrs. Chesnut continued" Chesnut, 708.

p. 257 "On February 7" McMurry, 185–188.

p. 257 "Trouble with another" McMurry, 188.

p. 258 "When Hood went" McMurry, 188.

p. 258 "In June, a depressed" McMurry, 192.

p. 258 "In the winter of" McMurry, 193–195.

p. 259 "On April 13" McMurry, 195.

p. 259 "Very little in known" McMurry, 195–196.

p. 259 "Hood's business provided" McMurry, 196.

p. 259 "Hood was very active" McMurry, 197.

p. 259 "In 1874, Johnston's book" McMurry, 198–200.

p. 260 "In 1875, Hood's" McMurry, 200.

p. 260 "Hood returned to" Keenan, 48.

p. 260 "Hood's friends decided" McMurry, 203.

p. 260 "Hood's memory would" Patterson, 21.

p. 261 "Hood proved to be" McMurry, 190–191.

p. 262 "He seemed an unlikely" Davis, et al., 419.

p. 262 "Most believed that" Davis, et al., 420.

p. 262 "The lofty dreams" Davis, et al., 421.

p. 263 "Joshua, called Lawrence" W. Wallace, *Soul of the Lion*, Gettysburg: Stan Clark Military Books, 1960, 17–18.p. 263 "Lawrence's mother was Sarah" Wallace, 18–19.

p. 263 "Lawrence's mother was altogether" Wallace, 19.

p. 263 "Joshua and Sarah" M. Perry, *Conceived in Liberty*, New York: Viking Press, 1997, 41–42.

p. 264 "Young Chamberlain was" Davis, et al., 421.

p. 264 "But life was not" Wallace, 20.

p. 264 "Joshua sent Lawrence" Wallace, 21.

p. 264 "By the end of" Wallace, 22.

P. 264 "Lawrence's academic record" Wallace, 23.

p. 265 "It was at" Wallace, 27.

p. 265 "With his marriage" Wallace, 28.

p. 265 "Having decided that" Wallace, 29.

p. 265 "Chamberlain remained at" Perry, 100.

p. 265 "During his Bowdoin" Davis, et al., 422–423.

p. 266 "Lawrence watched the war" Perry, 118.

p. 266 "The Bowdoin people" Davis, et al., 423.

p. 266 "Governor Israel Washburn" Wallace, 36.

p. 267 "Despite Chamberlain's patriotism" Perry, 141.

p. 267 "The colonelcy of" Davis, et al., 424–425.

p. 267 "In September 1862" Davis, et al., 425.

p. 267 "The 20th Maine" Davis, et al., 426–427.

p. 267 "At around three o'clock" Perry, 187.

p. 268 "The 20th Maine moved" Perry, 188.

p. 268 "Chamberlain and his" Davis, et al., 427.

p. 268 "The 20th Maine stayed" Perry, 188.

p. 268 "By the spring" Davis, et al., 429.

p. 268 "On July 1, 1863" D. Cross, "Mantled in Fire or Smoke," *America's Civil War* (Jan. 1992): 40.

p. 269 "Advancing against them" Cross, 41.

p. 269 "Chamberlain had sustained" Davis, et al., 431.

p. 269 "The sight of two hundred" Davis, et al., 431.

p. 269 "By the time" R. Pindell, "The 20th Maine," *Civil War Time Illustrated* (Feb. 1983): 19.

p. 269 "Chamberlain viewed war" Pindell, 19–20.

p. 269 "Taking over a brigade" Davis, et al., 433–434.

p. 270 "Defensive fire from" K. O'Brien, "Personality - Joshua Chamberlain," *Military History* (Aug. 1996): 72.

p. 270 "The attack failed" Davis, et al., 435.

p. 270 "After lingering near" O'Brien, 72.

p. 270 "By March, Chamberlain" Wallace, 144.

p. 271 "As Chamberlain slowly" Wallace, 145.

p. 271 "Chamberlain had quite" Wallace, 149.

p. 271 "Chamberlain had little" Wallace, 149–150.

p. 271 "On March 31, Chamberlain" O'Brien, 72.

p. 271 "Chamberlain continued to" Davis, et al., 439.

p. 272 "After Lee's surrender" Perry, 296.
p. 272 "The morning of April 12" Korn, 153.
p. 272 "Chamberlain ordered his" Korn, 155.
p. 272 "After the exchange" Korn, 155.
p. 272 "On the morning" Davis, et al., 435.
p. 272 "When the war" Davis, et al., 441.
p. 273 "During the year" Perry, 315–319.
p. 273 "Chamberlain and his wife" Perry, 315.
p. 273 "Chamberlain went on" Perry, 315–316.
p. 273 "Chamberlain's opponent in" Perry, 333.
p. 273 "Fannie was not happy" Perry, 333–334.
p. 274 "Chamberlain enjoyed being" Perry, 338.
p. 274 "She took no action" Davis, et al., 442.
p. 275 "Despite Chamberlain's rebuke" Perry, 353.
p. 275 "After his four years" Wallace, 230–235.
p. 275 "The next academic year" Wallace, 237.
p. 275 "When spring came" Wallace, 237–238.
p. 276 "When Chamberlain learned" Wallace, 238–239.
p. 276 "The revolt at Bowdoin" Wallace, 240.
p. 276 "In 1876, Democrat" Perry, 361–362.
p. 277 "At Bowdoin, Chamberlain" Wallace, 242–243.
p. 277 "Chamberlain was indeed" Wallace, 246.
p. 277 "Although Chamberlain recovered" Wallace, 247.
p. 277 "While president of Bowdoin" Perry, 390.

p. 278 "Chamberlain then threw" Perry, 390–392.
p. 278 "In 1885, Ulysses Grant" Perry, 393.
p. 278 "Chamberlain had good" Perry, 394.
p. 278 "Before his testimony" Perry, 394.
p. 279 "After Grant's funeral" Perry, 396.
p. 279 "In 1888 and 1889" Perry, 398.
p. 279 "In the latter part" Wallace, 288–289.
p. 279 "In March, Chamberlain" Wallace, 292.
p. 279 "In March 1900" Wallace, 295.
p. 280 "The position allowed" Davis, et al., 442.
p. 280 "During the Summer" Perry, 421.
p. 280 "During Chamberlain's last days" Perry, 422, 424.
p. 280 "President Hyde of Bowdoin" Wallace, 311–312.
p. 281 "No single battalion" J. Wert, *Mosby's Rangers*, New York: Simon & Schuster, 1990, Cover.p. 282 "John Singleton Mosby" Wert, *Rangers*, 25–26.
p. 282 "On October 3, 1850" K. Siepel, *Rebel, The Life and Times of John Singleton Mosby*, New York: De Capo Press, 1983, 25.
p. 282 "In the course" V. Jones, *Ranger Mosby*, McLean: EPM Publications, 1944, 21.
p. 282 "Mosby was arrested" Wert, *Rangers*, 27.
p. 282 "Mosby served nearly" Wert, *Rangers*, 27.
p. 283 "When Abraham Lincoln" Editors of Time-Life Books, *Spies, Scouts, and Raiders*, Alexandria: Time-Life Books, 1985, 115.
p. 283 "Frail and weighing" Editors of Time-Life Books, *Spies*, 115.
p. 283 "Mosby's first six" Davis, et al., 397–398.

p. 283 "When Colonel Fitzhugh Lee" Davis, et al., 399.

p. 283 "Mosby had a keen" Wert, *Rangers*, 33.

p. 283 "Mosby possessed untiring" Wert, *Rangers*, 33.

p. 284 "Sometimes during the" Davis, et al., 399.

p. 284 "Mosby's Rangers were" Grimsley, *Hard Hand of War*, 112.

p. 284 "Unlike the true" Staff of *Civil War Times Illustrated*, "John S. Mosby, An Appraisal," *Civil War Times Illustrated* (Nov. 1965): p. 4–5.

p. 284 "Mosby's chance at" Davis, et al., 399.

p. 285 "Men flocked to join" Davis, et al., 403.

p. 285 "Mosby's first notable" Davis, et al., 400.

p. 285 "The riders—twenty-nine in all" B. Brager, "Combative to War's Very End," *Military History* (Oct. 1986): 55.

p. 285 "Get up, General" Brager, 55–56.

p. 285 "Mosby's exploit raised" Editors of Time-Life Books, *Spies*, 119.

p. 285 "The terrain in Mosby" Wert, *Ranger*, 35.

p. 285 "The effectiveness of Mosby's" Wert, *Rangers*, 105.

p. 286 "No matter how" Wert, *Rangers*, 105.

p. 286 "News of the Rangers'" Wert, *Rangers*, 115.

p. 286 "Despite the danger" Wert, *Rangers*, 117.

p. 286 "Each safe house" Wert, *Rangers*, 121.

p. 287 "Mosby expected his" Wert, *Rangers*, 124.

p. 287 "Mosby's authority extended" Wert, *Rangers*, 124–125.

p. 287 "In June of 1863" Wert, *Rangers*, 87.

p. 287 "After his narrow" J. Wert, "Inside Mosby's Confederacy," *Civil War Times Illustrated* (Sept.–Oct. 1990): 41.

p. 288 "For Mosby, Union" Wert, "Inside," p. 42.

p. 288 "In August 1863" Davis, et al., 407–408.

p. 288 "By the beginning of" Davis, et al., 408–409.

p. 288 "In May, there was" Davis, et al., 409–410.

p. 288 "In August, Sheridan" Davis, et al., 411.

p. 288 "Shortly after arriving" M. Martin, "A Match For Mosby," *America's Civil War* (July 1994): 26.

p. 288 "When Sheridan found" Martin, 28–29.

p. 289 "By November, Blazer's" Martin, 30.

p. 289 "Mosby continued to be" Brager, 57.

P. 289 "When Mosby learned" Wert, *Rangers*, 245.

p. 289 "Mosby rode to Rectortown" Wert, *Rangers*, 245–246.

p. 289 "Not all the men" Wert, *Rangers*, 248–249.

p. 290 "The escape of two" Wert, *Rangers*, 249–250.

p. 290 "Mosby had many" Staff of *Civil War Times Illustrated*, 5354.

p. 291 "Mosby, however, never" Davis, et al., 416.

p. 291 "After disbanding the battalion" Davis, et al., 417.

p. 291 "On June 29" Jones, 275–276.

p. 291 "By early September" Jones, 278–279.

p. 292 "While in Richmond" Jones, 284–285.

p. 292 "Mosby was a devoted" Siepel, 176.

p. 292 "Mosby had few vices" Siepel, 176–177.

p. 292 "Politics during the" Jones, 286.

p. 292 "It was during this" Jones, 287.

p. 293 "As the conversation" Jones, 287–288.

p. 293 "The South refused" Jones, 288–289.

p. 293 "When Grant's second" Jones, 289–290.

p. 293 "In 1876, Mosby" Jones, 299.

p. 294 "For the next seven" Jones, 301.

p. 294 "Once back in" Jones, 301.

p. 294 "Throughout the waning" Jones, 302–303.

p. 294 "He continued, saying" Davis, et al., 417.

p. 295 "On a lovely summer" Jones, 303–304.

p. 295 "In January 1897" Siepel, 249.

p. 295 "Mosby, now sixty-four" Siepel, 252.

p. 295 "In a letter" Siepel, 252.

p. 296 "By early August" Siepel, 253.

p. 296 "In 1901, in an" Jones, 304.

p. 296 "As Mosby aged" Jones, 305.

p. 296 "Despite all his peculiarities" Jones, 305.

p. 296 "As the years passed" Jones, 306.

p. 296 "In June 1910" Siepel, 278.

p. 296 "Occasionally, in his" Jones, 307.

p. 297 "In 1915, a delegation" Jones, 307.

p. 297 "By the close of 1915" Jones, 307–308.

p. 297 "Two days later" Siepel, 277.

p. 297 "It was a bloody" Wert, *Rangers*, 292–293.

p. 297 "In the end, Mosby" Wert, *Rangers*, 293.

p. 298 "Mosby's military record" Wert, *Rangers*, 294.

p. 299 "At daylight on April" J. Wert, *Custer*, New York: Simon & Shuster, 1996, 13–14.

p. 299 "Custer was without" M. Katz, "A Face in History," *American History Illustrated* (Oct. 1985): 38.

p. 300 "George Armstrong Custer" Wert, *Custer*, 15–16.

p. 300 "Emanuel did not wait" Wert, *Custer*, 16–17.

p. 300 "As a boy, George" L. Frost, *The Custer Album*, New York: Bonanza Books, 1964, 17.

p. 300 "Autie's father was" Frost, 17.

p. 300 "Although Custer's interest" Frost, 18.

p. 301 "At the age of six" Wert, *Custer*, 19–20.

p. 301 "At the age of sixteen" L. Barnett, *Touched by Fire*, New York: Henry Holt & Company, 1997, 12.

p. 301 "Twenty-six dollars" Frost, 20.

p. 302 "About the same time" Wert, *Custer*, 24–25.

p. 302 "Custer achieved considerable" R. Utley, *Cavalier in Buckskin*, Norman: University of Oklahoma, 1988, 15–16.

p. 302 "Custer did well" Utley, 16.

p. 302 "On at least one" Utley, 15–16.

p. 302 "This episode revealed" Utley, 16.

p. 303 "Custer was very popular" Barnett, 15.

p. 303 "Cadet Custer was" M. Phipps, "Come on, You Wolverines," *Custer at Gettysburg*, Gettysburg: Farnsworth House Military Impressions, 1995, 7–8.

p. 303 "After the Surrender" Wert, *Custer*, 38–39.

p. 303 "Looking back on" Barnett, 18.

p. 303 "Second Lieutenant George Custer" Wert, *Custer*, 42–44.

p. 303 "The Bull Run debacle" Utley, 17.

p. 304 "Again Custer got lucky" J. Wert "Custer on the Rise," *Civil War Times Illustrated* (June 1996): 59.

p. 304 "Custer had great" Wert, "Rise," p. 59–60.

p. 304 "Staff duty involved" Wert, "Rise," p. 60.

p. 304 "Two characteristics marked" Utley, 18.

p. 305 "Libbie had a beautiful" Utley, 19.

p. 305 "Libbie was Custer's" Ward, 233–234.

p. 305 "They were married" Utley, 26.

p. 305 "Warfare seemed to" Phipps, 9.

p. 305 "After helping General" Utley, 20.

p. 306 "At the end of June 1863" Utley, 22.

p. 306 "Pleasonton had not" Utley, 22.

p. 306 "Less than a week" Utley, 22.

p. 306 "Under General David Gregg" Utley, 23.

p. 307 "Stuart launched another" Utley, 23.

p. 307 "In September, Custer" Utley, 25.

p. 307 "The spring of 1864" Wert, Custer, 145–147.

p. 307 "Custer was troubled" Wert, Custer, 148.

p. 308 "Sheridan, meanwhile, prepared" Wert, Custer, 150.

p. 308 "In early May" Wert, Custer, 152–153.

p. 308 "Custer's fame continued" Utley, 27.

p. 308 "Just as Custer" Utley, 28.

p. 308 "In September, Sheridan" Utley, 29.

p. 308 "The views of Custer's" Wert, Custer, 187.

p. 309 "In October, Custer" Utley, 30.

p. 310 "In the spring of 1865" Utley, 31–32.

p. 310 "By April 8, Custer" Utley, 33.

p. 310 "After the meeting" L. Frost, "Fateful April Days," *Military History* (April 1988): 32.

p. 310 "Fittingly, the symbol" Wert, Custer, 225. p. 310 "Custer loved war" Utley, 36.

p. 311 "Custer's first test" Frost, "Fateful," p. 69.

p. 311 "Custer quickly realized" R. Conrad "Custer's Long Summer," *Civil War Times Illustrated* (May–June 1993): 37.

p. 311 "Things reached crisis level" Frost, "Fateful," p. 70–71.

p. 311 "Preparations were made" Frost, "Fateful," p. 71.

p. 311 "The benefit of Custer's" Wert, Custer, 234.

p. 312 "Within twenty-four hours" Wert, Custer, 233.

p. 312 "Custer was determined" Wert, Custer, 233.

p. 312 "Custer's orders to desist" Wert, Custer, 235.

p. 312 "Custer's troops never" Wert, Custer, 235.

p. 313 "Nothing in Custer's experience" Wert, Custer, 235–236.

p. 313 "Despite Custer's problems" Wert, Custer, 237.

p. 313 "Meanwhile in Washington" Wert, Custer, 238–239.

p. 313 "Custer, uncertain about" Crutchfield, et al., 249.

p. 314 "Custer was ordered" Wert, Custer, 244.

p. 314 "Custer reported for" Utley, 45.

p. 314 "The 7th Cavalry fell" Wert, Custer, 246.

p. 314 "From its inception" Wert, Custer, 250.

p. 314 "By government estimates" Wert, Custer, 250.

p. 314 "The army saw its role" Wert, Custer, 251.

p. 315 "While on this" D. Nevin, *The Soldiers*, New York: Time-Life Books, 1973, 185.

p. 315 "Whenever he went" Nevin, 185.

p. 315 "Catching Indians was" Ward, 234.

p. 315 "Custer had no qualms" Nevin, 185.

p. 316 "Custer had been duped" Wert, Custer, 256.

p. 316 "Custer had been" Ward, 234.

p. 316 "Eventually, the remainder" Wert, *Custer*, 262.

p. 316 "In August of 1867" Wert, *Custer*, 262-263.

p. 316 "Custer pleaded not guilty" Wert, *Custer*, 263.

p. 317 "The court's punishment" Nevin, 189.

p. 317 "The Custers reacted" Ward, 234-235.

p. 317 "Before Custer's suspension" Ward, 250.

p. 317 "To head the Winter" Barnett, 155-156.

p. 317 "In the course" Barnett, 158.

p. 318 "Despite Custer's victory" Barnett, 158.

p. 318 "The Battle of the Washita" R. Utley, "Custer: Hero or Butcher?" *American History Illustrated* (Feb. 1971): 8.

p. 318 "After a time" Crutchfield, et al., 250-251.

p. 318 "In 1873, Custer led" Crutchfield, et al., 251.

p. 318 "Just a week later" Crutchfield, et al., 251.

p. 319 "In 1874, Custer" Crutchfield et. at. p. 253.

p. 319 "On June 25, 1876" Crutchfield, et al., 253.

p. 319 "The two commands" W. Taylor, *With Custer on the Little Bighorn*, New York: Viking Penguin, 1996, 65-66.

p. 319 "In the meantime" D. Brown, *Bury My Heart at Wounded Knee*, New York: Holt, Rinehart & Winston, 1970, 294.

p. 319 "Custer took a position" Nevin, p.220.

p. 320 "The smoke of" Brown, 296.

p. 320 "The report of" Brown, 296.

p. 320 "Red Horse's report" Brown, 296.

p. 320 "On the 27th" Nevin, 220.

p. 320 "The battle of" Nevin, 220.

p. 320 "Newspapers editorialized about" Wert, *Custer*, 355.

p. 321 "When Libbie learned" Wert, *Custer*, 356.

p. 321 "To Libbie Custer" Wert, *Custer*, 357.p. 321 "From Gettysburg to Appomattox" R. Utley, "The Enduring Custer Legend," *American History Illustrated* (June 1976): 44.

p. 322 "The North went" W. Davis, editor, *The End of an Era*, Garden City, NY: Doubleday & Company, 1984, 368-369.

p. 323 "Retribution was inevitable" McPherson, 486.

p. 323 "How different it was" Davis, *End of Era*, 374-375.

p. 323 "The reception to" McPherson, 486-487.

p. 323 "There was joy" Davis, *End of Era*, 376.

p. 324 "Even before the" Davis, *End of Era*, 376.

p. 324 "The war's impact" McPherson, 493.

p. 324 "Coming first as" Davis, *End of Era*, 383.

p. 324 "Republicans went south" Davis, *End of Era*, 383-384.

p. 325 "In the United States" Davis, *End of Era*, 386-387.

p. 325 "Of course, the old" McPherson, 486.

p. 325 "The states in the North" Davis, *End of Era*, 390.

p. 326 "Time would be" Davis, *End of Era*, 390.

p. 326 "In time they would" Davis, *End of Era*, 391.

p. 326 "The president of the Confederacy" Davis, *End of Era*, 391.

Bibliography

Alexander, Porter. "With Lee at Appomattox." *American History*. September, 1987. 51.

Ambrose, Stephen. *Duty, Honor, Country: A History of West Point*. Baltimore: Johns Hopkins University Press, 1966.

Anders, Curt. *Fighting Confederates*. New York: Dorset Press, 1968.

Bailey, Ronald. *Forward to Richmond*. Alexandria: Time-Life Books, 1983.

Bailey, Ronald et. al. *The Time-Life History of the Civil War*. New York: Barnes & Noble, 1990.

Ballard, Michael. "Cheer for Jefferson Davis." *American History Illustrated*. May 1981. 9–14.

Barnett, Louise. *Touched by Fire*. New York: Henry Holt & Company, 1997.

Batty, Peter and Peter Parish. *The Divided Union*. Topsfield: Salem House Publishers, 1987.

Bonekemper III, Edward. *How Robert E. Lee Lost the Civil War*. Fredericksburg: Sergeant Kirkland's Press, 1997.

Boothe, F. Norton. *Great Generals of the Civil War*. New York: Gallery Books, 1986.

Brager, Bruce. "Combative to War's Very End." *Military History*. October 1986. 55–57.

Brooksher, William, and David Snider. "Surrender or Die." *Military History*. February 1985. 29–33.

Brown, Dee. *Bury My Heart at Wounded Knee*. New York: Holt, Rinehart & Winston, 1970.

Buell, Thomas. *The Warrior Generals, Combat Leadership in the Civil War*. New York: Crown Publishers, 1997.

Carroll, John, ed. *Custer in Texas: An Interrupted Narrative*. New York: Sol Lewis & Liveright, 1975.

Castel, Albert. *Decision in the West*. Lawrence: University Press of Kansas, 1992.

———. "George B. McClellan: 'Little Mac.'" *Civil War Times Illustrated*. May 1974. 9–11.

———. "The Life of a Rising Son—Part I: The Failure." *Civil War Times Illustrated*. July 1979. 4–7, 42–46.

———. "The Life of a Rising Son—Part II: The Subordinate." *Civil War Times Illustrated*. August 1979. 16–20.

————. "The Life of a Rising Son—Part III: The Conqueror." *Civil War Times Illustrated*. October 1979. 9–19.

Catton, Bruce. *The American Heritage New History of the Civil War*. New York: Viking, 1996.

————. *Mr. Lincoln's Army*. New York: Doubleday & Company, 1951.

————. *Never Call Retreat*. New York: Pocket Books, 1965.

————. *A Stillness at Appomattox*. New York: Doubleday & Company, 1957.

————. *U. S. Grant and the American Military Tradition*. Boston: Little, Brown, 1954.

Chesnut, Mary. *Mary Chesnut's Civil War*. New Haven: Yale University, 1981.

Commager, Henry Steele, et. al. *America's Robert E. Lee*. Boston: Houghton Mifflin, 1951.

Conrad, Robert. "Custer's Long Summer." *Civil War Times Illustrated*. May/June 1993. 37.

Cooke, John Esten. *Wearing of the Gray*. Bloomington: Indiana University Press, 1959.

Cranfield, Cass. *The Iron Will of Jefferson Davis*. New York: Harcourt Brace Jovanovich, 1978.

Cross, David. "Mantled in Fire and Smoke." *America's Civil War*, January 1992. 40–41.

Crutchfield, James et al. *Legends of the West*. Lincolnwood: Publications International, 1995.

Cullen, Joseph. "Richmond Falls!" *American History Illustrated*. January 1974. 11–19.

Davis, Burke. *The Long Surrender*. New York: Random House, 1985.

————. *Sherman's March*. New York: Random House, 1980.

————. *To Appomattox, Nine April Days, 1865*. New York: Rinehart & Company, 1959.

Davis, Danny. "Tumult in the Gaps." *America's Civil War*. November 1988.

Davis, William, et al. *Civil War Journal: The Battles*. Nashville: Rutledge Hill Press, 1998.

————. *Civil War Journa: The Leaders*. Nashville: Rutledge Hill Press, 1997.

Davis, William. "Confederate Exiles." *American History Illustrated*. June 1970. 31–43.

————, ed. *The End of an Era*. Garden City, NY: Doubleday & Company, 1984.

————. *Jefferson Davis, The Man and His Hour*. New York: HarperCollins, 1991.

Di Nardo, R. L., and Albert Nofi, eds. *James Longstreet: The Man, the Soldier, the Controversy*. Conshohoken, Pennsylvania: Combined Publishing, 1998.

Domer, Ronald. "Rebel Rout of Streight's Raiders." *America's Civil War*. September 1996. 36.

————. "Sooy Smith and 'That Devil Forrest.'" *America's Civil War*. May 1998. 40.

Donald, David. *Lincoln*. New York: Simon & Schuster, 1995.

Dowdey, Clifford. *Death of a Nation*. New York: Alfred A. Knopf, 1958.

————. *Lee*. New York: Bonanza Books, 1965.

Dubowski, Cathy. *Robert E. Lee and the Rise of the South*. Englewood Cliffs: Silver Burdett, 1991.

Dunphy, Owen. "March to the Sea." *America's Civil War*. July 1990.

Dyer, John. *The Gallant Hood*. New York: Smithmark Publishers, 1995.

Eckenrode, H. J. and Bryan Conrad. *James Longstreet, Lee's War Horse*. Chapel Hill: University of North Carolina Press, 1986.

Editors of American Heritage. *The American Heritage Pictorial History of the Presidents*. Great Neck, NJ: American Heritage.

Editors of Time-Life. *The Time-Life History of the Civil War*. New York: Barnes & Noble, 1990.

———. *Spies, Scouts and Raiders*. Alexandria: Time-Life Books, 1985.

Editors of the World Book Encyclopedia. *World Book of America's Presidents*. Chicago: World Book Encyclopedia, Inc. 1982.

Eisenschiml, Otto. "Sherman: Hero or War Criminal?" *Civil War Times Illustrated*. January, 1964. 35.

Faeder, Gustav. "The Best of Friends and Enemies." *Civil War Times Illustrated*. October 1987. 23.

Fellman, Michael. *Citizen Sherman*. New York: Random House, 1995.

Fishwick, Marshall. *Lee After the War*. New York: Dodd, Mead, 1963.

Fleming, Thomas. "The Big Parade." *Civil War Chronicles*. Summer 1991. 64–66.

Flood, Charles. *Lee, The Last Years*. Boston: Houghton Mifflin, 1981.

Foner, Eric. *Reconstruction, America's Unfinished Revolution*. New York: Harper & Row, 1988.

Foner, Eric and Olivia Mahoney. *American Reconstruction*. Baton Rouge: Louisiana State University Press, 1995.

Foote, Shelby. *The Civil War*. 3 vols. New York: Random House, 1958–1974.

Freeman, Douglas Southall. *Lee of Virginia*. New York: Charles Scribner's Sons, 1958.

Frost, Lawrence. *The Custer Album*. New York: Bonanza Books, 1964.

———. "Fateful April Days." *Military History*. April 1988. 32, 69–71.

———. *U. S. Grant Album*. New York: Bonanza Books, 1966.

Glatthaar, Joseph. *Partners in Command*. New York: The Free Press, 1994.

Govan, Gilbert and James Livingood. *A Different Valor*. New York: Bobbs-Merrill, 1956.

Graff, Henry. *America, The Glorious Republic*. Boston: Houghton Mifflin, 1988.

Gragg, Rod. *The Illustrated Confederate Reader*. New York: Harper & Row, 1989.

Grimsley, Mark. "The Great Deceiver." *Civil War Times Illustrated*. November/December 1993. 37.

———. *The Hard Hand of War*. New York: Cambridge University Press, 1995.

———. "Leader of the Klan." *Civil War Times Illustrated*. January/February 1994. 41, 63–72.

———. "Millionaire Rebel Raiders." *Civil War Times Illustrated*. September/October 1993. 60–68.

———. "Robert E. Lee: The Life and Career of the Master General." *Civil War Times Illustrated*. November 1985. 14–19, 47–50.

———. "Ulysses S. Grant." *Civil War Times Illustrated*. January/February 1990. 21–31, 47–63.

———. "We Will Vindicate the Right: An Account of the Life of Jefferson Davis." *Civil War Times Illustrated*. July/August 1991. 33–74.

Grinnell, George. *The Fighting Cheyennes*. Norman: University of Oklahoma Press, 1956.

Groom, Winston. *Shrouds of Glory*. New York: Atlantic Monthly Press, 1995.

Hasler, William. *A. P. Hill: Lee's Forgotten General*. Chapel Hill: University of North Carolina Press, 1957.

Hattaway, Herman. *Shades of Blue and Gray*. Columbia: University of Missouri Press, 1997.

Henry, Robert. *"First with the Most"*: *Forrest*. Indianapolis: Bobbs Merrill, 1944.

Hoehling, A. A. *After the Guns Fell Silent*. New York: Madison Books, 1990.

Hoehling, A. A., and Mary Hoehling. *The Day Richmond Died*. New York: A. S. Barnes & Company, 1981.

Horn, Stanley. *The Robert E. Lee Reader*. New York: Bobbs-Merrill, 1949.

Hurst, Jack. *Nathan Bedford Forrest*. New York: Alfred A. Knopf, 1993.

Hutton, Paul. *The Custer Reader*. Lincoln: University of Nebraska Press, 1992.

———. *Phil Sheridan and His Army*. Lincoln: University of Nebraska Press, 1985.

Jones, Katharine. *Ladies of Richmond—Confederate Capital*. New York: Bobbs-Merrill, 1962.

Jones, Virgil. *Ranger Mosby*. McLean: EPM Publications, 1944.

Julian, Allen. "From Dalton to Atlanta." *Civil War Times Illustrated*. July 1964.

Katz, Mark. "A Face in History." *American History Illustrated*. October 1985. 38.

Katz, William. *An Album of Reconstruction*. New York: Franklin Watts, 1974.

Keenan, Jerry. "Fighting with Forrest in the Tennessee Winter." *America's Civil War*. November 1995. 72.

———. "The Gallant Hood of Texas." *America's Civil War*. March 1994. 43–48.

Kimmel, Stanley. *Mr. Davis's Richmond*. Toronto: Longman, Green, 1958.

King, Perry. *Jefferson Davis*. New York: Chelsea House Publishers, 1990.

Korn, Jerry, et al. *Pursuit to Appomattox: The Last Battle*. Alexandria: Time-Life Books, 1987.

Lee, Richard. *General Lee's City*. McLean: EPM Publications, 1987.

Lewis, Lloyd. *Sherman, Fighting Prophet*. New York: Harcourt Brace & World, 1958.

Lewis, Thomas. *The Guns of Cedar Creek*. New York: Harper & Row, 1988.

———. *The Shenandoah in Flames*. Alexandria: Time-Life Books, 1987.

Litwack, Leon F. *Been in the Storm So Long: The Aftermath of Slavery*. New York: Vintage, 1980.

Longstreet, James. *From Manassas to Appomattox*. Philadelphia: Lippincott, 1896.

Luthin, Reinhard. *The Real Abraham Lincoln*. Englewood Cliffs: Prentice Hall, 1960.

Luvaas, Jay. "Joseph Johnston." *Civil War Times Illustrated*. January 1966. 29–30.

McDonough, James, and James Jones. *War So Terrible*. New York: W. W. Norton, 1987.

McFall, Arthur. "Grant's Early War Days." *America's Civil War*. November 1994. 34.

McFeely, William. *Grant*. New York: W. W. Norton, 1981.

McMurry, Richard. *John Bell Hood and the War for Southern Independence*. Lincoln: University of Nebraska Press, 1982.

McPherson, James. *Battle Cry of Freedom*. New York: Oxford University Press, 1988.

———. *Ordeal by Fire*. New York: Alfred A. Knopf, 1982.

Mapp, Alf. *Frock Coats and Epaulets*. Lanham, MD: Hamilton Press, 1963.

Marrin, Albert. *Unconditional Surrender: U. S. Grant and the Civil War*. New York: Macmillan, 1994.

Marshall, Michael. "A Soldier No Longer." *Military History*. December 1990. 10–14.

Marszalek, John. *Sherman, A Soldier's Passion for Order*. New York: Vintage Books, 1993.

————. "Was Sherman Really a Brute?" *Blue and Gray*. December 1989. 46–51.

Martin, Michael. "A Match for Mosby?" *America's Civil War*. July 1994. 26–30.

Merington, Marguerite, ed. *The Custer Story: The Life and Intimate Letters of General George Custer and His Wife Elizabeth*. Lincoln: University of Nebraska Press, 1987.

Miers, Earl. *The General Who Marched to Hell*. New York: Collier Books, 1951.

Morris, Roy. "Editorial—John Bell Hood," *America's Civil War*. September 1998. 6.

————. *Sheridan*. New York: Vintage Books, 1992.

Morrison, James. *The Best School in the World: West Point, the Pre–Civil War Years, 1853–1866*. Kent: Kent State University Press, 1986.

Mosby, John. *The Memoirs of Colonel John S. Mosby*. (rep. ed) Gaithersburg: Olde Soldier Books, 1987.

————. "Retaliation: The Execution of Seven Prisoners by Colonel John S. Mosby—A Self-Protective Necessity." *Southern Historical Society Papers* XXVII, 1899.

Murfin, Richard. *The Gleam of Bayonets*. New York: Bonanza Books, 1965.

Murphy, Richard, et al. *The Nation Reunited*. Alexandria: Time-Life Books, 1987.

Neul, Robert. "Battle Most Desperate and Bloody." *America's Civil War*, January 1995. 31–32.

Nevins, Allan. *The War for the Union: The Organized War to Victory, 1864–1865*. New York: Charles Scribner's Sons, 1971.

Nevin, David, et al. *The Road to Shiloh*. Alexandria: Time-Life Books, 1983.

————. *The Soldiers*. New York: Time-Life Books, 1973.

Nobbitt, Phil. "Confederate Breakout Attempt at Peachtree Creek." *America's Civil War*. September 1998. 56–57.

Nye, Wilbur. "Grant—Genius or Fortune's Child." *Civil War Times Illustrated*. June 1965. 8.

O'Brien, Kevin. "Personality—Joshua Chamberlain." *Military History*. August 1996. 72.

O'Connor, Richard. *Sheridan the Inevitable*. Indianapolis: Bobbs-Merrill, 1953.

Patrick, Rembert. *The Fall of Richmond*. Baton Rouge: Louisiana State University Press, 1960.

Patterson, Gerard. "John Bell Hood." *Civil War Times Illustrated*. February 1971. 12–21.

Perret, Geoffrey. *Ulysses S. Grant, Soldier and President*. New York: Random House, 1997.

Perry, Mark. *Conceived in Liberty*. New York: Viking Press, 1997.

Phipps, Michael. "Come On, You Wolverines." *Custer at Gettysburg*. Gettysburg: Farnsworth House Military Impressions, 1995.

Pindell, Richard. "The 20th Maine." *Civil War Times Illustrated*. February 1983. 19–20.

Piston, William. *Tarnished Lieutenant*. Athens: University of Georgia Press, 1987.

Poggiali, Leonard. "The Death of U. S. Grant, and the Cottage on Mount McGregor." *Blue and Gray*. February 1993.

Potter, Robert. *Jefferson Davis, Confederate President*. Austin: SteckVaughn Company, 1994.

Preston, Margaret. "Robert E. Lee after the War." *Civil War Times Illustrated*. January 1969. 5–6.

Randall, J. G., and David Donald. *The Civil War and Reconstruction*. Lexington: D. C. Heath, 1969.

Reeder, Red. *The Northern Generals*. New York: Duell, Sloan & Pearce, 1964.

Rickarby, Laura. *Ulysses S. Grant and the Strategy of Victory*. Englewood Cliffs: Silver Burdett, 1991.

Robertson, James. *General A. P. Hill: The Story of a Confederate Warrior*. New York: Random House, 1987.

Rogge, Robert. "Devil at the Crossroads." *America's Civil War*. September 1990. 41–49.

Roland, Charles. *The American Iliad*. Lexington: University Press of Kentucky, 1991.

Royster, Charles. *The Destructive War*. New York: Alfred A. Knopf, 1991.

Sanborn, Margaret. *Robert E. Lee*. Philadelphia: J. B. Lippincott Company, 1967.

Sanger, Donald, and Thomas Hay. *James Longstreet*. Gloucester: Peter Smith, 1968.

Scott, John. *Partisan Life with Colonel John S. Mosby*. Gaithersburg: Butternut Press, 1985. (Reprint)

Sears, Stephen. *George B. McClellan, The Young Napoleon*. New York: Ticknor & Fields, 1988.

———. "Lincoln and McClellan." *Lincoln's Generals*. Ed. Gabor S. Boritt. New York: Oxford University Press, 1994. 1–50.

———. "McClellan at Antietam." *Blue and Gray*. November 1985. 20.

———. "McClellan vs. Lee: The Seven-day Trial." *Military Quarterly*. Autumn 1988. 11–12.

———. *To the Gates of Richmond, The Peninsula Campaign*. New York: Ticknor & Fields, 1992.

Sefton, James. *United States Army and Reconstruction, 1865–1877*. Baton Rouge: Louisiana State University Press, 1967.

Sell, Bill. *Leaders of the North and South*. New York: Michael Friedman Publishing Group, 1996.

Sheridan, Philip. *The Personal Memoirs of P. H. Sheridan*. New York: De Capo Press, 1992.

Sherman, William. *Memoirs of General William T. Sherman*. New York: De Capo Press, 1984.

Siepel, Kevin. *Rebel, The Life and Times of John Singleton Mosby*. New York: De Capo Press, 1983.

Smith, Carter. *Presidents of a Divided Nation*. Brookfield: Millbrook Press, 1993.

Smith, Gene. *Lee and Grant: A Dual Biography*. New York: McGraw-Hill, 1984.

Smith, Page. *Trial by Fire*. New York: McGraw-Hill, 1982.

Staff of Civil War Times Illustrated. "John S. Mosby—An Appraisal." *Civil War Times Illustrated*. November 1965. 4–5.

Stanchak, John. "Behind the Lines." *Civil War Times Illustrated*. November 1985. 52.

Stern, Philip Van Doren. *Robert E. Lee, The Man and the Soldier*. New York: McGraw-Hill, 1963.

Stokesbury, James. *A Short History of the Civil War*. New York: William Morrow, 1995.

Street, James, et al. *The Struggle for Tennessee*. Alexandria: Time-Life Books, 1985.

Strode, Hudson. *Jefferson Davis, Tragic Hero*. New York: Harcourt Brace & World, 1964.

Sword, Wiley. "The Other Stonewall." *Civil War Times Illustrated*. February 1998. 38.

Symonds, Craig. *Joseph Johnston*. New York: W. W. Norton, 1992.

Tarbell, Ida. "Disbanding the Confederate Army." *Civil War Times Illustrated*. January 1968. 5–13.

———. "How the Union Army Was Disbanded." *Civil War Times Illustrated*. December 1967. 5.

Taylor, William. *With Custer on the Little Bighorn*. New York: Viking Penguin, 1996.

Thomas, Emory. *Robert E. Lee*. New York: W. W. Norton, 1995.

Thornbridge, John. *The Desolate South: 1865–1866, A Picture of the Battlefields and Devastated Confederacy*. New York: Duell, Sloan and Pearce, 1956.

Trefousse, Hans. *Andrew Johnson*. New York: W. W. Norton & Company, 1989.

Trudeau, Noah. "Last Days of the Civil War." *Civil War Times Illustrated*. July/August 1990. 64–67.

———. *Out of the Storm, The End of the Civil War, April–June, 1865*. Baton Rouge: Louisiana State University Press, 1994.

Tucker, Glenn. "Forrest—Untutored Genius of War." *Civil War Times Illustrated*. June 1964. 36.

———. "Longstreet: Culprit or Scapegoat." *Civil War Times Illustrated*. April 1962. 6.

Utley, Robert. *Cavalier in Buckskin*. Norman: University of Oklahoma, 1988.

———. "Custer: Hero or Butcher?" *American History Illustrated*. February 1971. 8.

———. "The Enduring Custer Legend." *American History Illustrated*. June 1976. 44.

———. *Frontier Regulars: The U.S. Army and the Indians, 1861–1891*. New York: Macmillan, 1973.

———. *The Indian Frontier of the American West, 1846–1890*. Albuquerque: University of New Mexico Press, 1984.

Wallace, Willard. *Soul of the Lion*. Gettysburg: Stan Clark Military Books, 1960.

Ward, Geoffrey. *The West, An Illustrated History*. Boston: Little, Brown, 1996.

Ward, John. "Forrest's First Fight." *America's Civil War*. March 1993. 51–56.

Waugh, John. *The Class of 1846*. New York: Warner Books, 1994.

Weigley, Russell. "Philip H. Sheridan, A Personal Profile." *Civil War Times Illustrated*. July 1968. 8.

Welch, Richard. "Book Review—Joseph E. Johnston: A Civil War Biography." *America's Civil War*. November 1993. 58.

Wert, Jeffry. *Custer*. New York: Simon & Schuster, 1996.

———. "Custer on the Rise." *Civil War Times Illustrated*. June 1996. 59–60.

———. *From Winchester to Cedar Creek*. New York: Simon & Schuster, 1987.

———. *General James Longstreet*. New York: Simon & Schuster, 1993.

———. "General James Longstreet." *Civil War Times Illustrated*. November/December 1993. 106.

———. "Generals at Odds." *Military History*. August 1994. 52.

———. "In One Deadly Encounter," *Civil War Times Illustrated*, November 1980. 12–19.

————. "Inside Mosby's Confederacy." *Civil War Times Illustrated*. September/October 1990. 41–42.

————. "Lee's Old War-Horse." *American History*. March 1998. 17–24.

————. *Mosby's Rangers*. New York: Simon & Schuster, 1990.

Wheeler, Richard. *Voices of the Civil War*. New York: Meridian, 1990.

————. Witness to Appomattox. New York: Harper & Row, 1989.

Wiley, Bell. "Jefferson Davis, An Appraisal." *Civil War Times Illustrated*. April 1967. 8–9.

Williams, Harry. *Lincoln and His Generals*. New York: Alfred Knopf, 1952.

Williams, Harry, et al. *The Union Restored*. New York: Time Incorporated, 1963.

Wills, Brian Steel. *A Battle from the Start: The Life of Nathan Bedford Forrest*. New York: Harper-Collins, 1992.

Wilson, Ronald. "Meeting at the McLean House." *American History Illustrated*. September 1987. 48.

Woodward, W. E. *Meet General Grant*. New York: Horace Liveright, 1928.

Woodworth, Steven. *Jefferson Davis and His Generals*. Lawrence: University Press of Kansas, . 1990.

Wyeth, John. *That Devil Forrest*. Baton Rouge: Louisiana State University Press, 1989.

Index

Photo Credits